ISBN 978-1-331-11330-0
PIBN 10146572

Forgotten Books is a registered trademark of FB &c Ltd.
Copyright © 2018 FB &c Ltd.
FB &c Ltd, Dalton House, 60 Windsor Avenue, London, SW19 2RR.
Company number 08720141. Registered in England and Wales.

For support please visit www.forgottenbooks.com

AMERICA'S DAY

STUDIES IN LIGHT AND SHADE

BY

IGNATIUS PHAYRE

What hath this Day deserv'd?
What hath it done
That it in golden letters should be set
Among the high tides in the calendar?

NEW YORK
DODD, MEAD AND COMPANY
1919

THE FOREWORD

MY aim is to lift the note of the United States above the clamour of a world-war, its man-killing, restoration, and rearrangement. It shall be throughout an impersonal aim. I teach nothing—I only relate, conscious of a certain insight into America's music, though the sound of it be incongruous as a Bach fugue on the guitar. After all, more than a hundred million souls dance to this tune and try to make new harmony by inspired violation of the old.

The Great War affected this looser continent in various ways: business and bosom were searched with many-sided appeal. "Keep your harvesters and ploughs," Chicago heard with dismay. "What we need are thermite bombs to burn the growing crops. Or send us pedrail tractors to dig a ditch for the living and the dead." It was the shriek of madness in American ears. Forty million men were flung into the furnace of war. Europe was seen shaken and distorted, like a reverend friend that foamed with sudden epilepsy. I cannot speak of America's wonder, for the sight so dazed her that "Keep Away" was a compelling instinct which quelled all the rest. . . .

The live light of Christ was eclipsed with cave-man vengeance. The olden pillars tottered; our common sanctuary was soon a smoking heap involving the United States in the wicked futility of its fall. These people were aghast; they were also confirmed in their own ways —"Et voir autrement que les autres, c'est presque toujours voir un peu mieux que les autres." America was

vii

strong and sure in this perception of her own good. Who had seen it more clearly than her own First President, whose "Keep Out" policy in regard to Old-World tangles took a new lease when the rape of Belgium began with headlong fury? The prairie farmer gave Woodrow Wilson a second mandate on Washingtonian lines—the lines of Prosperity and Peace which reseated "that proven man" in the White House—the first Democrat of double term since Andrew Jackson's day.

Europe had run amok. America's millions stood far off in dim espial, deafened with partisan cries at home, where German bombs went off and the German Embassy was organized as a focus of conspiracy and crime. It was all so crude, this vengeful welter; startling as the flash and clap of storm out of a cloudless summer sky. So unaccountable to the naïve American mind; so unexpected of twentieth-century man, who rode the clouds and made the ether speak without wires. . . . Old seats of grace were gruesomely transformed. Rheims Cathedral was ablaze, Venice and the Isles of Greece were rained upon with fire like Sodom and Gomorrah.

America shed her youthfulness in those dreadful days and developed an impulse to save herself. No longer diffident, she was now mature and grave, surging with pity and timid ministration. How should it end, when would it end? The older and once-wiser world was become a slaughterhouse, crashing with satanic gear. All flesh was as grass over there; each levy of men mere *Kanonenfutter,* or meat for guns that were great as factory-shafts, with godlike youths high in the heavens guiding them. There was a waste of money beyond any Wall Street telling. The massed wealth of nations was now turned to devastation, with malign Science directing all— under water, in the air, and across tortured lands, black with refugees whose prayer to God sank into sullen blasphemy and bloody vows of vengeance. Such was America's vision of the calamity. . . .

At the same time, she reflected, the London poor continue to live like dogs. Trench heroes, pictured in the papers for glowing deeds, returned from the King's Palace to homes unimaginably vile. The Children's Hospital was pawning its last security and advertising the fact: "Unless help comes at once we must close our wards." America could only stare at it all, and reckon the cost of each day's killing which would surely heal a world's woe. She heard of girl-babies collecting for the blinded and maimed with an empty bomb as a money-box. Mother's fur coat was officially branded as a crime against the nation. Why? Because the cost of it would give the hidden sniper sixteen thousand chances of shooting his German brother!

Alas, that Bellona's robe should be the only wear in Merrie England—"O moissoneuse des prémices du ciel!" And America turned away from this shearing of the human race. Bright streams of joy lay stagnant; the fraternity of man was but a memory, known by its tribute of tears, like the Shrine of Pity in Athens. In the glare of war our striving frailty was a baleful thing; our divinity an august lie, our efforts to rise mere twisting of a rope of sand, "which was a task, they say, that posed the devil." Depressed and bemused by it all, America took comfort in the better part which was unmistakably her own. Therefore the philosophy of George Washington was taken down from its dusty shelf and re-read as the gospel of salvation.

"We are reasonable creatures," America insisted with Grotius. "Therefore our works may be moral or unjust, even in the rough grapple of war." It was a hint to all the belligerents. For by this time grief had given place to grievance as the United States steered a worried course

between the German devil and the deep sea where Britain
was enthroned. America blamed both sides with biting
impartiality. Why were they so "national" and not rational at all? America's creed was the reasonableness of
man, and this she preached to exasperation. It would
yet transmute the greed and guile that loosed this wither-
ing blast. Scoffed at now, it would yet lure Evil from its
lair into a shadowless White House day.

America was moved with Pauline sense of duty: "Necessity is laid upon me." She must somehow try to heal
humanity, long rent with hate and bloody aberration.
"Let us keep our heads," was Wilson's counsel—as a man
might urge when caught in a maniac surge and swept
away. "America is about to be thrust into the economic
leadership of the world." Let her stand clear of the
wreckage if she were to serve and rebuild when this European brain-storm was overpast. The genial Bryan (most
typical of all Americans) laid stress upon the spiritual
side of this future. "Some nation," he felt, "must lead
mankind out of the blackness of war into the light of
day. Why not make that honour ours?" Here was the
voice of America in her neutral time. One caught it in
all keys, from the Executive Mansion to the sod-shack
of the Nebraskan plains.

From Vienna to Van, America assuaged the misery of
war with grain and meat and shelter. From Douglas to
Dantzig she mothered the prisoners of war, hearing the
plaints of all and marvelling how God saw eye to eye with
each belligerent. "The Throne of the Most High," America thought—distracted enough herself—"must be like
Jove's whispering-place in Lucian, where prayers criss-
crossed in conflict, some for rain and others for shine"!
And so, deafened with contending claims, the big Republic
turned away from them all. She was ill at ease and angry
to find that her neutral *rôle* was in Allied eyes that of the

grafter and poltroon, battening upon the world's woe and
cursed from every side. . . . On the whole, she thought,
Europe was best left to the God that watches over the
afflicted and cares for drunken-men in the murderous traffic
of city streets.

Then lust of cruelty, America feared, was a very real
passion. Witness the Turk with his victims—say at Tre-
bizond on the Black Sea, where a whole nation was to
be destroyed. They were taken out in shiploads and
scuttled in a wholesale way. . . . Cruelty! The child
with a worm, the boy with a wounded bird—what flower
of evil blossomed here in dark abysses of our nature?
It was no sacred flame that moved the white hunter in
Uganda and made him drop the elephant-gun for a
Service rifle and the greatest game of all, which was the
killing of men. Why, the very curates "had to be held
down," as the Bishop of London announces. "I should
like to get back quick," Charles Lister wrote from Gal-
lipoli. "I've seen just enough to tantalize. . . . And
there's no sound like the scream of enemy shrapnel through
the sky." Or hear another paladin—young Julian Gren-
fell, "when the burning moment breaks"—

> "And all things else are out of mind
> And only Joy-of-Battle takes
> Him by the throat, and makes him blind."

Such is the lure of war. This fever was not infectious
in the United States, though sporadic cases were to be
found: I mean American volunteers in the French and
Canadian Armies. "It is well that war is so terrible,"
mused Lee, the Confederate leader; "otherwise we'd grow
too fond of it." Washington himself could revel in the
bullet's song—"There is something charming in the
sound!" It is an acquired taste which present-day America had thought outgrown in a more enlightened age.

She tried to understand it—to say of modern war what Shelley said of the Medusa's head: "Its beauty and its horror are divine." But only the horror emerged. Messrs. Swing and Swope, America's privileged correspondents, wrote of trench scenes discreetly glozed over by their European rivals. The dry-land drowning of the gassed Canadians, for example. The wild-beast rattle of their end; their purple faces and starting eyes with blood and tissue welling from dying mouths in torment that broke down the veteran nurse and surgeon. Here was Science enlisted in the war; it was the wraith of Science that hovered at sundown over the gas-graveyard of Poperinghe.

There came a time when America yawned over the war. News from the Great Ditch became drab and samely. So did cries from the sea where ships were shattered and the crews took to leaky boats amid German jeers. There was no longer a public for wolfish fights between the wounded and the dying out there in No Man's Land. Nor for the suicide of crazed men who exposed themselves deliberately on the parapet "to get it over." Haggard scenes in the dug-out hospital ceased to fascinate the American reader, with sweating surgeons cutting and hacking amid eerie screams or the cigarette-smoke of resignation from rows of stretchers on the floor.

There were ghouls that robbed the dead, it seems. There was a crash and din of shells that robbed the living of their reason, so that they bombed or shot the pals at their side until these in turn destroyed them, as they might the swarming vermin of the trench. There were few horrors left in the inkwell when the American reporter was done, so adept was he in sounding the horrid crannies of our nature.

Custom can (and does) brass us all with ease. The widow's tears are quickly dried; her mourning passes from harsh crêpe to dull decorous silks and serge, to shine

at last in pearl and gold. It is the way of the world; it
was America's way when she knew the worst of war that
her Swings and Swopes could tell her. And then, like
Tommy in the trench, she developed a talent for forgetting.
From over the water I caught the carol of Prosperity; it
was care-free as a dug-out serenade:

"The Bells of Hell go ting-a-ling-a-ling
For *you*—but not for me."

The stupidity of war became a fluent theme when the
horror of it no longer made the American cables burn.
"Who's going to profit?" was a query that rose from
President and car-conductor. "The Cause," they were
told, was in every case "My Country." O the consecrated curse that put the State before humanity and made
of each nation's flag a shroud that meant more than dia-
dem and robe to those damn-fool patriots! So this was
the lay-religion of the Old World? It put America in mind
of a noble fane reared in a pagan land; the light of it
streaming vainly, like a lamp in a sepulchre.

"When shall I do a decent day's work?" asked the
pruner of vines of a New York reporter on the Marne.
When would his mother do a decent day's work?—that
patient soul in lace cap and clogs. She was now stamping
steel and filling endless shell-maws out of dread alembics—
sticky stuff brewed *pour les Boches* by the learned Turpin,
and tried upon silly sheep in waste places of the Saône.
America mourned with the peasants of France, who saw
the very earth defiled by stinking warrens in zigzag rows—
thousands of miles of them, with deep galleries here and
there in which half a division could assemble and defy the
guns. Then there were enormous craters and shell-pits
in which you could hide a house. The patient fields
were turned inside out; the vineyard churned to chalk
by ceaseless drum-fire, and little homes ground to dust

and rubble under the leprous moons of war. . . . Look! There was the white-haired curé trying to trace where his village street had been.

"We must send over implements," America said in her cheery way. "We'll ship you a lot of frame houses. We'll renew your farm-stock, too—we'll send you seeds and pigs and poultry." It was no use. The top-soil of the Somme was swept away. Just as it was an army's job to make them, so it would be an army's job to level these lunar landscapes, scooped out as they were and heaped up like a frozen sea. They *might* grow forest seedlings—beech, and the like. But God help the cultivator who tried to wring a living from vengeful hectares in *les régions actuellement liberées de l'ennemi*—say, in the Oise, the Meuse, the Vosges, or Meurthe-et-Moselle.

This slaughter of the soil was a phase that shocked America in a new way. It was abhorrent to every instinct of the United States, now thrilling with regret that she had any art or part or profit in this crazy surge—that her Texan cotton, kneaded and nitrated, should fill the war-head of German torpedoes. Why, in her own waters half a dozen ships were smashed on the Lord's day, and terrified souls cast upon stormy waters sixty miles from land!

Then American steel—fine stuff for rails and bridges—was being frittered in gun-tubes and armour plates. A British artist (in khaki, of course) was cutting new masks and faces for the hideously maimed out of Arizona and Montana copper. America's wheat and meat were too often snatched from starving Poland and Syria to feed the poison-gas fiend and peeping assassins of the Turkish trench. America was abased at her own trade, haunted by dim eyes of women that outwept the clouds with anguish. Who could grasp the totality of it in this wartime world? Here is Emma Wilkins, the white-haired

widow, who begins life over again as a cook in far-off
Winnipeg. Her husband fell at Modder River, in the
Boer War. Six times in succession had the British War
Office wired to this woman to say that a son was killed.
To these add three stepsons and a brother-in-law, as well
as a sister who "became a raving maniac before my eyes
when she heard her husband was lost in the Jutland fight."

Acres of print were published in the United States about
the twin arts of killing and curing until America was
stultified with a sense of crime. She lost interest in those
surgical miracles: how bone was taken from the rabbit
and grafted on the pet of the hospital ward; how blood
was transfused, and the calf robbed of nerves for the
sake of the V.C. bomber, or the palsied lad who had ripped
up a dozen Huns in a minute's "haymaking" with the
bayonet. Such wonders grew more than stale. So did
pictures of the Hughes balance; the electro-magnet and
the microphone for locating steel fragments in the living
tissue.

Against these America set the German flame-projector
that burns men alive as they face the foe. How perverse,
when all was said and done; how revolting to men of
sense was this endless game of hurt and healing! Here
was Dr. Barthe de Sandfort who made a sound job of the
flayed poilu—"barely recognizable as a human being"
when brought in for the ambrine treatment to the famous
hospital at Issy-les-Moulineaux. America had no enthusiasm for this wanton mending. Nor had she any
pride in her own undoubted skill in the production of
artificial limbs. It was an added reproach, indeed, being
primarily the result of her own industrial speed-up, whose
casualties vied with those of Verdun and the Somme.

You will gather from my Foreword that America was
an unmilitary Power, with a policy diametrically opposed

to the Might before Right of Bismarck. "We are a very rich people," Theodore Roosevelt reminded them. "We are a fat, untrained, and helpless people. We have treated money-getting, soft ease, and vapid pleasure as the all-sufficing ends of life. We have let our Navy run down, we have refused to build up our Army. We have acted as if wealth and wordy sentiment atoned for the lack of those stern virtues upon which alone true national greatness rests. There is no surer way to court disaster than to be opulent, disliked—and unarmed!"

But that reproach has passed in a Day of violence of which no man can see the end; it was passing when Roosevelt wrote those words. For the first time nationhood was being born in the United States. New seeds and sparkles glowed in the melting-pot, and all eyes were fixed upon its ferment. For the older nations were now pale with the sickness of war. They were indeed "among the graves," as the prophet said, "and broth of abominable things is in their vessels."

Having said so much, let me light my candle at the cannon's mouth and show the Land of Opportunity, its striving castes and problems, together with the perils which beset the people's chosen path, and for the first time thrust them into a mighty struggle overseas.

CONTENTS

CONTENTS

AMERICA'S DAY

AMERICA'S DAY

CHAPTER I

"KEEP OUT" AND "KEEP OFF"

THE apostle of Preparedness was early abroad in the
United States preaching the god of war to Stoics and Epi-
cureans of capricious hearing. For these, their President
feared—with relucting mind, you understand, forced to it
by the press of fact—had been too long aloof "in provincial
isolation." It was a revolutionary saying. The many
Americas debated it back and forth—here with assent,
there with dissent or discord, dying away to complete indifference in the great food-acres of the Middle West.

In the United States we have the hugest assembly under
any civilized flag. They muster well over a hundred million souls scattered through sixty degrees of longitude, and
they include every race upon earth. "We are to play a
leading part in the world-drama," Dr. Wilson announced,
"whether we wish it or not." But the last election showed
no crusading zeal among the masses. America, her Chief
Executive told us, was vitally interested to secure universal
peace and save the smaller nations from violence and
wrong. But there are many Americas: who knew this better than Woodrow Wilson? Knightly champions there
might be along the Atlantic fringe; there were none at all
in the intermountain States east of the Rockies and west
of the Mississippi Valley. Here Freedom's pibroch had a
soothing sound; the price of beef on the hoof was more
than all the tortured Armenians.

When you mentioned war down in Texas or Arizona, it

was Mexico that became the fluent theme. On the Pacific Slope the Japanese bogey brooded as an abiding menace. So that each America was immersed in matters of its own; it was the Federal Government's affair to unite them all, and call a country's pride out of the continental immensity. The prime purpose of the United States, as Dr. Wilson reminds us, was to crystallize—"at any rate in one government, the fundamental rights of man." . . . "America," he said again, "must be ready hereafter as a member of the family of nations to exert her whole moral and physical force for the assertion of those rights throughout the earth."

So did the President prepare his people for that "leap in the dark" which Senator Lodge and many others condemned. Certainly Wilson was throwing to the winds of war the great principles of his predecessors, above all, the "Keep Out" counsel enshrined in Washington's Farewell Address, and handed down as America's gospel! "Europe," the Liberator explained, "has a set of primary interests which to us have none, or a very remote relation." Again and again the First President warned the infant State against foreign wiles. "Our detached and distant situation," he was glad to say, "enables us to pursue a different course." America might extend her commerce, but she would do well to have "as little political connection as possible" with the older Powers, their devious unions, quarrels and intrigues.

Such was the advice of the greatest American. To the "Keep Out" of Washington, James Monroe added his famous "Keep Off" in 1823, thus completing America's aloofness. It was with vague unrest that Monroe heard the pious vows of Prussia, Russia, and the Holy Alliance. Those precepts of Christ, those principles of justice, charity, and peace were thought to hide the devil's own designs upon Spanish America.

"We owe it to candour," Congress was told in Monroe's famous message, "to declare that any attempt on the part of the Allies to extend their system to this hemisphere will be considered dangerous to our peace and safety." With existing Colonies in the New World the United States had no concern. But any fresh adventure would be viewed as an unfriendly act.

"Keep Out" and "Keep Off" were the guiding politics of the United States down to the fateful year of 1914. The Great War put an end to this isolation, though the masses would not admit as much. America was so secure in the old days, so free to develop herself in ways of her own choosing. For nearly a century each Administration sang the praise of this policy. On the 4th of July silver tongues (like Bryan's) blessed the care-free hugeness over which Old Glory waved. What happiness was here, what lofty theories of life and man's duty to his brother! American envoys abroad were set apart from their colleagues. They were glad to be mere crows amid the paradise-birds around a throne; black-coated democrats in a gorgeous rout, decked with the gold lace and jewelled orders of a guileful and secret service.

The election of 1916 altered the political map of the United States, to the confusion of the Old Guard. For the first time something like a nation's voice was heard, but not even a Quixote would construe it as that of a champion of the world's woe. "He kept us out of war," men said of Wilson. There were wonderful times ahead, with America thrust into leadership and Europe a chaos of mourning and spilt blood. The election revealed the strength of the "Keep Out" tradition. Wilson's first term was full of it—though he veered and changed with every beat of the storm. His Message to Congress in 1914 opposed preparation for war. That of 1915 called upon the people for whole-hearted efforts "to care for their own security and that of the Government they have set up to serve them.'' Twitted with inconsistency, Wilson owned to a receptive mind, ever alive to fresh streams of thought. He was serene as Lincoln under these anxious digs. ''Yes,'' said the Emancipator calmly, ''I've another opinion now. I don't think much of a man who isn't wiser today than he was yesterday.''

''Always learning'' was Wilson's motto, as it was Michelangelo's. But could he impart his knowledge to the devotees of Prosperity and Peace? Would his people accept his prompting before it was too late? ''We can no longer indulge our parochialism,'' the President told them plainly, with no hint of his own regret for the old American way. They must pile up ships, he urged. They must patrol their coasts with aircraft, and not play the foolish virgin, caught unprovided in the stormy dark. So said the cautious Wilson to the States of the Union—those easy-going sovereignties which to the average Briton are ''something like our own counties.'' America's vastness is seldom grasped, though most of her problems spring from it. California alone is bigger than Great Britain and Ireland. So is Montana—though its population is not much more than Bristol's.

In Texas—the Lone Star State—you could stow all the kingdoms, principalities, and Grand Duchies of the German Empire, leaving room for Holland and Belgium in the semi-arid Panhandle, which is now a field of corn. Unless this immensity is borne in mind, with its range of climates, crops, and races—European, Asiatic, and African—no attempt to reveal America is of any avail.

Isolation was over. The ''Keep Out'' counsel of Washington was well enough for three million settlers strung out along the Atlantic coast. But now—! And even Washington had something to say about Young America's risks and liabilities. These, it seems, grew with ''our rising prosperity." "There is a rank due to the United States," her first President declared, "which will be withheld, if not absolutely lost, by a reputation for weakness." So the pursuit of peace might become an abject aim—far worse, indeed, than any lust of war for its own sake on Clausewitz lines.

Slowly, then, conviction crept through the United States that God was on the side of big battalions, and that Justice, in the last resort, spoke with giant guns and bombs. I say the conviction "crept," for it was not a welcome thought. The "Keep Out" advice died very hard in spite of urgent warnings. It survived the *Lusitania* shock and many another, bobbing up serenely with all the toughness of a timber-laden derelict. A word from the State Department, and "that easier feeling" supervened, as it did after the *Nebraskan,* the *Arabic, Hesperian, Persia, Silius, Sussex,* and *Marina.*

Beyond question the desire to Keep Out delayed the "strict accountability" of President Wilson's First Note to Berlin. Two minor tragedies—the *Falaba* and *Gulflight* —came before the *Lusitania* and involved American lives. As the list grew longer, fury rose in the Eastern States— only to die away in vast spaces west of the Alleghanies. On the other hand, New York and Washington laughed at the prairie politics of Hickory Creek, where the cowboy-statesman started a war-withering simoon in his local paper, comparing the American soldier to a watchmaker on the Congo—a man who should change his job at once lest society turn upon him as a useless drone.

We are all familiar with Roosevelt's fulminations against Wilson, the man of peace.

"Nothing permanent," he told the people in one of his early moods, "is ever accomplished by force." Then how were the British expelled, the dissentients asked. How was this continent won from the Indians? How was Secession crushed, and the Union saved in the Civil War? . . . Wilson was hedging at last, and changing his tune: "The United States can never be the same again." Here was the new note. "From across the Atlantic, from across the Pacific, we feel in our heart new calls and currents that touch our very life.".

No wonder the professional soldier increased his demands. Here was the Federal Chief of Staff, General Hugh L. Scott, proposing a standing army of 250,000, expanding to three millions in war-time and drawn from the whole manhood of the continent. General Leonard Wood, Commander-in-Chief of the American Army, was equally blunt in answering Mr. Bryan. "No wolf was ever frightened by the size of a flock of sheep. . . . If you have ideals worth defending, then words alone will not avail you. . . . We have far too many orators—too many Fourth of July flowers about a million citizens leaping to arms between dawn and dark. We of the War College sat up all night for three weeks in 1916 hoping to see thirty thousand volunteers take that leap for service on the Mexican border at the President's call. Take my word for it, it was a heavy jump they made with seventy-five per cent. of failure among the athletes we had counted on."

The President's party was well provided with answers to all reproach. Elihu Root accused them of not making timely provision "to back American diplomacy by actual or assured naval and military force." But Mr. Root and his colleagues, the Democrats said, had had twelve years of control in which to make this very provision. Not even Roosevelt, the most forceful of Presidents, could rouse enthusiasm for his Big Stick, which America was to carry and speak softly if she were to win her way and command the world's respect.

"Is our nation one, or a discordant multitude?" Mr. Root flung at the State Convention in New York. "Have selfish living, factional jars, and love of ease obscured our spiritual vision? Has the patriotism of a people never summoned to sacrifice become lifeless?'' Here were searching questions from a great American. They went to the very source of a continental apathy which has long been the despair of statesmen in a loose federation of sovereignties. "Here's a hoop to the barrel!" was the bitter toast of General Washington's officers long ago. It was a caustic allusion to the disruptive tendencies of the thirteen original States. This lack of cohesion persisted until 1916, baffling and obstructing the national government.

It is no easy matter to make a nation with three thousand miles between two of its capitals. The ideals of Ireland and Albania are no further apart than those of New York and Nevada. Far more than distance divides subtropic Florida, its orange-groves and palms, from bleak Montana, where the very wolves perish in their winter lairs. As for social contrast, let me set on one hand the Babylonian splendour of Newport, and on the other hand negro squalor in the "Black Belt" of Mississippi, where the white man is in a minority, and racial hatred is for ever smouldering.

I hope I convey some idea of the problems confronting the Federal Administration in 1916. President Wilson's appeal for unity to the League of the Foreign-Born had high significance. "A man or a woman," he said, "who becomes a citizen of the United States is not expected to give up his or her love for the land in which they were born. But we do expect them to put their new allegiance above all others." Nor should the foreign-born (Dr. Wilson hinted) continue to live by themselves—using their own language, having their own newspapers, and passively refusing to merge with America, where the "good mixer" has the best chance in opportunity's arena. It was the foreign-born who warred upon their adopted country in a season of strange malignance.   Infernal machines wrecked American docks and Allied ships.   About the factories were set barbed wire; armed sentries protected the plant from citizens whom the President, in a famous Message to Congress, "blushed to admit" as Americans.   They "poured poison into the very arteries of the United States," the National Assembly was told.   It was an onslaught of which America had never dreamed: "And we are without adequate Federal laws to deal with it."   Here was a frank confession of impotence.   The judgment of crime is a matter of States' Rights.   A fugitive murderer must needs be extradited, as from a foreign land.   It was so with the notorious Harry Thaw, whom New York could only arrest after long and costly litigation with the States of Vermont and Maine.

There are, indeed, myriads of American laws, most of them easily evaded because framed by amateurs and inoperative beyond the State line.   Thus the bachelor in Reno (Nevada) fresh from the "nisi-mills" of the Desert State, may find himself a bigamist in Spartanburg—for South Carolina has no divorce law at all.   A girl child of twelve can be a wife in Kansas and Kentucky.   She must be eighteen in Idaho and New York.   It is hard to imagine the chaos made in this way by forty-eight Parliaments electing over four thousand members, all of them anxious to please local supporters in a novel field.   At the last legislative session in Sacramento (Cal.), 2877 new Bills were introduced, and 771 were added to the Statute Book. The Sessions Laws of Arkansas for 1915 fill a volume of 1046 pages, those of Massachusetts one of 1100 pages.   I write of a New World isled in its own immensity, and impossible to grasp in a single *coup d'œil*.   It is a politico-social experiment on the hugest scale, preferring its own mistakes to our experience.   America is a noisy palæstra of sleepless wit and unresting hands.   Its strenuous aura is best felt in the personal formula of George W. Perkins, the insurance magnate, who retired at fifty to devote himself and his wealth to public welfare, education, and art. "My own method," Mr. Perkins says, "has been to live every day as though it was the only day I had to live, and to crowd everything possible into that day. I gave no heed to the clock, nor to what I was paid. I worked and lived for all there was in it."

Here is business efficiency defined by a master, with the speed-up focussed into a burning spot of corrosive power. For many years this was America's gospel, but today it is questioned for the first time. The colossal waste of life in Europe set up waves of constructive sympathy in the United States. "Over here," says Mr. Darwin P. Kingsley, of the New York Life Insurance Company, "the human machine begins to go to pieces at fifty-five. It is the price of our peace, and nobody counts the cost. So marked is the death-rate increase that all the companies have revised their rules for accepting lives at fifty-five and over."

Physical unpreparedness was hailed by professional soldiers as a factor in their favour. They argued that a stiffish course of training in early manhood would fit the American for every emergency of modern life, whether in peace or war. Governor Whitman of New York declared that compulsory service was in no way inconsistent with American tradition and aims. The revered head of Harvard University, Dr. Charles W. Eliot, also defended this step, since "the oceans are no longer barriers but highways inviting the passage of fleets." Besides, a citizen army on the continental scale was America's duty towards the peace of the world. Force was still supreme. And, reviewing the Great War, the old scholar reminded his people that: "Neither religion nor popular education has shown any power to prevent this lapse to savagery."

The American masses not only loathed war; they mistrusted the panoply and ritual of it. Congress has always suspected soldiers and placed them under a ban. The General Staff—a recent creation—was not loved in Washington, where the War Department has thus far been in civilian hands. "Keep away from Congress," General Wotherspoon warned his colleagues on his retirement. For he also was an alarmist; a man of conscience and plain professional speaking about a small and dwindling army, and a system of State militias worthy of the comic stage, and all the anathema heaped upon them in the report of Generals Wood and Barry.

There was something unmartial in this New World atmosphere. American history shows an inveterate reliance upon citizen levies, from Bunker's Hill to the Mexican Border of 1916. The army was abolished—re-established, reduced to 6000 men, and throughout regarded as a nuisance. One result of this was a war of seven years against the Seminole Indians, who, with 2000 braves in the field, called for over 60,000 American troops to put them down, at a cost of $70,000,000. The larger war in Mexico, the Rebellion of the South, and the clash with Spain—these taught America little in the way of armed preparation suited to the needs of a growing Power. "It is unhappily true," says Major-General W. H. Carter, U. S. A., "that in none of our wars has the Government been able to count upon the active support, or even of the good-will, of all the nation . . . even when the very life of the Union was at stake."

It was ignorance of these facts which made our own newspapers ask "What will America do?" after each new affront put upon President Wilson by Germany. What else could he do but "Keep Out" if that were the wish of his people? When he pictured them as champions of the weaker nations—quick and ardent custodians of the world's peace, "with every influence and resource at their command"—Dr. Wilson was careful to add: "But the war must first be concluded." He showed marvellous insight into the many-sided Republic. No doubt he hoped to educate the masses in preparedness, with wasted Europe before them, and a growing power in Asia fast closing the once "Open Door" in China, and heaping up fighting forces by sea and land and air. But in the flush time of 1916 Wilson admitted frankly that America had no world-policy at all. "To carry out such a program we need unity of spirit and purpose." And the "unified strength" upon which the President harped was not as yet in sight.

The New World was wholly misunderstood in Europe. Why, it was asked, had not the Big Neutral given a moral lead to the rest? Why had she fussed over her cotton and grain; why had she taken up Prussia's catchword about "the freedom of the seas"? It was because (one heard) of that trade neutrality which made Sweden protest so sharply over her mail-bags, Holland over her herrings, Spain over her oranges and cork—bulky cargoes in a time of tight tonnage and ruthless submarines. If America had only thrown her ægis over Belgium when the scrap of paper was torn, and the German hordes began to martyr the most innocent of all nations! So ran the reproaches on this side, whether expressed or implied.

European poets and scholars scathed neutrality of every shade, from the Pope's to that of American people. "The world is watching," Maeterlinck called across the sea, "to judge if the strength of your fathers is also yours." But America was not aroused; she was not in fighting trim at all. She would feed the hungry and care for the father-less and prisoners of war. Beyond this she was power-less. "What can America do?" asked the German papers, with an easy contempt that was almost incredible, addressed as it was to a continent of a hundred millions—

the richest on earth and the most insistent upon moral
claims and covenants. America must needs win her masses
to whole-hearted preparation if she were to be among the
guarantors of universal peace. "It is inconceivable,"
President Wilson told the Senate, "that we should play no
part in that great enterprise." For if peace were to endure, it must be secured by "the organized major force
of mankind." And in the same address Dr. Wilson dwelt
upon the limitation of armaments by sea and land as "the
most intensely practical question connected with the future
fortunes of nations and mankind."

It is plain that America has strong views upon this
subject. It was the piling up of weapons which menaced
"the sense of equality among the nations." Therefore the
President favoured a reduction, advising the world's rulers
to "plan for peace and adjust their policy to it." But he
could not be consistent in this matter. He was plainly
in a strait between the ideal of disarmament and the defence of the United States, which was an urgent affair upon
all grounds.

Wilson, indeed, went further than Roosevelt in his naval
aims. He declared himself in favour of "incomparably
the greatest Navy," since America's coast-line is so exten-
sive. The Cabinet's new five-year program called for an
outlay on ships of $661,000,000, with twenty per cent.
above specified prices for speed in building and general
efficiency of all craft. Professional advisers of the Government insisted upon these measures; the masses either
resisted or were listless and unconcerned. It was the in-
terplay of these active and passive forces which gave rise
to so much confusion. Official Washington had to walk
very warily, doling sympathy and blame to all belligerents
with the apathy of the larger Americas ever in view.

Britain was aghast at the detachment shown in the President's early speeches. So was France, where Freedom

blazed in the very heart of desolation. And she signalled
mute reproach to her sister Republic across the seas:

"I am she that was thy sign and standard-bearer,
    Thy voice and cry;
She that washed thee with her blood and left thee fairer,
    The same am I!"

Still there was no sign, and the amazement of Paris
broke into open reproaches. "When England tried to op-
press you with the help of hired Hessians, the peasants
of France came to your aid. They fought by your side,
they died for you. And yet, today in our agony. . . ."
It roused nothing but vexation, as the memory of a debt
so often does.

As a well-wisher, the *New York Tribune* was sorry to
record this sentiment. However, there it was, faintly moving America in the mass. It would be well for the Allies,
·the *Tribune* said, "to renounce all thought that America
is a sympathetic country, or one in which community of
ideas exists with regard to the present clash." It was
true that both France and Britain had warm friends in
the United States. "But they are in the minority; they
have not been able to mould American feeling." The old
French alliance, ties of British race and of language—
these were but frail exhalations from history's page. "The
sooner the Allies think of America as a foreign country—
not necessarily friendly, and certainly not of their way
of thought—the better for all concerned."

It was "reparation for the *American* lives lost," that
Dr. Wilson demanded in his first *Lusitania* Note. And
if in his next he warned the sea assassin "with solemn
emphasis," it is well to remind British readers of hot
American protest against the "vexatious and illegal prac-
tices" of our own blockade. All nations were foreign when
viewed from neutral Washington, whose outlook may be
expressed in the mild phrase of Lincoln, "With malice towards none, with charity for all."

CHAPTER II

A QUAINT episode in American history is the offer of a crown to General Washington by the officers of the Revolutionary Army. It was almost a mutinous army, ill-clad and ill-fed; dismissed at last and scantily paid in paper worth two per cent. of its face value. Only Washington's influence prevented an open revolt. It is curious to survey America's dislike of the "standing army," and later on of a navy—that added evil due to crescent power and the new duties that came with it. It has always been a point of honour with Congress to lop and prune these noisome growths of the State; it was at one time a moot point whether they were necessary at all.

In 1810, when Europe flamed with the Napoleonic wars, John Randolph of Virginia rose in the Lower House with the familiar motion "to reduce our naval and military establishments." "With respect to war," cooed that Bryan of his day—poet, orator, and wit—"we have in the Atlantic a force wide and deep enough to ward off peril from the land." Two years later that moat was crossed by a hostile army; before the war was over the very chamber in which Randolph had spoken was burned by British soldiers. But nothing altered the traditional mistrust of Congress for an armed host; the consequence is seen in America's unreadiness for all her wars.

What alarmed her advisers in 1916 was that the first onset of a modern enemy might be a lightning stroke, like the German sweep towards Paris. Leisurely war was a thing of the past; so was the raising of levies by bounties or reluctant drafts, as in the long-drawn Civil War. "The

14

records show conclusively," says Major-General W. H. Carter, the military historian, "that the theory of citizen volunteers ready to march in our defence is wholly fallacious." When the nation's fate hung in the balance, only 46,626 men over twenty-four years of age could be found for the Union Army; the vast majority were boys of sixteen or less. It took two years to train these troops and develop a Gettysburg from the dangerous rout of Bull Run, where disaster was only averted by eight hundred regulars who fought a rearguard action. In the war with Spain the volunteers, with few exceptions, were unfit to embark. Their lack of discipline, the failure of supplies; the disease and chaos at Chickamauga and Key West Camps—these are today as ghastly as they are fresh in the memory of professional soldiers.

The Commander-in-Chief, General Leonard Wood, warned the House Committee on Military Affairs in the usual way. "To send our troops into war as they are, without guns or ammunition, would be absolute slaughter." It was the Federal Army to which the speaker referred. Of the National Guard, or forces of the several States, called out on the Mexican Border, General Wood reported to the War Department that "only 25 per cent. of these can be reckoned as reasonably instructed soldiers." The Kentucky and Georgia Guards showed 50 per cent. of physical rejections. Of the 8th Ohio Infantry, 500 men were unfit. It was no wonder, therefore, that on the march Virginia lay down in companies; New York shed 90 men in 6 miles of the open road. Thousands had no uniform; thousands more had never fired a service rifle in their lives.

But why were such troops employed in a national emergency? In order to give the Regular Army a chance to recruit and make ready; it was at that time 34,307 men below its peace strength under the new law. On the other hand, the Navy was 2000 officers and 60,000 men short, so that when the *Arizona* went into commission she retired three older battleships, absorbing their crews and putting to sea short-handed herself. Such is the monotonous story of both Services.

The Washington Bureaux are full of secret reports pigeon-holed by a genial sin of habit. Here is one such warning from Secretary of War Dickinson and his Chief of Staff: "A foreign country," the House Committee was informed, "could land 200,000 veterans on our Western Coast in thirty days. To meet this invasion the three States west of the Rockies (California, Oregon, and Washington) could only muster 3000 Regulars and 5000 Militia; these last of little use, and all lacking transport and munitions." Still more alarming were reports upon the coast-defence artillery. The whole continent was more or less defenceless, although millions of money were spent, and the Washington Bureaux issued rosy reports to the papers.

The condition of the Navy was very bad. A Committee of Congress was its real ruler; the fighting Staff could only report defects and hope for the best, though with no illusions about promise or performance. Five battleships of the *Kentucky* class and five destroyers of the *Alwyn* class were accepted with defective machinery. Admiral Fletcher found the submarines in a "deplorable condition." At times not more than five were ready for duty. They could not reach their assigned stations 75 miles south of Nantucket, nor could they maintain their surface speed in moderate weather. Some of them leaked, others broke cylinders and cranks, or else they could not submerge at all. Rear-Admiral Grant assured the Naval Committee that "twenty-two of our K submarines are about equal to three of the German U-39."

Target practice by the larger ships brought bitter comment from Admiral Winslow and Captain Sowden Sims, two of the ablest officers in the Navy. Admiral Edwards pointed out that there was not a dry dock in the South Atlantic or Gulf coasts capable of taking a superdreadnought. Nor was there a single crane there that could install or remove a heavy gun. It may be taken for granted, on the best professional authority, that both Navy and Army were at all times unready for active service against a modern enemy. To America, war was a preposterous thought. Therefore soldiers and sailors, guns and ships existed only on grudging sufferance. They ate up millions, America was ashamed to say; so the wise thing was to keep these dragons as feeble as possible by denying their demands. "Ten of my twenty-one 5-in. guns cannot be manned," mourns the captain of the *New York* during manœuvres. Shortage in the engine-room staff of the *Arkansas* caused a serious explosion. It crippled the ship, and caused the admiral to declare himself unable "to meet on equal terms similar types in foreign navies."

It was this repressive rule which made Roosevelt say that "the whole Service is being handled in such a way as to impair its fitness and morale." But the American people would have it so; their whole complexion and quality of life was rosed over with peace and strenuous joy. Only the statesmen and professional fighters were anxious over the new era of armed sanction. Elihu Root impressed upon the Yale students that "while democracy has proved successful under simple conditions, it remains to be seen how it will stand the strain of those vast complications upon which the country is now entering." In other words, America was at the parting of the ways, and her men on watch had a delicate task to break the unwelcome news together with the sacrifice of comfort it would entail.

This accounts for President Wilson's vacillation and his slow abandonment of the "Keep Out" policy. After all,

Washington himself foresaw a sweeping change; there was comfort in that for the present White House occupant. The first President traced young America's growth along inevitable lines. He dared not hope that his impress would remain for ever, or his guidance "control the usual current of the passions, or prevent our nation from running the course which has hitherto marked the destiny of nations."

America's new destiny was soon the insistent theme of President Wilson. "The business of neutrality is over," he assured the farmers. This war of peoples was the very last from which America could hope to refrain. As things chanced, however, Fate was kind—kind to the United States, equally kind to stricken Europe, who looked overseas for a friend on the grey morrow of her dreadful orgy. "They will need us," the Ohio folk were assured by their President. His hearers agreed, recalling how King Albert asked the late Jim Hill, of the Northern Pacific, to rebuild the Belgian railways when all was over.

There would also be Russia and East Prussia to renew, with Northern France, the two Polands, Serbia, Rumania, Bulgaria, and Montenegro. Here were wide marts, and with them high mission to comfort the sore and scattered races. It was a lattermath of service which appealed with peculiar force to America. Already she felt the fires of war falling away. Uncle Sam would yet be the hierarch of a nobler altar, one built of Vermont marble and Nevada gold, overlaid with silks from the New Jersey mills! Business first, and with it Samaritan ministry for all the belligerents. There was "infinite prosperity ahead," as Dr. Wilson assured his people in election speeches. "We have bought back two thousand million dollars' worth of securities. In the first two years of war we amassed one-third of the world's gold."

And yet—? This riot of riches seemed to bring anxiety in its train. Official Washington, as nerve-centre, felt auras of fear chilling the wide elation of the continent. Military weakness was no longer a joke, neither was the endless "war" between Committees of Congress and keen officers of both Services who had America's honour and safety at heart. Even the State guardsman, a purely political figure, disappeared from the comic papers upon whose coloured covers he had capered with a javelin and a stone ax. "We must Prepare," men told each other—without any alarm, however, for there was no hurry. This was the new note that flickered from Bar Harbor to San Diego—which is now an aircraft station on the Pacific. "We shall be called upon to defend this Prosperity of ours." It was at once a nuisance and a novelty. There was talk of Preparedness— just talk and little more—all the way from Puget Sound to the Florida Keys.

Out at Sheepshead Bay the New York police manœuvred with bombs and maxims before an admiring crowd. Naval Secretary Daniels invited likely citizens to take a three weeks' cruise on a warship with a view to increasing the Naval Reserve. But when all was done, it was a languid campaign. To the Slovak farmer twelve hundred miles from any sea, Preparedness for war was pointless babble. In the Atlantic tier of States men were awake and aware; they were also carping at ways and means, like the rich burgess of other days who peered from the coach and spied robber horsemen in the chilly dawn. There were "Get Readys," and there were "Let Bes." Between these and the anti-British and pro-Germans, the President steered a precarious and troubled way. His position reminds one of the Pope's own, with the gentle Mercier of Malines upon one hand and Cardinal Hartmann of Cologne on the other, rolling out a very different tale of the Herrenvolk and their ways in a conquered land.

" 'Tain't easy, bein' Pres'dent, I guess," was a sympathetic hazard flung at Lincoln in his darkest days. The great man agreed, with gaunt simplicity. "I feel like the Irishman," he explained, "who was ridden on a rail and tried to keep his dignity all through. 'Ef 'twasn't f'r the honour o' the thing,' Pat called to his friends, 'I declare to God Oi'd rather walk!'" With the queerest of wars in Mexico, with German defiance at sea and rabid hyphenism at home, centring in the Imperial Embassy at Washington, Dr. Wilson's was indeed an unenviable lot.

There was much to be feared from the German-Americans. Nationalism had lain dormant in these exiled millions; it woke to frenzy the whole world over at the Fatherland's call.

"Don't you *dare* declare war on us," panted the Milwaukee German to his half-brother, the American. "If you do, you'll have the Japs on your back and ourselves in your guts!" It was not a pretty speech, but it was characteristic of the hyphenate in his early heat. Military weakness, then, as well as mixed races and unconcern for the issues, account for the humiliations heaped upon America during the first two years of the war. Her newspapers— those of the East should be understood—fretted and fumed afresh over the havoc wrought by U-boat 53 in home waters. How Gay of the *Benham* was waved aside by Hans Roze, who smashed ship after ship, leaving the American to pluck his citizens from a watery grave if he chose. "Here is congenial use for our warships," wailed the *New York Herald*. "They shall pick up women and children, while these German sea-wolves blockade our coasts and wreck our commerce. A noble task for the successors of Oliver Perry and Isaac Hull; Stephen Decatur, Farragut, and Dewey!"

Comment of this kind had as yet but little weight. President Wilson expressed his views in an identic Note to the warring nations, and subsequently to the Senate in Washington. The calamity oppressed him: "Every part of the great family of mankind has felt the burden and terror of this unprecedented contest of arms.'' In that contest America would take no part, but so ardent was her concern for the ensuing peace, that she was (her Chief Executive said) willing to forego her isolation and join an overwhelming coalition to preserve the sanctity of a new era.

The President spoke pontifically, and raised a great to-do. He had no censure for the submarine, no condemnation of chlorine gas or liquid flame; no abhorrence of the Zeppelin airships, nor of torture and killing from Louvain to Lake Van, where the Kaiser's Kurdish allies had done their damnedest to wipe out a nation. None of these things did President Wilson condemn, but there was pointed allusion to ''the freedom of the seas'' which was clearly intended for Britain. The presence of her cruisers was ''vexatious and uncourteous to the United States.'' The observer is struck by the different treatment meted by America to the two leading belligerents in this war. Mr. Lansing's Notes to Von Jagow contrast oddly with the sharp ring of protest to Sir Edward Grey over the stoppage of mails and the like non-vital issues.

The British Minister, Crampton, was given his passports in '55 for no greater offence than enlisting soldiers for the Crimean War. Sackville-West was dismissed for replying to a decoy-letter, to which he replied advising Americans of British birth to vote for Grover Cleveland. Whatever be the cause—clever propaganda on a great scale, homage to success, or hyphenate influence in Congress and the country—it cannot be denied that German and British transgressions were judged by two different standards in the United States. Count Bernstorff could boast of his ''Army''—an army of crime that terrorized industrial America. ''They have formed plots to destroy property,'' was the President's own plaint about them. ''They have entered into conspiracies against the neutrality of the Gov-

ernment; they have sought to pry into confidential trans-
actions in order to serve interests alien to our own.''

But for the time the hyphenates were able to baffle that
Government. Their violence had a longish run because, as
the President reminded Congress, ''We are without adequate Federal laws to deal with it.'' It was a German
axiom that ''Frightfulness paid'' and that German insight
into national motives was superior to that of any other.
There was much to support this view: for example, the
astonishing spectacle of a pro-German Spain, with an
officer of the General Staff drinking to the victory of the
Central Powers. ''Many people in Norway,'' said M. Nils
Vogt, a well-known publicist and brother of the Norwegian
Minister in London, ''admire Germany's power''—the same
power, you will recall, that sank fifteen of Norway's ships
in a single week to the tune of $4,200,000, to say nothing of
drowned men, or of lingering death and torment in the open
boats.

Beyond question America was impressed; millions admired the German machine, and at one time backed it to
win. Consider the gifts and banquets offered to Captain
Koenig of the subaqueous liner, *Deutschland,* which offered
to carry the American mails. ''There's nothing like Success to win over these people,'' said the *Muenchener
Zeitung.* The writer went on to purr over the ''atmosphere
of victory'' with which Deutschtum enveloped itself in all
lands, but especially in the United States. It was a solid
asset, one invariably neglected by that ponderous dunce,
John Bull.

I know nothing so curious as the rousing and regimenting
from Berlin of German forces overseas. In Bismarck's day
they were despised expatriates. ''America,'' the Pan-German stalwart, Hasse of Leipzig, used to say, ''is the grave
of Deutschtum.'' There was a big army there, but it was
an army of deserters, which had to be organized by the

Pan-German League. So far back as 1896 the Emperor
was appealing for help in the matter of linking these lost
forces.   There was at first no more enthusiasm for this than
for the Navy League, whose mission was to convince the
Empire that ''Our future lies upon the water.'' German
opinion had to be educated to these movements. It was to
the adhesion of learned men that Pan-Germanism owed its
rise at last.   There was a time when Mommsen dismissed
members of the League as ''our patriotic madmen.'' Yet
the cult continued to gain, even in the Reichstag, where it
won men like Hahn of the Agrarians, and Bassermann, the
head of the National Liberal Party.

It was Pan-Germanism that informed with new fire the
local Liederkranz of American cities; the Saengerbund, the
Verein-for-this, and the Gesellschaft-for-that. Devotees
were soon raising *schoppens* and *steins* to ''Der Grossere
Deutschland,'' which would one day stretch from the
Scheldt to the Persian Gulf, embracing the ''Kaliphate of
Berlin,'' which Sazonof outlined in the Russian Duma. As
a dream it was magnificent, and of course it meant war.
What mineral treasures lay in those Taurus depths! Assy-
ria and Babylonia should rival Oklahoma, California, and
the Caucasus as producers of oil. Cilicia and the Syrian
plains were to grow cotton for the German Empire. There
was to be wool from Anatolia, seas of wheat from the Meso-
potamian flats; flocks and herds beyond count upon classic
pastures now given over to the rascally Bedouin. The
whole face of Western Asia was to be changed. German
States were to be erected well out of Britain's reach and
beyond that hated ''Seegewalt'' which hampered Deutschtum's every move.

In 1900, when the German-American ''Army'' was organized, Von Holleben was Ambassador in Washington. A
very truculent envoy—no willow-back man like Bernstorff,
who succeeded him—Von Holleben defied Roosevelt over the

Venezuela dispute until the President massed his fleet at Guantanamo, and gave the Germans twenty-four hours to clear out. It is interesting to follow the German-American in those days, and watch him develop into the rabid hyphenate of 1914-15, whom the serious New York press styled "The most disappointing symptom of our national life since the disloyalty of the South in the ' 'sixties.' . . . No nation has ever been called upon to suffer so seditious a press as that published in the United States in the German tongue."

Yet before the present war no citizens were more esteemed. Germans and men of German descent had enormous influence. You found them in Congress and in the State Legislatures; they were bankers and railroad kings, manufacturers and traders on the largest scale.

The German-American Alliance had over two million members; Herr Hexamer, its President, wore the Red Eagle Order conferred by the Emperor "for diffusing German Kultur in the United States." But what was the part which Bernstorff's "Army" was to play as citizens of the divided allegiance? America was their home, but the Fatherland must be "over all"! In the first place— as Bernhardi pointed out—"the German element forms a political centre of 'gravity in our favour." They were really missionaries. The National Alliance was charged with the task of introducing the German language into American public schools; and how this is done is told by Dr. H. H. Fick, of the Cincinnati Education Service. The cities were bombarded with circulars urging the elect to: "Speak only German in your home, in your club, and in the stores. And speak German *loudly* in the street cars."

Political power was also sought. Herr Weismann, of Brooklyn, set the hyphenate machine in motion to defeat the election of a New York Congressman, and a Judge. In this he succeeded, and set out the moral in a rescript to all concerned. "The returns have proved that Deutschtum is armed and able, when the word goes forth, to seat its chosen men." So Germanism was already a menace to America's peace. Reckoning all enemy races, all shades of Teutonic sympathy and descent, I suppose there are nine or ten million adherents, beginning with the newly arrived Posen Poles and going on to State Governors and mayors, chiefs of police, and members of Parliament, whether of the Federal Assembly or the State Grange.

It was startling to see an ex-Cabinet Minister of the Roosevelt Administration—the late Von Legerke Meyer— prancing as a priest of Deutschtum, and warning America not to goad "his Fatherland" to extremes! This frenzy was a crippling disability in the body politic—especially . so when joined with the Irish forces, and those of pure pacificism in farming areas of unrealized vastness. Here was a trinity which, consciously or unconsciously, hindered all preparation for national defence. And that this was the aim of Pan-Germanism is shown by the correspondence between Professor Appelmann of Vermont University and Dr. Paul Rohrbach, the protagonist of the Berlin-Bagdad "Kaliphate," which is Germany's dearest dream.

The Professor wrote "home" to ask a question that troubled him: "Was Deutschtum in America justified in supporting these movements for a big army and navy?" To this Dr. Rohrbach sent an emphatic negative. "It is quite possible," he wrote to Appelmann, "that in an American-Japanese war we might act as benevolent neutrals towards the Asiatic, thus making it easier for him to defeat the United States. Therefore I cannot believe that our ends are in any way served by German-Americans lending themselves to domestic schemes of armament."

Well might the *New York Tribune* describe the rise and reign of the hyphenate as "the most shameful period of our history." "One thing is certain," said the powerful *Herald*, as stroke followed German stroke at home and abroad —"the tide of popular wrath is rising higher." But the journal was mistaken. There was as yet little trace of any such tide beyond Herald Square. America had grown accustomed to the horrors of war. She quivered a while after each shock, and then was still, just as parted water reunites after the waving of a wanton hand.

Frightfulness furnished table-talk; and this was excited or mild according to the zone and temperament of the America discussing it. "We shudder at it the first time," as Goethe said of the Merseburg beer, "but after we've drunk it a week or so we can't do without it." I know nothing so strange as the detachment with which grievous national insults were discussed, from the Great Lakes down to the Gulf.

Meanwhile Johann von Bernstorff, as director of an internal "war," went his way with wonderful unconcern. Not Hangman Peters in the heart of Africa ever pursued a policy of crime with less regard for "the natives." Washington itself might have been Windhoek; the President and his State Secretary, a couple of influential chiefs whom it were well to conciliate with suavity and the *beau geste* of a good-humoured boss. To this unique Embassy the Americans were of no account, as we know from Von Papen's captured papers. "I always tell these idiotic Yankees to hold their tongue," this apostle of Deutschtum wrote to his wife.

What could the President do in such a welter? "America has never witnessed anything like this before," he told the hushed Houses of Congress. "Never dreamed it possible that men sworn to her allegiance . . . would ever turn in malign reaction against the Government and people who welcomed and nurtured them." But new purpose glowed in Wilson's moves to filch power from the States and concentrate it in the national authority at Washington. For, after all, if democracy was to be saved, the President must needs become a "despot" as Lincoln did in his darkest hour.

CHAPTER III

NEUTRAL America, uneasy and beset, hoped that Preparedness was not a very urgent issue. And, whilst endorsing the theory, she put the practice from her, feeling sure that the world's Peace would hereafter enforce itself through vivid memories of tedium and terror drawn from these ghastly years.

Meanwhile, unpleasant truths were swallowed with a meekness entirely new. Girding and goading became the order of the day. Even the Hearst papers scolded the Americas, from Boston to Los Angeles. That odd farrago, the New York *American,* examined external dangers and rejected them all as negligible compared with the native lethargy that stifled military effort. It was not the yellow man nor the black man who was to be feared; there was a more insidious foe than Germany or Britain, the Hearst paper found. "The great white danger is here at home— the danger of national conceit and heedlessness of all things outside our continental circle" . . . "We cry out against the barbarism of Europe's war, well knowing that an army is only a mob. At the same time, our own mobs catch men and burn them alive. We call ourselves a Republic, yet any one can name a dozen rich men who have ten times the power of all the officials in the United States, because the Big Dozen stand for organized Money, which is the real ruler in our midst."

"Our abiding peril," the *American* concluded, "is not in this or that bogey overseas, but in the home-bred hydra of extravagance, self-satisfaction, inefficiency, and military

28

weakness which will make a walk-over of any foreign attack.'' In this vein was the new literature of Preparedness conceived; it flooded the continent, and then receded, apparently without leaving a lasting trace. It brought the dreamer back to earth; it killed the high hope of a new social order handed down by the early New England settlers. For a season you could scarce open a book or a magazine, a pamphlet or a newspaper, without finding the national fear shivering up and down the page. ''The American people is today in the plight of a man with a dull knife and a broken cudgel in an ever-growing circle of wolves.'' Statecraft pulled this way and Pacifism the other; the listless masses pulled no way, but wanted to be let alone.

''We implore your help in humanity's name,'' was agonized Belgium's cry, cabled to the Great Neutral by M. Carton de Wiart, the Minister of Justice. But official America was powerless. Her own citizens called in vain as they drowned, nearly two years after the *Lusitania* crime. ''Roosevelt is right,'' you heard men admit in the Eastern States. ''We've relied too much upon moral suasion. What fools we were to throw his Big Stick in the ash-barrel! Now here's Europe dumping her devilry at our door, and no doubt perfecting trans-oceanic aircraft for an invasion.'' Pacifism was weakening at last, even in States of the Central West—those exuberant Edens of beef and grain. Here orators became shy of painting a divine dawn when ''the lion shall eat straw, and dust shall be the serpent's meat.''

Those orators had many jars in the new day and found the old pose derided; their platform flags and water-pitchers, their stuffed doves and rolling periods about ''citizens leaping to arms,'' and licking a leagued world of wicked aggression. It was embarrassing to have ''Get Ready'' leaflets showered from an armed plane upon beatitude like this. Shortly before the war, Friederich von Bernhardi appeared on the Pacific Slope, having come from Japan and the Far East on a secret mission to the German-Americans. Dr. David Starr Jordan, a Californian pacifist of note and Chancellor of the Leland Stanford University, was invited to meet the famous General, who was instructing Bernstorff's hyphenate army.

The German visitor was business-like and curt at these private meetings. "Law is but a makeshift," he told his hearers: "the only reality is Force." And quite as frankly Bernhardi dwelt upon the tenuous nature of international treaties when the first shot rang out and German pledges melted like a dicer's oath. *"Not kennt kein Gebot"*— which is to say that need covers any deed; and reasons of war excused all things, from the poisoned well and the sinking of a hospital ship to slave-raiding and extortion among the heart-broken peasants of a conquered zone.

Upon these tenets America brooded in wonder and disgust. The people grew bored with all the prompting. Preparedness lost its edge: surely the thing was overdone by these politicians? Practical men put aside alarmist leaflets and turned again to the literature of power, such as drops like dew from the Department of Agriculture in Washington. *On the Value of Muck* is a worth-while guide to the worthy farmer. *On Hog Cholera* and *Grain Smuts, The Best Number of Hens in One Pen, Black Rot of the Cabbage, Fungus Troubles of Fruit Trees,* and *The Toad as the Farmer's Friend.* There was more for humanity here, it was argued, than in shrill appeals for machine-guns and bombs.

The conversion of President Wilson to militarism came as a real shock. So did the echo of German taunts in Democratic mouths that were trying to rouse the nation: "You have no Army. And such Navy as you have—a costly collection of ships—must stay at home." "It is our

wooden sword," the people were told afresh, "that is the
source of all dispraise, all flouting of our pride and honour. So it behooves us to arm, and to arm *now* ere the night
of our undoing be upon us." It was a strange turn of
Fortune's wheel that would heap weapons upon the Land
of Peace, just as Germany, the Land of War, sickened with
surfeit of that "drastic medicine," which her Saxon historian prescribed for a sluggish world. And how radiant
Prussia's war appeared in 1914, with its dazzling dementia
of overweening! What flaunting and flapping there was
in pedlar Britain's face, what fanning of Deutschheit to
white flame of passion by virtue of the sword!

"If you sink," cried ecstatic Fichte to the Fatherland,
"all humanity sinks with you." Hence the cocksure onset
of the German Michael in shimmering armour. But war-
weariness stole away his fire; the trampling mania grew
tamer until *Wir halten durch* (We're holding out) was the
master-word of the German masses' iron time. Last Christmas saw no cards sold in the Wertheim store showing the
Christ-Child knocking nails into Hindenburg's wooden
boots. All had changed, and from war's abyss nothing rose
but plaint and rue. For in the depths no shining milliards
of indemnity showed, but only trainloads of beloved corpses
tied with steel wire in stark naked fours, ready for pitching
to hell in the blast-furnaces of Seraing.

It was the creep of this cure in the very shrine of war
that America watched as one under a spell. She read
letters from mutinous German mothers; she weighed the
world's torment, and meted its tears all the way from the
Somme to the Tigris, and from African trails back to Verdun where Prussian *macht* lay like a broken moth, self-
shrivelled in its own flame.

An unlikely season, one had said, in which to bid America
pile up arms. And how did she take all the urging? Very
variously. Here excitedly; there disputatiously or feebly;

with a shrug elsewhere, or a blank stare across seas of corn
where "God an' Natur'" for ever wars against the farmer.
The "Get Ready" goading was often resented as treason
against the summer mood of a people concerned with output and results, and beyond these with the uplift and the
better life of man as they conceive it.

"It behooves us to keep our heads," said the Western
stalwart, whose feelings I want to interpret. And, mark
you, he was a power in the land, as President Wilson was
aware throughout. "Let *us* hug the real American hero.
He's no bomb-and-bayonet butcher; no gas-masked Thug
who lies in ambush where broken men sway and drip from
the barbed wire. No, sir. He's a benefactor to the race;
he's the lad who brought out of Switzerland the alfalfa-
seed which has transformed our empty West."

America's new Civil War was one between the "Let' Bes"
and the "Get Readys." These last were stern realists
entrenched in the hard angularity of facts. "Human nature," they owned sadly enough and with due disrelish for
the fact, "is the same now as in the first Olympiad. We
love war as little as you dreamers do, but we see it now as
an immedicable sickness—one that must endure until God's
own artillery shall blow away the stars. We're forced to
accept the Fichtean maxim that Right has no reality unless
fenced by Might." Between the two schools passed the
men of graft and "pork," mainly concerned with petty loot
and local power.

It was therefore a time of parry and thrust, of plain
words and sharp exordium, that withered America's olden
pride. Her wealth was no longer extolled as a shield or
an agent of defence at sudden need. Rather was it now
a flaring lure, one that called down destruction as careless
lights will do when the airship rides aloft in the dark.
"America is an undefended gold-mine," was the note of the
National Security League. And from both oceans (to say

nothing of the air), with Science in diabolic ministry, claim-jumpers were pictured closing in upon piled-up treasure worth $250,000,000,000. Meanwhile ten million citizens, untaught in arms, stood idly by, with the ghost of Lincoln renewing his reproaches of the Civil War and all his lonely desperation.

"Are we degenerate?" the Emancipator flung at citizens who refused to defend America in her darkest day. "Has the manhood of our race run out?" Equally blunt were appeals from the statesmen of 1916, yet the martial spirit remained anaemic and cold. "Look at China," was a hint from the Security League. "That unmartial giant is now the helot of Japan." "Look at ourselves in the 'sixties," urged the Navy League, which took up the call. "We had to let the Monroe Doctrine lapse in the chaos of our Civil War. And see how France took advantage! She marked out Mexico as a sphere, just as Germany fastened on Brazil in our own day. The Third Napoleon set Maximilian on that tragic throne, and we had to wait till our naval arm was free before we could reassert our authority."

All this should have been moving stuff at such a time. Yet Preparedness fell upon listless ears. "Speaking in all solemnity," said President Wilson at Kansas City after his conversion to the cult of force, "I assure you there is. not a day to be lost." Within twenty-four hours of that speech a vote in the State Grange put two million farmers cn record as being dead against a single dollar of increase in the Army and Navy appropriations. Sea-power had little meaning for the inland cultivator. What cared he for shadowy foes, Asiatic or European, when he wrestled night and day with "God an' Natur"? There is never any truce in this war with the soil; no rest, no decisive victory, but eternal grappling with mysterious, elusive hosts of heaven and earth. There are cyclones and hailstorms, drought and floods; frost and snow, wild beasts and poisonous plants. A single family of Montana wolves will destroy $3000 worth of stock in a year. The State of Colorado fought in vain to keep down the costly loco-weed that withered her horses with a slow, incurable marasmus. One campaign against this weed cost $200,000. There are also the fruit and grain-eating birds—plagues like the sand of the sea for multitude. There are rabbits and rats, bob-cats and "bugs," or insects. Of these last the American farmer faces a monstrous host—a hundred thousand differ-ent species, and of each kind legions beyond any counting. These scaly foes exact a toll of $700,000,000 a year from forest and farm, so that Prosperity calls for a valour of its own if it is to win and maintain its tide.

This peculiar valour the American possesses in a high degree. Moreover, he adds to it a rugged joy of battle which turns every obstacle into hope. I would call this strength the very mainspring of American character; it is the test by which all men are weighed and appraised in that strenuous land "Ef our woes had a Million Club, the same as 'Frisco has," a grim Texan put to me in Gal-veston, "they'd be out o' business in no time. As it is, they jus' sharpen our wits. Wha's the boll-weevil to *me,* man? Why, he's a noble inseck boostin' the price o' my cotton! As f'r the green-bug, he's an angel in disguise that forces the farmer to vary his crops. I tell ye tha's the true Amur'can sperit." And so it is—a spirit of gem-like hardness and nimble flame, focussed on the day's work and oblivious of all else.

Men upborne by this force are naturally slow to add fellow-workers in other lands to the crowding pests that prey with devilish ingenuity upon labour and life. Here, it seems to me, is the secret seat of that languor in the matter of America's defence. In the election of 1916 Wil-son ruined his rival's chance with a simple phrase, followed by a damning question: "He wants War; what other alternative is there to the policy I have pursued?'' Upon this a political revolution was wrought, soothing the unrest of a prosperous people vaguely impelled and drawn against their will into the seething vortex of the older nations. But the cocksure days are over, the days of beaming and spread-eagling, with happy assurance that potency and privilege lurked in the American name. During the war newspaper envoys were sent abroad to seek counsel and guidance in all quarters, from Vatican halls to Verdun itself, where democratic Joffre (that saviour of France) was asked to judge between America's men of peace and those who would ''Prepare'' with ships and guns and men for some tremendous Day.

In burly silence the soldier heard the case for Peace and War. It was the old dilemma of a demos swayed by every wind of words; a people fatally fond of its own ease and now tossed with dim dismay.

There was a frank parade of this before the French Generalissimo. Misgivings were quoted, from those of Hamilton to Wilson himself. . . . Now had he any fetters, Joffre was asked, to put about these free-footed fears? No, he had not. That captain of hosts had nothing to say about the people's control of foreign affairs, or the demand for russet Yeas and honest kersey Noes, instead of gold-laced guile in chariots and grand saloons, with princely precedence at Court and table. The great soldier was not to be drawn into a ''story,'' any more than the late King Oscar of Sweden, whose aid the American editor sought ''on the exceptional terms of twenty dollars a word.'' On the whole it was a meagre interview. All that fell from the Gallic oracle was quiet insistence upon ''the quality of self-discipline!'' There was need for it, this man of few words explained, in a Republic where the claims of liberty and the individual were unduly loud. Joffre extolled the suppression of self—*L'oubli de soi pour l'idéal*—which all the

world saw in the stricken heart of France. After all, what
was the love of country but the white flame sprung from
the mystical union of race and soil—*Par l'immémorial et
sévère hyménée.* . . . Discipline—just that and no more.
The stifling of weedy caprice; the calm *O France, tant que
tu voudras* of young poets and painters, already swallowed
in the ditch of deadly eyes. And what artists they were,
what ministers of grace and high gifts! Of these lyric
souls—*écrivains morts pour la Patrie*—France had a shining
legion. They left the sunlit heights for a vile sewer of
butchery; they chose a bloody death before the Chopin-life
of beauty, incense, and dreams. . . .

After all, that lovely spirit and unswerving choice was
not peculiar to Europe. It glowed in George Washington's
life as the American caller was reminded by his soldier-host.
It was seen in Lincoln's faith when his friends fell away in
the night of terror. There was little need for the United
States to seek advice abroad, for she had heroic voices of
her own. "A nation is not worthy to be saved," President
Garfield told the Lower House in '64, "if in the hour of its
fate it will not gather up its jewels of manhood and go
down into the conflict, however bloody and doubtful, resolved upon measureless ruin or complete success."

Nevertheless, Joffre's "quality of discipline" proved a
hard saying to the prosperity of the United States, where
military service was ever a hateful thing. In the stormy
'Sixties it was called "unconstitutional"—an attack upon
liberty which inflamed the mob to murder and madness.
Boston, Philadelphia, and Chicago ran red with riot against
the Lincoln "drafts"; the New York streets were full of
furies carrying firearms, iron bars, and knives. Federal
troops were clubbed to death with their own muskets; and
when Colonel O'Brien drew a pistol to defend his men he
was hanged upon a lamp-post and his body beaten by the
outraged proletariat. Yet one and all knew America's

future was at stake on that fateful April day when Beauregard's guns opened fire upon Fort Sumter.

Down to 1917 the panoply of war was decried by the zealots of moral suasion, of whom Mr. Bryan was the great exemplar.   At dove-and-brotherhood meetings these men deplored the genius wasted in war devices and proposed a more rational use for them.   Thus aeroplanes might locate the forest fire—that summer curse of the wilderness—and warn American settlers in the path of the flames.   The submarine was given a clear commercial future up and down the Alaska coast, where the winter floes prevent ordinary craft from landing Uncle Sam's mails.

So the first idea of a national army vanished, and with it went War-Secretary Garrison, whose plan the President would not openly endorse.   For Woodrow Wilson, with perfect knowledge of his people, was a slow and cautious convert to the "Get Ready" creed.   He knew that America in the mass was indifferent to a huge army, if not actually hostile to it.

His attitude to the notorious Hay Army Bill was a serious error.   It was a deplorable measure; the largest and most recent looting of the Federal Treasury by politicians who love "pork"—America's name for graft which use and custom have made respectable, especially in the State centres that profit by it.   Never has Washington seen such flagrant lobbying in both Houses of Congress as that which marked the passage of the so-called Army Reorganization. Never were the meanest of provincial interests arrayed so cynically against the nation.

The forty-eight States have armies of their own.   I shall not dwell upon the performance of these troops, for the story is tedious as well as grotesque.   As soldiers they were all but entirely negligible—untrained, unequipped, ill-disciplined, and physically unfit.   They were a social as well as a quasi-military body; on festal days they gave the

Governor's estate a certain figure and equipage. The Militia or National Guard could be called out to quell riots, but they were not under national authority, and swore allegiance only to their several States. The Dick Law of 1903 brought a certain measure of Federal control, and this was carried further by the National Defence Act of 1916. But the State Militias were still forty-eight easy-going armies. They served the local politicians, but were of little use to Federal officers worried over the problems of invasion and all-American defence.

"Could anything be more scandalous," asked General Butt, "than to take green men off the streets and send them down to the Border half-equipped, or with no equipment at all?" The men of Arkansas left with umbrellas and straw hats. Minnesota had "everything but uniforms and guns." The Illinois cavalry had no horses. Iowa boggled over the Federal oath; so did New Jersey, Maryland, and Massachusetts—whose Guardsmen were presently poisoned by their own rations! It was an aggrieved citizen army that kept watch on the Rio Grande and wrote letters to Colonel Roosevelt, of which the burden was "Never again!" . . .

The Hay-Chamberlain "pork" Bill was jockeyed through Congress by parochial lobbies and local champions, who are the worst enemies of their country, and are now thoroughly discredited. The idea underlying "pork" and political loot is that the Federal authority exists, not to be loyally served, but to be milked and plundered whenever possible; that Federal taxation of the States is really a system by which money flows to a common centre, and is—or should be— piped back again for distribution in "our district." A typical case was a bill to appropriate $75,000 for a post-office in McKee (Ky.). This turned out to be a village with a population of two hundred souls! But the appetite for "pork," like other ugly symptoms, is not so keen as it was.

There is everywhere a desire and demand for decency and social service among the mixed communities of this vast land.   Thus the little town of Ripon (Wis.) renounced an appropriation for a public building that was to cost $75,000. Ripon's Commercial Club asked to have that sum applied to Preparedness for national defence, preferably in the matter of aircraft.

CHAPTER IV

"STATES' RIGHTS" VERSUS THE NATION

IT is no easy matter to present in brief a clear idea of a "country" whose frontier has advanced two thousand miles in a single life-span. Let me take that of Colonel W. F. Cody, better known as "Buffalo Bill," because of his task of feeding with buffalo-meat the trackmen of the Kansas-Pacific Railway. Advancing in years, the Colonel settled down at last as farmer and irrigator in the dry lands of Wyoming. But the man's real *nunc dimittis* came in 1883, when he put his big Show on the road and knew the Wild West for ever tamed.

Dan Boone, Dave Crockett, Kit Carson, and Bill Cody—here in four dare-devil names is evoked the fascinating story of pioneer conquest in the United States. Her epic period is strangely near to us. The figure of Lincoln has all the magic of myth for America's younger generation, yet their fathers knew the Slave-emancipator in the flesh. Colonel Cody's life saw the passing of the Redskin, with his teepees, and squaws and scalps. Today the Shoshone brave wears a billycock hat and a Semi-Ready suit by Kuppenheimer "as advertised for dressy College men"! The Five Civilized Tribes—Choctaw, Chickasaw, and the rest—are now demurely herded and taught in the Reservations. Black Hawk and Sitting Bull of 1918 are flourishing dentists and attorneys; the smaller fry accept bread-and-blanket doles from a paternal Government in Washington. The big chief, once lord of the lonely horizon, now scuds abroad in a Ford car hunting a drink of bad whisky in some corrugated iron cave, far from the omniscient eye of Prohibition. *Sic transit gloria mundi!*

40

Many States, like Texas and California, are potential empires in area and natural resources. All of them lay claim to sovereignty, and this is clearly defined in the original Constitution. When the Peace of Paris closed the War of Independence in 1783, there were thirteen autonomous States with no common bond at all, and certainly no thought of Federation. New York especially opposed the idea.

To the eloquent Hamilton, the early Continental Congress presented an "awful spectacle" of stormy disunion and jealous watch upon State prerogatives and rights. Delegates eyed each other as foreigners, alert and wary as Prussian envoys at a Hague debate upon Disarmament. None was a patriot whose aims outsoared the boundary of his own State: Federation, Government from a common centre for the common weal—here was a notion long and violently resisted. A "League of Friendship" was put forward instead, as between striving nations of a virgin continent, beset with dim perils and engaged in a *sauve qui peut*.

Washington and Franklin, Madison and Hamilton, had an all but impossible task, but at length they won the States to a Federal Constitution. It soon fell into utter chaos. Congress alone could decide upon war, but it was powerless to raise or equip an army. In case of dispute, Congress was to arbitrate between the States, but either party could (and did) flout the Federal decision. It rested with Congress to make foreign treaties, yet any State might violate these with impunity. Washington himself wrote to the autocratic governors urging the need for a national revenue to be raised by Congress. To this there was only a stinted and grudging response. Some of the States pleaded poverty, and fell into arrears. Others offered their own woefully depreciated paper. A few declined with wrath until delinquents had paid their share.

It was a phase that could not last. "We are labouring hard," wrote Alexander Hamilton, "to establish in this country principles more and more national . . . so that we may be neither Greek nor Trojan but thoroughly American." The task is not yet complete, for States' Rights have always had their champions, of whom the most noted was that sturdy Democrat, Thomas Jefferson, the third President of the Union. A more formidable advocate was Jefferson Davis, who, in a dramatic Senate speech, announced the complete severance of his own "nation" from the United States. On February 9, 1861, Davis was elected President of the seceding Confederation. He desired to live in peace with the older Union, but there was a growing menace in his professions. If he were not "let alone," Davis at length declared, those Yankees should "smell Southern powder and feel Southern steel." Which, indeed, they did during the four years of America's domestic war.

I shall not venture far into the maze of American politics, but I must show both parties warring in the several States, whose internal affairs are beyond the control of the Federal Government. The result is confusion and much frittering of the national spirit in unworthy ways. Each State is the battle-ground of unseemly forces, and there is call for a Man, as there was for Hughes in New York and for Taft in Ohio, against Boss Cox and his evil works. It is in State crusades of this kind that national careers are made. Twenty years ago Wisconsin was in the clutch of the brewery-ring of Milwaukee and the railroad ring of Madison. In this case Robert La Follette was the liberator of the State. New Hampshire broke the bonds of her railroad ring through Robert P. Bass; and, after many years of shameless corruption and misgovernment, the great Keystone State of Pennsylvania threw off boss control with the aid of Governor Brumbaugh.

But the most notable instance of the oppressed State and

its champion is California and Hiram W. Johnson; he was twice Governor, and is now a Senator in Congress. For a generation the political rottenness of this glorious land was beyond belief. In municipal looting the San Francisco gang out-Tammanied Tammany Hall even in the classic reign of Boss Tweed. Under Abe Ruef and Mayor Schmitz (who wound up in gaol) the great city sank to sordid depths unparalleled in the history of American robbery and graft. The Pacific State had long ceased to be a republic, far less a democracy. It was ruled by the Southern Pacific Railroad with a tyrannous grip which is difficult for the European reader to realize. First Huntington and then Harriman was absolute "Tsar" over a country three times the size of England, and iron rule was directed from a Wall Street office three thousand miles away.

The State Legislature in Sacramento was made up of voting machines nominated by the Southern Pacific. California's laws were matters of bargain and sale. It was the Railroad that appointed judges, and broke them, too, when they disobeyed. . . . Here enters Hiram Johnson. How that Quixotic orator captured the Republican nomination and smashed the preposterous machine is too queer and tedious a tale to tell fully here. First of all he got in touch with the farmers, as the reform party did in Kansas. There were times when the young Governor despaired of success, so securely were the Southern Pacific interests entrenched, so lavish and unscrupulous were their agents in the doling of bribes. Ignored by the press, Johnson set out like a religious revivalist, spouting at the street corners and haranguing 'wayback farmers under the shadow of Mount Shasta, where railroads and politics were all but unknown.

It was a typical American crusade, but at long last the prophet found honour in that sunny land. At his meetings there were now reporters and advance agents. And from citrus-groves and fields the cultivators came running at the sound of cow-bells on the Johnson cars. They heard him gladly, if a little dubiously at first. "Will you keep faith with us?" the people asked of their new apostle, when he showed the way to brighter things, and the crippling of the Corporation autocracy that ruled them all. Johnson said he would—and he did. The reformer led his democracy against the big business and overthrew it. Today California is the freest and most progressive State in the Union; its new Senator in Washington is even hailed as "Presidential timber" for the 1920 election.

Such are the issues and interests that draw men from really national affairs. The central Government is well aware of this weakness; and there is a quiet but forceful tendency to break down State control and merge more and more authority in the Federal Congress. It is recognized that forty-eight sovereignties working at cross-purposes must hamper America's development, both internally and in foreign affairs. Industrial justice is not possible with forty-eight different codes governing accidents in factories as well as sanitary conditions, old-age pensions, and social welfare in general. A trading company may register in one State and operate in another, with serious results alike to debtors, creditors, and customers. A valid marriage in one State may be held null and void in another. There are thirty-five different causes for absolute divorce recognized by the various States of the Union. But not one of these is recognized by all!

Nor is there any uniformity in the *per capita* taxation, which ranges from $9.47 in Nevada down to $1.72 in South Carolina. In some States the Judges are elected by the people, in others by the Legislature; or again, they may be appointed by the Governor. In Texas and Arizona the Mexican *vara* of thirty-three inches is used in land measurement; of course it is unknown in the North. Legal holidays vary in all the States. Jeff Davis's birthday is a holiday in Virginia, but Good Friday is ignored in New York. In fact, each State is a law unto itself, and looks harshly upon its neighbour when that neighbour is stricken with a deadly disease. The old days of shot-gun quarantines disappeared with the yellow fever; but during the mysterious plague of paralysis in New York in 1916 there was a panic over the water in New Jersey, where boats and trains full of convalescents were turned back with senseless cruelty.

Inter-State quarrels crop up at times, like that between North Dakota and Minnesota over the marketing of wheat. But far more serious are the conflicts between individual States and the Federal authority in Washington. The gravest of these was the stand which California took (and still takes) over the penal laws which she passed against the Japanese settlers in her midst. This brought the shadow of secession again, and even the menace of international war with this I deal elsewhere. But the cleavage of States and peoples was a condition which could not last. Berlin was aware of it; the German Embassy in Washington traded upon it for two years of the Great War. Thus far the national consciousness showed no flame; the far-flung States were immersed in problems of peculiar diversity. Thus Iowa was warring on her rats, Nevada on her mad coyotes and the rabies in her flocks and herds. Louisiana was concerned with the hyacinth that choked her waterways. Rural Minnesota talked of model farms, West Virginia defied the Supreme Court to collect her *ante bellum* debt of twelve million dollars. And that mountain fastness, Wyoming (it is larger than Britain), was forming a game preserve for the greater antelopes and bears.

These things were real; the world-war came as a tiresome yarn to be swallowed on the Tertullian principle: " 'Tis impossible, and therefore to be believed!" These people praised Lord Fisher and shut his genius from their Hall

of Fame. But there we shall find Lord Lister, the gentle
healer who "with one gentle stroking wiped away ten thousand tears out of the life of man."

It was curious to see how America grew tired of war in
war-time, and fell back upon her own isolation. The great
topic was now tabu, being a source of social friction and a
business bar. "Leave *it* outside!" became an office door
appeal in New York City. One heard hyphenates dilate
upon the German primacy in war, its novel engines and
twisted technics of destruction. But these speakers were
quickly tamed; there seemed no prospect of universal service even on the Swiss lines, except after some invasive *coup*
such as was planned by Von Edelsheim in 1901, and debated in the Army and Navy Club of Berlin. In this
scheme stress was laid upon the fact that Germany was,
of all Powers, the one best fitted to conquer America. Ref-
erence to the weakness of the Regular Army, to the untrained Militias, and "the inexperience of the American
Staff" showed how well informed the Baron was when
outlining this adventure.

It was the State patriot who all but defeated the idea
of a unifying Constitution; and after sixty years he all
but ruined the national structure over the questions of
Secession and Slavery. States' Rights have been pleaded
to delay or defeat urgent laws relating to pure food, child
labour, transportation, and the conservation of natural resources. These Rights have also been invoked to rally and
shelter anti-social forces and to arouse sectional bias and
local prejudice. But they have no place in the new Americanism of 1918. In the Supreme Court the utterance of
Justice Hughes in the Minnesota and Shreveport cases lays
down the all-American law in a classic decision: "There
is no room in our scheme of Government for the assertion
of State Right in hostility to the authorized exercise of
Federal control."

Serious thinkers and leaders of public opinion are every-where alive to this peculiar danger. Thus in the Senate Mr. B. R. Tillman of South Carolina, Chairman of the Committee on Naval Affairs, condemned the State patriot in forcible terms: "It is as though men were crazy over local affairs," he declared, "and had no broad national grasp at all." Each State has its own floral emblem: Alabama, the golden-rod; Florida, the orange-blossom; Mississippi, the magnolia; Wyoming, the gentian; Utah, the sego lily, and so on.

Before the Great War the ablest thinkers were afraid the United States was less of a nation than it was when Washington wrote his political testament over a century ago. Senators, professors, and social reformers pointed to alien forces that were fast corroding the finer traditions and setting up standards that clashed with them. "You have in a common cause fought and triumphed together," the First President wrote in his historic Address. The new-born nation's independence was "the work of joint councils and efforts, of common dangers, sufferings, and successes."

But many of the newer States know nothing of such bonds, largely peopled as they are by Europeans of every race, intent upon material success and the good time denied them in the older lands. These settlers also tend to become State patriots. They show little or no interest in foreign affairs; they have Jeff Davis's own desire to be "let alone" by the Federal Government in Washington. "We are still sectional," Senator W. G. Harding of Ohio was sorry to say. "Not divided on the old Mason and Dixon line, but by East and West, North and South, coast and interior; financial and industrial on the one hand, and agricultural on the other."

This parochial spirit survived the dismissal of Bernstorff and the rupture of relations with the Central Powers.

It was the despair of men of larger grasp who would have had the President take a bolder line and fling at the masses the calm Lincoln-query: "What is our Duty?" They pointed to France, their sister Republic, just then "a-tingle with grief and glory," as her prose-poet said. What a pity Wilson was no incendiary of souls, voicing the *jeunesse endiablée* of Verdun and the Somme to a quick-witted, warm-hearted people like the Americans! A man of apostolic fire would have pictured the women of France upstanding in the nave of Notre Dame with streaming eyes and rapt senses on the burning appeal of Père Janvier; it rang like a challenge to the eternal Throne: "Justice for France, O God!" This appeal the organ lifted with stormy splendour to storied windows and darkling heights above the sworded statue of the Warrior-Virgin in the apse.

But Wilson erred on the cautious side. The world-war was to him a mystery in these neutral days. "Its origin and objects," the President said, "have never been disclosed." The Wilson of that time was a shocked spectator of the scene, with Mediation in his left hand when returning sanity should prompt an exhausted Europe to sue for it. ... "With its causes and objects we are not concerned. The obscure fountains from which the stupendous flood burst forth we are not interested to search or explore." How different it was when the rising waters threatened the speaker's native land!

It was this *incuria* which made America reckon the Allied cause in headlines and press sensations. The European battles were at length no more than "movie" features. They eclipsed the home-made thrills of colliding trains and men who leaped from sky-scrapers or tackled sharks on the sea floor. But it was mainly on business lines that the colossal struggle was judged. "War films faked" was an urgent telegram from Little Rock (Ark.) to an agent for the Somme pictures. "No smoke and soldiers laughing."

. . . "Sending another," was the prompt reply: "Clouds of smoke and men sobbing.   One dollar a foot—*guaranteed American make!*"

CHAPTER V

AMERICA IN THE MAKING

FOR two years or more, a lively press and a listless people were discrepant features of the United States. They were also the subject of puzzled comment on this side. The *New York Herald*, the *Sun, Tribune,* and *Evening Post* expressed themselves impeccably throughout, and with due wrath against German methods. Yet the American masses were but faintly moved. If they were stirred at all it was only between editions, so to say. One should not forget that the New York papers spoke for the cultured East alone. They did not reflect the masses at large any more than the London *Times* may be said to speak for Tyneside, or the *Morning Post* for the Norfolk farmer or the mechanics of Woolwich and Canning Town.

I am aware of the paradox which maintains that a metropolis is unrepresentative of its own nation. One hears this of London and Paris, of Rome, Vienna, and Madrid. Whether it be true of Europe is here immaterial; but let me say with all emphasis that no intelligent American can be found who will claim that New York City is in the smallest degree "American." It is, in fact, the most foreign of all the world centres; a native of Manhattan Borough is by no means easily found. Foreign names predominate in New York. All the races of Europe and Asia live here and labour in vortex rings of nationality. Over in Brooklyn you may lose yourself in a new Naples. Williamsburg is wholly German; Washington Street is Syrian, and reads a *Daily Mirror* in the Arabic script (*Meerat el-Gharb*). Mott Street and Pell Street are Chinese, with throngs of yellow men slipping past each other like eels in a tub.

In a thousand night-schools English is taught to new citizens who have formally "asked for their first papers." But these hordes are all apt to lapse into their own tongue; or they take no interest in study after a day's work at the highest tension. It is above all New York which deserves the name of "the melting-pot." It contains nearly a million Jews—a type of immigrant who will not be lured out on to the farms. The Jew loves New York City, where ninety per cent. of America's money is. Here in truth is an Israelitish camp to awe the modern Balaam: "Who can count the dust of Jacob?" One person in every four is a Jew whom you meet on Manhattan Island.

It is largely in her make-up, then, that the secret of America's apathy must be sought, apart from causes that are more obscure. If the special correspondent from London would take the ferry over to the Ellis Island Immigration Station, he might see America in the making and understand the swamping of the United States by alien stocks which became a problem so far back as 1885. It is astonishing that this Door of Hope has been neglected by British editors and enlightenment sought from the "men higher up" who live in wholly different spheres. Let me present the rushing of these foreign floods, for surely no such human portent, no politico-social factor was ever so strangely staged.

I shall go no further than the Franco-Prussian War, when the population of America was less than that of Britain at the last census. And Britain is smaller than the single States of Nevada, Oregon, and Arizona. Today America musters over 105,000,000 souls, white, black, yellow, and red. It is a welter of contradictions, a riot of inconsistency; and yet there is something in the very atmosphere which makes for national traits—the clash of races, immensity of area, "States' Rights," and local patriotism notwithstanding. In thirty years America doubled her population, such was the spate of foreign peoples tumbling in by the shipload. The Immigration Commissioner was once expecting two million new citizens a year.

Ellis Island, out in New York Harbour, was well named "Uncle Sam's Sieve," and I shall show it in pre-war operation. It is a breezy, emotional place, with vistas of sparkling waters; great ocean ships and fussy tugs, scows carrying railway-cars, ferry-boats, black with passengers, and a procession of double-decked barges plying between the island and the latest arrival of the immigrant fleet. There are sea-noises and land-noises, shrill whistlings and distant boomings. The roar of the city drifts over from Manhattan, with its sky-line of pinnacles and deep cañons full of fierce endeavour. Behind is the Statue of Liberty, whose torch is now ablaze in the dark; the colossus by day has a background of factory shafts and trailing smoke.

Here is the first barge-load from the ship, and a fantastic crowd pours out to the tune of "Presto!" from a cheery American inspector. The big red building yonder is the gateway of the United States. Go in with the awestruck rabble and ascend to the gallery. Now look down into the vaulted hall where future Americans are sorted in two and twenty pens, with high steel railings in between. All are examined by doctors and the unfit weeded out; the rest pass from fold to fold, answering questions at each official desk.

Listen to the languages in this busy hive of citizenship. In these pens are races that have never met before; people far apart as the Sicilian and the Hebrew patriarch from the Russian Pale. Three-fourths of the crowd are from southeastern Europe—from Italy, Austria, Hungary, Bohemia, Poland, and South Russia. Seventy-five per cent. are farm and village folk, with an average of twenty dollars between them and that "dependency" which means deportation.

The men are mostly under forty, pioneers in this magical land; their families will come on later, when Fortune's trail has been blazed, and the father is doing well. They are not pretty people to look at, these of the Ellis Island cages. They are primitive creatures, coarse and crude—too often illiterate, and on that account not so acceptable to America in her day of doubt. . . .

A Polish dwarf is prompting a nervous giant near the inspector's desk. A Magyar girl in a dull red shawl, with a guitar under her arm, stares up at the Stars and Stripes of the gallery. On the seat beside her is a cane hamper, with a pillow, a blue teapot, and other belongings. There are muffled fights between the Greek and Irish children. Picturesque dudes of Bessarabia and the Bukowina are busy with mirror and comb, oblivious to all else. There are burly Finns and Bulgars; gaunt Armenian women, Syrian maids of real beauty from the Lebanon, odds and ends from the *rayah* races of the Kaliph in Europe and Asia Minor.

Steady streams of immigrants are passing out. A waiting-room is raucous with relief in many tongues; shrill inquiries are made for the Jersey City ferry, and the New Citizens' train in the Pennsylvania station. Their baggage is quaint or mediaeval; humpy sacks, boxes of tin, and gaily painted wood secured with rawhide strips. Hundreds of them have no heavy baggage at all. These are mere straws in humanity's tide; sad-eyed waifs with all their worldly goods tied about their persons, and rattling oddly as they pass to and fro. There is one cage marked "Temporarily Detained"; telegrams must be sent to friends about the occupants of this place.

They may be young girls, to whom Uncle Sam stands *in loco parentis*. His officials are very suspicious of "domestic agency" men, who may be . White Slave raiders doing a big home trade as well as exporting victims down to Rio and Buenos Aires.

The telegraph operator has at last a sheaf of messages to send: "Detained Ellis Island, steamer ——. Need ten dollars. Also proof of your ability to support." For America has a horror of paupers and prostitutes. The pen of the "Detained" is at once a gay place, and a sad. Boys and girls are merry enough, buying cakes from a Polish pedlar; but in shadowy corners sit the old and weary, in every attitude of dejection. Some of these have been detained for days, well enough lodged and fed by the authorities. Before the week is over they must go before a Board of Inquiry. . . . Haply there is no answer to that appeal flashed into great American spaces. If the immigrant be old and feeble, he is deported—a word of damnation in the Ellis Island pens. . . .

An official in uniform calls names from a list, and the hall seethes with excitement. Four or five nondescripts step forward, tremulous with glee. These pass down a corridor into the "Lovers' Lane," which an inspector tells you "holds more kisses to the square inch than any other spot on earth." Here in a room walled with wire-netting the "American" pioneer, incoherent and overdressed, greets his people from overseas. He has already prepared a home for them in the jostling arena. Over-ardent swains are not allowed to claim their sweethearts when these young persons arrive alone. But the Island has a marriage-bureau of its own that works all day and makes love respectable from its outset on American soil.

Three judges hold session upstairs in the Board of Inquiry, and before them sit doubtful cases—red-eyed or listless folk, indignant or full of dread. In the Deportation-Room are some contract labourers—Bulgarians hired for the anthracite mines. They were marked down at Varna by an official of the American Federation who advised Ellis Island by cable of this infraction of the law. For such cases there is no hope; all are sent back to Europe at the steamship company's expense.

Now "a wise man's country," as Zeno says, "is where he finds happiness," so it would appear that this migration flatters the United States. But sentiment in the matter has long since flown. It stands to common sense that many of these people are not the best citizens of the nations they have left. Think what it means to tear up home by the roots; to leave one's own land and sail across the ocean to begin life anew in a continent of strange ways and foreign language, with extremes of climate which are very trying to the European.

It is depressing to watch the bitterness of the disinherited in these sorting-pens; the surliness of outcasts and trade-fallen failures—yet no sooner do they step ashore at the Battery than they fill their lungs with American air, which has a marvellous effect. Giani or Pietro, from Ajaccio or Messina, is soon a transfigured man; a hustler—a devotee of America's dare and do, poring upon success-books or studying law between each pair of boots he shines (at five cents) outside the corner saloon. At home in Corsica, Giani dreamed his life away in a hot sun with no more fortune, no more future than a few goats and a crop of chestnuts that dropped into his lazy mouth as he lay in the shade.

What is the secret of this sudden aspiring—of this young Rodin-passion—haunted day and night with the idea of doing *quelque chose de puissant?* It is the mysterious American element that favours the transmutation. One is reminded of the trout which in a Scottish burn may never exceed a fingerling size, yet when placed in New Zealand waters attain a weight of five-and-thirty pounds. All the same, America's pride and satisfaction in these hordes has long been jarred, especially when the million-mark was passed in 1905.

The insistent theme of thinkers was that, as immigration grew in volume, the quality of it fell off until the "men (and women, too), who are to vote" were eyed in the mass as questionable Americans. Statesmen began to discuss and classify the various races in the throng. Some were more industrious than others; some more ambitious, more assimilable. Others, again, would not respond to the American challenge. They herded together; they lived doubtfully, even calling for special police and secret agents of the law in polyglot squads, such as one finds in New York, Chicago, and San Francisco. This falling off in quality may be said to coincide with the rise to power and wealth of the German Empire, which checked and withheld the most desirable of immigrants.

So early as 1885 Teutonic and Celtic sources were thinning out; a prosperous Ireland could only spare 20,000 of her sons in 1914, whereas she sent 60,000 in 1891. As Northern and Western Europe began to keep their people, there was an abrupt migration of Iberian and Slavic stocks from the South and East; and these, America tried to tell herself, would be at least a passable substitute. The statistics of the change are remarkable. Thus in 1885 Germany showed an immigration percentage of 31; by 1900 it had dropped to 4. The Scandinavian nations fell from 14 in 1880 to 4 in 1905. Meanwhile the "ramshackle empire" of Austria-Hungary was readjusting the balance with Magyar and Czech, Ruthenian and Serb, Croat, Ruman, Slovak, Slovene, and Jew. Here the American table shows a percentage of 1 in the year 1870, leaping to 13 in 1895, and a decade later to 27. Italy's percentage was 2 in 1875 and 22 in 1905. In the same period the Russian influx rose from 4 to 18, whilst Britain's contribution crumbled from 30 or 40 to 13.

Applying the dollar test, it was seen that the German or Dane brought with him twice as much money as those stagey figures from South-Eastern Europe. The average Sicilian or Greek or Jew who landed at the Battery with $15 in his pocket was voted poor American stuff.

Worse still, out of a million aliens more than one-fourth could neither read nor write. Accordingly, the restriction screw was given further turns, and the steamship companies responded, having grown tired of taking back to Europe undesirables whom America refused to admit. It is beyond question that, in spite of all precautions, thousands of aliens have invaded the country who were on the verge of dependency, defectiveness, and crime. Then came the perplexing task of distribution, so long the crux of statesmen and social students; of professors of economies and sociology, the press and pulpit, the learned and industrial bodies, and the Labour Unions. At Immigration Conferences evidence of shocking congestion in the cities was produced. The Jewish immigrant especially will go no farther afield than New York, where his race has enormous power. Out of 694,172 Jews landed at Ellis Island, 504,181 remained in the city and settled there. Out of a million foreigners admitted, the Census Bureau shows that well over one-third claimed the State of New York as their "ultimate destination."

Most of that million were bound for the cities or suburbs of New York, Philadelphia, Chicago, and Boston. America was vexed to learn that seven-tenths of these citizens-to-be settled in centres already thronged, instead of "going West" which has long been held classic counsel for the ambitious. Five years of residence is the term for citizenship. It is preceded by a declaration of intention "to renounce for ever all allegiance and fidelity to any foreign prince, potentate, state, or sovereignty; and particularly to the one of which he may at the time be a citizen or subject."

Here let me note that there is much changing of names

on the part of the new American. The Magyar and Pole must not be unpronounceable among his fellows, so Rabbinovitch is neatly trimmed to Robins. There is wholesale shedding of "skis" and "offs." Jangling consonants of Bohemia are dropped, so are smooth vowels that mark the "Dago," and whole slabs of syllables that show the Greek: Spyridon Paraskevopoulos is a serious handicap in the hot American race for Success. The Jew will often drop a too "Sheeny" name—and with it much of the olden faith, which his children frequently lose. Aliens who take to prize-fighting adopt Irish names—Murphy, Sullivan, or O'Brien.

The last census showed altogether 13,515,886 persons of foreign birth in the United States. To this one may add ten or twelve million negroes in order to gauge the hugeness of elements that clash with, or merely hamper, the true American ideals.

One learns casually that Norway has in the United States a population nearly as large as its own, and that M. Paderewski forwarded a Polish protest from America representing 4,000,000 citizens banded together in societies and organizations.

Altogether over five hundred journals are printed in foreign languages, thus fostering "national" feelings which conflict with the new citizenship. America shows an increasing dislike of the many quarters in her midst, ruled as they are by the padrone and the ward boss. Some reformers would press compulsory English upon the newly-landed immigrant. He should be guided and taught, they say, as one teaches children; for it is in the intelligence of these people that the future of democracy lies. On the other hand, to neglect them means a listless electorate and weakness in the body politic.

"Americanization Day" was last year celebrated in 150 cities. The women's clubs take a hand in the process of

moulding new citizens; and a Forward-to-the-Land League,
with experimental tracts in Florida, tries to coax the Ellis
Island hordes out of the Eastern cities into the real America beyond. But the immigrant question bristles with
difficulty. The labour market is in chronic rebellion
against a flood of workers who compete with the native
on un-American bases. And those interested in the purity
of politics see in these docile mobs a new supply of cor-
ruptibles upon whose votes (often secured with forged
naturalization papers), "machines" may be reared and
supported for the purpose of municipal loot. So serious
a matter had immigration become that America was glad
of the respite given her by the war. During the second
half of 1915, there were only 169,291 arrivals. As against
these, there were 166,899 departures for Europe, leaving
a net increase for the half year of only 2392.

It was one of war's few blessings, this abrupt exclusion
of unskilled labour. Restrictionists were glad to see there
was less unemployment than ever; fewer claims upon public and private charity through the checking of a human
tide which had become a danger. Of course, America dis-
cusses immigration after the war, and that with renewed
anxiety. Some thinkers contend there will be a great migration from the "militaristic" nations; that men, heart-
sick at the very thought of war, will turn eagerly to
the land of peace and the serener uplift of life. Others
are that the older nations will need all their sons to repair
the wastage in man-power and material; that all the won-
drous gear bought and built in America, and long employed upon munitions of war, will in the Old World be
turned to productive labour, so as to reduce the enormous
debts under which the warring Powers must groan for a
generation.

Nor is America sorry to see her supply of Jewish citizens
cut off. Jewish influence permeates the United States,

and is pacific to the point of emasculation. Jews own great newspapers like the *New York World* and *Times*. Jews are elected Governors of States. There is "Honest Mose," the reformer of Idaho, who once sold cheap togs in a wooden shack of Boise City; and Simon Bamberger, the first Democratic Governor of Utah, who is still a "Gentile" in the Mormon State. A Jew—Louis Brandeis—sits in the Supreme Court of the United States. As for ambassadors at foreign Courts, one has but to mention Oscar Straus, Henry Morgenthau, Abraham Elkus, and Lewis Einstein. But it is in the realm of finance that the Jew is supreme; a notable exemplar is Jacob Schiff, the philanthropist, who played a leading part in the League to Enforce Peace.

My point is that Hebrew pacifism is opposed to vigorous measures of national defence. "Over yonder," the generous Jews were told in Carnegie Hall, "Despotism rallies its victims to a bloody death. Here in America we set in motion vastly different armies. Behold our 20,000,000 school children laughing as they go. See yet another army of 20,000,000 stalwarts who march out each morning to the anvil, the forge and the loom." So what with Jewish and Gentile pacifism, the influence of the women, and German intrigue from Cuba to Colon, and thence to Mexico City, Preparedness for war had "hard sledding" indeed in its early days.

It was this feebleness of the national will which engaged the ablest American minds. It also accounted for the feeling of relief when immigration stopped, and the alien torrent was shown to be a factor which the country could do without. For many years American students of this problem have been of three schools—restrictionist, selectionist, and exclusionist; these last weighed police revelations of unexampled crime, as well as horrible crowding in the slums. But the demand for cheap labour, for illiterate, non-English speaking serfs, was both insistent and fierce. Beyond doubt the poor devils of aliens were cruelly exploited. Until quite recently (and the change of spirit is startling to one who knows the facts) no nation on earth held human life so cheaply as the United States, in spite of professions to the contrary which were conventions and little more.

"The casualties of our peaceful industries," wrote President Roosevelt to Josiah Strong, the statistician, "exceed those of a great and continuous war." In round figures they amount to 50,000 killed and 500,000 injured every year. Such is Prosperity's toll; this is the seamy side of America's speed-up. According to Dr. W. H. Tolman, "the Pennsylvania coalfields alone furnish a Bull Run Battle of deaths year by year." And so reckless are the railroads that their foremost expert, Mr. James J. Hill, remarked to a Cabinet Minister: "Every time I take a journey I expect it to be my last, so uncertain has the thing become."

"Ah, Bawss," said the negro brakeman to me at Fort Worth, "w'en soldierin's as deadly as switchin' I guess we'll have disarm'ent at hand!" The railway havoc for one year was 10,046 killed and 84,155 injured. Angry protest appeared in the papers about this, but public opinion was never roused. The Interstate Commerce Commission collected almost incredible facts and figures. The Sunday journals had whole-page articles on "The Price of Peace"—"Every time the second-hand circles the dial of your watch, an American is slaughtered or maimed."

"It's cheaper to kill men than to protect them," said the disappointed inventor to Dr. Josiah Strong, who gave his whole career to preventive work in this direction. "When I produce a thing that saves time and labour, it goes off like hot cakes. But directly I make a device to save human life and limb, I've only wasted energy;

and I can't *give* the thing away!'' It is undeniable that
the alien immigrant was no more than raw material,
cheaply held, mere unconsidered gun-meat in America's
eternal war.

I saw an Armenian arrested for begging on Third Avenue, New York. The man had both hands destroyed by
the machinery of a harvester concern in Chicago, and he
was soon thrown on the community as a public charge.
The flesh-and-blood havoc of bursting fly-wheels in the
factories is another reckless tale. So also are the casualties
in lead and copper mines; in city subways and in the
streets, where motors and trams take a fearsome toll.
Chemical works and quarries, laundries, foundries, and
textile-mills—the slaughter and crippling of workers in
these places has long been the despair of social pioneers.
The farming and lumbering trades had awesome records of
their own; so had construction-work, especially in bridges
and skyscrapers. ''Count the storeys,'' your guide told
you impressively in the down-town tour of New York, ''if
you want to know how many human lives the So-and-So
Building cost.'' And truly, from the deep caisson to the
fiftieth tier of windows, these towers have a dreadful record in killing and crippling for life.

It is for this reason that America became proficient in
the making of artificial limbs. And here we found her a
useful ally in the aftermath of war, offering the Carnes arm
to Roehampton Hospital, as well as mechanical legs and
jointed feet that hid all deformity. ''Success is a fine
goal,'' says that typical American, Mr. Darwin P. Kingsley,
of the New York Life Insurance Company, ''but in our
eagerness to win it we lash out right and left, trampling
and wounding in ruthless concentration. We destroy far
more than we afterwards redeem by our public and private
beneficence.'' Mr. Kingsley heads the ''Safety First''
leagues of America, which now preach a saner gospel of

values, and point out "the brutal and costly inefficiency of a speed-up that defeats itself." The last ounce of output is exacted of the worker—and then the bit beyond, which brings disaster on so huge and frequent a scale throughout the American sovereignties. /

I have explained how the laws are made by forty-eight Parliaments, laws which are not uniform and are quite beyond count. In this connection I may quote Secretary Trefz, of the U. S. Chamber of Commerce. "In the last five years," he says, "our national and State Legislatures have passed 62,550 laws, as compared with 1500 laws passed by the British Parliament in ten years." It is not so much new laws that America needs as what Elihu Root calls "the organization of the nation." Lincoln himself had this at heart when he conferred with General Dodge about the new trans-continental railroad—"not only as a military asset, but also as a means of holding the Pacific Coast to the Union." To foster a really national spirit came before all else in President Wilson's war-time plans. "What I am striving for," he told Labour delegates at the White House, "is to blot out all the lines of cleavage in America. To sweep away groups and camps, and caste distinctions; to close up our ranks and kindle fresh unity of purpose." This was the foundation of Americanism in 1917.

There should be less exuberance and more reflection in an era that broke with the past before all men's eyes—that rollicking past when Macaulay found "all sail and no anchor" in the Constitution of the United States. I know no symptom of this effort more striking than the new relations of capital and labour—of master and man; even of the helpless alien who was so lightly regarded in the heedless America of yesteryear. I heard a Pennsylvania coroner, Mr. J. C. Armstrong, of Allegheny County, express himself sadly in this matter. "The number of

alien deaths in our furnaces and mills is truly distressing.
But nobody cares—they're only Hunks or Dagoes. Why,
there's more fuss made over the loss of a horse or a
mule!" Thirteen Hungarians were killed in Pittsburg
by one blast of molten metal. The furnace was known
to be defective, and some of the men were wary enough
to leave their work in time. At the inquest the foreman
explained that "a rush of orders had kept the company
from making repairs in time."

What did it matter?—They were only Hunks. That
day an Austrian Lloyd steamer landed a thousand more at
Ellis Island from the port of Fiume; the morrow or next
day would see groups of them squatting at the gates, glad
of $2 a day and a life of withering hardships. I suppose
the valley of the Monongahela from Pittsburg to McKees-
port (where the Hungarian colony is) shows industrial
America in its most terrifying aspect. There are no words
for the vileness and flame of this hissing Gomorrah. Fifteen thousand factory-shafts spout smoke and soot. In
the vengeful reek of this place the dead Hunk is buried
in an unceremonious ditch to a dirge of psalms, oddly
confused with the crash of steam hammers and blast-
furnace roars of imminent menace.

The half-naked Hunk, wrinkled and wan, half-blinded
by the glare of liquid steel, gasping and scorched, streaming with sweat as well as half-gassed with the poisonous
reek—this is no picture piled up for effect, but a fact
from which the onlooker turns away. No negro, no Chinese coolie would undertake this foundry and rolling-mill
work; it is too heart-rending. But the Hunk is dumb;
he knows no English. Fifty per cent. of these industrial slaves are Ellis Island pioneers. They come over
alone, and do not send for their families till they have
a pittance put by. I called upon these outlaws in their
shacks by the drear churchyard. Here they lived like

swine, in an atmosphere of murk and damnable tumult. Their patient acceptance of it all was to me more moving than any rage. Was not this America—the only America they knew? The joyous Old-World days were over; the blue Adriatic, and fair Carpathian valleys, too unreal now for any dream. Between Transylvania and Pennsylvania, hell's own gulf was yawning—and this was called the Valley of the Monongahela! . . .

Yet even the worm, we are told, will turn. These aliens have shown fight in murderous strikes, especially where they see miniature standing armies maintained by employers for their own repression, as in the coal mines of Colorado. An affray of this kind broke out two years ago at the big plant of the Fertilizer Trust in Roosevelt, N. J., barely twenty miles from New York's City Hall. At the first volley fired by the private guards eighteen unarmed strikers fell dead or wounded. But here again they were only Hunks and Dagoes; and tradition of American capital rates these below the beeves and porkers of the stock-yard. Tradition of this kind dies hard in a land where business has become a god. But such conduct is bound to react upon the community. The criminal records of these aliens are of peculiar flagrancy; they call for police-squads and special agents, like those of the famous Petrosino, who had a detective bureau of his own in Lafayette Street, New York. Petrosino was murdered in Sicily whilst following up a Black Hand trail.

Here I touch those secret societies which the immigrant floods bring with them from Europe. I refer to the Armenian Henchakist, the Chinese Tong, the Athenian blood-pact, and Neapolitan vendetta; as well as the Mafia, Camorra, and La Mano Nera or the Black Hand. One hesitates to mention the exploits of these murder-clubs, for they surpass the crudest fiction and reveal fatal flaws in the civilized polity upon which they prey. There are over half a million Italians settled in Greater New York, and the Black Hand Society had extraordinary license among them. In four months fifty-four persons were killed or maimed by pistol, knife, or dynamite: the victims had ignored the usual Black Hand letter demanding money under pain of death.

Big corporations, like the United States Steel, have detectives of their own to protect their industrial army. At one time $25,000 a month was extorted by threats from the foreign workmen of this huge concern. But the Secret Service agents crippled the system by seizing the bandit leader, Pagnato, and ten of his assassins at the pay-office of the Hillsville Quarries. It is remarkable what license all classes permit themselves in the slack immensity of this New World. Even the city police are apt to consider the brothel, the gambling den, and saloon as lawful sources of income. It is a point of view very difficult to deal with, based as it is upon custom and a peculiar ethical code.

New York City has for many years tried to reform her police, pointing out the scandal of the lowly officer who could advertise the loss of his $1500 diamond ring. Then there was the discovery of forty-three bills, each of $1000, in the desk of a captain who fell dead in the West 47th Station. And a corruption fund was raised by the force at large to defeat the Anti-Graft Bill in the State Legislature at Albany.

It was strange to see sober journals in so great a city as New York referring to their police as ''a semi-secret, semi-criminal association that fosters and battens upon crime, and will not stay its hand at murder.'' But all such crudity is passing, as well as the docility and unconcern which has long been a marked trait of citizenship. This was glaringly shown in New York's acceptance of the ruffian rule of Tammany Hall, its thugs and thieves, and criminal "Grand Sachems." Inaugurated long ago as a "friend of the poor," this singular body turned to politics under Aaron Burr and bossed New York for generations. Tammany Chiefs were brigands of incredible boldness and absolute sway. Boss Tweed died in gaol, after looting the city of millions. But the hateful dynasty was far from extinct. It began to decline in 1901; entire control of the New World's greatest city passed from Tammany with the evil days of Van Wyck. Under Mayor Mitchel— a typical crusader—New York was not only "free," but aspired to be America's model municipality.

CHAPTER VI

THE intelligent immigrant has a great desire to survey New York from the Singer building, which is forty-seven storeys high, and towers six hundred feet above Broadway, between Liberty and Cortlandt Streets. It is an awesome experience for the simple soul, rapt heavenward in the "Observatory Express." And the panorama below him at last is overpowering. It makes real all the wonders that glowed in those letters from America, which were read aloud to neighbours at cottage doors in the Black Forest, where toys are made, or in hot Sicilian steppes where the slaves of the sulphur-mine hear the Statue of Liberty calling them in their sleep.

A glance at Lower Manhattan from this height shows the difficult building problem of New York, and how the skyscraper has solved it with characteristic daring. Business interests of enormous range are here squeezed into an area less than two square miles, bounded on the south, east, and west by the waters of the Bay and the Hudson and East Rivers. Here huddle the offices of the trans-continental railways. Here is the stronghold of the Standard Oil—that giant among the giants of American trade, with mysterious claims reaching from California to Rumania, and from the Black Sea to Siam. Here the Steel Trust is financially at home beside famous corporations with skyscrapers of their own. On this narrow tongue are the big exchanges, the banks, trust companies, and brokerage offices. Land has fetched as much as $700 a foot in the Wall Street district.

The only outlet was gained by the steady pushing of

non-business dwellings to the north end—and by going up in the air. Hence the skyscraper, a cage of steel beams carried on sixty or eighty legs which are thrust down to bedrock, ninety feet or so below New York's famous Broadway. These legs are the wind-anchors of a land-lighthouse which is without a peer in any nation. If there were no wind, a skyscraper of a hundred storeys would be possible. As it is, there is talk of a tower a thousand feet high and a hundred feet square, swaying with perfect safety in a gale of a hundred miles an hour. This is the estimate of Mr. Ernest Flagg, the architect of the Singer building; he has no love for these monstrosities, by the way, though he admits the necessity for them. The steel skeleton is weighed in advance—every beam and bar and bolt; the furniture, too, and the safes, together with the population of a country town. Upon the legs of the Singer tower rests a weight of 86,000 tons.

It is these tremendous buildings which make New York unique, and turn the streets into profound chasms, with dizzy troglodyte walls that blaze at night with dim and weird effects. The progress of the skyscraper, as one might suppose, was bound up with the elevator, which dates from 1870. The vertical cylinder hydraulic lift was developed in Chicago with an eye to safety and certainty of control; a speed of 600 feet a minute was soon demanded in the twenty-storey structure. Real estate values rose with the height of these new buildings. Owners and architects, engineers, builders, and inventors hailed the steel construction, for it increased the price of sites prodigiously. It also produced a new race of workers from the "sand-hog" of the pneumatic caisson deep in the bowels of the earth, to the reckless riveter who would pose for a "stunt" portrait on a swaying, crane-lifted girder, seven hundred feet above the curb of Lower Broadway.

The skyscraper is a complete city under one roof, with

racing elevators carrying sixty thousand passengers a day.
Such a pile has its own electric light and gas plants, its own
waterworks and fire brigade; a police-force, mail-chutes,
telephones, telegraphs, banks and clubs. A business man
need never leave his lofty suite. Here are restaurants
and bedrooms; bathrooms and barber-shops, news-stands,
safe-deposits, and all professional aid—manicure, medicine, and the law, together with minor stimuli ranging
from candy and chewing-gum to cigars and soft drinks.
The aura of the skyscraper favours exact and continuous
concentration. Nevertheless responsible men foresee ·dis-
aster to the swarming cliff-dwellers of New York, and
also to the city itself—especially since San Francisco was
destroyed by earthquake and fire. The Board of Alder-
men have a Building Codes Revision Committee, and this
body met to consider the limitation of the skyscraper in
view of repeated protest from experts of undoubted standing. Architects, builders, and insurance men were invited
to state their views. An important witness was Mr. G. H.
Babb, President of the New York Fire Underwriters.

"San Francisco has taught us," Mr. Babb declared,
"that our so-called fire-proof buildings will not resist an
uncontrolled wave of flame. We know that these lofty
shafts nurse the fiercest fires of all. And we do fear
an outbreak in that down-town nest. It would beat and
drift across the narrow streets, involving other pinnacles
at their topmost floors. The firemen could do nothing;
no system of sprinklers would avail, nor all the attempts
at fire-proofing. We dread a blaze involving whole blocks,
and therefore menacing the city. The money loss might
amount to billions, and so cripple the insurance companies
that they could offer no more than twenty-five cents on the
dollar to owners and mortgagees."

But America will not stay to consider these things:
heedlessness is a trait peculiar to the genius of the people.

Risks are ignored, so that present ease be assured. A lurid morrow there may be, but it lies on the lap of gods who have always been kind to America!

It is New York that sets the pace for the continent. Here notions are born with abrupt caprice that alters a woman's gown or the income of her man. Or even the too orderly topography of the trees, which are torn up and pulled down with uproarious glee. There were no new aliens, as it chanced—no Ellis Island Americans to witness the moneyed invasion which marked the New York of 1916–17. Nothing like it was ever known, even in a land of freak spending and mushroom millions. Of course, it was war money. October promised a fairish season without any hint of the orgy ahead. Giant hotels, lavish restaurants, and cabarets made ready for the election crowds; for dancers and skaters, for lovers of the theatre and music-hall, who sup at two in the morning and cry, "What's a hundred dollars?" with their whole heart.

Those election throngs remained in the city, and to them were added visitors from all the States, until New York swelled and sang with carnival. Families from Buenos Aires piled in; from Rio, Havana, and the Central American capitals. For Paris was now an unattainable goal. There were also the idle rich who are, I must say, a diminishing caste; there are signs of penal laws against them. There were brokers and speculators, celebrating a revival with "any-price" dinners and Neronic gifts to the ladies. There were quite new types seen in this invasion: families from the Central West, farmers, contractors, and manufacturers intent upon circulating some of the money which deluged America, and now taxed even New York wits to devise new ways of melting it.

The city's floating population was more than doubled. Seven hundred thousand "purses" came into New York, asking for genial robbery and a good time therewith. The

hotels overflowed; a mattress in a bath-tub fetched five
dollars a night; rich men lay on the floors or sat contorted
in the corridors awaiting the dawn of new delights.   Grad-
nally guests were driven out of the city.   They might sup
on Broadway, or in Fifth or Madison Avenues; but for
beds they were billeted afar off—in Yonkers or in New-
ark, in dingy Hoboken, or Long Island City, and the
other "nowheres" of New York.   It is not possible to
exaggerate the nightly riot, nor the outrageous prices
asked and gaily paid for food and wine, amusements, and
souvenirs bought in shops which in normal times are the
most expensive in the world.

Money appeared to have lost its value.   There were
yellow-back tips (of $100) for the bowing *maître d'hôtel,*
five dollars for the boy that "boosted" an overcoat and
handed out a hat from the cloakroom.   Two dollars was
paid to enter a noisy cabaret; here one sat down exhausted
to a supper-dish of eggs at one dollar a plate.   Champagne poured freely as ice-water on a sultry night.   The
men who speculate in theatre tickets got fifty dollars
for a stall.   Beggars of yesteryear were now telephoning
madly to order banquets in princely suites at ten dollars
a plate. . . . The manager would put the receiver down
and dwell with wonder on the meteoric rise of men whom
no fate could floor, since they "came back" with unquench-
able *élan* to astonish the natives—an all but impossible
feat in sated New York.

I am bound to deal with this tiresome phase; it was
a phenomenal reflex of the Great War, and one which
American thinkers would be glad to forget.   Moreover,
New York, though voted un-American by all, is yet America's playground, and therefore an index to flush or tight
times throughout the continent.   Above all others this
city is sensitive to the drift of European affairs.   Dramatic events of the war were calmly received elsewhere;

only New York was really excited in the early days, and crowded to the bulletin-boards debating belligerent chances the whole night long. This is the American metropolis. Washington, the political capital—the Westminster of the United States—is 220 miles away in the south. It is a beautiful, uncommercial city of sleepy avenues and broad sunlit leisure, contrasting sharply with New York. The Federal seat, in its brief and vivid season, is a wholly delightful centre of sets and cliques and aristocracies. Washington is, in fact, America's "Court," at once informal and prim—not to say rigid in rule; hospitable, witty, and sown with American *salons* of surprising and diverting range. If it were possible to unite New York and Washington, the result would be a capital of unique allurement and zest for a brief stay.

The note of New York is impermanence; it never is, but always to be blest with civic and architectural perfection. Last season's hotel, with an amusement-annex that cost a fortune, is this year already under a cloud. For another is projected—one of fifteen hundred rooms and the soaring splendour of eclipse. It will cost fifteen million dollars. Before it opens a still more attractive palace is planned and talked of—not necessarily larger— but with novelties that take the town and are flashed for thousands of miles to maintain the siren fame which has been New York's since Revolutionary times.

It is a city of noise, of course, with electric railways borne upon iron pillars over tram-laid streets paved with granite blocks. The passion for altering is everywhere seen. Great pits yawn here and there—perhaps for the leg-rests of yet another skyscraper. Or the hole may be part of a city tube. Bombs explode; there is quarrying in the building lots—erection, demolition, carting away of débris, and the dumping of new and costly materials.

The "Great American Novel," so long expected and

discussed, lies here ready made, expansed for every nation to read, each in its own tongue. The glamour of New York invades the prairie farm; it fires young ambition in the cross-roads store thousands of miles away in the Oregon sage or Nevada sands. There is but one Fifth Avenue, only one Broadway, and no room in either for the ill-dressed or glum; they would be out of place as a bully would be in the nursery.

New York is a city of late hours, a temple of airy intoxication, where the drunken man is a rare bird indeed. Extravagance is a game in this place, haply encouraged in the young folks by dad, who beams amid the nightly glitter recalling the day he landed at Castle Garden with all his worldly goods in a ragged handkerchief. Quaint tales are told of spendthrift "stunts" that vied with one another, until folly fell exhausted for a space of new germination. There was the hostess who bought boxes for three plays, that her guests might choose according to their after-dinner mood. There was Mrs. So-and-So's ball with costly jewels for cotillion favours; the banquet with dancers on the table, and stocks and bonds folded in the serviettes as little gifts. There were ballets on the Long Island lawns brought *en masse* from the Metropolitan Opera, with Caruso himself to sing "Hail Columbia" at the close. There was the special train from Los Angeles to New York which enabled young love to keep its tryst; there were the famous monkey-and-horseback dinners, with many another prank and curvet to outshine all the revellers from Caligula to Louis Quatorze:

> "Why should the gods have put me at my ease
> If I mayn't use my fortune as I please?"

The answer is that today this riot is voted bad form. It is a crudity of jaded senses which the best people leave to the unsophisticated newly-rich who block Broadway at night with a tangle of sumptuous cars.

It is for her invaders that New York displays electric signs so glaring that the native citizen cultivates blindness, hoping to save his soul alive and keep his limbs from the mercy of Broadway joy-riders. For here night shineth as the day. There is blazing publicity for all manner of wares. Ebullient rainbows leap and race, flicker and flash, as for a Fourth of July that never ends. Fabulous glow-worms crawl up and down. Zigzag lightnings strike an acre of signboard—and reveal a panacea for over-eating! A four-storey Highlander dances a whisky-fling; another pours out a highball, with a hundred feet between his bottle and the glass. Household words race with in-visible pen across a whole city block. An electric kitten plays with a mighty spool of Somebody's silk, then jumps at a bound to the top of a skyscraper. The man does not live who could clearly record his impressions of New York's phantasmagoria.

"More light" is the city's motto; the blaze of it is another form of idealism which dispels the gloom of life. It is certain that restaurants, theatres, and shops have been dragged out of ruin by sheer glare. "Do it electric-ally" is now a familiar exhortation, and the thing is done with ferocious glee—not alone on the Great White Way, but also in countless homes that cook and clean at five cents per kilowatt-hour. New York has a mania for this unseen force. Her missionary fervour carried an Elec-trical Week into fifty-nine other cities, passing thence to the farms, where 108 new applications of electricity were speedily found. Thus the milkmaid is an electrician; the prairie goodwife runs a mysterious churn and chats at her work with a lonely neighbour twenty miles off by means of a telephone visor on her head. It is a country of marvels, of tip-toe expectancy, and impatient scorn for all the older ways of "dad an' the ox-cart."

Liberty's torch blazes electrically above the bay. All manner of irksome tasks grow easy when done electrically. In this way is the baby's bottle heated and mother's curling-iron made ready once a day for two weeks with one cent's worth of wired magic. Another cent makes ten rounds of toasts, a third runs the sewing-machine for two hours. The electric range produces a tempting dinner; and there is a dishwiper to deal with the plates in the scullery and coffee is served from an electric percolator on the table. A washer and wringer makes short work of the week's linen; electric irons follow it up the same day and give languid maids a "boost" which there is no resisting. In this manner is the domestic problem solved in New York where menial service is hateful to a joyous democracy. "Rare as an American waiter" is a phrase of high significance.

The matter of hired help has driven city folk to live in hotels, apartment-houses, pensions, and tenements. It is hard to imagine the range of these communal dwellings, from the alien squalor of Avenue A to the ultra-Roman magnificence of the Plaza by Central Park. In middle-class buildings the janitor is an autocrat collecting his rake-off from tenants and traders according to custom. The American inventor busies himself with household chores, knowing that even moderate success in a labour-saver will mean a fortune. These domestic aids bring comfort to a woman's life in a land where home service is only for the rich.

"She's leaving you!" is a poignant thrust printed in huge letters in advertisements on the servant question, issued by electrical concerns. "Leaving her job disgruntled; leaving *you* discouraged and down." It was a true enough statement of pre-electric days. The sick-at-heart mistress would tramp Third Avenue in search of "help." She rang Sullivan's bell and went up—and down she came again with a flushed face. She climbed four dirty flights to a frowsy room which had *Dienstmädchen* on the door. Within sat Frau Schmidt, a female bully with an odd platoon before her of Finns and Swedes, Poles, Italians, and Syrians. "Jus' landed alretty," the Frau explained, waving a plump hand at the menagerie, and adding a warrant that all in the squad were free from kitchen vice. The crudest of these asked five dollars a week, although more familiar with a spade or a plough than a saucepan. And to this demand the creature would add (through the Frau interpreter) conditions and privilege of unexpected guile.

Another agency tempted the mistress with "real Southern help." But first of all there was first a matter of $20 rail-fare to pay the coloured mammy in the corner. That savage grinned engagingly, and praised her own fried chicken and waffles. . . . If they only *knew* of her at the White House. . . ! Alas, she turned out to be a dope-fiend given to cocaine; a notorious "rounder" of the agencies well-known at The Island—which is not Ellis Island at all, but another place of penalty and shame. On the third day it took three policemen to remove this Ethiop from a stricken kitchen and strap her in the station wagon outside.

No wonder the true American housekeeper is the most efficient of all, though you will not find her in New York. She relies upon her own wit. She is without any servant, and quite likely runs a prosperous business into the bargain, apart from her husband's, or else in partnership with him. Of course the telephone is a great help, alike in the hot weather and on zero days; in fierce New York gales, torrential rains and snowstorms, such as London and Paris will never know.

As a developing agent the telephone has played a vital part in the United States. Here in New York you meet middle-aged men who remember the birth of it. They tell you how, on a March day in '76, Alexander Bell spoke to Tom Watson over a few feet of wire in the top floor of a Chicago office building. Today America has twelve million telephones, a smooth and perfect service of astonishing range. Portland, Me., talks to Portland, Ore., over a continental stretch equal to that between Stockholm and Stamboul. This New World chatters electrically; you cannot escape the telephone in New York City. It is to an instrument you speak in your hotel bedroom. The receiver is rarely out of a business man's hand; the Wall Street titan, the Trust, or railway king is photographed "on the 'phone" with millions of money in his rugged frown, for the 'phone is the sceptre of American sway.

My lady has a telephone in her boudoir. Here she can shop in cosy peignoir and slippers. She gossips with her friends in this way; she orders opera tickets, or calls her husband from the office dictaphone to speak of a change in the dinner-hour or measles in the nursery. At the smart restaurant the ever-ready mouthpiece peeps at you from the roses and lilies of a silver-set feast. There is a telephone in the smoke-room of the luxurious limited train going down to Palm Beach, or across the continent to Los Angeles in California. It is a habit in this wide-awake land where things happen as the avalanche falls, and market panics leap and race like forest fires at the merest whisper. Witness the result of leakage from the White House over the President's famous Peace Note.

I would even call the telephone a New York instinct; the "Hullo-girl" knows this to her cost as she sits at the switch-board watching the tinted bulbs glow with endless inquisition. "Where's that big blaze? . . ." "Say—is it really true that Senator Smith is dead? . . ." "*Would* you mind calling me tomorrow at five-thirty? My alarm clock's busted, and I've a train to catch.'' There are schools of politeness and patience for the young ladies who receive these impetuous calls. But the telephone service is seen at its best in country districts, far from any railway—perhaps in a region where no roads exist, and the trails are impassable through bad weather and furious storms. Here the farmer is "neighbourized" by the friendly wire. These rural lines have a regular news service supplied by a general call after supper at night. Widely-scattered subscribers gather round in their own homes, whilst the far-off Central first of all gives out the correct time—a greater boon to these lonely folk than the city dweller might imagine. Next comes a condensed report of the day's home and foreign news; then the current quotations for wheat and cotton and corn, oats and eggs, butter and all sorts of live stock, from the Jersey cow to the laying hen. Country teachers give lessons over the 'phone to pupils who are blizzard-bound in their own homes for days together. The deaf have telephones in their church pews; even the marriage ceremony has been conducted over sympathetic wires, with a lady reporter as bridesmaid and the press photographer as best man.

Electricity is the god in America's car, solving every crux of today and tomorrow. She regards Thomas Edison as her greatest genius. Her editors never tire of sending star men over to that wizard's den at West Orange, N. J., to hear the latest miracle—actual, potential, or merely desired for humanity's sake. . . .

"The future of electricty?" echoes the mage; he is old and very deaf, yet America made him chairman of her new Naval Consulting Board. "Why, the sky's the limit! One day *everything* will be done by electricity. Our railroads will be electrified, so will the labour of farm, factory, and fireside. The miners will turn their coal into current at the pit's mouth. The sea's tide will be harnessed to our needs; we shall call down nitrates from the air to fertilize our fields. Hydro-electric engineers will take hold of water now running to waste, and evoke from it the strength of sixty million horses.''

The Athenian appetite for ''something new'' is a keen American trait, and keenest of all in New York, which is the most inquisitive and acquisitive of cities. She expects Europe to serve her, and is lavishly served, with every art and craft and inspiration. Few foreigners realize how New York combs the earth for luxuries, paying a princely price for each flash of conceded rule. Every cult and whim comes here—an Eastern faith, preposterous frocks and Paris follies, like diamond heels and the torpedo toque.

Or it may be the Houses of the Children; tenement blocks on ideal lines for parents with large families only. Here we touch the ''race suicide'' question which Mr. Roosevelt has at heart. Married couples with a big brood are hard to find among the New York natives; landlords and janitors will have no truck with people thus encumbered. The native birth-rate has declined since the Civil War. In 1860 there were 634 children under five years for every 1000 women of child-bearing age. By 1900 the figure had fallen to 424; and flush times, as the Central Bureau shows, result in a still greater decline. The Southern States have a better record in this respect than the North; New England has the lowest birth-rate of all. On the other hand, the Mormon State of Utah is unique, for it has 233 children per 1000 women more than Colorado, and 309 more than California. The contrast between town and country in this respect is very striking. Out of 160 cities of 25,000 population and more, 390 children under five were found to every 1000 women; whereas in the rural districts outside those centres, the proportion was 572 children for each thousand possible mothers.

The causes contributing to this state of things are four-fold: the migration from country to town, the facilities with which divorce is granted, the increase of wealth and luxury, and the constant vying to maintain or exceed one's social position. A mortgage on house or farm for the motor-car's sake is a symptom of these times. But in the matter of birth-rate, lavish New York deserves a space of her own, so curious are the facts. In eleven months only thirteen infants were born in the four-and-a half mile stretch of Fifth Avenue, from Washington Square to Ninety-Fifth Street. This magnificent Avenue houses the fewest children of any residential quarter in the world. In the section observed, there were over seven hundred rich homes and four immense hotels. In strik-ing contrast with this is the record of teeming Avenue A, where in the same period 445 children appeared.

An elaborate system of tubes has of late years improved the New York transit systems out of all knowledge. It is not so long since a blizzard was able to throw the city into hopeless confusion, especially on the Brooklyn Bridge and the Elevated lines, where frozen switches and ice-covered spurs defied the most resourceful of engineers. Hosts of city workers were driven at the rush hours to the surface cars; these had their snow-ploughs and sweeps, with ingenious engines for scattering kerosene and salt in the outlying districts. It is well to remember that Greater New York covers 315 square miles, and disputes with London the primacy of the world: it musters more than six million people.

The transit companies receive weather-warnings from Chicago and St. Louis. When a storm is signalled, cars are run all night, so as to keep the tracks open. A blizzard is a very costly as well as a disagreeable city visitation. To remove an inch of snow means an outlay of $35,000 for labour. In case of a great fall, perhaps eighty miles of main streets in Manhattan and The Bronx are promptly cleared, and rather less in Brooklyn; the rest—a thousand miles or more—are necessarily left "to God and the rain."

But when the worst is said, it must be owned that New York gets plenty of sun, even in the severest winter. And when the weather clears—towards Easter, say—the city flames with a new blitheness which there is no resisting. She is now all smiles—"like a cotton-patch after a spring shower"—to quote the Texan visitor, as he climbs into the sight-seeing car outside the Flatiron Building where Broadway and Fifth Avenue converge. New York is at all times hopeful, but more so than ever at this season. You may dwell upon the war with its latter-math of hate and a future full of guns and smouldering revenge, New York will agree to some extent, and then confound you with jets of life and laughter from Walt Whitman . . . "Yet how clear it is to me that those are not the born results, influences of Nature at all, but of our own distorted, sick, or silly souls. Here amid this wide, free scene—how healthy, how joyous, how clean, and vigorous and sweet!"

New York looks all this and more to those transient pilgrims who buy a two-dollar ticket and seat themselves in the Rubberneck Wagon—a sort of grand-stand on wheels which "does" New York, from Grant's Tomb ("ten minutes for prayer and meditation") to the Temple of Confucius down in Chinatown. Here the timorous are assured that "no vice or dens shall be shown, no immoral phases, but only the curious shops and homes." Perhaps a Chinese opera too, and a chop-suey feast of barbaric cates.

The Rubberneck Wagon is so called because the rows of sightseers crane this way and that at the sonorous bidding of the megaphone man—"a bright, entertaining, well-informed, and courteous gentleman, who provides a brilliantly-told tale of history and romance.'' One learns this from the program. But surely the personal experience of that historian—the rich humours of his daily trundling through the town with America *in petto*, wide-eyed and tense under his monster trumpet—would make a far more acceptable yarn! *The Memoirs of a Rubberneck Man* should command a great sale; only none but that genius himself should have a hand in the script.

This is a slow-moving wagon. Its cicerone stands up with his back to the driver, and from his 'phone fall measured accents which the hindermost can hear: ''On the right are the twin Vanderbilt houses'' . .. ''On the left you have the famous St. Regis Hotel, which cost Twelve—million—dollars!'' To all which the rubbernecks attend, with periodic buzz of eager babble ere the next marvel shall come into view. . . . Was not this the hotel that suffered from too-exuberant advertising when it opened? Publicity o'erleaped itself in the case of the St. Regis—not publicity of the paid-for kind, but a jocular inspiration of the newspaper wags.

This stately pile was overwritten, overpraised. New York and all America was soon gorged with the ''gorgeur'' of the St. Regis, so that the ordinary visitor fought shy of it as a New York headquarters. It was a monument, one gathered, in all manner of precious marbles and bronze, reproducing the glories of Versailles and the Petit Trianon. What damasks and tapestries were here; what far-fetched ivories and cloisonnés, silken carpets, rare silver, and fragile Sèvres! Such music and wines, with exotic meats prepared by artists equal to the great Soyer or Vatel!

A lady reporter slept one night in the famous tulip-wood bed of the State suite, so as to record her regal dreams. Without sleeping there at all the cartoonist of the Sunday supplement recorded a nightmare of anticipation over his bill in the overwhelming hostel. Lightning zigzags were seen in the picture, hitting the victim as he slept and confirming his worst fear with legends like these: "Beef and sinkers—$15!" Manager Haan, of the St. Regis, protested against this nonsense, for which there was little or no foundation. But New York would hāve her jest. It was soon forgotten, of course, and the St. Regis has long been ranked as one of the foremost hotels in this eccentric city.

In considering New York, her spendthrift season, her white lights and "glad hand," it is well to remember that she is also the metropolis of the New World. Here are four hundred miles of docks, with roaring marts and factories so efficient that psychology is brought into play to get the uttermost out of the human machine. As a financial centre, New York hopes she eclipses London already. Since 1914 money has flowed this way as water flows down hill. "Only by the most careful and constant extravagance," as the native humorist explains, "can we keep it from bursting the banks!"

"My only despair," M. Prosper Grévilot told me at Delmonico's, "is to plan dishes costly enough for the tastes and bottomless purses of our patrons." It is chiefly the visitors who maintain this standard of splash. They bring with them the old traditions of freak-spending upon which Mrs. Astor frowned long ago; then she regimented the "Four Hundred" into a new American aristocracy. "There are degrees here as elsewhere," a Hindu reminded me in Olympia, Wash. "It must ever be so, since the fingers of the hand cannot be all of one size."

I found caste-marks everywhere in America, and heraldic searching was a profession that paid handsomely.

"There is a fad for armorial bearings," I was told by

a vivacious lady with a tidy business in this line. "You'll see a big display of shields and quarterings on our cars as well as on plate, china, and linen. One season there were crests and mottoes on our stockings! But you know New York's weakness for notions." I do indeed. But no man lived who knew them better than the late George Boldt, manager of the Waldorf Hotel—"a singular genius" was President Wilson's tribute to the inventor of Peacock Row, which is the women's parade in that Fifth Avenue temple of frocks and food, music, fine wines, and good cheer.

Although social centres shift in the queerest way, the Waldorf was for many years a sort of court or palace: a rendezvous for the wealth and fashion of the United States. By the way, the social ebb and flow is very disconcerting to property owners in New York. Sold under the hammer recently, the highest bid that could be obtained for Madison Square Garden—the Olympia of New York— was only $2,000,000. This was less by $1,375,000 than was paid for the building in 1911. Twenty-third Street has steadily declined in value; Sixth Avenue is a still more striking instance. In three years a tract across Manhattan Island, from Fourteenth to Fortieth Street, showed a depreciation of $65,000,000.

Twenty years ago the social axis of New York was at Fifth Avenue and Thirty-Seventh Street. It is now in the Sixties and beyond. Even Newspaper Row is dissolving and dispersing. "Nothing stays put" is the good-humoured plaint of this restless city. People of wealth give up their mansions, and pay tens of thousands a year for a wonderful suite in the latest skyscraper apartment-house. Then they grow tired of it. They complain they have "no more privacy than a goldfish," and find repose at last by taking a country home after the manner of the English, importing furniture and works of art through agents in

New York, London, Paris, and Rome. The American country house, at any rate on this scale, is a recent portent. It
is also a fashion likely to endure, as the agrophobe traditions of the cities break down and green trees are found
to be more companionable than skyscrapers.

It is well to remember that what New York says "goes,"
in the terse American meaning of that word. Her visitors
roam up and down in the true pilgrim spirit of veneration
expressed in the modest "I'm from Missouri, and you must
show me." They take home to Podunk and Bird Center
impressive facts that fell from the megaphone man on the
Rubberneck Wagon. How, for instance, New York has
thirty fires every day. How her burglars make off with
$20,000,000 worth of property in a year; how her railroads
provide marble halls and terminal stations beyond the
palace dreams of Tsar or Sultan. How glad also is New
York to see the man with money—and how glad to see *her*
is the man who has no money at all! For it is after all
a very kindly stepmother that America has here. The
municipal charities begin with the babe's milk, and end
beside the nameless alien's grave out there in the Potter's
Field.

"Look prosperous" is the tacit order of the metropolis.
You read this on the box of matches given away at the foot
of the "L" stairs. "Wear diamonds" was another prompting on the label. "Come and choose a nobby gipsy setting
and pay us as you please"! To stint and save in New York
is said to be the maddest extravagance of all, if a man is to
win. Yet free food is offered to the destitute with impulsive cheer. There is free lodging too, and good books,
with the hand of uplift extended to the sinking soul. As
for entertainment, where will you find such a movie-show
as New York herself! Why, it rivals all the films of Los
Angeles—pretty Maud in the leopard's den, bold Romeo's
fall from the fortieth storey, and the long, long kiss of

reunion—which must not, however, be prolonged beyond eight feet of film! The States of Ohio and Kansas are more generous in this respect; there the censor will permit a ten-foot kiss.

Is it any wonder, with all these facts before them, that New York's visitors are reluctant to return to their native obscurity? There is a glamour in this place for provincial America. There is wit everywhere, if only you understand the language—Hungarian at the sidewalk cafés of Second Avenue, Yiddish in Canal Street; German, Italian, Greek, Arabic, and Russ. And the theatres and halls, what a range of distraction is here, from the *Diamond Horseshoe's* blaze at the Metropolitan to the howling mob that assails the hobo singer or dancer on "amateur night" down the Bowery, or over on Eighth Avenue. What talk of plays and players around breathless tables at night in the restaurants, cabarets, and hotels! How Maude Adams earned $10,000 a year more than the President of the United States. How any sum was paid to anybody for *anything,* so long as it drew a crowd. How Bronson Howard pocketed $100,000 the first year as his share in *Shenandoah.* How the *Old Homestead* just "growed," with no author at all to its name and therefore no royalties to pay on production.

This classic play began as a shapeless sketch somewhere in the slums. Then it changed its name, and took on more acts; it developed snow-scenes and chimes, and choruses of home until at length it got on Denman Thompson's nerves. The "old rustic" that New York adored would have no more of it; he retired to a country castle and lived as a bucolic lord. The younger people hear father recall these simple far-off times. How remote they seem to the New Yorker of today! That negro phrase, "befo' de Wah," strikes quite a new note now. It is not of Lincoln's time at all, but of Wilson's, with memories of the Twelve Days

in August, 1914, and the frantic scramble of stranded
Americans abroad to get home before Germany came to
blows with the Mistress of the Seas.

The Rubberneck Wagons and yachts still toured New
York in war-time; the city was fuller than ever, indeed,
because the pleasure resorts of Europe were closed. Palm
Beach became the Monte Carlo of these times. San Diego
did duty for Cairo; and instead of the Alps there were the
Colorado Rockies to climb, with a "See America First"
society behind this new domestic travel. But what resort
could eclipse New York, if numbers are to count and the
length and cost of stay? There is no such arbiter like New
York City for laying down the law—or more strictly, *being*
the law in all things, from business ethics to dress. Now
the matter of women's clothes I may for the moment leave;
whereas the correct wear for men is a shrewd New York
concern calling for comment here and now. "A new suit,"
as the suasive announcements tell you, "is more than a
purchase; it is an investment." And the psychology of it
is fully explained in the many books and magazines which
deal with salesmanship, efficiency, and success.

"It is an axiom," the student is told, "that when a man
looks successful, he finds it easy to feel and to act successfully. On the other hand, when he feels shabby his power
to do a deal falls off appreciably. Even a detail may af-
feet a man's mental and moral state; a wrinkled tie or a
dusty hat can upset the salesman, and so business passes
to a smarter rival. Do we not hire a cobbler to build up
the heels of a tramp's shoes? There's more in that than
meets the casual eye." . . . The composer Haydn thought
so, too, you remember, and sat down to do ambitious work
in his best clothes. Now the mass of men's wear in New
York City is of the ready-made variety. British goods cut
by a tailor of Fifth Avenue are only for the gilded youth,

to whom the London cachet means as much as that of Paris to his mother and sisters.

This "semi-ready" trade is in the hands of Jews, and the advertisements are a great joy. The New Yorker, it seems, must always look young, so the jacket suit is most in vogue. Morning coats and silk hats are unusual wear; the walking stick is rarely seen. The Ready-for-Service people have an ideal model; it is that favoured by the exigent college man, "but any youthful mind and figure can wear it." It is "bred in the lap of science." You are asked to mark the "vigour and character" of a double-breasted sack which is subtly attuned "to the wave of clothes-culture now sweeping the continent." Over it you wear "a sort of bantam ulster with all the bulk tailored out of it, and the snap and virility of a form-fitting coat tailored into it." "Knee-length and double-breasted; half-belted, plain or inversely pleated and finished with slash pockets and a convertible collar that operates as easily as an electric push-button."

"Made in both dark and colourful fabrics; skeletonized, with a flash of satin in the blades; cut with an eye for curves, tailored with an eye for trifles, and finished as finely." . . . Such a garment clearly needs "a swagger hat to top it off." And here it is—"a new soft felt made for us by Stetson, and lending itself to the most rakish twist." There may be a fancy vest with this radiant outfit—one "that comes in pearl or tan, or Cuba brown." There must be a suitable shirt "of four-ply bosom with split neck-bands, felled seams and placket sleeves." From this meticulous attire down to the "Trousers Mecca" in Fourteenth Street is a heavy fall, but I must deal with the great sources of men's dress in New York.

Those Arabian offerings seem to sell themselves. Here they are—"the togs of stunts and outsizes." You may take them or leave them at $2.50 with no guidance but the one sign—"Green is the latest caper!" This is no place for the 'varsity man with "sixty years of knowing how" behind his "bench-tailored clothes-craft." The Trousers Mecca is just a plebeian hoard of pants—"the stout, chubby sort, the tall slender kind," which need a lot of finding amid the pants of normal men. A Shoe Medina is next door to the Trousers Mecca. Here is a giant dude in card·board at the door; a gay Charlie Chaplin of insinuating smile, who bids the prowler "Be Good to your Feet this Fall"!

It is in these poorer parts of the town that one sees New York's kindliness in operation. Here a college settlement, out there in the river a floating home for mothers and babes, with trained nurses and dainty food for the suffocating summer nights. There must be no mention of charity in America—only what is due from the Haves to the Have-nots. Even the New York slums are sensitive, and are quick to resent a tactless exploitation. Some years ago the Rubberneck Wagon went down Canal Street and toured the East Side—a very different East Side from today's—to "do the depravity" of that section between Allen Street and The Bowery. The natives were highly indignant, and got an express-man to fit out a retaliatory expedition at fifteen cents a head.

Soon Fifth Avenue and Riverside Drive beheld the queerest portent creaking by—a crazy van full of happy, dilapidated folk, men and women, boys and girls, and infants in arms. All were hilarious and ragged and noisy; all hugely interested in the palaces they passed, in astonished faces at the windows, and in the racy yarns—social, financial, and matrimonial—which their cicerone fired off about the gazing exhibits in a fluent Babel of many tongues. It was a great success, and thereafter the Rubbernecks confined themselves to Chinatown, leaving white America severely alone.

The benefactions of the metropolis, whether left in wills or given in the donor's life-time, are truly staggering. Millions of money rain upon the city's institutions—educational, pathological, religious, and philanthropic. There is money for art, and false teeth for the poor; money to cure consumption and "the hook-worm of laziness," which is said to affect the Southern negro. There is money to fight all things which America dislikes, from despotism to old age: there is a Life Extension Institute with ex-President Taft at the head of it. And there is money without stint—millions untold—for scientific research, the kind that lightens labour and brightens life. For no limit is set to possibilities of science in the United States.

There are free lawyers to assist the Ellis Island immigrant in the most unlooked-for plight. Here, for example, are three Russian women, from whom the Appraiser of Customs is claiming $170 duty on the bales of feathers they have brought with them, and which rank as "merchandise." It seems these peasants had long been plucking Volga geese and packing their household treasures in between the feathers, in anticipation of the day when they should sail for America. Embedded in the bales were cooking-pots and candlesticks, holy books, gilt ikons, and smelly clothes. The Legal Aid Society pleaded successfully with the Port Collector, and the feathers were at last admitted as "household goods," though there was enough in the bales to bed a whole street.

Such is New York, whose war relief work in the neutral Day covered Europe from Brussels to Belgrade, and thence to Beirut and starving Palestine. Through the Federal Council of Churches the city appealed to 35,000,000 Americans, and through Cardinal Gibbons to America's 16,-

000,000 Catholics. It was New York, in short, that mobilized the impulsive generosity of the continent. There were In-aid-ofs of inexhaustible ingenuity; "chain-letters" crossed over to the Pacific, gathering millions of dollars as they went. You were bidden buy eyes for the blinded soldier, milk for the Armenian babe, clothing for Serbian refugees, an ambulance for the Somme; a soup-kitchen for Berlin, or Warsaw, or Paris.

At emotional meetings women gave the jewels from their necks and wrists. The illiterate immigrant threw twenty cents on the platform. Jacob Schiff handed up $100,000; the Rockefeller Foundation voted $1,000,000 for relief in Poland and the Balkans.

The Clearing House Wharf at the foot of Charlton Street showed how great was New York's anxiety to alleviate Europe's woe with some of her own prosperity. But the metropolis, like the rest of America, longed for peace, and the ceasing of a havoc too strange for transatlantic minds to grasp. "Yes," said the typical New Yorker at a naval review, "the *Pennsylvania's* a wonderful gun-platform; so is her sister, the *Arizona*. The new *Mississippi* will be greater still, I guess. But we'd rather have the *Mauretania* racing in once more for our Christmas mails. Can't you *see* her, man, sighted from Nantucket in the tail-end of a December blizzard? What a vision of power and utility in grey-white tones, shining with frozen spray! Her towering bows awash, cascades of water streaming from her scuppers, and four enormous funnels belching flame and smoke. A regular Pittsburg tumbling through our wintry bay. . . . Watch her back up the Ambrose Channel, her course lit with blazing buoys, her upper works higher than the roofs on the wharfs! Ah, my friend, that's the old-time social link—the giant shuttle of brotherhood between the Old World and the New!. You may keep your destroyers, your *Revenges* and *Warspites* and

Iron Dukes. Only send us the *Mauretania* again, and by God! we'll give her skipper such a welcome as Columbus never knew!''

CHAPTER VII

"DARE AND DO"

"ATMOSPHERE" is an intangible thing, yet it can mould new men. Call it environment if you will, or the radiant aura of place and people. The working of it is surprisingly seen in America. I have entered a Syrian restaurant in Washington Street, New York, and been all but mobbed for language lessons by *rayah* shepherds and small cultivators from the Metawileh villages around Ba'albek. The keenness of these men amazed me, for I have known them at home—slow, apathetic, and resigned to the wicked tyranny of the Turk. Here they were free. Here life has a blue-eyed, cheery look; all were striving and thriving, as waifs and strays have done since the first steamer *Sirius* crossed the Atlantic in 1838. It is an inspiring sight, this widespread impulse and aspiration.

"Where were you last night?" I asked the Lithuanian Jew boy, who sold me the *Evening Post* outside the Subway. "At the Law School," he replied. He was saving his money, that earnest lad, not frittering his dimes and quarters at the movies or at Coney Island shows. You will meet hundreds like him in the Canal Street cafés. And Manhattan's Ghetto is the surest place to look for poets, musicians, and painters. My paper boy will soon be at the New York University, where nine undergrads out of ten are Jews. But the zeal for knowledge is universal here; it is the key to all success, and that elation which sings in Chopin's letter—"I move in the highest circles, ana don't know how I got there!"

The spirit and process are well shown by the Texan

94

student who arrived at the State College with two Jersey cows of a good grade. "We've lots of cows at home," he explained to President Bizzel, "but we *are* a bit short of money, so I'm going to sell milk on the college campus to pay my way. All I ask is the use of a barn and a little pasture." It was pretty cool, but the freshman had his way. At nine cents a quart he cleared $54 a month, and wrote off $14 for the cows' feed. In this way did the Texan boy secure a college education, at the same time offering to others a living lesson in ways and means. "I will study and get ready," Abe Lincoln said, "and maybe my chance will come."

This motive is plainly seen in a party of immigrants roaming the New York streets to gain ideas and weigh their own chances. They have an air of independence since they landed. They are like Daniel and his fellow-aliens in the gate of the Babylonian king, with notions of their own about the worship of the golden image. The newcomers are not only thinking; they have already begun to read. They are spelling out Success-books which tell how, from a wooden shack on the water-front at St. Paul, James Hill saw an empire in the wilderness—a railway system which was to cover half the continent. It was the same Hill who went to a bush school as a boy, and lived to promise aid to King Albert in the rebuilding of his ruined kingdom. "There is no substitute for hard work," is a saying of this man which the immigrant takes to heart in his early stages.

"Organize your leisure" is a hint from people with books to sell, the right sort of books. The great thing is to acquire knowledge, and to buy an outfit for the game. Quite likely the immigrant's education began on board the ship. Here he had nothing to do but listen, and compare what the teacher said with the letters that Franz wrote from the Florida groves and Lucia from the Little Italy of

Brooklyn, where she had a fruit stall at the side of a saloon. On the big immigrant ships trained social workers gave classes in English and talks on American ways; social, civic, industrial, and political. Such a missionary was the friend and guide of perhaps fifteen hundred souls, who were soon to be caged and sorted in the Ellis Island pens.

Even illiterates show new aptitude to learn on board the ship bound for America. There are cinema shows, dealing with the wonders of town and country life, and warning the immigrant of danger to body and soul in the siren-city of New York. There are friendly tips and exhortations to the queer crowd on deck, much as the veteran sergeant gave as "the Kitchener Crowd" drew near the firing-trench for the first time. . . . A little colloquial English would get a man a job; it would also help him to find his way about the town, and open new avenues of betterment. This ship-board schooling was an excellent plan. It roused the interest of these aliens; they were encouraged to continue in the night schools of New York and complete the process of Americanization.

In those night schools the teacher needs no language but his own. He knows his adult pupils personally; their daily work, ambitions, and tastes suggest new drills in phonetics and English conversation. It is surprising what progress these people make, especially the Germans, Syrians, and Greeks. The ideal tutor of a night class shows sympathy and perseverance; he is a fervid, ingenious organizer supplementing the routine in a social way, and turning his school into a club. Debating and singing societies are formed. There are musical evenings, addresses from public men; recitations, theatricals, visits to the library, art-gallery, and museum.

As for the immigrant women, they are a handful for the domestic educator. Mainly peasants from field and farm, they know no more than an ox of sanitation and hygiene; of food values, home nursing, or the sewing-machine. They need instruction in the very A B C of city life; their New York teachers have a tragi-comic tussle with dirt and flies, queer customs, and superstition deep as life itself. It is different with the children, of course. Their former ways melt readily enough in the public schools. Here the clash of races so often seen in adult classrooms—the impatience of Latin with Teuton, friction between Asiatic and Slav—is rosed over with cool reason and tact. This softens strife in the playground, and the races quickly blend.

All through the elementary grades in school the love of home is fostered, and reverence for the parents inculcated with anxious zeal. And for this there is special need. Illiterate or careless parents and quick, clever children are all too prone to fall apart in this land of *"Presto,"* where *"Adagio"* is the inveterate note of a slum home. Gradually the breach widens through a lack of sympathy and understanding on both sides. Sons and daughters grow ashamed of uncouth fathers and mothers, who refuse to mix with America, and cling to the older life. A little girl from the Ghetto wants to go on to high school from her graduating class. She is already a great reader, and father hides her library-card, hoping to avert the disruption he sees ahead.

I am here reminded that the American money-lust—the eternal hunt for dollars which tradition abroad has fastened on these people as their *anima mundi*—is very largely misapprehended.

It is not so much money that these people laud as energy, efficiency, and success in all walks of life, public and private; civic, industrial, artistic, or humanitarian. It is in the earning—in the matching of wits, the vying in a breathless race, that the American finds his crowning satisfaction. This is well put by an industrial lord like Charles M. Schwab, of the Bethlehem Steel-works, a concern with 70,000 hands and a pay-roll of $72,000,000 a year. "What is it," asked the ironmaster, "that drives us on to great enterprise? It is not for the money's sake, but for the thrill of accomplishment. Whenever I see a man out for nothing but wealth, I ask myself—as the brakeman did of the little dog that chased a train—*What* the devil will he do with it when he gets it?" Let America, therefore, be believed when she defines her Get-rich-quickness as the greatest game she knows. Mere money these prodigals cannot keep. "While we are the wealthiest people," says the American Bankers' Association in its Thrift Campaign, "we are still a nation of spenders."

A man who saves his money is voted mean; the thing is hardly respectable and certainly un-American. Social standards rise and surge with the flush time. Establishments swell with new accretion of income; the same is freely spent and capital encroached upon with gay disregard for the future. A successful neighbour must be "gone one better" in the way of frocks and jewels for mother and the girls; and sonny must have the car of the hour—"an Aluminium Six that rides like a liner and leaps to the gas like a blooded horse under the whip!" There are seasons at Newport and Palm Beach where money is shed as a garment. There is also the visit to New York. Here, as we know, riches are put "on the toboggan"; and the hotter the pace, the more it is appreciated.

There are signs of slowing up, however. This free "circulation" is questioned now, as so many American traits are at this time. It is a hundred years since savings banks were first established in America; and a nation-wide effort was recently made to educate the people in personal preparedness for the bad times which may be ahead. Five Thrift Days were observed in the public schools; special pamphlets were read to the children, and then given them to take home to their parents. There were Thrift Sundays in the churches, with suitable sermons and appeals. Thrift called to citizens and farmers from all the papers and magazines. There was Thrift in the street-cars and subways and L-trains; advertising on bulletin-boards all over the United States. Illustrated placards, changed every month, appeared in the factories, offices, and stores. The wage-earner found in his pay-envelope a thumb-nail folder suggesting novel ways in which he might save. And, of course, the movies preached Thrift on the continental scale. America was impressed by all this, and still more by the feckless record of one hundred typical young men, set out by the Savings Bank Section of the American Bankers' Association. These were real cases from the courts and insurance companies; from the poor-farms, charity societies, and credit departments of large concerns. This "Light Brigade" consisted of normal Yankee blades, sound enough in body and soul; quick and keen, but with no more idea of saving money than they had of loafing their young lives away. Their downhill "charge" begins at the age of twenty-five, when these knights of the golden spur prick forth on the high emprise. Twenty years later fifteen have fallen out and are dependent upon their children, or the neighbours, or some benevolent society. At the age of sixty-five, fifty-four of these have become thus dependent. Out of the hundred only five become rich. Sixty of them leave enough to pay for their own funeral; thirty-two fail even in this miserable respect.

This is not a wholesome example for the immigrant, whom I have pictured schooling himself in New York and drilling for the business fray. He is a glutton for knowledge, this citizen-to-be; his children develop with pushful

Americans in the common schools, which are purely democratic.   In Illinois a dual method of education was mooted, one for the well-to-do, another for the working-classes. But the Chicago Teachers' Federation defeated this scheme, and at the same time fought the School-book Trusts.

There are, however, hundreds of private academies for the sons and daughters of wealthy people.   These are lavish establishments—''schools of personality,'' in which the elegant arts are taught, from leadership to entertaining; how to make a speech or ride a horse, or play the violin with the pearly purity that Sevcik taught in Prague.   In the hot weather such schools as these dissolve into summer camps, where the young people frolic in idyllic surroundings by lake and wood and mountain.   The States vie with one another in this matter of education; private gifts and bequests to the college and university run into millions every year.   The rural school is a genial community centre; and there is now vocational training for the Indian children in twenty-four Western States, with headquarters at Santa Fé, N. M.

Only the South has been backward in this regard, but she is showing improvement, even as regards the black children and those of the ''poor whites'' of the mountain districts.   Education must be above all things practical, and much ingenuity is locally shown to make it so.   Thus a school in Portland, Ore., has twenty-four acres of model garden.   Arithmetic is taught in a ''play-store,'' which is, in fact, a well-found shop, complete with groceries, canned goods, and dairy produce.   There are business-like counters for the little salesfolk; an automatic till, too, and a cashier's desk, where accounts are paid and change given out in real American money.

The Bible is barred from the schools through fear of sectarian teaching and consequent discord in the homes. I have heard many protests against this, as a system which provides no spiritual or ethical ideals beyond a patriotic hymn and an occasional salute of the Stars and Stripes.

Thus far I have considered the married immigrant and his family. But what of the alien bachelor, lingering in America's gate, which is New York? He slips into a job the day after he lands—any sort of job. And then he looks round to take his bearings. He dresses gaily, as young Montaigne did to humour a world that likes a brave show. This Aladdin city takes hold of the man. Anything is possible here, he believes. And this spacious faith, this pervasive wonder and tip-toe looking for "the next" forms the groundwork of a patriotism that grows until the day of citizen papers, with its pageant of music and flags, and general felicitation.

The five-year interval has been well and shrewdly spent, for America works like a charm on the receptive man, and spreads the will-to-win with infectious zest. His earliest reading was the literature of self-building, and those books of power which fairly shout from the advertisement pages of every newspaper and magazine. "Which is *YOU*"— is a typical challenge—"the Man in the Street, or the Man in the Car; the Man with a grand home and a string of servants to do his bidding?" A picture at the top shows a poor devil nearly run over by a fur-coated plutocrat with panicky hands on the steering-wheel and a diamond "headlight" in his tie. "You can't get on by *looking* on," is a caustic reminder. "From Pick and Shovel to Consulting Engineer" is the tale of a lonely alien who gave up his evenings to a correspondence course. And again: "The Boss is Sizing You up!" The boss of the salesmen, whose star lad (the text informs us) is now on the road to earning $100 a week with a bacon-slicer which enables the grocer to sell bone at twenty-five cents a pound.

These appeals carry portraits of great men who were "all poor boys and missed a college education." Thus the

Carnegie family are pictured in Barefoot Square, Slabtown, Pa. Here little Andy got a job as bobbin-boy in the cotton mill at $1.20 a week—the mighty Andy who was one day to mould millionaires and give away $300,000,000.

Joe Pulitzer, the Hungarian Jew, was another humble‐ alien whose career is set out as a model. He was soon a prince of the press, the owner of the *New York World,* and the donor of a couple of millions to Columbia University in one lump. And so with all the big fellows. Henry Frick came of folks so poor that as a child of eight he was sowing corn on the farm, with no boots and only a precarious winter schooling. Now behold Henry Frick today, buying Rembrandts and Flemish tapestry; bronzes of the Renaissance, and rare furniture by great *ébénistes* of the eighteenth century! What capital had these strong souls to start with? What culture or social "pull" as they set foot on the first rung and stared at the stars? . . .

Consider the career of "Plunger" Gates! Or the cattle baron, whose herds range over a bovine empire; the mail-order man whose suasive leaflets fall like snow in every town and prairie hamlet between the two oceans. How assiduous they all were! How unwearied in pursuit, poring and experimenting with incredible pains; the Lionardos of a business era, determined to "get there" and rule the rest—"Better be the head of a mouse than the tail of a lion!"

Such is the printed word that kindles the young American—"the man who won't stay down," as the rousing pages of power describe him. There is no conceivable calling, it seems, which may not be taught in his leisure hours through Uncle Sam's mails. Thus the New Yorker can study song-writing under the Tsar of Rag-time, who lives a thousand miles off in Chicago. There are postal courses in forestry and law; in dentistry, chiropody, and aviation. The aspirant merely makes a choice and pays his money; books and postal lessons do the rest. He may incline to plumbing or poultry; to mining, railroading, or the dressing of a draper's window. Here again the ambitious are fired with golden facts, such as the fees paid to famous professionals. "They have no more ability than you, only they're trained in grip and go."

In this way are high hopes of his own career raised in the restless youth who feels within himself the "hundred per cent. efficiency of a goal-getter." For three dollars he can buy a book of secrets which will change his whole life. The author of that book is not modest; indeed, "How to have Nerve" is one of his leading chapters. He claims to be a builder of back-bone; the deviser of a system which dispels all fear and plays upon the small man's diffidence as "a ghost-scattering searchlight on the rich fields of life." His book will galvanize the weakling into activity. It will mass the cell-forces into new power to "put things over," and fox the foxiest neighbour until that neighbour laughs at his own defeat and hails his master in that studious fellow.

All this for three dollars! But there are deeps beyond mere knowledge, and the reader is promised "a bodily buoyancy—a tingling zest which you never felt before." The mention of physical fitness reminds me that America puts health even before this hypnosis and drill of the mind. There are stringent food and hygienic laws, ranging from clean milk to mad dogs. There are weird diets for the fat and the lean, the neurotic, dyspeptic, and sleepless; Mr. Edison has his own "Insomnia Squad" helping him in the problems of electrochemics and naval war. "Health first—pleasure follows" is the arrestive slogan of the Corrective Eating Society. One is amazed at the publicity given to "preparedness" of this kind, together with tips and warnings from all manner of men—the prize-fighter and an ex-President of the United States, Mr.

W. H. Taft. During his term at the White House his
great bulk was a real trial to Mr. Taft. It may be remembered that his fabulous trousers were borne upon a pole
by admirers in the Inaugural Parade. That genial statesman tipped the beam at 342 lbs. when he re-entered private
life, and then he began a regimen which reduced his
weight by 75 lbs. in ten months. Mr. Taft himself tells
the story.

I know no people so keen as Americans upon physical
vigour, and the causes supposed to promote it. Of course
it is the last of the speed-up which accounts for this; the
business world's message to all is "Make good or get out!"
Hence the artillery of tonics and dope for the man who
feels "all in" from overwork or strain. Hence the best
dentists and the worst quacks in the world—the vitopath
and hypnotic healer; the magic potions and electric belts
which "charge the body with the bubbling joy of wingfoot
manhood."

An addiction to drugs and bracers is decidedly on the
increase, especially those containing cocaine, morphine,
heroin, and opium. The Harrison Act of 1914 has failed
to stop the traffic in these narcotics; and Dr. C. B. Towns
of New York has urged upon Congress a Federal Commission to study the growing evil and stamp it out with
drastic laws. It is not so long since America was startled
with vital statistics, and the causes behind them, from the
Association of Life Insurance Presidents, a body entitled
to attentive hearing. At their convention the Public Service Commissioner of the Equitable flatly declared that
"the physical force of our people has declined." This was
partly due to the great increase in wealth, partly to the
time- and labour-saving devices which had altered American
habits and made all forms of exercise unnecessary.

At the same time, the consumption of rich foods had
increased; the sedentary worker took far more than the

2500 calories a day prescribed for him by Professor Lusk, of the Cornell Medical College. The result was alarming, as seen from the insurance records. These showed far too many people over forty who were from fifteen to eighty pounds above normal weight. And among these the death-rate was from nine to seventy-five per cent. in excess of the average.

Revelations of this kind tend to increase anxiety and fads, and to multiply experts of dubious fame. In the schoolroom boys and girls—with the aid of cardboard skeletons—are taught how to drive "the internal combustion engine" of the body through a strenuous American life, with due regard for the nerves which are "the sparking plugs or energizers" of the whole machine. Meanwhile mother vows she will buy no food at the grocer's which is not put up in sealed packages. And father is warned by the physicians not to cultivate any hair on his face. What is the moustache but a focus of infection in the office, workshop, and factory? "You may not *feel* the bacteria that flock to your face, but all the same you take home a choice collection of belligerent bugs"! The Menace of Whiskers is the theme of an M.D. in a popular paper, and he thanks God that "the Americans who sport a trellis-work of this kind are as rare as Irish royalists"!

Chicago was the first metropolis to start a municipal Diet Squad of twelve men and ladies. They were well fed on forty cents a day; they were frequently weighed, and the figures flashed to all the cities of the continent. It was an heroic regimen for Thanksgiving Day, when all America feasted on turkey and mince pies, while a devoted squad drilled with Dr. Robertson, the city's principal physician.

"Don't hurry," he ordained, as the hominy and codfish balls were disappearing. "You must Fletcherize, and chew each mouthful at least twenty times." This sort of thing is taken seriously in America. "Don't hurry; don't worry''; this is the latest official counsel. Even Federal Government concerns itself with these social aspects and their bearing upon the national soul. ''Worry weakens our mental forces,'' the U. S. Health Service explains in a special pamphlet for popular circulation. ''It tires and undermines us by doing nothing. The mind's engine runs idle under these vague fears, at the same time delivering no propulsive force. Worry is the protective instinct become abnormal. Consider the lower creatures. No bird that we know ever tried to build more nests than his neighbour. No fox ever fretted because he had only one hole, no squirrel ever died of anxiety lest he hadn't laid by enough nuts for two winters instead of one. We are quite sure no dog ever lost any sleep because he hadn't buried enough bones to provide for his declining years.''

The campaign against the liquor traffic is only a fight for clear thinking and productive power, with the moral aspect an ''also ran,'' on the great industrial course. Twenty-three States are now bone-dry; nine more are drying up; and by 1920 the Bryanites may easily win the thirty-six State votes which will place 105,000,000 people under nation-wide prohibition. The long battle between alcohol and industry is well worthy of notice, for the issue is pre-eminently American. It recalls the complacency of Ben Franklin, who, as a ''water-American'' in the London printing-shop, proved himself a stronger fellow than the beer-drinkers. That was nearly two centuries ago.

The tenets of the citizen on this question are not those of the fanatic, or the Anti-Saloon League, but rather those of the Tin Plate Trust and the Pennsylvania Railroad. Throughout the vast works of the Illinois Steel at Joliet and Gary, electric signs shower discouragement upon drink —''Did Booze ever get you a better job?'' Promotions are only made from among abstainers by the company's foremen and inspectors. The social change in this respect is more than sweeping; it amounts to a revolution. There was a time when the town bell rang for the labourers' grog; there was rum provided by farmers at harvest-time "to ward off the sun." In winter the ice-cutters, the masons and carpenters out in zero weather, drank hot toddy as a matter of course. Grog-shops followed the railway gangs and the miners and lumbermen of the West, as well as the prairie pioneers of Boomtown, where crude petroleum spouted over the tops of the derricks. The Labour Union, as Samuel Gompers reminds us, at first met in a saloon; the steel mill managers were sure that workers in the blast-furnace would die unless they were dosed with whisky between the heats. Even the engine-driver on the railway took a bottle into his cab, and after an awful accident one heard that "some one had been drinking."

It was Science which altered this—the science that saves time and converts every atom of human energy into output, efficiency, and results. But it was the employers' liability for compensation which set that science in motion. The injured workman had to be paid, no matter what the cause of the mishap. So if the employer tolerated tippling it was his own look-out. And he began to look very keenly indeed into the matter. He was soon interested in appliances and safety campaigns. Then came the war upon alcohol. In this the railroads led, for here if anywhere was need for clear eyes and nimble wits. A switch misplaced, a signal ignored, a telegram misread, and a hundred human beings were killed with every circumstance of horror. Yet the pioneers of teetotal reform had an uphill climb; "personal liberty" was not to be interfered with in Liberty's own land. The railroads persisted, however. They exacted pledges, and went further still—they dismissed from their service the man who entered a saloon. The logical sequence was to cut out the drinks served in the dining-car; and in this reform the Pennsylvania Railroad led.

Today there are over two million employés who are strictly dry, and well catered for by railway clubs and centres of cheer. One hundred and fifty steel and iron magnates gave their views about the old-time vice of "rushing the can"; all were agreed that it reduced the men's labour, and was a source of serious accidents. Some large employers buy up the saloons near their works in order to abolish them. "A man with a bottle of whisky," says the Du Pont Powder concern, "is as perilous in our plant as a bomb-thrower."

In some centres cold milk and tea, and cost-price meals are provided as an offset to the old lure. The Philadelphia Quartz people put the matter on a dollar-and-cents basis, and now pay the total abstainer—as the better workman—ten per cent. more wages than the moderate drinker. It is in the main a commercial crusade, and the results surpass all expectations. No moral zealousy could have worked the miracle which these business men have wrought, and the wonder spread like a religious revival. Temperance advocates talk to the men in the dinner-hour. Anti-liquor literature is given out for home reading. There are bulletin boards and flashing signs to make new converts, and keep the wobblers and backsliders on the dry line. Medical men lecture to the assembled hands on alcohol as a depressant; and the time spent in listening to this is paid for by the company at the highest rate.

Make no mistake about this teetotal taming of the American. He is above all things a practical man. He has harnessed the Niagara Falls to electric turbines, and now asks of the flood another two million horse-power. He would unweave the rainbow if it paid him, or empty the haunted air and the gnomed mine with a shrewd "What's-in-it-for-me?"

The American contends that his meat and grain have done more for mankind than all the schools of philosophy. Look at his little daughter—say, Minnie Rohmer of Beaman, Ia. Minnie was given a calf to rear in a feeding contest which was not to exceed $6.50 per hundred pounds of meat gain. Within a year the child stood beside a monster that was hailed as champion by the Iowa Beef Producers. Even the negro preacher—the prize orator at Tuskegee College waves a prize cabbage in his black fist as he roars, ''De cart' am full ob dy riches, O Lord!'' And therewith he kicks a bushel of giant maize on the pulpit floor at his ecstatic feet.

All the great stores read dollars and cents in the weather, just as the electric power people do in the scenery of the Rocky Mountains. Trade advertisements are displayed or withdrawn in accordance with predictions from the Bureau. Thus rain in the early morning is bad for the shops, whereas afternoon showers give the counters a welcome boost. A summer that is cool until late June means a heavy loss to the stores, for the women refrain from buying. And when it gets warmer they still waver, uncertain now whether they will ''get the good of their clothes'' in what remains of the season. Gloomy weather, the dentists say, keeps their parlours empty in spite of the appointments made. On the other hand a lowering day keeps the drug-store clerks and telephones busy with orders for liveners and dope. The insurance agents also bless the clouds and the squalls, for these seem to chasten exuberance and give even American life a more sober outlook in which a ''policy talk'' is feasible. A tobacco company of New York City with a chain of shops, looks to lose $4000 on a stormy day, simply because smoking is disagreeable in a high wind and rain. It is not alone the farmer and grain-gambler who follows the forecast of the U. S. Weather Bureau.

And yet for all his shrewdness, the American remains the

most sentimental of men, with social and ethical aims beyond any 1 know in the older nations. Those aims may be unrealizable—the mirage of expectancy and national youth; nevertheless they remain a potent factor in a people to whom the day's strife is a rebellion with banners, a triumphant march towards betterment of man's estate. Here is inconsistency which is not easily explained in a paragraph. In these people qualities of sense conflict oddly with the spirit. The most literal perspicacity is mixed with a visionary exaltation which in this New World recalls the singular antithesis of the Middle Ages. The Germans have judged America correctly in this regard as one sees from the opinion of Dr. Dernburg, who was their propagandist in the United States.

"It is wrong," Herr Dernburg told his Berlin audience, "to regard the American as a pure materialist. True, he is English in language and habit (which was bad enough, indeed!) but, he does carry a great deal of moral baggage with him." The point is aptly put, and force is lent to it by President Wilson's Notes and speeches during the war. "I would fain believe," Dr. Wilson told the Senate, "that I am speaking for the silent mass of mankind everywhere, who have had no place or opportunity to speak their real hearts out concerning the death and ruin they see already upon the persons and homes they hold most dear." In the same address the Upper House was reminded of America's special mission "ever since we set up as a new nation in the high and honourable hope that in all that it was and did it might show mankind the way to Liberty." This is the note of America's schools. It is also the lesson which the immigrant learns with much of the patriot faith of old Japan: "There is no need to pray, for the country itself is divine." America is considered apart in destiny, with higher ideals and unique facilities for attaining them.

Therefore all things combine to foster hope in the humblest citizen, if he keeps his body fit and his brain keyed to the high American tension. With this end in view the State Governments rain hygienic guidance on their communities. But their leaflets are now eclipsed by the Moving Picture Health Car, which North Carolina sends on a rural round where a guarantee of $90 can be got for a month's service, and go-ahead county boards, rich farmers, and local housewives often start a fair for the purpose. This laboratory on wheels carries a trained mechanic and a medical lecturer who announces the show with a megaphone. The car has a camp and kitchen outfit for the crew's use in the remoter wilds. It generates electric light, and strings the village hall with cables full of coloured bulbs. The program is changed every fortnight for the edification of country folks; and these look for the car as their children might for a circus. It is an event, a distraction, a novelty. It is even good for trade, because a film on the care of the teeth increases the sale of tooth-brushes; the fly-fighting pictures induce folks to order screens for their doors and windows.

Typhoid, malaria, and tuberculosis are some of the subjects flashed upon the screen, with cunning embroidery of human interest, lest they prove "deadly" in the showman's sense as well as in the doctor's. It is now proposed to extend this service to agriculture and domestic science— even to religious and uplift themes, such as make for better rural homes, and a happier and richer country life. All this ministry sharpens expectations and gives the charlatan unbounded scope among simple people who look for miracles, and are often robbed on a great scale. There is no land so afflicted with bogus doctors as America, thanks to the welter of laws in her self-governing States. I know no scandal so insidious and huge, no American reform more urgent—especially on account of the foreign born, who are and the magic of science which can do all things but raise the dead.

Consider New England as a quack field, now swarming with alien labour. Here the foreign born are thirty-one per cent. of the population, with 81 newspapers of their own in thirteen different languages. It comes as a shock to learn that one-third of the great and cultured city of Boston is made up of foreigners. I know a small Massachusetts town whose seven thousand people you may sort out into twenty-one races, speaking as many different tongues. These are the communities reached and fleeced by bogus doctors, who spend $40,000,000 a year in the newspapers, playing upon credulity and anxiety with merciless cunning.

The mischief done by these pests is heartrending. Here is a Polish boy of nine, discharged from the New York Orthopædic Hospital, securely trussed in iron braces. These, the mother was warned, were on no account to be removed for fear of straining the cripple's spine. Then came the quack advertisement and the fond mother's reply; the visit to a palace of magnetic healing with $100 in her hand—all the savings of a little bakery in the slums. Next day the child was back in hospital in a dying state, and the wizard skipped off to his Baltimore branch until the fuss died down.

"We have no definition in this State," Mr. C. S. Andrews told me—he was prosecuting counsel to the Medical Society of New York—"as to what constitutes 'the practice of medicine.' We have often asked the Legislature in Albany to define this for us, and they have as often refused. We do what we can, of course, but our best effort is no more than a drop of remedy in an ocean of infamy. Some of the quacks employ qualified doctors to make false diagnoses, or even to produce wounds upon healthy tissue by means of erodent acids. These are kept open as long as the money flows. It is very difficult to convict these men. In any case they set up afresh in another name and another State, perhaps two thousand miles away. Then Little Italy has its quack healers. So has Little Russia, Bohemia, Hungary, Greece, and the rest. How are we to get at these?"

Perhaps by "tapping new springs of democracy," as President Wilson urged in the domestic program which is so dear to him in these crusading days. "The votes of far-sighted men must be recruited by the votes of women, so that we may have fresh insight into matters of social reform, and move more certainly and promptly in all the problems with which our government must henceforth deal."

"Legislation will be a vain thing until the antagonisms of industry give place to generous rivalries in the pursuit of Fair Play. Labour and Capital, with angry insistence upon their rights, have entirely overlooked their obligation."—PRESIDENT WILSON.

THE outbreak of a world-war threw the United States into profound distress and gloom; it is curious to recall this fact in view of the roaring times that followed. The South was in despair, unable to sell its cotton. New York, for all its wealth and careless pride, was afraid it could not pay its debts, and therefore closed her Stock Exchange for four months. "In all previous panics," says the official chronicle of that institution, "the markets abroad were counted upon to come to the rescue and break the fall. Imports of gold, foreign loans and foreign buying were safeguards which prevented complete disaster. But now our market stood unaided. An unthinkable convulsion had seized the world. Our boasted bonds of civilization burst overnight and plunged us all into barbarism."

The savings banks fell back on a panic law, and would only pay deposits upon sixty days' notice. For the first time bankers called to their aid the Aldrich-Vreeland emergency currency. And Clearing House certificates were issued as in the dark old days. The great steel industry was turning thousands of hands into the streets; and Government was appealed to on behalf of the unemployed who were soon an army of millions. Soup-kitchens and public charities were besieged in a manner wholly un-American. . . . How the scene changed in 1915 as an industrial drama of historic interest! For three months the export of food-stuffs rose; and by April the first big order was placed for $83,000,000 worth of munitions of war. Thereafter the clouds lifted with dream-like swiftness until America had paid off a mortgage of five thousand million dollars, thanks to Europe's ravening needs. The export trade of 1916 was nearly $2,000,000,000 beyond that of 1915; the excess of exports over imports was ten times greater than in 1914. There are no records comparable with these in the whole story of American commerce.

Great fortunes were made in a night; a concern like the Bethlehem Steel could declare a dividend of two hundred per cent. The humblest alien found work at unheard-of rates, and buyers for the Allies were outbidding each other in frenzied contracts. It is not possible to exaggerate the chaos and confusion of this transition time, when agents with unlimited credit burst upon traders who had been whistling to keep up their courage after the first collapse. One Government gave an order for a chemical which was five times greater than America's entire production of it. I cannot deal at any length with the "war-brokers" and their games. The mechanic with the lathe, the clerk with a can of coal-tar—these became shell-makers or dealers in dye. They talked in millions, dogging the buyers from London and Paris, Petrograd, Rome, Belgrade, and Bucharest. Short of cash, though long of nerve and wit, many a bright young man dealt mysteriously in horses and mules, in rifles, machine-guns, and explosives. In cotton, too, and woollens and hides; in machinery and food-stuffs, cartridges, copper and war-inventions of awesome range.

It is a peculiar fact that Labour troubles multiplied in these flush times. In the fiscal year of 1915 the Department of Labour dealt with forty-one disputes involving 138,100 hands. By 1916 there were 227 cases, affecting

350,800 men. And yet large increases had been granted to the workers, in most cases voluntarily, to offset the cost of living, which had soared. There were economic causes for this, of course; but there were also artful corners in food, and the trickery of petty trusts like that of the potato-men up in Maine. There were also cold storage-stunts and a general shyness to part with supplies. The farmers were hanging on for a rise.

Here, as in Europe, profiteering was a great game, and the man with food to sell extorted the last penny before he would market his hoard. The result was that the dollar bought less than at any time since the Civil War. Flour went to $12 a barrel, or more than double what it fetched in 1914. The mine workers of Ohio came to President Wilson, demanding a nation-wide inquiry into a rocketing of food rates, which left the extra wages far behind. "He didn't keep us out of war-prices," was now a rueful caption below the President's portrait. The truth is there was no thrift shown, and the carpenter at $50 a week spent every cent of his increase. With Europe's millions withdrawn from productive labour; with its youth in the trenches, and millions more (to say nothing of the women) turned to the arts of destruction, the immense American workshop found fierce demands upon its energy, and economic chaos was the result.

Factory bosses of the Middle West vied with each other in tempting schoolboys with $15 a week for screwing common nuts in place. A hurry call to the skilled mechanic meant two dollars an hour—or say $5000 a year. All industrial concerns made haste to raise wages. The U. S. Steel added ten per cent. to the pay-roll of 318,000 men, a matter involving $20,000,000. The Standard Oil did the same, so did the Westinghouse and the General Electric. Banks and insurance companies, the New England mills, and the motor-shops out West all followed suit, until 25,000,000 workers had an increase amounting to $7,000,000,000, distributed all over the continent. Even Government salaries were raised—for the first time since Walt Whitman was a Treasury clerk half-a-century ago.

And still Labour was dissatisfied. Strikes and lock-outs were declared in the unlikeliest quarters. An eight-hour day· was the issue in Pittsburg. In New York even the garment-hands walked out. Strangest of all, the typists and stenographers of the American Federation of Labour asked for a minimum wage of $3 a day, and were backed up by the Central Union. But the gravest trouble—the shadow of a national calamity—was the threat of a general railroad strike throughout the United States, paralysing the good time and bringing everything to a standstill. This menace came in the midst of a Presidential campaign, and Dr. Wilson handled it with a boldness quite unlike his usual caution. He sided with the Four Brotherhoods of railway labour in their demand for an eight-hour day. Strike funds totalling $15,000,000 had been mobilized for a conflict which should spread like a storm, involving many other trades.

President Wilson hurried to Congress as champion of the Brotherhoods and twelve other Unions· all linked with the Federation of Trade, and representing 700,000 men. Mr. W. C. Adamson framed the Eight Hour Bill, which bears his name, and this was passed as the new unit of a day's wage for all workers operating trains in Inter-State commerce.

But the new measure was promptly challenged by the railroads as "an unconstitutional interference with the liberty of contract." Meanwhile the strike was called off, leaving the employers sore and the men suspicious that President Wilson had "tied a string" to the prize he had given them. And so indeed he had. For when the Adamson Law was passed, the President urged that in future an inquiry into industrial disputes should be made compulsory; and that, furthermore, until the investigations were complete "no strike or lock-out shall lawfully be attempted." The President's model was the Canadian Industrial Disputes Act, which has worked fairly well—though the Dominion Trade and Labour Congress claims that "it pinches only one foot," and binds but one side in these industrial wars.

In no nation have Labour troubles been so frequent or so bloody as in the United States, where strike-breaking is a regular craft employing thousands of armed men. Disorder has often been on so great a scale as to pass beyond police control and call out the State Militia, or even the Federal troops, as in the Chicago "battles" of 1894, which began in the Pullman Works and spread to the Railway Union. It is now hoped that such strife belongs to the past. There is a gulf not measured in years alone between Henry Frick of the Homestead "war," and the Henry Ford of 1917, with his profit-sharing schemes and his minimum wage of five dollars a day for a staff counted in tens of thousands. As a Peace apostle Mr. Ford had no success: as an employer of labour the ascetic little man is a power in the United States, where he aspires to employ a hundred thousand hands and turn out a million cars each year.

Thomas Edison paid a visit to the "Detroit mechanic," who was busy with farm tractors, such as the maimed soldier might use after the war. "Ford is the most humane man I know," was the great inventor's verdict. "He's all machines, of course; but what he talks about most is his men. Are they doing their work easily as well as efficiently? Henry's critics take him to task for the high wages he pays. Why, they work out at America's lowest! I pay less, but Henry gets more for his money." Mr. Ford is the pioneer of shorter hours on quite new (and mechanical) lines. In February, 1913, 16,000 of his men, working ten hours a day, produced 16,000 cars. Just one year later, with other aids and systems—with task analysis and "progressive assembling"—15,800 men produced 26,000 cars.

This man is the Messiah of the Central West; an industrial dreamer, a benevolent despot, with fifty-three different nationalities in his employ. "No workman," he contends, "will take pride in his work if he's underpaid, or has no leisure in which to enjoy his life." And therewith Mr. Ford cut a Christmas "melon" of $850,000 which he shared among his foremen and department chiefs. These are the new ideals of American business. They go much further than the installation of a well-equipped hospital in the mill, or the display of signs urging "Safety First," and total abstinence from booze. The speed-up remains, of course; it is even intensified in queer scientific ways. But "welfare" is now a great word between employer and employed. It is carried to extremes in that marvellous "foreign" city of Detroit, where every third man you meet is an alien.

The coloured map of the Board of Commerce in this place, showing the location of the different races, is like a war-chart of Europe in 1918. The Slav splash of colour looms largest of all. Other areas show the habitat of Italians and Jews; of Magyar and Ruman, Belgian, Armenian, and Greek. Detroit is above all cities the best in which to study the process of Americanization, as well as that new "spirit of the hive" and specialized labour, which can turn out a six-cylinder car at $1000, with a constant tendency to raise the power and reduce the price.

"Keep your workers happy" is the watchword of American capital today. But the happiness must pay its way; it is a commercial aim on peculiar lines, satisfying both sides—for a while. I know a factory in Rochester, N. Y.,

where it takes seventy hands to turn a South American
ivory nut into a trousers button. The work is very monotonous, but the girls who do it are cheered with music—
with lilting melodies from batteries of gramophones installed in airy rooms. Ventilation, by the way, is a typical feature as a dividend-payer; for bad air is more tiring
than hard work. "What's the matter?" asks the boss at
three in the afternoon. "Not so much snap and drive
as at eleven o'clock. Production seems to sag. What's
the cause?" And fans and blowers are installed; heating
and cooling systems whose cost is carefully weighed against
the extra output which energized workers will show.

"The only way to mend a bad world," says Henry Ford,
"is to create a good one, and give the workman his due
in a generous spirit." Hence the profit-sharing principle
and the higher standard of life insisted upon by the
Ford Educational Department. This is an inquisition of
peculiar powers, like the company itself, which is independent of banks and has its own deposits of iron ore on
the Pacific Coast.

It is worth recording that his polyglot army show no
great gratitude to this singular man. "I don't owe nathun'
t' Henry Ford," snapped the rugged Pole at the Detroit
night school, where the motto is "Learn English and get
better pay." "When he pay me tree dollar, I make tree
hunnud bolts in ten hour. Now I work eight hour an' get
five dollar. *But I make nine hunnud bolts!*" Even the
alien worker has no illusions on this score. None the less
a profound change of relations is manifest. It was clearly
stated in an address to Cornell University by Mr. John D.
Rockefeller, Jr., who hoped that "the personal element in
industry would soon be regarded as an important part
of the college course, which aims at fitting a man for business life."

"Hitherto," Mr. Rockefeller pursued, "the chief execu-

tives of our great undertakings have been chosen chiefly
for their organizing or financial capacity. The time is
come, I think, when the best men for such positions are
they who can deal successfully and amicably with Labour,
which is, after all, the natural partner of Capital. And
personal contact of the right sort gives us the greatest
promise of bridging the chasm which opens between employer and employed!'' The speaker had just visited his
coal mines in Colorado, where downright slavery existed
not long ago, and a bloody warfare broke out which scan-
dalized all America. Mr. Rockefeller went from camp to
camp among the aliens, talking with their families, visiting their schools and places of amusement. ''These men,''
he reports, ''and many in the State besides, had formed
their opinion of any one bearing the name of Rockefeller.
. . . Because of the disturbances, bitterness and hatred existed in a high degree.'' And no wonder. The exploitation of cheap foreign labour is a fact which no American
disputes, though he hopes the worst of it is over. The
labourers, especially in foundries and mines, were enslaved
in the most literal meaning of the word. And when they
rebelled they were shot down by armed guards, or by strike-
breakers, as at Lawrence and Paterson; and at Everett,
Wash., where on ''Bloody Sunday'' the casualties were five
killed, thirty wounded, and a hundred more in gaol.

Many of these aliens realize that, although they escape
one form of militarism in the Old World, they are seized
by another in the New—the militarism of money, and the
vicious concept of the human machine. Here they found
the titans of trade using men as the cottager at home used
bees. They were creatures of profit; the study of them
had a cash value, and was reduced to an exact science.
That the wage-earner's life and limbs were cheaply held
admits of no doubt. The American Institute of Social
Service collected industrial casualties for four years, and

set them in telling array against the fours years' slaughter of the Civil War. It was then seen that money's militarism was by far the bloodier, exceeding that of the armed strife by eighty thousand deaths.

In the quarries and mines—coal and iron, lead, copper, silver, and gold—Mr. John Mitchell, of the United Mine Workers, reckoned 11,986 cases of killed and injured in an average year. By no means all the States record their accidents, and official returns are questioned by unbiassed observers like the late Dr. Josiah Strong, whose motto was: "Better a fence at the top than an ambulance down below!" Indiscipline and ignorance account for much of this industrial havoc. Thus, out of 448 collisions on the railway, three-fourths of them were due to negligence on the part of trainmen and engineers. One hundred and seven more occurred through heedless signallers and despatchers. Then foreign workers in the mines are careless of safeguards, and are too often left to their own ways. So their death is accepted as a daily event, and their friendless bodies sold for dissection to the medical schools.

There remains the question of overwork and fatigue. Science is not everywhere alert in the United States; and the speed-up strains flesh and blood to the breaking-point and beyond. An inquiry into the Terra Cotta disaster on the Baltimore and Ohio line, near Washington, showed that the engine-driver had been on duty for forty hours out of forty-eight, with no chance of any rest. Moreover, the railroad time-sheets for the two previous months gave fourteen hours as the working day of six hundred train-crews. On the Southern Railway the President of the system lost his own life in an accident caused by a track-man who was too weary to flag the train.

This phase of prosperity has long been a theme of the social reformer. "A perpetual war upon humanity," Theodore Roosevelt called it. As Chief Executive he had many a tilt against employers because of their callous view of all this murder and maiming. Roosevelt also brought it to the notice of Congress, pointing out that "in legislation and the use of safety devices we are far behind the European peoples." But for business reasons this was a ticklish target for the American crusader—unless he were a mechanical genius like Henry Ford of Detroit.

It is the passion for results—a love of short-cuts and spectacular methods—which accounts in part for the cheapness of life and limb in America. Her greatest holiday—the Fourth of July—was, until recently, a lurid and deathful orgy. Luckily it engaged at last the drastic attention of both State and Federal Governments. Before "a saner Fourth" was forced upon the nation, the day's fun cost the lives of fifty persons, besides injuring five thousand more, and inflicting anguish upon the sick in hospitals through the din of giant crackers, cannons, and revolvers. Many of the injured died later of blood-poisoning, lock-jaw, and burns. This strange sacrifice has been gradually reduced since 1899, when the *Chicago Tribune* first began to count the casualties of Independence Day.

I am well aware that these things sound preposterous to the British reader, but my task is to present the facts and seal them with American testimony which there can be no gainsaying. I shall pass lightly over the death-roll of city streets, only remarking that in New York I rode in the car of a wealthy speedster, whose record is, I hope, unique. That car had already killed two men; it figured in thirteen accident cases, and had injured nine persons, of whom five would be crippled for life.

Police Commissioner Woods looked for, at least, one death each day, and a case of injury every twenty-three minutes. Yet his traffic squads were picked men, each with special knowledge of his own zone. Block systems, new semaphores, and safety-isles are tried, so as to reduce the street accidents; but the traffic-courts of the city tell woeful tales of lawless men (and women, too) who never drove a car before, yet essay a 'prentice hand in the rush-hour at Forty-Second Street and Fifth Avenue!

European readers have a habit of dismissing queer or monstrous happenings in America as mere Yankee yarns. It is a mistaken frame of mind, an incredulity which is resented over there as conveying a superior pose *de haut en bas*. What seems to us grotesque and strange is, to an American, the commonplace of his daily paper. This democracy claims extraordinary license, and chafes under the new discipline lately urged upon it by leading men. It is, indeed, a wayward people, following the feet of change and revelling in the polyphonic surf of novelty. Evasion of the law is a general symptom, coupled with irresponsibility and the pursuit of individual aims. And this entails calamity on a huge and frequent scale. Take the burning of the pleasure-steamer, *General Slocum,* which sailed past the foot of the New York streets with a blazing holocaust of a thousand souls—surely the most dreadful sight which a great city ever witnessed. The inquest showed that every known rule and regulation had been broken by the owners of the boat. And, to crown all, the life-belts were found loaded with metal in order "to give them the required-weight"!

Then there was the defective steamer *Eastland,* which rolled over at her dock in the heart of Chicago for a horrified populace to see. "There is not now," was the official verdict on this disaster, "nor has there ever been, an inspection service of the Federal Government for judging the stability of these boats." The result is that in the last ten years thirty-one vessels have been lost on the Great Lakes with every soul on board. A lawless spirit in "the man higher up"; indifference or ignorance among employés—these are contributing causes in a waste of life and limb which has no parallel elsewhere.

The American worker of whatever grade is selected, trained, and improved in a strictly productive way. There are in the workshop taskmasters and efficiency engineers, just as there are soil and crop intensifiers sent round to the farms by the Department of Agriculture. The man laying bricks, or feeding a furnace with coal; the woman pasting labels on jars or cans—here is scope for highbrow aid and the psychological laboratory of the University. Or, again, here is a girl folding handkerchiefs. Somehow she falls slack in the early afternoon; her output is below that of her neighbours. Why is this? Here enters the expert—if necessary with a cinema camera whose film will reveal human frailty and fatigue in microscopic detail. The reason for fewer folded handkerchiefs is that old chair upon which the worker sits. It is too low, imposing extra strain upon the girl to maintain her hands at the proper level. Now enters the carpenter with four blocks for the chair-legs—and lo, the automaton's output reaches the normal again and surpasses it.

Or, again, here is a Detroit motor-shop where twenty-eight men assemble four thousand pistons a day, each man putting piston and rod together in three minutes. The operation is a simple one—incapable, one has said, of any further speed-up. Yet the analyst has his eye on it. A sleuth-hound of time is this omniscient plotter; he detects each flick of a finger which "does not pay," and forthwith enlists it for service. Those twenty-eight assemblers, it seems, spend four hours of their nine-hour day walking back and forth. They are now reshuffled. The task is still further subdivided; the result is that fourteen men are reported to the foreman as "free for other work." Such is the speed up, which has become an extraordinary mania in the United States—at any rate on the employer's side.

Its ideal is to conciliate labour as it goes, selecting bosses
who are born for control. "Tact," says the staff pioneer of
a big concern, "is the sweet oil of business. *So keep your
can full!*"

Many of the big concerns catch their employés very young
and drill them with vocational insight. This is especially
true of the electrical industry. The New York Edison
Company is supposed to choose its youngsters "in the
nursery." They are weighed in the balance of heredity
and environment; they are appraised and educated, cred-
ited or debited with plus or minus marks.

Health and a good appearance are factors insisted on.
So are perseverance and energy; the "Hold on" and "Try
again," with all concentration, enthusiasm, observation,
memory, understanding, and will. This strenuous gospel
—this sleety faith and all its fruitful works—may be said
to be the real religion of the United States. "There will
soon be no more priests," Walt Whitman exulted. "Their
work is done. A new order shall arise, and they shall be
the priests of man, and every man shall be his own priest.
. . . They shall arise in America, and be responded to from
the remainder of the earth."

Here I am reminded that once, and once only, did Wall
Street reach out to save souls, with Mr. James Cannon, the
New York banker, as chief apostle. Five teams of well-
drilled scouts were sent out in advance to attack the strongholds of sin in the Eastern States, and that on highly
original lines. Even that difficult man, the late Mr. Pierpont Morgan, gave $5000 towards this novel mission, for
he was impressed by maps and figures, and by a card-
indexing of the redeemed which promised rich results.
The manager of this campaign gave up a fine position in
Detroit to act as the spearhead of assault; and his action—
paradoxical as it may seem—was characteristically American. "We're going after souls," that zealot told me, "exactly as the Standard Oil goes after business. And we're

backed by the best money and brains in America." But the Standard Oil success was not forthcoming when the first flush of novelty was gone. However, that soul-saving is possible "on business lines" has been demonstrated for years by the famous Billy Sunday, the ball-playing evangelist who must be a rich man now, with a fervid following which no orthodox preacher can ever hope to win.

Mr. Sunday's methods are lurid beyond all American records, which is saying a good deal. "He has the bellow of Edwin Forrest," an admirer says: "the glare of Edmund Kean, and the flip modernity of George M. Cohan." Billy's manager will enter a great city and form a joint-stock company to guarantee expenses; these may reach $50,000. A board tabernacle seating 18,000 people is rigged up on a vacant lot, and then the show begins. Mother may take her baby and have the little one checked, just as father checks his hat and coat. There is no describing the vast audience; it is simply America. Here are shop-girls, and members of the Hod-Carriers' Union. The rich man is in the front row; so is the music-hall manager, who follows the uproarious scene with envy. "Billy Sunday's act is the greatest ever," he sighs, and tries to profit by it on the boards.

As a pulpiteer the unreverend Billy Sunday is at once actor, acrobat, and mime. His hearers are in tears over the sob-story of booze,—when lo, the preacher convulses them with antic mirth! He plays upon all the emotions. He sounds all the human stops with a power that must be seen to be believed; he uses the rich vocabulary of baseball and prize-ring. See him picturing the eternal war of the weak against the strong. "There's young David," he screams, "soakin' Goliath on the coco, clean between the lamps! Down goes the big stiff for the count. An' while the kid's choppin' off his block, the whole bunch behind the big feller skiddooes!"

What milder pastors think of "Sunday salvation" makes very mixed reading. Billy had shattered Springfield, Ill., when a university graduate reported upon the moral aftermath of the orgy. "Our community seems disillusioned and burnt out. The sacred power of souls to respond to the gentle voice of Christ has been strained and coerced by these high-pressure methods."

Now for their cash returns. Concerning these the famous evangelist is very frank. "Do as you want with your own money," he roars as the collection pans go round, with a Fitzsimmons reach. . . . "Give if you will. It's none o' my business what you do with your dough, an' none o' yours what I do with mine!" Philadelphia's dough came to $51,156; Pittsburg gave Mr. Sunday $44,000, Boston beat them all—though Cardinal O'Connell warned his flock against Billy's bizarre performance. Here the collections totalled $90,436.

These large offerings are chiefly from the masses, to whom closeness in money-matters is the meanest of traits. Thrift is today set before America's millions, and was none too welcome at first, even when masked as "efficiency" or "conservation." The wealthy were asked to set a more sober example; the worker was besought to save his money so as "to prevent his wife going directly from his funeral to a job at the wash-tub." So keen are the employers of labour upon the workers' thrift that they go to extremes of paternalism and stir up wrath by welfare schemes of drastic range.

Take the Educational Department of Henry Ford's plant in Detroit. "We estimate," an official said, "that sixty per cent. of the men can look after themselves. So we organize to take care of the rest." The affluent workman is here required to conform to a higher standard of life. He must prove himself "clean, sober, industrious, and thrifty." "It is not wise," says the chief inquisitor, "for working men to spend money on things above their station." Employés must bank their surplus money, and domiciliary visits are paid to see that this is done. Passbooks and private papers must be produced when the Ford Investigators call. No profit-sharer may take in lodgers; and should he settle in an evil neighbourhood, well-meaning despots transplant him and his into a sweeter quarter of the town.

It would be absurd to suppose that this system was meekly accepted by tens of thousands of men: Ford himself knows quite well that it is not. He would like to see all the guidance, the advice and oversight of private affairs made less minatory, more optional and free. As a "Sociological Department" the inquisition goaded the men to mutiny. It set up a rigid code of morals, it had spies all over Detroit reporting lapses; it took testimony from children against their fathers, and from wives against their husbands. Mr. Ford was grieved over this tyranny, and he checked and modified its scope. He does not believe in Labour Unions, by the way, "because they mean war." The equality of men he will grant you—as a theory with considerable hedging. "But power of all sorts," he says—"business, financial and political—seems to centre round the big fellow; it has always been so, and I guess it will always be."

Henry Ford plays the democrat out on his Dearborn farm. It is a mistake to suppose he is greatly loved, or that his social views have any influence upon the municipal government of Detroit. This is an extravagant town, and men of the right civic kind will not "play politics," having a more alluring game of their own in the gas-blasts and automatic conveyers of their miraculous shops. No doubt Detroit is an exceptional instance of bossing and drilling the human machine; it is at once the most foreign of all, yet the most American of cities in spirit. Its population in 1900 was 285,000; today it has three-quarters of a million, and assimilates aliens in a magical way, chiefly through night schools, where Greek, Italian and Pole are tempted to learn English, and so "become a better citizen with a better job."

Printed slips of advice on these lines are found in the worker's pay-envelope. The saloons are plastered with similar hints; the girl who borrows a book at the library finds promptings on the first page. Preachers and editors, gangsters and ward leaders, all lend their aid to break up foreign ignorance and blot out hyphenism of all shades. The big motor shops put premiums upon adult education; some offer an extra two cents an hour to Italians, Hungarians and Poles who are learning English. Their teachers are themselves taught by experts in immigrant education, like Mr. H. H. Wheaton and Dr. Peter Roberts.

Here we see the "progressive action" which President Wilson sets before American employers. He would like to have an end made of anarchy-breeding inequalities, which are still so glaring a feature of the great Republic. The President also hoped that mutuality of interests will henceforth receive support—"and that men of affairs will lend themselves to the task of making democracy a more effective instrument of human welfare. It cannot be said that they have done this in the past." Here is a thrust which goes to the root of civic and social ills. Hitherto the ablest and most fearless of men—men of great wealth and moral strength—have not been willing to serve the community in public positions. The word politics conveyed a taint of trickery and graft. Then the newspapers were also feared. The result was that State and civic government passed to professional cliques of the Tammany type, intent only upon power and loot.

"Real remedies," as Dr. Wilson points out, "wait upon the development of a more honest and more discriminating public opinion." That big business is giving a good lead to the smaller concerns in the treatment of Labour is now undeniable. A notable instance of welfare-work was the laying out of the industrial city of Gary by the Steel Trust. This model town of 100,000 souls was designed and built as one builds a country house, amid the sand and scrub of the southern end of Lake Michigan. There were two square miles of furnaces, foundries, and mills; four square miles of tree-shaded streets, with parks, playgrounds, and dwellings of many grades, each one perfect of its kind.

The Grand Calumet River was turned from its course; all that science could suggest was here carried out to show what American capital could do for its labouring men. Industrial strife, it was hoped, would never mar the idyllic life of Gary. Here the skilled hand could earn high wages and rear a family, at the same time putting by a competence and enjoying life in the true American way. Squalor, poverty, and vice—these were to have no part in the Utopian city, with its fine boulevards and concert-halls; its libraries, museums, and gymnasiums. All sewers, conduits, and pipes were laid in thirty-foot alleys behind the town blocks, so as to avoid the noise and dirt attendant upon the tearing up the streets.

As for the minimum wage, this is now assured in ten States, and others will presently follow—though the American Federation of Labour opposes the idea, chiefly on behalf of the working women. President Gompers championed the cause of these before the Industrial Relations Commission. "I am very suspicious," said America's labour lord, "when I see Government agencies busy in this way." His reasoning is too long and complex to set out here, but undoubtedly there is confusion and evasion through the conflict of laws in the various States. Thus labour boycotts are forbidden in Alabama and Colorado— where a Federal Statute declares them perfectly legal.

There are laws against blacklisting in twenty-six States. Others have special rules against intimidation, or against conspiracy, or harsh conditions of employment like the barring of a worker from his trade union. This lack of uniformity hampers progress in unexpected ways.

The case for an eight-hour working day has established itself after five and twenty years of agitation. It was recently set before the Supreme Court in a brief of a thousand pages intended to uphold the legality of the Oregon Law. Tired workers and their diminished output were here represented, whether in a candy store or in the bituminous mines of Illinois. Shorter hours were eloquently urged upon a democracy that sets great store by the intelligence of its citizens. How shall a man vote wisely if he has no time for reading, or for study of the topics of the day? Of what use are night schools to the worker who comes home dog-tired after a complete round of the factory clock?

Long hours led to poor health, and symptoms of strain due to industrial speed and drear monotony. Cumulative fatigue was set up and to this were traced the serious accidents which figured so luridly in statistical tables. A shorter day, it was claimed, increased the quality as well as the quantity of work. It also promoted temperance; it encouraged education and the general uplift which America is for ever preaching.

The rank and file of workers are now shown the way to betterment; the biggest prizes of all are offered to intellects of devoted training, however lowly in station and poor in this world's goods. "There's not a man in power at our Bethlehem Works," Mr. Schwab declared, "who didn't begin at the bottom and work his way up. Eight years ago Eugene Grace was switching engines. But he out-thought his job, and that, as well as integrity, lifted him to the head of our corporation.   Last year Mr. Grace earned over a million dollars.''

The smaller concerns follow this lead, and seek to kindle in their staff a goodwill and interest which never existed before. ''Let's put up a Suggestion-box,'' a certan partner proposed.   For some weeks it was a nest of complaints and vile abuse—of course with no signature. ''They've got a grouch,'' said the smiling deviser of the plan. ''Now they're working it off. But we'll get some notions presently.''   And so they did.   An idea of great value was one day found among the mixed contributions, and a cheque for $1500 was quietly handed to the man as he worked at his bench.   He was of course astounded.   Two years' wages for a few lines on a scrap of soiled paper!   The news spread like fire.   A second man soon waved a $500 cheque; a third had $1000 to show, and was proud beyond any money at this tribute to his wit in the utilizing of waste products.

Yet, in spite of this movement, America remains the land of giant strikes fought out with firearms and dynamite. How is this to be explained?   Perhaps by the inequality of distribution which here presents quite monstrous contrasts.   Mr. Rockefeller is reported to be a ''billionaire.'' Certainly the man's riches are beyond any dream.   Against him and his may be set the ''poor whites'' of Kentucky and Tennessee, a folk who live as illiterate savages in a bleak and dismal squalor passing all belief—even the belief of most Americans.   It is the record of the Standard Oil and other Trusts which have set up those ''antagonisms of industry'' which President Wilson deplores.

''We find,'' says the Preamble of the Industrial Workers of the World—a Labour body of seventy thousand members —''that the centring of the management of industry into fewer and fewer hands makes the trade unions unable to cope with the ever-growing power of the employing class.''

That labour laws are nullified is beyond doubt; the sovereignty of States and the powerlessness of the Federal authority are great temptations to the unscrupulous in this direction. "You must watch them!" cried little Sarah Shapiro to the Women's Trade Union League of New York. Sarah was a garment-worker over on the East Side, and could read the greedy employer like a book. "I shall take you to our factory after hours, when the doors are locked and all the windows darkened. Yet inside are the girls and children—working, working, working!"

The Federal Government prohibited from Interstate Commerce the products of all mines, factories, and mills employing child labour. But there are still two million working children not protected by this Act. The Southern Senators opposed its passage in Congress as likely to clash with existing local laws. Mr. Tillman, of South Carolina, found the Child Labour Bill not only unconstitutional, but also an infringement of States' Rights. New Mexico, North Carolina, and Wyoming have no child-labour laws at all. And nowhere does the Federal Act apply to farm-work. On the whole, there is ample ground for Labour's cynical attitude in the face of princely gifts from million-aire employers. I was astonished at the spirit in which these benefactions were received. "He'd steal the cow," said a superintendent grimly of a very great man indeed, "and give away the horns for the love o' God!"

At the best time of the year there are 7,000,000 wage-earners in the factories, at the worst time only 4,500,000. Therefore, according to the Census of Manufactures, there is a regular human "slack" of 2,500,000 workers. The number of men who lose four months or more out of the year totals 3,300,000. Now, to regularize this drifting labour baffles all investigation, so immense is the area to be covered. Subway construction may be finished in New York, whilst California figs and oranges are waiting to be

picked.   But the distance between these two points equals
a journey from the Old World to the New

There are fine chances for the small cultivator in the
Yazoo Valley of Mississippi; the flour mills of Minneapolis send out hurry calls for hands.   But it is nobody's
business to handle the floating forces of labour and distri-
bute them in strategic and seasonal areas of the continent.
American prosperity is, therefore, an elusive condition.   No
man lives who will guarantee it for two successive years.
Desolation dawned with 1915—only to melt into the prodigal riot of 1916.   Bubble finance and frenzy were rampant in the cities; the farmer was rolling in money with
his cotton at twenty cents instead of ten, his wheat at
two dollars a bushel instead of ninety cents.   It is perhaps
this uncertainty which fosters in the United States a
gambling spirit which I have not seen equalled in any land.

"We are a composite and cosmopolitan people," President Wilson owned in his Inaugural Address to Congress.
"We are the brood of all the nations now at war."   A note
of regret runs through this grave message, because counsel
and action had been turned from "the great problems of
domestic legislation" to "other matters lying outside our
own life as a nation."   America had no control over those
gusts, "which have shaken men everywhere with passion
and apprehension."   It was a disappointment to Dr. Wilson
who had set his heart upon the unity of the nation and
internal reforms of crying need.   "We have sought very
thoughtfully . . . to correct the grosser errors and abuses
of our industrial life, to liberate and quicken the processes
of national genius and energy, and to lift politics to a
broader view of the people's essential interests."

When all has been said about welfare schemes we still
have to consider the armed guards and strike-breakers
whose work it is to crush uprisings and disrupt the industrial Unions.   Now this strike-breaking and gunning

is an ugly symptom of that cleavage which the President deplores. A Labour Board may be in full session over a dispute, but both sides will take no chances. The employers order out their secret armies, with weapons and without; the Unions have trained corps watching the professionals who would force the open shop upon them.-- A typical strike-breaker was the late James Farley, of Philadelphia, who was a rich man with a blood-stock farm at Plattsburg, N. Y., and a cheque which Wall Street would at any time honour for $100,000. Mr. August Belmont used to say that Farley was "a born soldier." Certainly he gloried in the fight; he was shot at five and twenty times, and received over five thousand threatening letters in a year. Railroads, street car corporations, mines, machine-shops, and factories all employ men like Farley and Harry Bowen—who took out a special policy upon his own life for $100,000. Strike-breaking bosses are on the pay-rolls in peace time; and as the first murmurs arise, secret agents scatter among the men to ascertain their case and their financial strength. Meanwhile the "breakers" are enlisted. -In a New York subway tie-up Farley was paid $5 a day for each man, and $1000 a day for himself as field-marshal of the strike army. It was a task of deadly peril, but Farley cleared $130,000 in this one campaign.

Today the strike-breaker has a gentler name. Mr. James A. Waddell is an "expert in emergency employment." This general has an armory of 1100 rifles in New York City, as well as barracks where guards are drilled and maintained. When a railway tie-up was in the air, Mr. Waddell mobilized in Chicago 13,000 trainmen and engine-drivers. For this force he drew the great sum of $65,000 a day, plus ten per cent. commission on the commissariat. How large a matter this may be is seen in a thirteen-day strike which called for $168,000 worth of provisions. In many cases, the Labour Union is beaten, the strike called off, and mortified men ordered back to work on their employers' terms.

It is against militarism of this kind that President Wilson has set his face. "Our industries," he declared, "have been under the control of too small a body of men. Business ought to be democratized, and made to see that aristocracy is bad for it, just as it is for governments."

". . . Men can assist Fortune, but they cannot resist her; they may weave her webs, but they cannot break them."—MACHIAVELLI.

I KNOW no stranger institution than the Lincoln Memorial College down at Cumberland Gap, in the lonely Appalachians. Here is a forlorn region of rugged spaces and wretched farms, which a negro would despise; of one-room huts where illiterate women spin, or barter hog-meat and feathers. Vendettas and feuds are the only break in a life of complete stagnation. There are no waterways in this mountain land, the railways have been careful to avoid it. Yet in these hills dwell Americans of the purest breed descended from pre-Revolution pioneers; a real peasantry, vaguely known to the outside world as the "poor whites" of Kentucky and Tennessee. They are unobtrusive, however. The poor whites are lost Americans; clannish and resigned, given over to tribal wars and a diet of " 'possum and peanuts, with occasional nips from a moonlight still."

From this unlikely stock have come some of America's greatest men. The greatest of all was Abraham Lincoln, who as a boy crouched at a "poor white's" hearth, and by the light of a blazing pine-knot pored upon the Six Books of his salvation.

When greatness came to the hero, he never forgot those days, nor the bleak abandonment of that life. The poor whites had no chance, so Lincoln asked his friend, Oliver Howard, to help, and in this way the University for Lost Americans was born. It has a farm of six hundred acres. All the practical trades of men are here taught, all the useful chores which a woman should know both in the home and out of doors.   Students at this College leave the plough-tail, the cow-byre, kitchen, and sty to take their final degree, then they walk home—fifty miles or more—to spread the new light in a darkness which is generations old.

It is not so long since Dr. Wilson took over the Lincoln hut at Hodgenville, Ky.; it is now a national memorial, enclosed in a granite temple.   That occasion was pecul-iarly solemn.   The speaker's fervour; the surroundings and historic associations all combined with the war-cloud to produce a deep impression.   Gradually the speech veered to the novel demands and duties of today.   ''Democracy will be great,'' the President said, ''and will lift a light for the nations only if we ourselves are great, and carry the lamp high for the guidance of our own feet.   We shall not be worthy unless we be in deed and in truth real democrats and servants of mankind, ready to give our very lives for freedom and justice.''   The speaker has often shown himself alive to the limitations of the older Ameri-canism, and he now appealed for a larger patriotism on the lines laid down by Aristotle: ''The salvation of the State is the business of all its citizens.''

Let me consider in passing the Americanism of yester-year which rested on individualism and the square deal for all.   It is best defined by the foremost of the intellectuals —Dr. Charles W. Eliot, who for a generation headed the academic world as President of Harvard University. ''Americans desire for each citizen,'' Dr. Eliot says—''what-ever his birth or station—adequate opportunity to develop the best there is in him, and to win a social position con-sonant with his capacities and character, both innate and acquired.   They are quite aware that men are not born equal in these respects; . . . but Americans insist upon the chance to rise and to do the uttermost.   Moreover, they long for a mobile and fluent community, in which men and women climb or fall quickly—as it were automatically—in accordance with their dower, whether this be strong or weak, virtuous or vicious. They have no objection to genuine leadership in politics or business—or even to distinctions of birth, provided that leadership is based upon superior mental and moral powers, and that birth means inherited force or transmitted culture. And Americans believe that society should give or maintain no privilege, save that which is founded upon capacity and achievement." This need now merges in new national consciousness, begotten by the war. What Emerson called "the sluggard intellect of this continent" is at last astir, and prepares to meet "the postponed expectation of the world with something better than the exertions of mechanical skill."

It is true that America has perplexity to face when we haul home the guns and open bloodless fire upon her and one another in the economic field, which is to say the whole earth. "Make no mistake about Britain," New York is warned by skilled observers, who went round our "shops" after a visit to the red litter and black cities of Northern France. "You wouldn't know her now. Britain is a new commercial and manufacturing Power—alive, alert, and plainly bent on conquest. When the crazy fight is over, Old England will have what she never had before—a race of business-breeders of the scientific sort. Such labour-saving machines as they have now! Such fresh ideas too, and enterprise that's postitively explosive! For the first time you meet high-brow professors in the factory; physicists, specialists, inventors concerned with Death today, but tomorrow with dyes, or drugs, or dolls.

"So prepare for economic war after the War. Are you ready for the coming tussle in Central and South America? Have you a clear-cut-policy for Far Eastern trade? Or was Prosperity just a pipe-dream of the war—one that vanished with the smoke of it, leaving Uncle Sam to bleat and trail blindly behind the band-wagon, like a brindle calf behind a Kansan hay-cart?'' Such fears as these have a certain following, but President Wilson takes a different view. ''Even when peace comes,'' he said, ''what instant rivalry is to be feared? Already the killed, wounded, and missing reach a staggering total. The reconstruction of industry and commerce is bound to be attended with confusion and delay. It stands to reason that the first task will be along the lines of repair, to make good the wastage and havoc of war. Then prodigious debts will burden the belligerents. And, aside from interest on money borrowed, each Government will have to care for millions of cripples, widows, and orphans.'' There was no reason, therefore, to fear a surcease of America's prosperity. ''Not only is there the part we shall be called upon to play in the rebuilding of shattered Europe, but the great markets of Latin-America and the Orient are also calling.'' And to hasten developments, the Ship Purchase Act was devised, and plans laid before Congress to assist American trade.

Here we have the President in practical vein, narrowing his vision to the material needs of the hour and trying to lay the ghost of business blues that stalks at every American feast. It is certain that the war-boom was no time for Quixotic strokes on the part of ''those who love liberty, justice, and right exalted.'' For no era had seen the Get-rich-quick craze so reckless and wide. It threw into the shade the mania for speculation which began in 1899 and died down in 1907. Hundreds of new millionaires were made in 1916. The cities were bulging with riches that ached to be spent. Small farmers up in Maine (to their own amazement) found themselves ''potato princes,'' with their land rich as Nevada patches where high-grade ore may begin at the grass-roots.

Now was the heyday of wild-cat stocks and fly-by-night ''syndicates for undisclosed purposes.'' The promoters of these withheld the very nature of their venture, and on that account reaped the larger harvest. Even shrewd financiers were badly "whip-sawed"—to use a Wall Street word—and wrote off serious losses in the spirit of the man who sent off a quarter for a "fine steel engraving of George Washington," and received in exchange a penny stamp bearing the hero's head! Why is it that Americans are so gullible? Why is the craze for short cuts so common a maul to men who aspire to be rich without any effort? Because the short cut is possible in this land of unique resources and spectacular coups. Nowhere in the world are the ups and downs of fortune so dramatic and swift as here. Consider Dan Sully, the bull operator in cotton, who bossed the markets of New York and New Orleans. He made millions a day—for exactly one week. Then the price broke, and Dan was forced to the wall with debts of $10,000,000.

Was he downcast at all? Emphatically no. Trade was fairly singing, and the defeated Cotton King sang with it from disappointed depths. He would "come back," as they say of the beaten pugilist. "Life springs anew," mused Dan sententiously, "from the grave of lost wealth. I'm down, but not out. I'll spring up again at the gong with a new gait, and then you'll see things leap where now they crawl!" It is the American spirit that bubbles here. Whatever is sent these men "receive in buxomnesse," in the old Chaucerian spirit. They let hazard reign, retaining their composure and the *mens aequa* amid stormy bliss that changeth as the moon.

James R. Keene won and lost his all in plunging style— not once, but half a dozen times. The Pacific Coast grew too small for Keene's operations; he must needs sell out and go East to lock horns with Jay Gould in the Wall Street arena where giants are for ever vying like the Broadway skyscrapers.

Wary and grim, the Railway King made ready for the

onset. "I hear Keene's coming East in a parlour-car full of money. Well, I'll send him West in a freight-car when the fight is over." The invader did have a bad time at first. He tried to corner the wheat market, and Gould squeezed him badly. Then Keene tackled Russell Sage, but his foes joined forces, inflicting a loss of $8,000,000 in a war of sixty days. But plume-plucked Richard came back in the grand manner. James Keene paid all his debts; then he began to juggle with sugar, tobacco, and railway stocks till his cheque was once more good for $30,000,000.

There was also "Bet-You-a-Million" Gates, a tragi-comic figure of the old school, now passed from the hectic scene. John W. Gates was a rugged fellow, a man of muzzle-loading maledictions whom Pierpont Morgan loathed. John had a grudge against the great financier, who denied him a seat on the board of the Steel Trust as a crude, indecorous person. Gates brooded upon this, and took his revenge by buying the Louisville and Nashville Railroad overnight from the Belmont family, afterwards forcing Morgan to take it off his hands at a profit of $7,500,000. In 1902, a whole cohort of these "Kings" came out of the West, scenting battle and power in Wall Street. There were Tin-Plate Kings, and Kings of Wire and Sheet-Steel; others again had kingship thrust upon them either by the Mc-Kinley Tariff, or the accident of cheap fuel on the Appalachian plateau.

But men travel by night, as the Moslems say, and Destiny travels towards them. Playing with our daily bread in the frenzied wheat-pit of Chicago, James Patten cleared $750,000 in a few hours. Joe Leiter's corner is an historic event, so is the railroad duel between Edward Harriman and James Hill. This was the strategy which allured America, though her leaders urged upon her the "competition of virtues" which Burke declared to be the only profit of war. In this land a penniless man may, by a clever stroke, make himself master of the game. A striking instance of this was the famous "postage-stamp bid" which Abe White of Texas made for Grover Cleveland's bonds in the panicky days of '96· The President appealed for gold to replenish the Treasury reserve, and a great idea flushed the red-haired lad from far-off Corsicana.

White was without a dollar in the world; yet behold him nosing in and out of Wall Street offices to estimate likely tenders for the emergency bonds. I ought to say that Secretary Carlisle exacted no deposit from patriots on this occasion. Young Abe, with characteristic daring, filled up a string of bids totalling $7,000,000, and sent them off to Washington by registered mail at the cost of 1.11. When the allotments were out, a sum of $1,500,000 stood in the unknown name of Abraham White of New York. The issue was a great success. Government credit rose, and the bonds were listed at a premium. But how was Abe to find this huge sum, with no more assets than a sure financial flair, and that *felicitas* for which the Romans looked in the genius of their generals? Mr. White took his allotment down to Russell Sage, and begged for a boost with a suasive tongue and argument there was no gainsaying.

The railroad giant was delighted to help. It was, of course, a gilt-edged deal; and as he listened, Sage recalled his own dim days as errand-boy in a grocer's shop up-state. He financed Abe's bid, and the resulting clean-up gave the Texan a handsome start. He had luck, and the multitude followed him for a time.

It is no use pretending that careers like White's have no influence upon the masses. "Abe can fly without feathers," his publicity agent said. "He'll run a shoe-string into a fortune. Look at his Bonanza Gold!" America looked very hard indeed at this ugly venture. To give Abe his due, he returned all moneys when nothing but "frost" was found in those shining sands and veined rocks, which were presently to dazzle the speculators.

It is of course a pity that wild-cat stocks are advertised at all—especially with such decoys as the Mohawk Mine in Goldfield, Nev. There was a time when Mohawk Mine was quoted at ten cents a share on the New York Curb Market. It soared to $20 when the ore in sight was paying $1,000,000 a month. Here, then, was a spring-board for the wild-cats in 1916. They appeared in all the cities with Denver, Col., as the fiercest of them all. For the Mohawk was a great name. There was the Red Top, too, that hopped from eight cents to five dollars. There was Great Bend and Silver Pick; Four Aces, Jumping Jack, and the Stray Dog. America rose at them all as a pike will rise at a spinning-bait. In boom-towns of the Sierras publicity-men were writing "human interest stories" of sudden wealth. Here, for example, is a mysterious waster who sold his little claim for six figures and lost all in Larry Sullivan's saloon. This prospector owed his laundress $40; he paid the poor soul with a bunch of worthless paper which she jammed into a cigar-box among candle-ends and scraps of string. A few weeks later they were dug out as ten thousand dollars' worth of property.

These were everyday events, and not concocted stories. One advertising agency spent $1,000,000 in newspaper advertising. Companies were floated in thousands, but not one of them made good. And some idea of the speculative spirit can be formed from that fact that this one boom inflicted a loss of $200,000,000 on the credulous American public. That Nevada rush had all the features of old-time Western life, and boomers made the most of it in a literary way. There were desert tents with snowy ranges in the background. Here was the tin bank with gay ruffians cashing in on the strength of sensational daily strikes.

Great sums were lost and won in the gaming-joints, where faro and roulette went on all through the drunken night. Bad men held up the mule-teams, and stole ore that showed "four noughts to the ton."

Pneumonia and poor food filled a God-forsaken cemetery; some of the camps were thirty miles from any water, and over a hundred from the railway. No timber was available for the mines. To crown all, there was no permanency in the patchy ores, and the boom collapsed at last in dismay and general wrath.

At every turn Americans are tempted by the science of investment, which Russell Sage used to say was "the most profound and complicated of them all." To make money quickly is an American obsession; one turned to rich account by swarms of sharks whose array of argument and appeal must rouse the student's admiration. Here again State barriers and conflicting laws intervene to snatch a rascal from the ball and chain of felony. The cheats had an unexampled harvest in the flush time of 1916–17. But there were fashions in the crooked game. Thus the old bucket-shop disappeared; it was killed by crusaders of the Stock Exchange and the Board of Trade. Another factor was the refusal of service by the telegraph and telephone companies. Bonanzas in cotton, and land-irrigation schemes; fake insurance and the bold "syndicate of secret process"—these also were missing. But the oil-well and the mine are perennial lures, tricked out with allusion to Rockefeller and Senator Clark, the Montana copper-king and patron of art, whose Fifth Avenue mansion so bristled with bronze that he set up a foundry of his own in West Sixteenth Street.

The motor-boom bred hundreds of fly-by-night concerns, run by veterans from the backyards of finance—often from the State gaols. One of these sharks, with handsome offices in eight cities, was recently raided by the

Federal Government for using the mails with intent to defraud. In ten months he had wrung over five million dollars from every known class. His literature bore the stamp of genius; his free book—*The Open Gate*—would have opened the purse of Hetty Green herself.

In another brochure, a handsome lad was seen haunted and dunned by outstretched hands—crude hands of tradesmen, dainty palms of women, expressive enough, but imperious or full of greed. "Where's the Money Coming From?" was the arrestive legend. "There's more due to you out of Life," the harassed one was told. "Get it—Get the Money, the repose and success which you ought to have."

This is a diverting subject. You may follow it through the bronze doors of the Stock Exchange in Broad Street, a place of clanging confusion and maniac cries. Membership here is so sought after, that $75,000 has been paid for a seat. I shall not follow the financial brain-storms of this money-mart, nor the records of panic and boom, with attendant scenes of ridiculous frenzy. However, the most recent deserves passing mention, for it preceded the famous Peace Note of President Wilson and quite demoralized the Exchange.

People who were rich on paper only—plungers in "warbrides" and munition stocks—saw their profit vanish as they stared; all manner of people, from the scrub-lady of the Ritz-Carlton to ranchers of the Western plains. "Funny thing," remarked the moralist of the coloured supplement, "but the moment the millennium bobs up—bang goes the bottom out of our stocks!"

I shall not dwell upon the scenes of the Curb Market at Wall and Broad Streets; they would read like a visit to Bedlam—though the annual business done in this roped enclosure exceeds a hundred million dollars. "The Curb" is a fantastic pandemonium of hardy stalwarts, whose garb varies with the season. For this arena is no place for invalids. Heavy rains find the brokers in sou'westers, oil-skins, and rubber boots. An August heat-wave brings them out in shirt-waist garb; and in the zero blizzard a chorus in Arctic furs serenades the luxurious towers all round with, "In the Good Old Summer Time!"

Communication between the offices and these men is very queer to watch. Excited figures lean from the sky-scrapers and shower pellets of paper, or even weighted notes, which sportsmen below catch before any one is hurt or killed by them. There are secret codes of gesticulation with the swift commerce of deaf-mutes. In all this mad-ness, however, is money method on sound lines; and the Dean of the Curb presides with eloquent fingers and a megaphone of heaven's own reach.

The dollar-hunt has lost some of its zest now that "big" Americans have left it and given themselves to that public service for which President Wilson has so often appealed. Already there are signs of change, though they are not demo-cratic signs. Afar off in California a thinker like Professor Ide Wheeler, of the State University, regrets the grouping of new "castes" and classes. At the other side of the continent a typical magnate like Charles M. Schwab would like to see an American "aristocracy": "The men who have succeeded—who have helped to build up the country, and now contribute to the efficiency and well-being of their fellows." There is less blatant vying of late years among the "cottagers" of Newport and Lenox. Mere dis-play in the House of Have is voted vulgar now, whether in yachts or racehorses, or lavish entertainments with details priced for the reporters—the frocks and jewels, the flowers and food and wines, even the massed money represented round the festal board in the persons of famous men.

One is surprised to pick up in *salons* of the great a sort of American peerage, with pedigree tables set out with regal circumstance, beginning with the Astors and the Vanderbilts. There follow the Goulds and Rockefellers, the Morgans, Mackays, Havemeyers, Fields, Lorillards, Armours, Harrimans, Du Ponts, Belmonts, Whitneys, Leiters, and Goelets. Mrs. Astor queened it in her day, calling the famous Four Hundred from the social mass as the cream of America's money-power. Mr. George W. Perkins set an example of civic spirit; the late Mr. Pierpont Morgan spent nearly forty million dollars in looting Europe of its art treasures for the enrichment of the United States. And in a later day we find Mr. Benjamin Altman, the Fifth Avenue draper, bidding seventy thousand dollars at Christie's for a Hoppner portrait of the Lady Louisa Manners.

The Rembrandts of Havemeyer, the Sugar King, are the envy of connoisseurs. So are the Pompeian bronzes which Mr. John Wanamaker gave to the University of Pennsylvania. For the portrait of Pietro Aretino by Titian, Mr. H. C. Frick paid $100,000. Well may the Old World fear the American millionaire, when he seeks such treasures with the best advice in Paris and London to guide saleroom bids which are not to be denied. Italy had to pass special laws to prevent her noble but faded families from parting with heirlooms and works of art. Mr. Pierpont Morgan restored to the cathedral of Ascoli its famous Cope, because he found it had been stolen for sale to the "mad American" who was in Rome with millions of lire to fling away for such things. When the harassed banker returned to the Grand Hotel, he found six thousand letters from people offering treasures of all sorts, from a Cellini dish to a Della Robbia plaque built into ancestral walls.

This is an acquired taste in America, yet the rough diamond seeks it—the social climber and men of mushroom wealth who follow a leader with blind faith, and pay great prices for unblushing fakes.

No collector can escape these things: witness the Moabite pottery which the faker, Shapira, foisted upon the German Emperor. But no nation in the world buys bogus works of art on the American scale. The subject has long delighted the comic artists of New York, who pictured the "well-upholstered plute" in his marble gallery on Madison Avenue, staring at a Cinquecento pax or a monstrous goddess "by Rubens" . . . "*Why* had the Old Masters no pretty girls among their acquaintance?" Yet there is hope for the plute who feels the bleakness of money, and regrets a life in which "Red-lined accounts were richer than the songs of Grecian years." There are many such converts in the United States today, where divine things are *not* held lightly, despite all appearance to the contrary.

Many of these money-kings have had none but the "ferocious education" which Louis Philippe bewailed, with physical torment too, a hard bed and never-ending battle with toilsome tasks. The city child thinks in terms of money, turning his spare time into dollars with precocious flair. It is the money standard which faces the home-seeker in the wilds when he presents his entry-claim at the Federal Land Office—say, in the rolling foothills of the Flathead Indian Reservation, which was opened to white settlers in 1910. Here is cut-over land disfigured with tree-stumps which must be blasted out with a low-freezing explosive in cold or wet weather. "The ground covered by a single stump," the State mentor tells the pioneer, "will grow from twenty-five to fifty cents' worth of food in a year. You may take it that an acre of a hundred stumps will produce $50 worth of a crop after clearing. So why leave these dollars under the stumps? Why pay taxes upon stump-land when the whole world cries out for American farm-stuff?"

So the speed-up is introduced to this jungle of yesterday. Mother Earth must now produce; she is encouraged and bribed and trained, her output watched and methods improved precisely as with the human element in Detroit shops. Most of the States send country advisers round on regular tours of counsel and inspection. These men are local Ministers of Agriculture, with social and uplift missions as a sympathetic side-line. The farm expert may make three hundred calls in a summer. He draws maps of the fields, showing drainage, fertility, and fitness for this crop or that. In passing he notes the barns and houses; the village school, the social and economic con· ditions of the community. Then he meets the folks at a peach and oyster supper, and in a hearty talk impresses all with cheery science and assurance of bumper yields—if his guidance be followed intelligently.

In this way pioneers are taught to know soil-types at sight, as well as insect pests and remedies for their extermination. Men learn how to test seeds and rotate the crops; also the value of rock phosphate and limestone. Social intercourse, promoted by that visiting genius from the world beyond, develops a spirit of co-operation in buying and selling to the advantage of all. Yet these rural sections need more than money, as Mr. Carl Vrooman testifies; he is Assistant Secretary of Agriculture in Washington. "I know farmers," Mr. Vrooman says, "who have broad fields, great herds, huge barns, and long bank accounts, yet their success ends abruptly there. They live dull, narrow, purposeless lives, devoid of all aspiration, happiness, or public spirit. The wealth of such men is like much of the fertility in our soil; it is not available. These farmers need instruction in the art of living just as their less skilful neighbours do in the art of growing and marketing their crops. For, after all, it is only the wealth we dominate and dedicate to some fine purpose that we can be said actually to possess."

What I may call the new America has no quarrel with

money-making, but does seek to endue it with high vision and aims. Yet Success remains an absorbing game in the United States; its votary is too often a hermit plotter, "as unsocial as a wolf taken from the troop," as Byron said of himself. This quest of profit is a peculiar peonage. It begins in childhood; it matures in the hard man of tabloid speech, whose real confidant is the cylinder of an office dictaphone.

Now come with me into the prairie spaces, and watch the American boy coining his wits into gold. Here is Charles, aged thirteen, with a nice little pony of his own and $40 in the bank besides. His first capital was a dying piglet with a broken back, presented by his father as a hopeless case. But Crip pulled through and lived, fed by his young master with pitiful care. Crip was soon sold for $4, and the money invested in other piglets with equally slender prospects of life; for Charles was now become an expert. He was constantly marketing porkers, and reinvested at last in sheep, with which he had great luck.

"I saved my pennies and nickels till I was six," the successful man will tell you in a reminiscent mood. "Then I had ten dollars. With that I bought a Jersey calf, earning money for its keep till it became a cow, and I was able to sell milk, prouder than any farmer."

The girls make and sell college flags to help their own education. A widow with sick children and a mortgage of $500 on her frame house will turn her last few cents into the nucleus of a little fortune. She becomes a "cake architect." Thousands of women have found "the cook-stove route to Success": Mrs. Ellen Kidd of Richmond, Va., with her pin-money pickles; Miss Mary Laverty, with canned and jellied fruits, now worth $7000 a year; Mrs. L. A. Schaaff, who sells marmalade by the car-load in every city of America. Man, woman, or child, these people will not be kept down, whatever disability may hamper them. Consider the case of F. R. Bigler, who as a railway servant lost his right arm below the elbow and his left foot above the ankle. "I was up against it," this gallant fellow owned to me in Kansas City, Mo. "But I had to forget the word 'can't.' What's more, I slid past 'I will' and froze on to 'I *must*,' whilst learning to write with my left hand.

"On leaving the hospital I walked miles after a salesman's job, with a 'hot box' in the new joint of my artificial leg. And a dandy salesman I became! When I called, I gingered up the 'Can't-See-You's' and 'Notbuu' Doin's,' till they gave me the glad hand as 'Expecting-You's' and 'Dee-lighted You've Come!' Mind, I've broken no skylights on my way to the top, but all the same I'm comfortably fixed."

The American spirit shines bravely here. It is a spirit of many facets, with an ethical code which, it must be owned, is lenient to "the 'cute trick that comes off." Many a time have I heard the late Edward Harriman unravel the tangled skein of American business with a sarcastic smile. He would tell of a State Legislature that blocked his plans. "These people are crooks," he would say, calmly; "and I can buy them." This frail little man was lord of fifty thousand miles of railroad and controlled a more powerful oligarchy than ever sat in Washington. A deep trader in the wash of Wall Street wars, Harriman was absorbed and cool at the desk, though fidgety and nervous in his private life. The ambit of his schemes overleaped the United States; he pegged out Mexico and China in enormous claims. It was strange, indeed, to hear this man dissect human nature and American graft, with all the frigid science and detachment which we associate with Guicciardini and Machiavelli. To the hot-headed Roosevelt (as President) this meteoric genius was "an undesirable citizen." But he was also a great American, carrying craft and force with him as Ulysses did the winds.

Huntington, Harriman, and Hill—here are three master-builders who "found desert and left a garden" in that mighty West where they carved out a group of the wealthiest States in the world, and shaped with steel rails the destiny of five-and-twenty million people. As companions these titans are far more interesting than their European compeers. They may care no more for poetry and art than Darwin did; they are probably eaters and hunters of facts, who

> "Contemplate the wisdom of the past,
> And see the splendid thing we've made of it at last."

But their whole life is in their work. Big deals are to them a delectation, just as painting was to Veronese; his water-colours to Turner, and to Gautier and Flaubert the magic of carven words and jewelled lines.

Sir Rivers Wilson once travelled West with James Hill, and for two hours sat with the statesman-strategist in his private car, soaking in statistics and economics of the prairie and its population. "I was mentally prostrate," the Englishman owns. "I left him at last with the excuse that I had letters to write, but really in order to sleep off the debauch! An hour later I was awakened by a knock on my door. It was Hill's secretary, with four foolscap sheets packed with figures, and commencing: 'Dear Sir Rivers,—Pursuant to our discourse. . . .' " So thought and action were inextinguishable fires! James Hill saw with sleeping eyes, and played the game in dreams by night as well as day.

To sit with a group of these men on the deck of a yacht in the Sound, or in the lounge of the Poinciana at Palm Beach is to realize that truth is stranger than any fiction in the matter of human experience and strife. The big fellows relax and expand on these occasions; they grow episodic and discursive, searching the detritus of years and recalling trifles with a tinge of regret in their mirth. Thus "A" left a poor man's camp in Arizona, and was soon digging out "gold bricks as big as an Iowa barn that assayed twenty dollars to the ounce." As a lad, "B" was in a copper boom on the El Paso and South-Western, a savage country close to the Mexican border. "C" was of the *ancien noblesse* of New York, with no rough corners in his career. He came of a family that waxed great as realty values grew in the most chaotic of cities. The C's had a pedigree that went back to 1801, when hay was mown in Astor Place.

"D" was once the slave of a cross-roads store in south-west Kansas, where railways were unknown, and broom-corn and milo-maize stretched in leagues to a brassy horizon: Here "D" doled crackers and tea to old-timers. He chewed calico, too, and spat balls of it on the counter before critical ladies to prove that the colours would not run. As a child of eleven "E" ran errands for the men in the Cambria steel-plant at Johnstown, Pa. At thirty-eight he was a millionaire. One night "E" met ten of his col- leagues in the Stotesbury mansion in Philadelphia, where he sold Cambria to the Midvale people for $72,900,000.

"F" is the head of a mail-order concern whose sales amount to $140,000,000 a year. Of this immense traffic, not one dollar's worth is sold over the counter; it is purely a postal business, with catalogues and lists of which 40,000,000 copies were issued last year. This idea was due to a boy station-agent in the Minnesota wilds. He sold cheap watches through the mails, and his advertising had an irresistible pull. Today "F" retails every known article from a button to a bungalow; for wooden houses in sections are commonly ordered through the post in the United States.

"Your staunch Aladdin home" (the advertisement tells you) "comes to you in a sealed box car, complete even to the key of the front door. All is ready for the carpenter to put up, with wide porch, a big parlour and dining-room;

three bedrooms, a work-saving kitchen, a bath and the latest hygienic closets. The price is $687." These are the homes which the Western cyclone so easily whisks away, often with serious loss of life. They can also be jacked up and removed on wheels by a team of horses—or by a motorcar which is photographed in the act of trailing a mansion in its wake. For this will be a double-edged advertisement.

I must not forget "G" in my group of magnates; he is the Timber King, perhaps the most distinctive of them all. His hosts of lumbermen in the Pacific North-West are turning American forests into cash with incredible speed. They sleep under pines that were towers of green when Columbus fell on his knees and kissed the earth of a New World. "G" is something of a recluse, with a silent empire of his own in the remote States of Oregon and Washington.

Here begins at dawn the song of the ax and hammer and saw; the crop of centuries is harvested with an ardour and method which has lately alarmed the Federal Government. "We are the champion wasters of the earth," Secretary of Commerce Oldfield told the Philadelphia Board of Trade. And he gave amazing instances, including the reckless havoc wrought by squatocrats of the timber lands, before whom noble forests melted away into a dismal tangle of sumach and blackberries.

I have spoken of ethical codes peculiar to men who have come to the solstice of honour and power. How these codes have changed one realizes as "H," the tram-and-train lord of New York, recalls the manœuvres of Belmont and Ryan, of Gould and Sage and Whitney. Historians of the City try to probe the tangled mergers and pools of those troublous times; the perfidious deals which considered everything but the common people. "The story of our street railways," says a New York authority, "is one of franchises stolen from the public. Of bribery and the corruption of officials; of debauchery in the Courts of Justice, of stock manipulation and the deliberate wrecking of rival roads, whereby hearts were broken and the innocent involved in direst ruin. A classic instance was the Thirty-Fourth Street tramway, which showed costs of $6,472,287 per mile, whereas the real cost was only $150,000. The sum charged for steel rails alone would have laid the whole system with solid silver bars weighing forty-seven pounds to the yard."

That era passed with the power of Tammany Hall. And today the Federal Government, whilst averse from undue interference—"Government by suspicion," as the President calls it—is determined to attack business of the "loaded-dice" variety: the description is again Dr. Wilson's own. Business of that kind is often allied with shady politics; and here an experience of the great Edison lends point. Apropos his first patent was a machine to record votes, and this he took to Washington, and showed to veterans in the Capitol lobby.

"It's mighty ingenious," one of these conceded—"an invention you couldn't monkey with if you tried. And that's just the trouble, me lad. If all things here were on the square, and no man tried to crook us,—why this invention would be a dandy find. As it is, it's useless." The crestfallen inventor asked, "Why?"

"Because we must leave a loophole," he was told, "a chance to block the fellow who seeks to railroad through Congress a little pork-barrel of his own. So you see, this machine is the last thing we want. Mind, it's a bright notion, all right for the Utopian State, but there's no idealism here—only just politics. So take the damned thing away!"

Mr. Edison owns that the lesson "broke him all up." He profited by it, however, and on the way home vowed that never again would he waste time and brains over an article which would not sell. There is much "Americanism" in both sides of this story.

With these dubious ethics we find a puritanical spirit in the people at large. This paradox is seen in the career of Elihu Root, who is one of the ablest of American statesmen. Mr. Root might have been Republican candidate for President, only the White House is for ever barred to him in public estimation. The counts against him are twofold: His defence of Boss Tweed before Judge Noah Davis, and his activity as leading counsel for the Metropolitan Street Railway—the most reckless of all the old-time traction gambles. William Tweed was the hugest embezzler whom even Tammany has known. He looted New York on a colossal scale; and the lawyer who defended him was rebuked by the Judge after the notorious boss was convicted. "Good faith to a client," came from the Bench to Mr. Root, "can never justify or require bad faith to one's conscience. It is well to earn fame as an advocate; it is still better to be known as an honest man."

CHAPTER X

PRESIDENT WILSON locates the real wealth of America in
"our great, flowering acres," and quite rightly points to
the farm as the greatest asset of all. In 1916, although
the crops were poor, agricultural products realized the
vast sum of $13,449,000,000. High prices made up for a
diminished yield, and the following season, in response to
Presidential appeals, the area under cultivation was
enormously increased. The city American knows little
about rural conditions. He is in the main an agrophobe,
and life in the country is to him inconceivable. Thus Rube,
the farmer, looms as a comic creature, whose ways are
drolly shown in coloured supplements of the Sunday papers.
He is scarcely real—a shadowy wraith, with scientific
guardians in Washington who teach him to tickle the soil
and so drown America with plenty.

Against this may be set the fact that Rube is leaving the
land for the streets of "white light," and the big industrial
centres; here he does less work and earns much more money.
This movement is remarked in all nations, but I cannot
stay to comment upon it. Even Germany is alarmed by a
flight from the land which has reduced her rural population
from 63.4 per cent. in 1871 to barely 39 per cent. today.
But that Rube, the American rustic, should forsake his
garden came as a real shock to the city folk. He was
thought to be a pampered person, turning over wads of
wealth with a pitchfork, and keeping old age at bay in
the great outdoors. Thirty dollars hung from his fig-tree.
A Texan acre gave him a whole bale of cotton, or cauliflow-

ers to the value of $900 where there was a well to wet the top. So at any rate the city understood.

What was the hog but a prowling dividend? The hen was worth $9,000,000 to Kansas alone. As for the goat, he cropped the worthless hillside and made grass-land out of it in the process. He raised his own kids, boarding them on brush and weeds, with much consideration for the farmer. Experts of the comic supplement showed the goat browsing on bits of paper and tin cans. He was said to weed the garden, and repair the fences for the feeble farmer who looked to Congress instead of to manure and the sweat of his own face. . . .

So the homeseeker of the plains was now bound for Broadway, and the intensive farming of human beings! Not alone from the Dakota Bad-Lands was he trekking, or the Oregon sage, but from that tropic paradise of the poor man—palmy, piney Florida, surely the fairest State in all the sisterhood of commonwealths? Florida was below the frost-line, the city man argued. It was an open-air hothouse of sugar-cane and citrus groves, where no man worked save for exercise and to feed the less fortunate Northern people.

With little in his pocket but rectangular holes, the merest hobo could buy orange land down here, and rich muck soil such as old Nile never made in its overflowing. For the terms of the agent were: "A dollar an acre down— that's all! a dollar an acre a month—that's easy." Florida's name evoked a Pindaric Elysian for the pure in heart. "A Garden of Eden without snakes," as the land-boomer called it feelingly—"A Riviera without swells." Here the lotus-eater shot big game in his back-yard, and hauled out of the sparkling Gulf red snapper, pompano, and the mighty Jew-fish of four hundred pounds.

Why, then, was Rube leaving the lush regions, and heading for Manhattan and the skyscrapers? The official reply surprised America. It was because of the drear serfdom of the farmer's lot; because of a host of foes beyond the scope and science of the Federal Entomologist in Washington. True, the Bureaux showed Rube how to fight the chinch-bug and the army worm; the weevil that spoiled his cotton-bolls, the tick that tormented cattle and pierced their hides to the farmer's loss. But human pests preyed also upon Rube: usurer, the big railroads, and a gang of commercial brigands who posed as middlemen and absorbed nearly all his profits. "Our normal life is on the land," says Henry Ford, speaking for America in the mass. Ford's earliest dream was the cheap farm tractor, with fuel distilled from the growing crops and not bought from the greedy Standard Oil. "The mechanical tractor will replace the horse and all draft cattle; it will do all the heavy work and make our farmer independent of short-haul freight rates. As things are, more than fifty per cent. is added to the consumer's cost after the crops are grown!"

"Efficiency in production comes first," this typical American pursues. "But not less important to Rube is the matter of handling, distributing, and marketing his stuff. Up to now the trusts have cheated our farmer. The cost of transport hampered him, the banks have soaked him an awful price for loans. I want to do away with all this. I'd like Rube to stay on the farm, for he's better fixed now than ever he was. The cheap car keeps him in touch with the outer world. He can hitch his telephone to the barbed wire fence; he has the phonograph, the moving pictures, and electric aids. Still, when all's said, our farmers do need a missionary government and influential friends in Congress." They have a staunch friend in President Wilson, whose Good Roads Bill and Cotton Futures Act, the Office of Markets and Rural Credits Bill, are all sound measures in the agricultural revolution which began with the greatest of wars.

America learned from her Government that Rube had been neglected. He was a kind of mujik, it seemed, whose very existence the intelligentsia of the East ignored, until high food prices brought him, together with his crops and "critters," on to the front page of the New York papers.

But who *is* Rube? Whence comes the most unmartial of all Americans, whose attitude to war is summed in the Chinese maxim: "We do not make swords of our best iron, nor soldiers of our favourite sons"? Rube is often enough an alien—a German, a Finn or a Swede, at his ease on the early homestead claim, which may be twenty miles off the rail in a primeval wilderness of dark pines and tamarack and fir. Rube is the landless man on the manless land; he squats with his women upon wild sod soil, where steam outfits are breaking a thousand acres a day. I saw Rube in the primitive stage at a dry-farm meeting of Poles on the prairie of Eastern Colorado. Here thirty families sat down to a basket dinner, with stack-covers upheld with boards to keep off a sun-blaze which imposed silence upon us all. There was not a tree to be seen as tired eyes swept a breathless horizon. This is how townships begin.

The next scene is a group of wooden shacks and sod-houses, with buffalo grass for lawns. Water must be hauled two miles; but the women are brave, and take their turn as path-finders, ploughmen and builders. Even so, Rube is a good American; he may even be a real American migrating from another State. In any case, there is keen competition to get him. Virginia makes an official bid. So do the rail-roads and land-agents of the South and South-West, going out by way of Kansas, Oklahoma and Texas; the semi-arid regions and the Pacific Coast—then back East through the Rocky Mountain States: Montana, Wyoming, and Idaho. The rural homeseeker is really an immigrant of a secondary type. He is one of the floating mass that studies, with a view to betterment, the literature issued by State agencies, as well as by realty-men of all grades.

Thus the intense cold of Michigan may prove too much for the Italian berry-grower. He is therefore attracted to the Pecos Valley of New Mexico, where the Reclamation Service have, by irrigation, made apricot orchards out of a desert of cactus and sand. On the other hand, a Dane or a native American may be driven from Arizona by the fierce heat; and he now surveys all America's range for a more temperate clime. There is constant migration of this kind; and to lure the settler on to the land is the special work of railway Industrial Departments charged with the development of new territory. With the rhapsodic boomer-salesman who buys part of "Section 32—Township 12—Range 14," I shall deal in more detail, as he deserves. For the land-boomer is a genius, as well as the most amusing rascal in America; he buys by the mile and dreams of selling by the square foot.

Booklets and maps, folders, pamphlets, and "letters of experience"—these are turned out by the ton. Written with skill and fervour, they are illustrated with photographs of a conventional type. Here, for example, is an early pioneer beside a crude hut on the roughest of land. On the opposite page is the same man assisting a large wife (and the girls) into a swell car outside a colonial mansion. He has made good in a few years. In the background a couple of whirling threshers are at work; and farm hands are driving buggies through oceanic crops, from which emerge only the men's heads and those of the horses. A glance at this farm literature is worth while, for it reveals an important phase of America's materialism. Nature and man's labour are here translated into dollars and cents; the versions varying from sober tables and reports to soaring raptures over "the golden pay-dirt which you handle with a hoe."

Virginia makes a dignified appeal, as befits the Mother
of States. Settlers are shown the tobacco-fields, and
tasselled maize which is fourteen feet high. Orchard
ledgers of Waynesboro are produced to show how each tree
filled ten boxes, at $10 a box, with "that sun-kist pippin
which we call the Young Man's Hope." Then come the tes-
timonials. Here is a doctor from California, disappointed
by coastal fogs and the heat of inland valleys. He had
lived in many States, and was now vowed to Virginia,
where niggers knew their place and malaria and mosquitoes
were alike unknown.

There was also the man from Iowa, to whom northern
blizzards and cyclones were now but an evil dream. He
was today the Water-melon King, filling standard cars
on the railway with Eden Gems of forty pounds apiece,
grown on deep phases of the Norfolk loam. These migrant
settlers are met by local agents whose strident offers call
from the official booklets. "The chance has come to You
—it will not come to your children." . . . "Be Careful!"
cries the Homeseeker's Friend. "You may encounter a
crook at the depôt, and of course he has a big bargain
just to toll you off. If he says he's the agent, and won't
let you see the seller, then it's time you sat up and looked
for horns and a tail!" The honest one tries to put this
warning into German, Magyar, and Italian. "You are *my*
guests, gentlemen," says he with the *beau geste*. "Your
board and livery will cost you nothing on the show-me
trip."

As we go South and West the exuberance of the boomer
rises. "It's mighty fine to be king of your own farm,"
says North Carolina, where deed restrictions "will for ever
prevent the land from passing to a negro": this clause is
never waived. "It's grand to know the future without
any fears, and that the man of fifty-five—the age of city
failure—is here at his best; his experience ripe, his judg-

ment good, with no lime in his bones—thanks to God's
sweet Southern air." . . . "How can any reader," a sudden challenge rings, "with red blood in his veins, scan the
leaping stories set down here, and not feel fired in the same
way? So fill up the contract-form on the last page—it is
your Declaration of Independence." Here is a Chadbourn
farmer who came in a prairie schooner from Indiana after a
voyage of six weeks and five days. He was a cripple, with
an invalid wife and eight children—"as forlorn a family as
ever sought the sun in this blessed garden spot, where
merely to breathe is to drink Ambition in camel-draughts."

That heroic cripple cleared the first three acres on his
knees, and was soon raising wheat at forty-five bushels to
the acre. "But he said 'Yes,'" the earnest agent hammers
at waverers. "He grasped the offer, as the city man may,
leaving all the turmoil—the battering, bruising strife of
office and streets. Come where the tomato ripens in mid-
May. Come where the hog only dies when he goes to the
smoke-house, after a riot in peanut fields where the 40-bushel
crop merges mystically into pork at four hundred pounds
to the acre."

Kansas, the core of the continent, raises an unblushing
pæan in her own praise. The Sunflower State is *not* the
treeless, sand-swept, cyclonic barren of city imagining, but
a granary "where the farmer has so much corn that he
can't find his way home!" There were no white men here
in 1850. The Indian hunted the buffalo; American soldiers
hunted the Indian; all the plagues of Egypt settled on the
soldier until the name of Kansas became a lurid reproach.
All that has passed, and today the State has nearly two million people who have done wonders to plough the Great
American Desert off the map.

In the semi-arid regions of the West, vast areas are now
"brought under the ditch" by the U. S. Reclamation
Service. And by the Carey Act, agreements are made with

the Federal Government for the development and sale of desert lands—"not exceeding a million acres in any one State." Irrigated farms are sold with water-rights from a system of canals, like that of the Arkansas Valley of Colorado, which cost $2,000,000. The result is very striking. Cherry-orchards here make $500 an acre. Senator Crowley's little fruit-farm of ninety acres at Rocky Ford cleared $20,000 in a single season.

But the boom State—the State of mushroom cities and fortunes—is surely Oklahoma, which was long ago given to the red man as a home "so long as the grass grows and the water runs." It was President Jackson who signed this domestic scrap of paper. But the Cherokees refused to budge beyond the Mississippi. The Seminoles went on the warpath for years; but at last the Five Civilized Tribes were settled in Oklahoma. Not for long, however. One April day in '89 an army of whites, 60,000 strong, invaded this No-Man's Land, and the city of Guthrie was born in a night with a population of 10,000 souls. Next the Iowa and Fox lands were thrown open. After these came 3,000,000 acres of the Cheyenne and Arapahoe Reservations. The Cherokee Strip was twice as big; and to it were added lands of the Kickapoo, Kiowa, Apache, and Wichita Nations. There was no rest for the red man. He is an American misfit; he vanishes slowly, out of sight and out of mind, with his tomahawk tamed to a pruning-hook, his buffalo-robe exchanged for an agency blanket. Yet some of these redskins are very rich. Braves of the Osage Nation draw millions of dollars from lands and royalties on oil and natural gas. A headright in the Osage tribe is worth $27,500; but I fear wealth only hastens the process of decay.

Restrictions upon Indian lands have been gradually removed in favour of the white pioneer. Soon there will be little left for the aboriginal tribes but "reasonable areas for homesteads." Meanwhile, the invaders develop Oklahoma with impetuous zeal. New cities are shaped in an hour. Newcomers dwell in tents and shacks and dug-outs until the township of Pawnee or Shawnee is fairly on the map— heated and lighted with natural gas, oiled in crude oil or grain, and of course with a live newspaper to record and boost the raw metropolis.

All the semi-arid States have irrigation schemes. Even Nevada tried to forget her lurid past, and now poses as "Uncle Sam's Nine Million Dollar Farm." Here land is almost given away, and water-rent charged for a ten-year lease of the dams and ditches of the Truckee and Carson Rivers. The idea is to supply the mining centres with fresh home-grown food. For here is a large non-producing community with plenty of money to spend. Nevadan towns and camps are largely fed with tinned stuff, imported in carload lots from more fertile States. This elusive treasure-house could never sustain herself, and at last the Reclamation Service came to her aid with canals and pumps and reservoirs.

Thereupon much of the desert bloomed. Diversified farms appeared among the sagebrush of Las Vegas; oases glowed in the Carson Valley, not far from the famous Comstock Lode. And a new Nevada called to the farmer, dressing the Sierras in orchard guise and denouncing as slander her old repute as an ash-heap freaked with gold and silver.

I fear she remains a volcanic desolation. After all, Nevada has her own bonanzas—her sudden pay-streaks of gold, and wild stampedes, as to the Kendall claim where ore was sacked assaying $10,000 to the ton. Farming in this Tom Tiddler's ground is a ticklish task. "You must have money to begin with"—even the land-boomer admits this awkward fact. "The capitalist can live here in comfort" is his victim's way of putting it. And therewith that victim works up to a crescendo of disillusion. He writes a letter that sears the recipient who sold the land and representing it as Nature's shrine, where a few twigs stuck in the rock became a bending grapefruit orchard. "The only trouble with pears is the breaking down of the trees." . . .

"Yes," sighed an agent to me in St. Louis. "Nevada *is* an imperfect Eden, with a soil-making process that tends to get on top of the water. It's a pity. The farmer out there needs real science as well as the push you can't keep in with a hog-tight fence. Strange, how the man of guinea-pig power *will* hear Opportunity knock along that rainless sand! He takes up three hundred and twenty acres under the Expanded Homestead Law, and then sits down to watch things grow! Of course nothing grows but disgruntlement. And the last chapter is a letter to the agent so hot that Uncle Sam needs an asbestos mail-bag to carry it."

Dry-farming and the ditch are also features of New Mexico and Arizona. Torrid arroyos and virgin mesas have here been made to yield; but again the process is not for the poor man. Both of these desert States are larger than Great Britain; their range includes the date-palm and the turquoise mine. Here also, I must say, the West remains very mild, and no boom literature can alter the fact. It is all very well for Arizona to advertise her fabulous copper mines, her new orange and olive gardens; her ostrich farms, and that Homeseeker's Ideal—the Salt River Valley, where irrigation has done flowery things. It is good to hear that the Houses of Parliament in Phœnix were "built without scandal, or even a breath of sus-picion"; that college men are ranching here; that the desert is "dry" indeed in a whisky sense, and wholly free from the toughs and yahoos too long associated with the Border State in uninstructed minds "back East."

Granting all this, the fact remains that Arizona is the un-likeliest place for farming. Moreover, judge and jury have *not* yet superseded the "hip pocket" court as an arbiter of equity and law. The Arizona Rangers, under Captain T. H. Rynning, could tell tales of frontier life madder than any yarn set out in the penny blood beloved of British boys. Grim encounters with smugglers and stage-robbers, moonshiners and cattle-thieves—Indian, Mexican, and American. For the Arizona bad man still haunts the Border; and at Douglas he has only to cross the dusty street to find himself in Mexico. Down here desperadoes still spur into town with pistols, rifles, and dynamite, intent upon the bank safe. And later they gallop over the Border with their haul. The lifting of horses and stock became so serious at last that small ranchers gave up in despair; and then the Arizona Legislature brought the Rangers into action. These are half-police, half-soldiers; crack shots, and cowboy sleuths well versed in the desert wiles and amenities. So the farmer in these parts has enemies in lurk, even though "God an' Natur' " be not ranged against him, or the.wolf and the worm—the flood and drought and tornado of the Northern States.

It is this eternal warfare which in part accounts for Rube's defection, and that growing distaste for life on the land which has alarmed the Federal Government. The symptoms are not merely local; they are fairly general from sea to sea. Over much of New England farming is unprofitable now; the hilly sections are worked out. New Hampshire and Vermont, northern New York and Western Massachusetts have "abandoned farms"; the process is spreading in Ohio, Indiana, Maryland and Virginia. Thousands of men from the Middle West have gone over into British Columbia or the Canadian North-West, in search of cheap and fertile lands. What is the cause of this? Partly the increase of population. The disappearance of public domains has had much to do with it. So have speculative abuses of the land-laws; the "tiring" of the soil by imprudent methods, and the havoc of floods due to reckless destruction of the forests.

Few Americans realize the damage done by soil erosion, caused by the cutting of timber on the hills. ''Will the lumberman straighten up,'' asks the booklet of the Woman's Club, ''and see what his fortune is costing us?'' No, he will not, so the destruction goes gaily forward. The present stand of timber covers 550,000,000 acres, or about one-fourth of the United States. Of this stand four-fifths is privately owned, and the present rate of cutting is three times greater than the annual growth. Forest fires alone cost $50,000,000 a year; and all efforts to rouse public sentiment have had little effect in reducing the prodigal waste of timber which attends the development of America: the extension of railroads, the settlement of public lands, the building of cities, and the opening of mines. In one year the State of Michigan alone cut 3,600,000,000 feet of white pine, with the result that her wheat crop steadily dwindled from 35,000,000 bushels to 8,000,000 bushels. Indiana's forests are but a memory now; a century of clearing forces that State to import eighty-two per cent. of her lumber. Disastrous floods are frequent in deforested areas, like the lowlands of the Southern Appalachians. In one year floods fed from this treeless tract caused $18,000,000 worth of damage, sweeping away bridges and dams and homes, as well as spreading barren sands over thousands of fertile acres.

The flood was a serious discouragement to the farmer, and he began to give up ownership of the soil. In a couple of decades one-tenth of all the holdings changed to a tenant basis; and nomadic renters hastened the agricultural decay. In 1902 the Reclamation Act was passed; and a Board of soil experts and Army engineers went out to survey the desert States, with a fund of $20,000,000 behind them for irrigation schemes.

Thirty million acres of likely land were mapped out by the Reclamation engineers; then rivers were dammed and waters impounded on a great scale. But from the first Director Newell sounded a warning note. No simpleton would succeed as a farmer in these arid zones. Labour alone would not do, for "if working took the place of thinking along the desert ditch, then every male would have a bank account."

Here the opening is for the few; and the fact should be made clearer to the trustful homeseeker, who is too often swindled by visions of an irrigated West, where the orange grows in dust and sleek kine turn the alkali-flats into a model dairy. There is too much of this hilarious stuff in circulation, and the rustic, native or alien, is all too apt to believe it. Is he not for ever absorbing miracles? He hears of a cow on the shore of Lake Huron milked by electric power from Niagara Falls; of moving pictures thrown on the screen in Seattle by means of melting glaciers in far-flung peaks of the Rockies. The wit of man—machinery—electricity; all things are possible through these, the wide-eyed rustic is told, until wonder has banished all mistrust.

"If your crops increase at this rate," said the agent to the Texan planter, "what'll they be worth ten years hence?" Rube was overcome, but managed to blurt out at last: "There ain't that much money in the world!" It is this bouncing spirit which makes the boom literature so easily accepted. A favourite State with the land-sharks and colonizers is Florida, "where wire nails will blossom in a sandy loam, which has a marl below it that shows eighty per cent. of lime." Florida is a magical name, linked with tropic fruits—the lemon and the lime; guavas, mangoes, and pineapples. Nevertheless it is no place for the average farmer, as a glance from the car window shows on the way down to Palm Beach, which is the Monte Carlo of America.

Here are miles of palmetto-scrub with sworded leaves;

miles of dismal cypress swamp, and of live-oak festooned with ragged moss; miles of grey wilderness too; and over all a sifting of fine dust which covers everything in the train as with a coating of flour.   An unpromising garden is this Florida, tricky and treacherous; rich enough in spots, though often ruinous to the experienced citrus-grower. Yet homeseekers buy land here which they have never seen, relying entirely upon the boomer and the Development Company who seem so fair and forthright, with their money back offers and pressing invitations to a Show-Me trip "in our private car, Millicent."

As many as fifty of these concerns have operated at one time in the "orange garden of the world."   They buy thousands of acres of sand-soaked stuff and sell it at $50 an acre to weaklings who drift from State to State in search of an easier life.   There is no resisting the boom literature, nor the follow-up letters mailed at intervals from an office in Chicago or St. Louis.   These are positively ecstatic. They anticipate each question and demur till it seems folly not to sign and remit a money order for a stake in "this predestined centre of wealth and population." . . .

"Here things grow for the sake of growing, and to make glad the heart of man.   Here noxious things call a hushed truce, and good growing weather lasts from March to December. . . . You're homesick for the South, so come out of bitter places where the thermometer gets white in the face with cold.   Come down to Punta Gorda and perfume-laden zephyrs of the Gulf.   The frail and feeble here get well, the well get rich; the poor live for nothing on game and fish and a little garden.   What you pay for coal up North will clothe your family in Florida.". . . And so the wild place is invaded.   The new homestead may look like a forsaken goat-walk in West Texas.   It may be in the tall timbers, or in raw cut-over lands—even in a noisome marsh, where a wagon sinks to the hubs in mire.   Still it is always

Florida, and the Show-Me tripper is easily overborne by the rogue's word. Just as dubiously (the shy visitor is reminded) did the "Iowa pioneers survey those treeless plains which now feed the world."

And then the boomer gets down to practical things. "If your hogs get wormy with over-eating, mix lye with their feed and so protect your profits. Don't wait till the hogs are dead. Try a quarter of a can to each barrel of slop. ... Your own health is assured. Doctors are the only droopy people in these parts. If you hear a cough, be sure it's imported. And you'll know the hearse horse when you see him, for he's downright ashamed of his job!" The comic side of this traffic has long been pictured in the papers: Mr. Homeseeker's first night in a languid heaven which turns out to be a floral swamp aflame with fireflies; the boom of bitterns heard afar, and frogs in all octaves. A bush township is on the map indeed, and there it will remain for a season. It will never materialize beyond the boomer's first improvements. Remote from railway markets, it is impossible to sell delicate and perishable fruits. So the lots merge once more into the jungle. And Mr. Homeseeker—"his face working, his mind yearning for likely curse-words"—is driven from an Eden where snakes curl on his doorstep and alligators bark in his backyard! ...

There is no need to harp on the mischief of these frauds. The failures drift back to the city, and for all time they kick and croak whenever "the land" is mentioned. For it calls up a hell of a life, with savings sunk and farming hopes gone down for ever. Such pessimism as this injures America badly. Meanwhile, the boomer swings another deal, being nobody's keeper but his own. Yet even this callous calling shows signs of grace in a time of flux and change. The new type of boomer is Ben F. Faast, of Eau Claire, Wis. He formed a company and bought 50,000 acres of brushy, cut-over land to retail in the usual way.

Most of the buyers were factory aliens and steel-mill hands; nameless creatures known to the furnace boss as a number— as a bull might be, or a convict. In the course of years these men had saved a few hundred dollars; they could peel off a few ragged bills to make the first payment on fifty acres of the uncouthest land.

But such "farms" are not quickly cleared; perhaps an acre a year is won. Knowing buyers will strip the brush from ten acres or so, and then grow clover and timothy among the stumps. Or they turn in cows and hogs and sheep to grub over the ground, and help the frost to dislodge the rugged roots. At any rate, Mr. Faast grieved over his clients' bargain. They could not support a family on the land; and, turning once more to wage-work, they fell between the two stools of livelihood. In this case the boomer decided to clear and develop the holdings; his company could do it better and cheaper than any individual settler. First of all the land was gone over with a steam stump puller. Then Mr. Faast built cottages and barns; he also stocked each forty-acre lot with a cow and two pigs; a dozen fowls, six rolls of wire fencing, and other needs. A ready-made farm was then offered on a long-time basis of purchase; and so low was the interest that the buyer could make a living from the start.

I cannot stay to trace the rise of Boomtown from its "unincorporated" stage to the order of Judge So-and-So, who proclaims it a city of the second class. But miracles of this kind never cease. Not long ago the Imperial Valley in Southern California was a tangle of tropic thorns and arid scrub, infested with tarantulas and snakes. Last year it sent out 100,000 bales of fine cotton, and 10,000 freight-cars full of melons and other fruit. The chapparal thickets of South Texas are conquered this way; so are malarial swamps of the Mississippi, which cover the richest of alluvial lands.

Yet no skill can ensure success, and the fact is strikingly shown by the cotton crop. Of this commodity the world's annual need is 20,000,000 bales, and America produces about three-fourths; the looms of Lancashire alone call for 4,000,000 bales. Now in the first month of the war, when the New York Cotton Exchange closed its doors, the staple stood at 7 cents, or $35 per bale of 500 lbs. Planters and markets were aghast. A pool of $135,000,000 was formed to steady the price, and ten cents were aimed at as desirable. As consumers the Central Empires were cut off, but the military needs of the Allies created a boom without precedent in the trade. For in scientific hands the stuff can kill as well as clothe; cotton is a prime factor in the high explosive of today which destroys merchant ships and turns Northern France into a crater-field. By the end of 1915 the price had risen to 12 cents, and Southern planters were mourning their reduced acreage and the careless handling of a growing crop which had been thought worthless.

The yield for 1915 had been over 13,000,000 bales, and farmers now set to work with furious zeal on the largest acreage ever sown to cotton in the United States. Meanwhile speculation and rumours of peace, with exhausted nations replenishing their stocks at any price, sent the staple up to 16 cents. The extra demand, it was thought, would exceed three million bales, apart from Indian and Egyptian supplies. But while man was proposing, Nature disposed. In mid-July, when all looked well, the whole cotton area of the Atlantic States was swept with storms of wind and rain. The rich bottoms were flooded for days, the uplands scoured and washed severely. To crown all, the dreaded weevil attacked the bolls in countless swarms; this insect flourishes in damp weather, and now it appeared in districts never visited before. There was great distress in Alabama, where the negroes were soon beating the woods for food; even white landlords had to mortgage their plantations. The crop excess of three million bales, so confidently predicted, now melted away. It was not even a normal crop, but about three million bales below; and the result was that cotton soared to 20 cents and over—a figure unapproached since the Civil War.

Even more serious was the falling off in wheat. With high prices ruling in the first six months of war, the American farmers added ten million acres to their wheat area. But much of the extra crop was so poor that millers refused to buy it; and there were many complaints from purchasers abroad. In 1916 it was hoped that wheat production would approach the normal, but here again Nature intervened, and Government forecasts came whittling down owing to losses from rust and blight, and other causes. In any case our daily bread is at the gambler's mercy. I know no stranger figure than that of the Chicago Wheat King, who never sees a grain of wheat and may be unable to tell a harvester from a plough. Yet he sways vast tides of the North-Western plains. Behold him in his skyscraper office, poring upon charts and wavering ratio-lines of population and production.

The Wheat King has weather reports from Chile and the Argentine. He knows the threshing conditions of India and Siberia; the "invisible" supplies in farmers' hands and the "visible" in grain-elevators and ships; on the railways, the canals, and Great Lakes. At the man's elbow is a crop-map of the United States. And all day long electric advices ring and buzz from his commission-men throughout the continent, but especially in primary markets like St. Louis, Buffalo and Duluth. The King is warned of coming changes, and he acts accordingly. A rising storm in Montana may reduce by two per cent. the crops of Northern Minnesota.

Of scenes in the Chicago wheat-pit it would be tiresome to speak. They are degrading; and in war-time they showed trade neutrality at its worst, with frenzied men screaming bids in each other's faces amid a tumult of indescribable violence. In a recent ten-day tussle "for future delivery" forty-four cents was added to each bushel of wheat. Millions of money were made and lost by dealers whom present-day America looks upon as enemies of the people and the farmers; the statesmanship of President Wilson is dead against these produce-gamblers; it may safely be said that their tricks and corners are a thing of the past.

In Secretary Houston the American farmer found a friend indeed outside the high-brow circles of Agricultural Science. Mr. Houston is a practical economist; his grading of crops and protective measures bid fair to restore to the land its old prestige. Since the passing of the Cotton Futures Act, the farmer is no longer at the mercy of local buyers, nor can the big operator raise or depress market prices at his own reckless will. In 1913 Mr. Houston had two hundred Kansan farms surveyed. It was then shown that with an average capital of $8800 the owner received—after paying five per cent. on his money—exactly $529 for the year's work. On a farm averaging $18,359 his share was only $659; and where the investment reached $32,231, Rube had $1028 for himself when the season's battle was over.

This revelation surprised the city folks. They imagined Rube planting dimes and reaping yellowbacks with the expert aid of Mr. W. J. Spillman, Chief of the Office of Farm Management in the Bureau of Plant Industry at Washington. The Department of Agriculture has been justly held in high esteem. It has spent hundreds of millions in research work, and heaped up records in agronomy and biology. Moreover, it sent trained pioneers into foreign lands for new things to grow. Here I touch upon America's "plant immigrants"; the story is quite a romance, and, so far as I know, unrecorded in Europe. It is assumed by the Department that there is not in this world any variety of grain, or a fruit or food-plant, which cannot be suited with a "stepmother" soil and climate somewhere between the bleak Dakotas and the Mexican Gulf; the cane-brakes of Louisiana, and the wine and citrus lands of California.

Therefore a corps of explorers is maintained; devoted men who will run any risks and use all means to send home scions and cuttings, seeds, and even useful insects like the kelep or Guatemalan ant, which it was hoped would prey upon the cotton-boll weevil: these live consignments go direct to the Parasite Laboratory at North Saugus, Mass. The work of plant introduction dates back to Franklin's day. So far back as 1770 we find that statesman-scientist (as Pennsylvania's agent) sending home mulberry clips and seeds. For many years American consuls did the same; and at last Congress voted $20,000 a year for the support of botanists at large—keen-witted legions of peace who should go forth to conquer the nations on their own ground

Here, for example, is David Fairchild, with a caravan in Babylon, and palm-suckers swaying from his camel-packs. "We pay $600,000 a year for dates to this very region," he told our consul in Bagdad. "Now we shall introduce the palm to our desert gardens at Yuma and Tempe, Ariz., and also at Mecca, Cal." Professor Hansen went to Turkestan for new foreign plants; Dr. Knapp brought the Kiashu rice from Japan; Carleton's prize was the dhurum wheat which suited the two Dakotas and Nebraska, and now is worth $10,000,000 a year, To transplant the Smyrna fig to Californian orchards took nineteen years; but the task was done by Explorer Swingle, who made a special journey to Asia Minor for the wasp-like insects which fertilize the flowers.

I cannot linger over the adventures of these free-lance farmers. Fairchild was arrested in Corsica; and in a cross-country flight he cut enough scions or bud-sticks from the citron groves to graft a small American orchard. At Saaz, in Bohemia, the same envoy was a suspected person among the hop-growers. Cuttings were secured in the dead of night. Fairchild packed these in a ruined barn, and sent them off as ''glass-ware'' to his agent in Hamburg. This work is but a minor branch of the Department of Agriculture, which may be styled the mainspring of rural America. It has an army of 16,000 men and women, including technicians and specialists in every branch. The past three years has entirely changed its methods—or rather added economic efficiency to the purely scientific side.

''It is all very well,'' says Secretary Houston, ''to teach the farmer to make two blades grow where one grew before; but if he can't sell the extra blades at a profit, he's a poor business man.'' And in this way ''we aim to help him.'' The farmer has wondered why he got less money for a larger crop. In 1912 America produced 677,758,000 bushels of maize in excess of 1913, yet the farmers received $171,638,000 less for it To solve this and other problems the present Government created the Office of Markets and Rural Organization. In 1915 this Bureau showed the cotton-planters of the South what their product was worth, and induced them to hold it for a better price. Land banks and good roads are amongst other features of the renascence; and the Agricultural Extension Act will spend $10,000,000 a year in direct education of the farmer and his family. This Bill places in each of the 2850 rural communities a couple of county agents—a man and a woman—specially picked for the task, and trained. These will work with the aid and direction of the land-grant colleges and the Department of Agriculture.

It was Secretary Houston who realized that too much science and too little sense had been shown by the Washington Bureau in their relation to the farmers, who were as far removed from their national guardians as they were from the State Department or the Coast and Geodetic Survey. Of what use was it to spend millions in research and pay no heed to practical application of the results? The farmers' bulletins were found to be too diffuse and technical. There was a treatise on the silver fox, but no popular paper on the raising of colts. Guinea-pigs and pheasants were learnedly presented, but there was no compendious pamphlet on the feeding of the dairy cow. Therefore concise and simple pamphlets were prepared, and of these over seventeen millions were issued to the farmers last year.

Moreover, an Office of Information was created to summarize for the local papers all the literature of the Department, and make popular the lessons of scientific agriculture. So the farmer absorbed knowledge with the day's news. He was taught the lesson of field tests undertaken by the county agents: how a crop of hay showed a profit of 257 per cent. on an extra outlay in lime; how to sort his potatoes and sell the best to the city hotels, getting as much for one grade as the entire crop used to fetch in haphazard days. A new system of killing and chilling poultry replaced the traffic in live birds; new methods of picking and packing citrus-fruits saved decay in transit which entailed a loss of $1,500,000 a year to the Californian growers. The functions of the middlemen; co-operative purchase and sale of all things from berries to seed, and from implements to coal—these and other phases of life on the land now engage the Washington Department.

CHAPTER XI

"AN HELPMEET FOR HIM"

THE "solemn emphasis" and "sacred duty" of the United States, expressed by President Wilson in the *Lusitania* Notes, set the Germans discussing a new enmity of inevitable drift.

"The fact is," concluded the Hamburg *Fremdenblatt,* after a caustic survey, "that so deep a chasm yawns between our Kultur and America's that only a bridge of swords can span it." "This New World," the German stay-at-home was told, "is bossed by the women; they are worshipped over there like the sacred cats of Thebes." And to show the American man's nonentity, Herr Doktor would quote a Texan paper: "If there's $10 to be spent on clothes, Daughter takes $5, Sonny gets $3, Ma grabs $2—and poor pa has his hat brushed!"

No land was more foreign to the Teuton habit than this huge gynocracy; the rulers of it waddled out today in Persian tubes, and tomorrow rolled forth like the hooped Infants of Velasquez. American women were spoiled by cockering and indulgence. They counted life by the heart-throbs of passion and caprice, yet in twelve States the polling booths were open to them; they swayed ninety-one votes in the Electoral College, and might well decide what manner of President should go to the White House and reign in their name.

Germany reviewed these facts with rising ire. For if, as Bismarck said, the Fatherland was the male element among nations, surely America was the female, owing to

the social chromosome in her make-up which gave her a
horror of the destroyer's *rôle.* How different was the
status of woman in Germany, where she was a source
of strength as the prime recruiter of an "Army with
a country"! Did not the German mother advertise her
new-born child as "another little soldier for the Fatherland"? Here the Kaiser set decent bounds to female
activity, naming church, children, and kitchen as the
proper spheres. On the land, even in peace-time, four-and-
a-half million women handled the hoe, clad in the Petrine
apparel of a meek and quiet spirit, and withal bred to
worship of the male. These pious souls, as well as matrons
and maids of high degree, were compared with the gay
scansorial birds of New York and Newport who were intent
only upon candy and clothes; the car, the *salon,* and the
good time, with its biting thirst for change and the switch-
it-off and fade-through of a life that was like a perpetual
movie-film. . . .

Now in all this German girding there is a modicum of
fact leading to false conclusions in the Teutonic way, and
ignoring incalculable factors. No sooner was war declared
than America's women rallied to the President with a
fervour which Berlin found disconcerting. The *bourgeoise*
of France was not more devoted, nor the modish maid,
who turned from the tango and tight skirts to become a
jusqu'au boutiste—a bitter-ender with the passion of
Jeanne d'Arc lighting her girlish eyes.

A joint memorial, pledging loyal service and support,
was offered to the President by eight of the greatest colleges for women in the United States, including Barnard
and Bryn Mawr, Vassar, Wellesley, and Mount Holyoke.
At the White House this vow was read to the President
by his two daughters, Mrs. F. B. Sayre and Miss Margaret
Wilson: "Although we believe that the settlement of international difficulties by war is fundamentally wrong, we

recognize that in a world-crisis such as this, it may become our highest duty to defend by force the principles upon which Christian civilization is founded."

In the long list of German mistakes, the American woman must be given a prominent place. Her adhesion ensured the full measure of military and industrial aid, to say nothing of the part played by the farmer's wife and daughters in the food-supply of us all. I shall not deny the supremacy of women in the United States, for it is a fact. She is a law unto herself, imposing her will in all directions, from the motor-shops of Detroit to the *ateliers* of Fashion in the Place Vendôme. Immersed in business, her men are apt to leave civic betterment to the women's clubs, as well as all the finer things of life, from music and æsthetics to the planting of shade trees. Women have much to do with the suppression of the liquor traffic as well as the promotion of better babies, with prenatal care and oversight for the poorest of mothers. In the West especially the woman in public office is a power for good. She is there concerned with prison reform and public recreation; with libraries and museums, city planning, local efficiency, and fire and police protection.

In America marriage is considered from the business angle, with a wealth of published anecdote and testimony from successful men who love to tell the story of their climb, and the part which their wives have played in it. The effect of marriage upon employés is debated: how it steadies the worker and helps the speed-up of factory production; why bachelors are less efficient and devoted; why the married man lives longer, with evidence upon the subject from Herbert Spencer and the Germans, the insurance companies, the Federal Census Bureau, and big employers of labour like Mr. Armour and Mr. Vail. Whether young love pays any heed to this prosy aspect I take leave to doubt. Certain it is that couples are wedded, divorced, or merely "separated" with surprising ease in the United States.

There is no attempt at uniformity in this matter. Some States forbid marriage between whites and negroes, whites and Chinese, and whites and Red Indians. Others allow all three. Marriage between first cousins is prohibited in sixteen States, and in some of these declared incestuous and void; other States are quite complaisant in this regard. In most of the States you may not marry a step-relation; but in seven of them (and in the Hawaiian Islands) no such veto is imposed.

Perhaps the greatest scandal of all is "easy alimony," as the result of a collusive bargain between the parties; the man willing to pay for freedom, the woman seeking a life of selfish sloth. In one New York court, alimony sets $4,000,000 a year in motion, and the evil has grown with the flush time. "Divorce is our subtlest social menace," says Judge Morschauser, of the New York Supreme Court. "The alimony system is the sanction of it by society and law, and it places a premium upon idleness and vice." "Do away with collusive divorce," said an eminent jurist to me in Washington, "and two-thirds of our childless couples will readjust their lives. Then we'll hear less of the 'I'm tired of him and he's tired of me, so why not fix a divorce?'" Last year in New York City the courts of Manhattan alone granted 1300 divorces, and twice as many separations. Yet the metropolis is by no means "easy" in this respect, whereas the "nisi-mills" of Reno, Nev., and Sioux Falls, S. D., are notorious all over the continent. Chicago's divorce rate is higher than New York's; America's fairest city—Denver, Col.—outpaced them all last year, having more than half as many divorces as there were marriages.

This unrest is found among all classes, from the New York motorman to the queenly "cottager" of Newport;

one of these dames threw her little son into the alimony bargain for an extra payment of a million dollars.

Meanwhile the war offers new and vivid interests for the women as for the men. Within a month of President Wilson's declaration, the women of thirty-two States had volunteered for substitute work in a way familiar to us all, but wholly novel in the United States. The Wireless League impressed many college girls; they sat with receivers on their heads, jotting upon pads the cryptic buzzings sent by Mr. Otto Redfern, the radio-inspector of the U. S. Navy. Then the suffrage parties formed National Service bodies on the usual lines—nursing and motor-driving, cooking, farming, and clerical work. New York had its War Substitute Department, calling for a unit of 100,000 women to replace in part the men who enlisted for the first Expeditionary Force.

America's upheaval was the most bewildering of all. The continent was soon adrift, groping for guidance and trying to follow precedent of appalling trend. A lead had already been given by Mrs. W. K. Vanderbilt. This great lady—a *decorée* of the Legion of Honour—worked as a scullion in the Lycée Pasteur at Neuilly. She was under fire at Pont-à-Mousson with Harvard *ambulanciers* and young free-lances of the American Field Service who were attached to the French Armies. Mrs. H. P. Whitney was another early worker in the French field; she hurried over with surgeons and nurses, motors, medical supplies, and clothing for thousands of refugees. At home the cloud of change spread slowly, till the state of war was a fact, and Liberty's torch glowed with new demands above New York Bay. Then it was that the pink tea vanished, and the Red Cross function became a social sign. Soon economy was a White House watchword; Mrs. Wilson and the Cabinet ladies were urging thrift and deprecating the extravagance in dress. Vanity's

mirror was seen shot to pieces by the European guns; the
rites of Beauty were now concerned with that test of the
nation which the President put so plainly "for the future
peace and security of the world."

Now the American woman is an able recruit, as the
German writers know, even when they present her in
the rainbowed spray of Folly's fountain. She is, in fact,
peculiarly adapted for management. Self-reliance is
developed in her from childhood. Her business head is
unaffected by a sentimental heart; the handling of affairs
comes more naturally to an American woman than any
other, not excepting the French. This applies to more
than the common trades and callings; it covers also the
learned professions, and the oversight of industry on the
largest scale.

A glance at the Census of any date shows hosts of
women doing work which was thought to be man's alone.
But this is a commonplace of American life. It has never
called for remark or borne any relation to war. Nowhere
else is the value and dignity of labour so respected, and
this esteem applies equally to the woman's share. I
take 303 occupations from the 1900 Census, and I find
women engaged in 300 of them. They are slaters and
plumbers, carpenters and house-painters; teamsters, electricians, masons, bricklayers, and mechanics of every grade.
Dentists, architects, and civil engineers are here in hundreds; commercial travellers and clergy by the thousand.
And these last are licensed to preach, and to marry couples
according to the State law.

But I cannot hope to convey in brief space a fair idea
of woman's activity; it is too huge a subject, too diverse
and full of surprise. Consider the case of Widow Warren,
of Silver City, N. M.—"General Contractor and Specialist
in Concrete-work." This typical Western woman has her
own quarries and saw-mills, her steam derricks, steam shov-

els and steam pumps, ready for the biggest job. She designed and built a dam of 50,000 cubic feet with the aid of Mexican gangs, whom she bossed with more than American tact.

My survey could be continued indefinitely. Turning to the South, we have Mrs. G. H. Mathis, of Alabama, the ablest soil-expert in the State, and a spreader of "pep and ginger" among all classes, from Governor Henderson himself down to the poor whites of the range, to whom this energetic lady introduced tomato-growing with excellent economic results. Mrs. Mathis has trebled the earning-power of farmers in this cotton State. She has multiplied values, introduced new crops, and wiped out the cattle-tick which was costing the stockman over a million dollars a year.

It is difficult to speak in general terms of the American women, as it is of any other phase in a land of such extremes and joyous novelty. Here caste and degree take the widest flights, from the school-marm of the oil-lands to the *grande dame* of the Newport cliffs, who breathes an oxygen denied to the baser sort and spreads a feast like the Eleusinian mystery for the elect and few. Such contrasts as America presents I have never seen elsewhere. The distance from Palm Beach luxury to the Polish hovel of the Panhandle is not to be measured in miles alone. And here let me say it is the wife of Rube the farmer who fills the asylums of the Middle West. Her lot is one of appalling toil, quite beyond the ken of folk outside the barbed-wire push of progress which is found beyond the Rockies.

Very different is the city woman's life. Of course, it varies with the cities, of which some are as far apart as Cork is from Constantinople, with all manner of climates in between. Speaking generally, the American housekeeper is the most efficient of all, whether as contriver, seamstress, or cook. Yet in New York—and here is a typical paradox—housekeeping is a lost art, save among the rich, who pay their parlourmaids more than we do our high-school teachers. The metropolis is a hive of communal living; of vast hotels and apartments which leave the housewife nothing to do, and are very proud of the fact. Less wealthy families frequent boarding-houses; but even the best of these depress the permanent home-seeker, whether she come from Europe, or from the Southern and Western States, where home life has peculiar variety and charm. A New York clerk with a wife and $2000 a year cannot look for a cosy suburban villa with a garden and a maid; he might as well expect a palace in Madison Avenue.

Life in the cities is not conducive to child-bearing, as may be seen from the falling birth-rate among American stocks, as distinguished from the foreign-born, whose fertility brings the general level up to that of France, and no more. The real American family has decreased surprisingly in the past hundred years. Franklin found an average of eight children to each married couple of his day, but when the present century opened the number had fallen to between one and four. It is the alien stocks that increase, and the older aristocracies of intellect and rank express dismay over the fact. In Massachusetts, taking all social classes, it was shown that the foreign-born had twice as many children as the native Americans. Then Dr. William Guilfoy, of the New York Health Department, showed that these alien infants were a more resistant stock, with a death-rate well below that of American children. Why was this? Because the foreign mother suckled her babe. "She is more likely," Dr. Guilfoy adds, "to stay at home and look after her family."

All manner of leagues have sprung up to study and solve the "race suicide," to which Roosevelt drew attention years ago. Maternity is encouraged in various ways; and much prominence is given to the so-called "twilight sleep"—the painless *Dämmerschlaf* of Drs. Krönig and Gauss, of the Frauenklinik in Freiburg, where the scopolamin-morphine treatment has been long in vogue. Then Baby Week, with its literature of hygiene and infant aid, became a national institution; it was proposed by the General Federation of Women's Clubs and welcomed by the Public Health officials in thirty-nine States. Next came Mother's Day, with its white carnation badge and homage in the home to "the best woman who ever lived." President Wilson proclaimed the first celebration, after a special resolution in both Houses of Congress.

But all this deference does not alter the fact that mother has a hard time of it as a housekeeper in the cities; she is very far indeed from being the toy and tyrant of man as set forth in the German papers. Even living in common brings her up against petty tyranny and graft on the part of janitors. Lack of steam heat and hot water leads to unseemly squabbles and "rent strikes"; there are disputes about the lifts which you would never suspect. For example—is Baby in her car to go up by the main shaft, or be relegated to the garbage-hoist, with the groceries and the coal? I was in the New York Supreme Court when such a case was fiercely fought out between landlord and tenant. On the other hand, to run a home on British lines means that the housewife must do her own work, for the American servant is a contradiction in terms, the alien charlady a trial too bitter to be borne. It is surprising what shifts even families of a good class are put to by this problem. Chinese and Japanese boys have been tried with poor success; and as for the negro maid, her "goings-on" would knock the breath out of a reformatory superintendent.

I have referred to electric devices in the home, from

shaving-mugs to raisin-seeders. "Nobody," declared Dr.
Eliot of Harvard, "should be employed upon a task which
a machine can perform": this is a very American maxim.
Certainly the city housewife looks for universal service
from the button at her bedside, which starts the day by getting breakfast without any drudgery at all. "Free yourself from the tyranny of servants" is a clarion note of the
electric companies to the women. "Get more time for
recreation—for worth-while family life and the things you
really *want* to do."

Now, as the finer vessel, the American woman does lean
to the higher things. She wants to read the best books,
to study music, and wander through Europe on the educational tour. Quite likely there is a husband to polish—
an earnest climber whose youth had known nothing of
art. "My carving was done at the wood-pile," he owns
with a new regret. Such a man will stand before the
costly Corot with the scoffer's "Only trees and water!"
Or he will agree with Walpole that the *Divine Comedy*
is like "the ravings of a Methodist parson in Bedlam."

Therefore much is expected of the women in matters of
culture and taste. It is for them that the Mentor Club is
formed, with a conversational course, "which enables you
to ignite a dinner party at fifty yards with Familiar Wild
Flowers, Three Weeks in Rome, and The Pictures We Love
to Live with." I find this an admirable tendency, though
it make the superior person smile. There is a story told
of a farmer's wife in Missouri, who wrought classic sculp-
ture in butter, as her familiar medium. Mrs. B—— sent a
Sleeping Iolanthe to the Paris Exhibition. It was politely
rejected by the Art Committee, and sent down to the Dairy
Products section, where it wilted when the warm weather
came, and comically disappeared.

Yet ridicule falls with broken sting before the childlike
purpose of these people, and their naïve pursuit of nobler

things, when the get-ahead game is over. Before the war one met American girls of quite humble origin in Milan, studying opera under a *maestro* of' unconscionable fees. But then America and millions are convertible terms in the Continental mind. In far-off Prague I found American girls in Sevcik's violin school in the Lindengasse. The Bohemian hermit took thirty kronen for an hour's lesson from the Chicago school-marm, who had saved her money for ten years in view of this tuition. Miss R—— went back at last in a low-necked gown that showed the "Sevcik mark," a little bruise that bore witness to eight hours' practice every day. It was the women who in pre-war days organized the grand tour abroad from Killarney to Darjeeling; from the Rue de la Paix to Plato's Academe in Athens—that mangy mound of picnic litter and tawdry memorials. Who was so frank as the American over the disenchantment of foreign travel?

The month of May saw the Exodus begin from New York City. There were more than a hundred magnificent ships in the service, and in ten weeks $7,000,000 was collected in fares. For many years the "See America First" movement was little more than a voice in the wilderness of joy. But with Europe closed, the tourists overran their own continent, climbing the Rockies instead of the Alps, taking cures at Hot Springs and Paso Robles; camping out in the Maine woods, and spearing giant tuna in the Pacific off Santa Cruz.

"Discover America" was now a shrewd appeal. "Switzerland is ringed with armies," the holiday folk were warned. "The peaks of Tyrol bristle with guns, so turn this year to Colorado and the Garden of the Gods." This America did, increasing the railway revenues by $326,-401,568. Hotels and farmers, ranchers and innkeepers, all had handsome hauls.

The "Discover America" literature of this year is cun-

ningly addressed to Mother and the Girls; and patriot
ladies support the movement with diverting tales of travel
disillusion. What a fraud the Orient was after all, with
dirt and squalor in the Christ-shrines, and in hotel beds
"old warriors with plated backs" of a less heroic breed than
Milton had in mind. . . . Here was the great Sikh, Patiala,
striding down the platform at Charing Cross to his car—an
incongruous figure for London town in flowered silks and a
chaplet of roses. The Mikado had sent his palanquin to the
Uyeno Museum; today that divinity shot forth in a racing
Twin-Six which could climb the castle wall "on high without a knock." Then reviewing her tour in India, Mother
was sarcastic over a call upon the Rajah of Faridkot, a
model State studded with schools, grain elevators, and other
agencies of hustle. The gorgeous nautch was non-existent
in Shahadpur; its place was taken by a movie-show which
exposed the evils of booze in the most rabid Kansan manner.

So it was better to stay at home and do the Grand
Canyon, the Big Trees, and Spouting Geysers, which no
age withered nor custom staled. Americans abroad—one
of the Girls declared—went in vicious ruts beset with vul-
garity and dollar-chasing fights all the way from the Giants'
Causeway to the Pyramid of Cheops. In Rome itself there
were Coney Island shows on the hoary Borghese acres. In
all the capitals were noise and heat, hurry and smells, with
sights which left the soul blind and the body limp in lands
where ice-water and the shower-bath were extravagant
wants. Nor was it true that "English will carry you anywhere"; or that the contadini of Tuscany will fetch and
carry at a bidding in Pennsylvania Deutsch.

It is safe to say, however, that American armies of culture
will always go abroad, even with the slim purse that boards
in Bloomsbury and "does" artistic Paris from a five-franc
pension in the wilds. As for the social climber, the cachet

of foreign travel is as necessary to her as the name of Carlier in a hat, or Worth or Paquin on the waistband of a gown. There are climbers of many grades, from the provincial élégante of the Middle West to the great lady of New York who aspires to the dazzling record of Mrs. J. J. Astor; that gifted hostess who received the King of England as a guest in her own home.

It would take too long to trace even a modest climb, diverting as the stages are, and the many stumblings in unfamiliar ether. There are social sponsors, of course; openers of doors in which even the rattle of golden keys can spell disaster. But the whole career—this shooting and shining through the London season like a star, belongs to another world, marked with the milestones of Ascot and Cowes, the moors and the Carlsbad cure; the Nice Carnival and a winter in Cairo, with orgies of dress and days of tumult too silly for belief in the deathful glare of 1918. This European triumph was very dear to the American woman, and doubtless will be again; it was the subject of cable matter to the New York papers, often with portraits of the victors and spicy details of intrigues and vying: "Our stars must glister with new fires, or be—today extinct." But the men cared little for these costly campaigns; the uplift at home was more to them than social gains abroad, and the idea spread that wealth were best regarded as an instrument for the common good.

Before the war the industrial king moved in a glare of publicity. His business deals were discussed in the papers, his cliques and projects, and the buzz of Wall Street rumour against him. The splendours of his wife were set down with Pharasaic micrology. Her ocean-going yacht was expressed in dollars and cents, its silver fittings and grand saloons; its crew of sixty men; a French chef in the galley, and on the shade deck a dozen Japanese valets in white silk tending men of awesome name on Astor Cup Day in the

Sound. Parade and pageantry at Newport was the papers' untiring theme; it was said to surpass all that went before, even in Byzantium or Bagdad. It was always the women who willed these modish stunts, whether as breaker-in upon the established powers, or as an *arrivée* of austere magnificence, more or less securely throned. The man was acquiescent and no more, having interests of his own in the home town or in the office.

Yet when success came he strayed joyward with the rest on conventional lines; in no country has the say-so of Fashion such unquestioned sway. The new millionaires sat to visiting painters, men who came over from Europe to give a pompous rendering of business humanity; then they boomed the portrait like professional barkers outside a show. For this was a further boost and counted in the social climb. Mother and the Girls favoured Art in like manner, so that suave painter-immigrants reaped a golden harvest with unsubtle and sentimental brushes. There was La Gandara and Chartran, Mucha the Czech, Zorn the Swede, Thaddeus the Irishman, and Boldini the Paris-Italian, who paints chiffons divinely and sets the insipid maid on a full-length canvas as the heroine for bold dragoons. There should be rich stuff in the American memoirs of these visitors.

Here I cannot escape Newport: it is amazing how this town has held American attention. For many years preachers and social reformers inveighed against its freakish riot. Newport life was the scandal and target of the masses all over the continent. "The expression we get of society in this place," Bishop Potter of New York used to say, "is quite beyond my comprehension." But it was well within the compass of reporters for the yellow press, who piled Pelion upon Ossa in preposterous yarns, as though the bare facts were not sufficiently absurd.

On these Newport cliffs, tracts of rock and scrub have

been sold by the square foot, as land might be around the Paris Opera or the Bank of England. Here "cottages" were built (like The Breakers) more stately than Dorchester House in Park Lane; here castles of marble or granite sprang up in the desert—like Grey Crag, the massy pile which overlooks Sachuset Beach. As there was no shade, huge trees were tunnelled and uprooted far inland, then hauled to Newport by tractors and Italian gangs, to be planted on the sea-lawn of America's Crœsus. The formula for a cottage on Bellevue Avenue is "A million for the house, a million to furnish it, and $100,000 for a stone wall or a steel fence that would defy the safe-breaker."

This exuberance needs a good deal of trimming, yet what remains is lavish enough; it is a fact that the wall around Mr. Berwind's château cost a fortune. Nor can it be denied that Newport is the playground of America's plutocracy; a none too wholesome influence in the nation's life, considering its antics and the devouring interest taken in them by the people, especially the women. When fortune smiled upon her man, Mrs. Break-in aspired to conquer Newport; and press and pulpit never tired of her pushful manœuvres. First of all the lady rents a cottage at $10,000 for the season: this begins in late June, reaches the zenith in August, and trails away after the Horse Show in September. Then the elect move up to the Berkshire Hills—perhaps the loveliest spot in America, when the autumn blaze of woodlands beggars all description.

But Newport remains unique among the resorts: it is the social citadel, its freedom and favour a precious guerdon bestowed upon very few. Dragons innumerable are here on watch; and let it be said at once that money is powerless to move them. Many a prodigal spender knocks in vain at Ochre Court and The Crossways; the season fades without any hint of an Astor or Vanderbilt invitation. There is indeed small hope for neophytes of the rough diamond order; the Western woman who is just *bon enfant* and a good sort, brimming over with hospitality and faith. Many such have played a waiting game at Newport and Palm Beach, aided by their Girls, who have no doubt attended the most exclusive (and expensive) of private schools. I refer here to the wives of mining magnates, or to those of men who made a fortune in munitions or the motor trade—or even in ways still more abrupt, like the produce gamble or an oil-strike in Texas or Oklahoma. Newport has no love for these sudden ladies; their career is not so much a climb as a rocketing, with inevitable fall in it from the first.

Behold Mrs. Break-in receiving in a Bourbon *salon* of green and gold; a merry and flaring soul in orchid brocade, with a social guide behind her, and in the kitchen a hierarch of pots and pans imported from Paris on his own terms. The lady's meat-bill is already $1700 a month, the retinue she brought with her a joy to the brigand tradesmen of the town. It was to resist the exactions of these that the richest members of the colony declared a boycott, and started markets of their own. Mrs. Break-in was at last shown checking her bills by the cartoonists of the Sunday papers, who knew the game by heart. She was discharging servants in desperation, or even cleaning her own tiara and cursing in Gehenna-torrents the butcher who sent twenty pounds of sirloin up to Reckless Castle and charged for a hundred on a crested and scented bill.

Behind old Newport rises the twelve-mile avenue of mansions in which American women rule. Here are formal gardens such as Lenoir laid out for Josephine at Malmaison. There are alleys and hedges, exotic trees and colonnades; aviaries, pagodas and fountains, with classic nymphs outlined against park-like thickets. A striking feature of the colony is its hostility to casual trippers and sight-seers. The most tempting paths are blocked with "Private—Keep off!" Alert attendants chase away the curious prowler who would invade the sanctity of Bailey's Beach, or survey the famous cottages from the street side. It was only the old law of Fishermen's Rights that saved Cliff Walk for the public; and the city fathers were asked to move a road which exposed to vulgar gaze the luxurious bathing-huts of the rich.

Some of the embassies have summer quarters here, and foreign diplomats play a leading part as arbiters of elegance and devisers of novel fêtes. The mania for novelty spread like a sickness: the starter of a new craze was acclaimed with brazen smiting, for Newport abhorred monotony as Nature does a vacuum. There was competition for the occult person with a turban and a mystic line of talk; he sat in a Chaldean boudoir, turning blood-red crystal and tracing life-lines that were badly tangled on the matrimonial side.

Brahminism and Bahaism had their day; so did coaching and polo and golf. Auction bridge enjoyed unfading vogue, with losses and gains on a staggering scale. At banquets the lordliest dish was voted dull at last. *Bécasse à la riche* and *Truite saumoné à la Monseigneur,* these gave place to heathen plats—perhaps a Canton puppy with bamboo-shoots and birds' nests; shark-fins to follow, and sea-slugs with as many legs as a centipede. These Apician tricks, we are told, will never again be played after the purging of a world-war on unparalleled lines. However this may be, the recorder of social America notes a great advance in taste and interests. Gone for ever are the days when jaded guests waded in the public fountains of Baltimore, or played leap-frog in the Washington streets after a smart dance.

Ten years ago the money-splash was rampant. The Newport hostess scoured history for spendthrift notions which should eclipse the Roman feasts of Horace and Petronius. Freakish pageants were weighed, from the "costlie braverie'' of Elizabeth's wooing to the mindless whim of a former Gaekwar who spent a million rupees on the marriage of his favourite pigeon with one belonging to his Prime Minister. The great thing was to outshine one's neighbour and maintain a loud lead in lavish entertaining. No wonder the yellow press showed ''How the Rich Live,'' with facts and figures procured from the Fifth Avenue shops. Here everything was set out, from Mother's rope of pearls to Baby's hundred-dollar doll, with its Paris hat and ''fluffy undies'' of fine silk and filmy lace.

But apart from strident folly of this kind it is a mistake to suppose there is no American aristocracy. Families of rank and breeding maintain ancestral pride with rigid hauteur, as any one knows who has even a nodding acquaintance with the *élite* from Charleston up to Boston— where, as the satirist says, ''a Cabot will only speak to a Lowell, and a Lowell only to his God!'' ''Your minds turn more to the past than ours do,'' Lord Northcliffe told America in a message of racy insight. And there is no abler or more intimate witness than he in matters relating to the United States. ''You have an astonishing cult of local antiquities, all the way from andirons to inscriptions on tombs. You have an incredible number of books devoted to family history, with lists of ancestors and enormous lists of descendants. You have also a unique array of patriotic clubs and societies—especially for women—to which nobody may belong unless descended from some special group of historic persons somewhere in the remote Colonial or Revolutionary past.'' Lord Northcliffe refers, of course, to such bodies as the Daughters of the Revolution, whose chapters have been recruiting for the Army and Navy. There are also the Society of the Descendants of the *Mayflower;* the Society of the Colonial Wars and the Daughters of the Holland Dames,

Descendants of the Ancient and Honourable Families of New York.

The American woman's view of the war is worth noting. As onlookers they surveyed it for more than two years, paying little heed to the martial or mechanical sides— the hero who muffled a bomb with his body, or the sea-plane which torpedoed a ship from the air. It was the bleak agony of Europe's women which most impressed their sisters in the Great Republic. The wailing of German *Klageweiber,* or Grumble-wives, such as shocked the Bavarian poet, Ganghofer, in letters found on the slain of his own side. "Barely a word of cheer," this recorder noted—"nothing but cries of misery and lamentation, with news of mutinous parade in the cities, and a shrill 'Give us back our men'; which defies the drawn sabres of the Berlin police." . . . "Our little Klauss has died of emaciation," was a typical passage from a letter found on a dead soldier. "And I should like those Herren of the Reichstag who tell us all is well, to have a look at my baby now."

American women wept over these scraps of paper. They knelt with the girl-wife in the slime of France, as the Last Post died down, and men with arms reversed turned away their faces from a figure of shaking desolation. . . . "Where is he? . . . Am I too late?—Oh, my darling, come back to me, I *can't* live alone"! Such scenes moved American women profoundly. So did the opinions of great ladies like the Countess of Warwick, who dwells on the eternal battle between feminism and militarism; the bleak dismay and new knowledge forced upon suffragists "belonging to families with a great military record."

"We must learn to hate war," American women were told by Ellen Kay, the Swede. "We must hand on the spark of hate till this evil thing is quenched for ever."

The revolts of hospital nurses were weighed in the United States; the glee and gladness of the shabby mother whose son was yet alive, although half his face had been shot away. And likewise the awful nescience of her who turned from God with unbearable ache: "If prayer was any use, would the child I bore with so much anguish have been torn limb from limb, and left to scream for death in a pool of filth and rats?"

This woman-view was seen with stark clearness on the other side of the water. Here Jane Addams and Julia Wales echoed Aletta Jacobs, the Dutch organizer, who called an International Congress at The Hague. "We women," Dr. Jacobs said, "judge war from our own angle. The men consider economic results—the glory, power, and so on. But what are such things to us beside our husbands and sons, the fathers and brothers, who march out and never come back again?" Here no comfort is felt "because they died in honour's lofty bed." The great test has come to all the women. And today even the German mother is no Spartan, but a blasphemer, standing with Death the reaper in the *hortus siccus* of a ghastly field.

I have dealt elsewhere with the American farmer's wife and her slavish lot, which is in glaring contrast with that of the idle rich in Newport. Theodore Roosevelt received a letter from Mrs. Rube, in which her outlook upon war is expressed in artless terms:—

"DEAR SIR,—When you were talking of 'race suicide' I was rearing a large family on almost no income. I often thought of writing to you about my hardships, and now when 'preparedness' may take of my boys, I feel I *must*. I have eleven of my own, and brought up three step-children besides. Yet in all the thirty years of my married life, I have never had a new cloak or a winter hat. I have sent seven children to school at one time. I had a family of ten for eighteen years, with no money to hire a washer-woman—though bearing a child every two years. Nine of my children (several are through or nearly so), got into high-school; two reached the State Normal, and one the University of Michigan.

"I haven't eaten a paid-for meal in twenty years, nor paid for a night's lodging in thirty years. Not one of my five boys—the youngest is fifteen—uses liquor or tobacco. I've worn men's discarded shoes; I've had little time for reading, so I think I have served my country. My husband has been an invalid for six years, leaving me the care and much of the work on our sandy little farm. Now I've bothered you enough. Only to me, race suicide has perhaps a different meaning when I think my boys may have to face the cannon.—Respectfully,

"MRS. ——"

Mr. Roosevelt thought his correspondent more worthy of salute than "any colonel of a crack regiment." He could only instance Belgium, whose sons were helpless when their mothers and sisters were abused. He could but reassert that law rested on force alone, and that "Preparedness no more invited war than fire insurance invites a fire." Here feminism and militarism are seen in hopeless clash. What the claims of women may be when this scourge has passed is a theme beyond my present scope. Certainly American women add to a social sway already unique, new political power in a dozen States. As a live issue Woman's Suffrage is endorsed by all parties, and may well be an important plank in the election of 1920. Girl workers of the sweat-shop talk about votes; it is in this direction that President Wilson seeks "new springs of democracy" . . . "that we may have fresh insight into all matters of social reform."

I must deal briefly with the old "indictments" of candy,

cars, and clothes. The consumption of sweetstuffs is, of course, enormous; in three decades the *per capita* stint of sugar rose from forty pounds to over ninety. Dr. Eugene Fisk, of the Life Extension Institute, advised American girls to "Cut out candies and ice-cream sodas" if they would carry good looks and elegant figures into middle life.

As to motors, these are counted by the million in the United States; quite humble folk will buy one, though it entail a mortgage upon their home. And as John N. Willys reminds us, "many refinements and conveniences of the best cars are due to woman's demands." "The final decision," this famous designer says, "often lies with a man's wife, or sweetheart or sister; so the woman's favour is a sovereign asset in the selling." For this reason the mechanism must be simple, for my lady loathes any "mussing or monkeying with the engine." All the advertisements dwell upon this, and the delights which should follow the touch of a button. "No exertion, no uncertainty, no bending over—an act which the well-groomed woman will ever resent." She will, indeed, for her corset's sake, rightly holding this garment as the basic truth of dress.

I have no doubt that American women are the best-dressed of all, though they follow the caprice of Paris with superstitious zeal. In the first flight I place the cosmopolitan aristocracy of the Eastern States; these are catered for by such artists as Jean Worth and Madame Paquin; Paul Poiret, Doucet, and the great Félix, whose *salons* in the Faubourg were-thronged by the beauties immortalized by Balzac and de Musset. American women of today have much to do with settling the current vogue for the whole world.

At stated seasons, buyers of unlimited credit and keen flair visit the *grandes couturières;* and great are the pow-wows held in sumptuary cabinets round about the Opéra.

Here graceful *mannequins* parade upon a stage in splendid raiment, with footlights to show night effects to professional eyes of the New York and Chicago Dressmakers' Clubs. These visitors are by no means easily awed. They have minds of their own, and the caprice of millions to humour when they get home. So they suggest alteration or modification. The Paris artist demurs, pleading inspiration from a sunset, an exotic flower, or some lovely portrait in the Uffizi or the Louvre. In this manner is the model "fixed," and with it a season's fashion for the United States, with repercussion down as far as Rio and Buenos Aires.

The say-so of Paris "goes" with American women of every grade. I was amused to hear the forewoman of a Baltimore factory testify in court that as skirts had become so short she had to wall her girls round with barrels so as not to distract the male operatives who worked near by! I am here reminded that Beauty and the Boss is a regular discussion in the New York papers, varying with the season and the modes. Hot weather brings out the famous "peekaboo blouse," a more or less diaphanous affair, and the anxious theme of employer and employed. "Does Docility go with Dimples?" is a typical headline, and both sides state their grievances and views. In other words, is the pretty girl a worthwhile servant? And just what relation does the vanity-box bear to the pay-envelope at the week-end? Such matters are quite gravely weighed in the United States.

Here also Dress is taken in the serious mood of the French, only there is far more spent on it. A designer like Lady Duff Gordon is struck with the aplomb and chic of the office girls in down-town New York. "Nothing in Paris can touch them," is the testimony of this *modiste*. "They have plenty of money, as well as the spirit for wearing delightful clothes." Home dressmaking is forced upon American women because skilled service is scarce and dear. Besides, the individual is a clever contriver, with all·manner of aids at her disposal, as one speedily learns in the Butterick skyscraper—an eighteen-storey workshop of fashion papers and patterns which cover the two Americas from Montreal to Montevideo. I will not deny that these women lean to the bizarre in modes; they follow "the latest" with neuromimetic faith, whether in dress, new dances, or pastimes.

The fact remains that they have a talent for adornment. Long ago discerning visitors like Réjane and Bernhardt found this out, and took home with them trunksful of New York creations. For many years American designers were aggrieved at their patrons' devotion to the Paris label. "If an earthquake levelled the Opera Quarter we'd have a chance," the Madison Avenue artist told me, with Cellini's own acceptance of a mad, bad world that forced ugly tricks upon the rarest craftsmen. "Our best people lay down the immutable law that tourists and trousseaux must cross each other on the seas. Right here in New York the creative impulse has a poor show. Rich women prefer to look a fright in a frock of Monsieur—without any regard to line or style or colour—than appear as a luring and gracious figure in an American frock. It's really sad." So the dressmakers said.

The great ladies maintained that New York was only a copyist and adapter, lacking the artistic atmosphere of Paris, and therefore obliged to import the models which it multiplied with such cunning and success. Some years ago Mrs. Stuyvesant Fish declared for Home Rule in Fashions, and war upon the French mark; the movement made a great to-do, because of the lady's rank. "We're like a lot of sheep," she declared abruptly. "We go over in droves and buy everything we wear, from silk hose to hats and frocks and jewels. Yet our own people have more skill and taste. I've often shown a French fitter how to pin a gown so as to get the best effects." . . . American *modistes* and *couturières* assuredly came into their own during the war, reaping and sowing in the flush time, and profiting—it may be permanently—by the stoppage of ocean traffic.

CHAPTER XII

"Especially in your country does it exert immense influence on the public mind."—POPE BENEDICT XV *to his American interviewer.*

THE front-page Person who sets out for America pre-pares for a stiffish ordeal, as one does who embarks for the Equator or the North Pole. But no vicarious hint, no experience at second hand, can make real the endless siege which a grand tour of the United States entails upon the distinguished visitor. Three royal names occur to me in this connection: Prince Henry of Prussia, Prince Louis of Battenburg, and the Duke of Abruzzi. It is safe to say these sailors will never forget New York, with night and day assaults upon their peace and patience, which baffled every known strategy. The stay of each of these was an orgiastic whirl not to be conceived by the European; an epos of stormy joy beyond the power of sober words. Those bulky mail-sacks, with epistles from soulful girls—and queer abuse from anarchist dives in the Black Belt of Chicago! Specimens of cigars and ties that sought a swell christening were sent along for the Lord High Admiral's blessing. So was the Semi-Ready suit, which was none the less "personal as a billet-doux; tailored entirely by hand, with intimate touches and endearments of individual effort in each hidden stitch and high-caste line."

There was a time when cynical and scandalous comment in the press drove prominent Americans abroad and kept them there. The ablest men were barred from a political career through fear of the newspapers. The Trust magnate saw his career dissected with frigid scorn; his 'cute law-honesty and stock-watering; his Borgian *virtù,* and the glorious villainies which had marked his rise to greatness. At no time could the reporter be evaded. Nor was he to be suppressed or censored, as the Government itself has lately found, and therewith bowed to a puffing humour which "put it over" on George Washington himself in the long ago. One day the Liberator attended a Council with a copy of the *National Gazette,* a lewd and daring sheet edited by Philip Freneau, who held a clerkship in the State Department under Jefferson. "That rascal," said Washington to his colleagues, "has been sending me three copies of his paper every day, as if he thought I would become the distributor of them." He probably did—especially as the Father of his Country was vilely abused in that day's issue! Freneau's paper died an appropriate death in the yellow fever outbreak of Philadelphia in 1793.

You cannot awe the American scribe. He pursues the biggest game with a child-like trust in the due and license which have never failed him; we saw these conceded in the first two years of war, when "big things" rained upon the American press until the veterans were sated. The New Yorker chatted informally with kings, as none other could do. Foreign Offices received him gladly, from the Quai d'Orsay to the mysterious Bab-i-Ali above the Golden Horn. Chancellors and Ministers gave exclusive stories to the Yankee, leaving the native scribe to pout with a sense of slight and chagrin. But New York was in no way elated, accepting each prize as a matter of course. In Berlin old Zeppelin was interviewed upon the aerial raids. Von Tirpitz was America's authority for the submarine exploits; at home Edison was asked about electric cures for all the curses of a chemical war.

It was to a Hearst man that the Crown Prince wept over the havoc and slaughter he had seen. At the Sublime Porte the Grand Vizier shook his hoary head over Veni-zelos; and complained about the Sherif of Mecca who hid the treasure of the Holy Places—a tidy sum, and one sorely needed by the Porte in a hungry time. America was bombarded with the sayings and sentiments of august Persons who had never previously spoken for publication. Newspaper envoys flitted back and forth in Europe with a naïve thirst for knowledge. As it happened, all the belligerents were anxious to humour him; so from end to end the firmament of war fairly blazed with American stars, tackling jobs which in 1914 were not even office dreams, but mere *pia desideria* too silly for editorial thought.

But of all the stunts, all the resounding scoops (how the English language limps behind them!) none quite equals that twenty minutes which the *World* man had with the Pope "in his magnificent private library on the second floor of the Vatican": there a Maestro di Camera trans-lated, as the Keeper of the Keys delivered his prayer and plea—"that this terrible carnage with its attendant horrors and misery may soon cease." That famous inter-view gave rise to caustic comment abroad. The Papal Secretary of State tried to explain "misunderstandings"; the Austrian prelate who arranged the audience was censured and dismissed. Certain it is that the Vatican was embarrassed by this Park Row feat. Dom Gasquet, the Benedictine historian, found the Pope depressed over the affair—and no doubt prejudiced against American reporters. But how came this New York Worldling to glide by the noble guards and arch-priests, the purple monsignori and princes of the Curia, who fence the Sover-eign Pontiff from the passing show? There was a prec-edent, it seems, and the *World* man played it well. Leo XIII (the American urged) had received Jim Creelman at no fateful time; so Pope Benedict might well speak to a hunded million neutrals through thirty thousand newspapers, all the way from Tallahassee to Spokane. Now what were the war-aims and views of the Holy Father?

To say that America believes in publicity is to state a fact too feebly. Publicity is America's blood and breath. The President is bound by it; a President's coffin cannot escape it. I have before me a page advertisement of the Springfield Metallic Casket, which at Canton, O., keeps the remains of Mr. and Mrs. McKinley "from the violation of the earth." Never before have I seen coffins flaunted in seventy-five styles, with hardware to match, and "burglar-proof vaults," which are surely peculiar to America. You will find all about them in a lavish catalogue called "The Final Tribute," which shows the funeral pomp of all mankind, from that of a Kansas Senator to the hairy Ainu of Yezo. This macabre business may be in doubtful taste, but it is gleefully characteristic. Down in Birmingham, Ala., I was handed an undertaker's card with the gay-grim legend: "I'll get you yet!" On the other side was this consolation: "But you'll have all the attention you'd expect from a friend."

This matter of publicity, I must own, appals me at the outset. The gleam of Liberty's torch, high over Bedloe's Island, is somewhat dimmed, when I reflect that a newspaper lit it, with the aid of Henry Doherty and the Society for Electrical Development. A great city like Baltimore takes space in the magazines beside the breakfast cereal and the safety razor. And the text tells you why. "Ask Charles M. Schwab, of the Bethlehem Works, who is spending $50,000,000 here to establish the largest steel plant on the Atlantic seaboard." A smaller town like Kenosha, Wis., makes a most modest bid for your plant and personal energy. "She offers low freights, lake transport, intelligent labour, and cheap electric

power." All over the continent statesmen and society
leaders have their own halo-polishers in the press. A
Presidential election is the most colossal task of all for
the publicity expert. He has a cabinet of movie-men,
an army of orators in a dozen tongues, including Magyar,
Yiddish, and Greek.

He partly edits ten thousand papers by means of extra
matter supplied in plate, and matrix, and proof. He
inspires a corps of cartoonists day by day, till the whirl-
wind finish rings out a blast of challenge from the rival
camps. Then it is that the best writers open fire with
pile-driving boosts for either candidate. No wonder the
Campaign Headquarters is like a great post office gone
mad. The Boss of all is now firing salvoes with a range
of three thousand miles; his target is nine million votes,
scattered from the Great Lakes to the Gulf and from the
Atlantic to the Pacific Ocean. America revels in the
strife which Success entails; the Edison formula for it is
"two per cent. inspiration, and ninety-eight per cent.
perspiration." Repose seems to mean stagnation in this
vivid land. One must do and drive, if one is to rank
among the live wires of business; how many American
figures of speech are drawn from electricity, railroads, and
mechanics?

The same qualities are looked for in the man as in the
car—"power and pep, pick-up and snap"; I quote from
an advertisement before me. "Life is too good to waste,"
the American gloats—and wastes himself in the using
of it. "If I can't make sixty-one minutes to the hour,
it won't be for want of trying!" It must be that extra
minute which the foreign visitor finds so wearing—even
the militant suffrage lady who never knew defeat before.
Poor Mrs. Pankhurst, hunted by reporters, hid from them
on the dock near the outward bound *Saxonia,* and went
on board at the last moment only to find the préssmen

waiting at her stateroom door! "I am very tired, and wish to lie down," was an appeal which even the sob-sisterhood respected.

That great soldier, Marshal Joffre, must have felt like that when he left New York for home:

"Un gros rusé compère
Qui cachait bien son jeu."

He was a *jusqu'au boutist* in that American Press campaign; temperamental calm sustained him, and the "Il faut tenir bon," which one notes in his early letters; that motto goes back to Colonel Joffre's trials among the Touareg of Timbuktu. The Allied Missions were made up of men who dislike publicity, yet they took naturally to democratic ways. Witness Mr. Balfour sitting on a box in the foc's'le of the *Mayflower*, chatting with the sailors, and handing out cigars on the way up the Potomac to Mount Vernon and Washington's Tomb.

The front-page Person is never allowed out of the public eye; he must always be on show for anecdote, opinions, and appraisal. "Not quite my type," was Walt Whitman's verdict on John Morley. "Not the letting-it-go kind. Rather too judicial; still, quite a man." Visitors nowadays show more tact and understanding than Dickens did in 1841. His *American Notes* gave umbrage to his inquisitive hosts—though Dickens did his best to placate them during a second tour after the Civil War. The famous Person is apt to become fogged with incense and deafened with the feast of trumpets. Cocktails are named after him; he eats and drinks too much, and gets very little sleep.

The flashlight fiend will take even genius unawares. There are shorthand scribes who report the statesman falsely, leading off with an Epictetus maxim, and winding up with prize-ring praise of the orator,—"he carried a

wallop like the kick of a mule!'' One of these days
perhaps Mr. Balfour will tell us of his pilgrimage with
penetrating play, and that charity of the mind which is a
sympathetic vision. It cannot be said of him, as it was
of Canning, that he was a ''ballroom failure''; a stingy
talker, and no ladies' man. I am always expecting some
Lucretian epicure to return from the United States and
write a classic book which shall be a joy to us all, alike
in the Old World and the New. Even Lord Bryce remarks
the noise and tremor which accompany American life.
He compares this people to a tree ''whose pendulous
shoots quiver and rustle with the lightest breeze, while its
roots enfold the rock with a grasp which storms cannot
loosen.'' The rustling, at any rate, is demonstrable by
a mania for publicity, which is all persuasive and unique.

''Is church advertising as necessary and fruitful as it is
in business?'' was a question put to seventy-eight factors
of all denominations. And seventy-five answered, ''Yes,
it is.'' But Barnum methods are over, it seems; the
Religious Press Advertising Bureau warns its wire-pullers
against ''aping the circus billboards.'' . . . ''The Church
does *not* run a bargain counter; and in our judgment
she soon reaches the limit of legitimate publicity. Is it
not still true that regenerated men and women are our
best showing? After all, the real Gospel is our main
attraction; and we doubt whether any side lines will
bring us a nobler profit.'' The boomer of 1918 is a skilled
psychologist as well as an artist of Rossini's own exuberance: ''He could set to music a page of advertisements!''
Everything in heaven and earth, from the night sky to
Niagara Falls, has been pressed into selling service.
Landscape and mountain are made hideous with mammoth
''calls'' from chewing gum and spotless cleansers. There
is a good deal of feeling, I must say, against this violation; it is passing in the new Day. Less odious, even

masterly, is the phrasing and display of advertisements in the newspapers and magazines. Besides these, the trade appeals of other lands look anaemic.

Great musicians who visit America are all the better for eccentricity of person, however pure and perfect their art may be. A great soprano will permit the boys to invade her hotel suite; on Sunday morning the lady is stupefied to read—not indeed an interview, but a signed article by herself on "Singing Shorn of Its Mysteries"! As for the President, his "public" life is not so wearing as it was. I have known Roosevelt retire to bed with a bruised hand and aching neck after two thousand hand-shakes at a garden fête. The White House of 1918 has no more welcome for casual callers than Buckingham Palace has, or the Elysée. But in Jackson's day a reception drew ungovernable mobs to the Executive Mansion which "belonged to all the people." Old Hickory could never have foreseen the result of his first free lunch. When he opened the doors his admirers surged in and trod his cheeses into a greasy pulp on the East Room carpet. The chipping of furniture for souvenirs; the removal of statuettes, cutlery, cups, and glasses—here was an enthusiastic vice which lasted up to Roosevelt's term. The Colonel and his lady worked wonders in White House reform. They put a stop to a traffic in invitations which brought seven hundred guests to a supper for three hundred, and drove a hungry President to raid his wife's larder for cold pie and pickles in the small hours.

America was rather restive over the war-time sovereignty which the Federal Government assumed. Thus a Press Censorship clause was inserted in the Espionage Bill with a view to ensuring reticence in regard to the plans and armed forces of the nation. Most of the newspapers, the President was glad to say, put national safety before mere news.

At the same time there were "some persons who cannot be relied upon, and whose interest or desires may prove highly dangerous to the country at this time." The penalty for indiscretion was a fine of $10,000 and ten years in gaol. Here was a revolutionary move in a land where the Press had unbridled power; it is not surprising that the Senate added a proviso that: "Nothing in this section shall be construed to limit or restrict any discussion, comment or criticism of the acts or policies of the Government or its representatives, or the publication of the same."

There were statesmen in that debate who had no illusions about the sacred mission of the Press. Senator Pomerene of Ohio quoted articles "so treasonable that had they been published in other countries the editors would have been shot." "Some people," mused Mr. Stone, the Chairman of the Committee on Foreign Relations, "seem to think there is something about a journalist which puts him above the law. I cannot understand why these men should be allowed to prowl at large after information." This is the view of a new aristocracy; it is by no means that of the masses, to whom the Press is a mighty abstraction, a more than Roman *imperium,* dancing through American history with the large exuberance of Liberty herself. American reporters and men of letters enjoy greater favour and fortune. Every avenue of public life is open to them. President Wilson won early renown as historian and biographer; he also wrote for the papers in his Princeton days.

Roosevelt passed from the White House to the office of *The Outlook;* and among Foreign Ministers who were writers too, I need only name John Hay and Mr. Bryan, who has been a journalist all his life. Colonel W. E. Edge, the Governor of New Jersey, was manager of the *Atlantic City Press.* Governor Cox of Ohio was first a farmer's boy, then a printer, and finally the owner of the *Dayton Daily News.* Reporters, publishers, and poets are rated as men of affairs, and appointed to important embassies and legations abroad. Mr. Whitelaw Reid, who lived in regal state among us, was for many years editor of the *New York Tribune*. And I first met his successor, Mr. Walter Page, in the office of *The World's Work*, which he directed, being at the same time a partner in a publishing house of high repute for the quality of its books and periodicals. The Ambassador to Russia, Mr. David R. Francis, owns the *St. Louis Republic*; Dr. Henry van Dyke, lately at The Hague, is a poet and essayist of international renown. The list could be extended surprisingly.

Enormous fortunes are made by men who own newspapers and periodicals; this is mainly due to the advertisements, which account for nearly ninety-five per cent. of the revenue. So cunning are these announcements, so artistic and lavish in scale, that there can be no reasonable comparison with the advertising of any other nation. The total sum spent in this way must exceed $500,000,000, yet this is by no means the money-measure of American publicity and salesmanship, which bring into play all the wiles and guiles, all the faith and hope and vigour of the national genius.

A million dollars is nothing for a breakfast-food campaign or the launching of a new car. The New York department stores contract for daily columns by the thousand; and $5000 is no startling price to pay for the "position" page of a magazine. The ability shown in advertising, the close watch upon results, the psychologic study and high pay given for text and pictures—these are matters to amaze the foreign expert who scans the page with knowledge of price and "pulling power"—say in the *Saturday Evening Post* or the *Ladies' Home Journal* of Philadelphia. As literary properties, apart from the daily papers, I consider these the most valuable in any country; and the last-named deserves special mention as a factor in the uplift of women's lot. I know no agency—political, civic, or social—which is such a power for good as the *Ladies' Home Journal;* though to understand this calls for intimate grasp of rural and provincial life in the United States.

The daily papers, with their overwhelming Sunday supplements, have to a large extent dropped those "yellow" features which made them so offensive to Americans of the better sort. "It is the task of a live newspaper," one was told, "to raise the devil in some way every day." Hence the craving for stunts, for daring personals and prurience, which the European could only survey with awe, seeing men defamed and women mocked for the fleeting amusement of the mob. This ugly phase belongs to the past. The monthlies, too, have given up the so-called "muck-raking" articles, of which the most notable was Miss Ida Tarbell's history of the Standard Oil concern. To attack the Trusts was once a paying vogue; to expose municipal graft and big business grabs, as well as the careers of industrial kings, their coups and counter-plots, which were cynical and crooked reading in the literature of power.

This missionary zeal is an American tradition; it was defined by Joseph Pulitzer, when he bought the bankrupt *New York World* in May 1883, after its failure as a religious journal.

Government by the newspapers was of real use in Boss Tweed's outrageous day; it is out of place in President Wilson's, and that of State Governors of a new type. Thus I find a fervid Churchman as Chief Executive in Maine, a Socialist farmer in North Dakota, a Doctor of Philosophy in Arkansas, and University men in Illinois and Indiana. It was already a changed America which took up the Prussian challenge; and since that day the all-absorbing theme has been Democracy's War, and the new world-order that must come after it.

From the very first—three centuries ago, indeed—the hunting of news was known for a prime sport. In 1680 Ben Harris of Boston resolved "to furnish the Country once a month (or if any glut of Publick Occurrences happen, oftener) with an account of such considerable Things as have arrived unto our Notice." In Colonial days, the papers had a lively time. There was British censure and stern visitation upon offenders; there were inter-office wars and editorial duels with bludgeon and pistol and pen. The famous Stamp Act killed many aspiring sheets. Among these the *Pennsylvania Journal* died with mournful glee— "In the pious hope of Resurrection, having departed this life on the 31st of October, 1765, through a Stamp in the vital parts." There were forty-nine of these casualties before American independence was won.

I must pass over the journalism of Revolutionary days, when the Boston bell-cart went through the streets collecting rags (at 10/ a lb.!) which a primitive mill made into paper for the *Massachusetts Spy*. Ink and type—any sort of a press—these were hard to come by in the new Republic. Moreover, readers were so few and shy that the seven dailies of New York could only muster a circulation of 9420 between them. Yet it was always natural for the Press to lead the nation. The big editor was already a political boss who took himself very seriously. "You must try to elect the President without me," cried old Sol. Smith of *The Independent*, with tears rolling down his massy cheeks. Sol. was just then amalgamating a couple of papers, so for a season America had to lose the guidance of her inky Tsar.

The birth of the *Sun* in 1833, the forming of the Associated Press in '48, and the invention of Colonel Hoe's machine are landmarks in the newspaper history of New York. Sunday papers were long resisted in the Puritan spirit; on the other hand, all attempts to establish a religious daily were foredoomed to failure. As a preaching sheet the *Sun* was a poor concern; the original founders of the *World* withdrew from an uplift venture with a loss of $200,000. With sensational coups and headlong vying for public favour—like that between the *Herald* and the *Sun*—I have little space to deal. There was no such thing as a dull season for news. When facts were few, reporters eyed the moon itself with wistful impulse that begot a monstrous yarn, which was fathered upon Sir John Herschel, who at the time was out of the way in South Africa. The astronomer was supposed to have viewed the moon through a new and mighty telescope which revealed weird valleys and forests, stupendous temples and strange birds winging stranger way over rivers paved with gold. It was Locke of the *Sun* who wrote the famous *Moon Hoax,* and the watchful *Herald* demolished it.

I suppose the *Herald* is the richest of newspaper properties. Its founder, the elder Gordon Bennett, was a humble proof-reader down in Charleston, S. C. How he borrowed $500, and produced the first number in a Wall Street cellar, at a desk made of bits of board upon two barrels, is a classic instance of American hustle. Bennett did everything himself. He secured advertisements and financial news. He haunted theatres and clubs for social stuff; at four in the morning he was writing leaders, or else sweeping and dusting out his editorial cave. All things were made to serve the *Herald;* an infernal machine addressed to the editor, or an assault upon his person by a visiting crank; the first gold of the Californian rush; and episodes of the Civil War, with its corps of *Herald* correspondents, who had $100,000 to spend. These men wrote of Union victories on the backs of rebel State bonds and Confederate scrip of enormous face value. So scarce was paper at that time, that more than half the Southern journals suspended publication. Others used crude wallpapers, with the news on one side and gaudy floral patterns on the other.

Under Gordon Bennett's son the *Herald* attained a wider renown, notably by the sending of Stanley to meet Livingstone at Ujiji. But it is Horace Greeley who stands out as the most powerful and truculent figure of the American Press. It was the dream of his life to own a newspaper; so far back as 1833 we find the man touring New York and boring young editors with his views on a one-cent paper of vast politico-social sway. Greeley was laughed at, of course. He started the *Morning Post* on a cash capital of $150, a promise of $200 worth of paper, and an agreement with a cautious printer to settle for the composing every week. After three stormy settlements the *Post* died out amid general execration. Greeley was now a precarious free-lance; he was also a Voice hired on easy terms by shady politicians at the State Capitol up in Albany. Yet this hack could bring out the *Tribune* on a mysterious thousand dollars, and the moral backing of petty statesmen who had faith in his stormy talent. The first number was published in 1841 with a lofty flourish which was not upheld. "No immoral or degrading police reports" were to pollute Horace Greeley's page; the *Tribune* was to reflect only "the virtuous and refined."

The famous pressman gloried in a fight and had recourse to the queerest circulation methods. He "donated" strawberry plants and steel engravings of himself, which gave his rivals scope for the drollest scurrility. In the summer of '63 the *Tribune* office was besieged by a murderous mob, and Greeley took refuge in a refrigerator. These riots were due to Lincoln's drafts for soldiers; and they broke out afresh in the following year. But already schooled in violence, the *Times* and *Tribune* now mounted real artillery on their office roofs. There were editor-gunners turning off real thunder, with ingenious hoists for the ammunition.

Greeley's fort was now stuffed with giant reels of paper; he poked Minié rifles out of loopholes, and had handy openings for grenades to be thrown at storming parties. Such was New York journalism during the Civil War. Henry Raymond of the *Times* is a familiar type, akin to Gordon Bennett and the rest. Here is Raymond writing his first leader in a windowless loft by the light of a guttering candle stuck on three nails in a wooden block. "It'll take five years," he said, "to put my bantling on its legs." He was soon greeting Kossuth on Staten Island, and devising stunts that put the *Herald* in the shade, and eclipsed the *Sun* itself.

It was the *Times* that shocked New York with revelations of the Tweed Ring, giving figures from the City Comptroller's books to show the huge extent of the looting. One item was $5,663,646 for "repairs and furniture for a new Court-House." In vain was a bribe of a million dollars offered to the *Times;* and so ingrained was graft that Bill Tweed surveyed the whole exposure with a bored indifference—"Well, what are you going to do about it?" was a classic question of the Boss. After Raymond of the *Times,* comes Pulitzer of the *World,* who once slept out on the park benches as a homeless hobo. It was this man's "Yellow Kid" whose antics in the Sunday paper moved Dana of the *Sun* to condemn "Yellow journalism" for the first time. Pulitzer was in turn defeated by the rich Californian, W. R. Hearst, who coaxed away the *World* staff, including the Yellow Kid artist, who was offered a Presidential salary.

Whatever may be thought of Hearst and his chain of papers—there can be no denying the skill and mob-knowledge with which they are conducted. None others approach them in circulation. None pay so lavishly for pictures and stories, whether news of the day or science and society features for the Sunday sections. The Hearst papers, as all Americans know, have their own code of ethics, and upon this I need not dwell. Setting aside questions of decency and taste, the Hearst journals are marvels of popular appeal; it is absurd to ignore them when considering the influences that sway the mixed peoples of the United States. Moreover, it is incontestable that Hearst motives and methods—political and social, technical and professional—have moved certain of our own papers to a discreet and pallid emulation of stunts and hunts, adapted to our less impressionable people.

Press publicity is quite a modern weapon, one forced upon the British Government like the flame-thrower and the chlorine-cylinder. It went against our grain, yet could not be ignored without serious disadvantages. So at last we find our Foreign Office receiving the American "boys," as President Wilson does after the Friday Cabinet in Washington. An interview with the British Prime Minister, our Foreign Secretary, or First Lord was no longer an impossible stunt, but a frequent fact, with big headlines and editorial comment when the feature reached New York. Even in Paris the rigid Protocol of the Quai d'Orsay so far unbent as to form a "Comité de l'Effort de la France et de ses Alliés," which was to counteract the world-wide ferment which centred in Berlin.

This covert arm of the Kriegsamt was for many years run by Dr. Otto Hammann, the supple tool of Hohenlohe, von Bülow and Bethmann-Hollweg. It was Hammann's work to create the "atmosphere of Victory" which should go before the German legions like a cloud of fire, tinging a timorous world with awe and admiration. Whether Britain and her friends will ever equal or surpass that Berlin Bureau is unlikely.

The stealing away of its "atmosphere" is not to be

denied. "Sooner or later one succumbs to it," is the reluctant testimony of Professor F. Sefton Delmer, who may be cited as an excellent witness. He is an Australian, and was appointed English Lecturer at Berlin University in 1901. "In Berlin I had constantly to remind myself that these were German reports, and full of German guile. The marvellous thing is that *this subtle influence is felt even by intellects which perceive its trend.*" Judge from this what its power must be where no bias exists, and where German rumour calls from every cave to the untutored masses.

Publicity is proven as a weapon of war. Here in England we have seen it used to call armies into being for the factory and field, to raise enormous loans and rally the nation to economy and thrift for a long and wearing fight. It is pre-eminently an American weapon, and plays a compelling part in the polity of a land where silence, dignity, and repose do not accord with the spirit of youth welling in a restless people. A recent skirmish between the Cabinet and the Press ended in official rout and a letter of capitulation from the Secretaries of War, the Navy, and Foreign Affairs. "While there is much that is properly secret," these Ministers said, "in connection with Departments, the total is small when compared with the information which it is right the people should have. America's present needs are confidence, enthusiasm, and service; and these are not completely met unless every citizen is given that feeling of partnership which comes with full, frank statements relating to the conduct of public affairs." This was the outcome of the "news-gag" clause in the Espionage Bill, which had been severely handled in both Houses.

At last President Wilson formed an Information Board, with Mr. George Creelman in charge. The Press was appeased and put upon its honour, with regulations on

the news-desk and hints from the Bureaux in each
reporter's heart. In a word, the Government was beaten;
the papers were self-censored indeed, but as free as ever
from "the dictation of superannuated majors who knew
no more about news than they did of giant ordnance in
the field." With this parting shot the Press withdrew
to engage in war-work and devise a Headline Policy
which should be common to them all. Here Columbia
University joined forces with them through the School
of Journalism founded by Joseph Pulitzer of the *World*.
A super-editor was soon instructing his colleagues from
academic halls on the Hudson heights. "It is to a considered and continuous policy of news presentation that
we must primarily look for the keeping before the American
people of the importance of team-play, and of the fact
that we are today a member of a great team of nations
whose success is ours, and whose failure would alike be
ours. . . .

"Keep news of the fighting upon the front page. For
it is *Our* fighting. It is the reason why all our local
energies—the raising of troops, the training of men here
or there, the manufacture of munitions and the issuance
of billions of credit—are conducted. These activities can
be understood only in relation to the end for which they
are undertaken. . . . That end is the defeat of Germany,
which is being accomplished on the battlefields of Europe
and on the high seas." Such was the new policy which
the official "blacking-brush" might have brought to
angry damnation. At the same time, the Government took
care to issue a daily Bulletin of its own. This was displayed in all post-offices, and marked the stages by which
a pacific continent took on war-harness by a social revolution.

Here publicity has a pride of place denied it in the
quieter lands. The University of Pennsylvania welcomes

a congress of Advertising Clubs. "Sparks will be struck," the advance agent said, "from the contact of keen minds, new fires of optimism will be kindled, new courage and understanding promoted among men." These live wires were able to draw a letter from the most conservative of Presidents. Dr. Wilson was glad to know that the clubs sought "to establish and enforce a code of ethics based upon candid truth." This was an aim which showed "good business judgment as well as a fine conception of public obligation." That such a crusade was needed, I will not attempt to deny.

But of late Truth has invaded even the Bargain Basement, where sober values have superseded the merely snatching legend: "These 25 c. Handkerchiefs are a trifle mussed, so we allow you 10 c. for washing them." I know a mammoth store in New York, whose publicity man began a Truth campaign which all but drove the managers to mutiny. Yet the fellow persisted in his heresy. "Sincerity," quoth he, "is the biggest word in the dictionary. Give me six months' run, and if I don't double the sales, put me in the discard as a street sweeper." He had his way, that revolutionary, and dollars followed "like trained pigs"—the phrase is his own. It was perplexing at first to the startled staff. The devotee of Truth knew that the average woman will refuse to buy "five-dollar" hats at fifty cents, whereas she will readily bite at $3.89. This tricky system was swept away,— though for a while Truth stood unheeded in frippery's halls, like the pedlar who sold golden sovereigns on London Bridge at a penny apiece.

Nowhere is publicity so profoundly studied as in the United States. I am willing to believe it is a "fascinating" art, since human frailty is its chief concern, and it carries a shifty code. Howbeit one must admire the play which these mages make with words. What insinuation equals the hand-camera hint: "Your friends can buy anything you can give them—except your photograph!" Or what is quainter than the shaving-soap that figures as a "Big Stick"—one of suaver utility than Roosevelt ever planned. "So husky to look at, so magical and soft in application! The metal grip grows daily in your affections as the Big Stick wears itself out in your defence."

In the underworld of advertising I came upon the letter-broker, an agent unknown over here. He deals in names and addresses; he rounds up and classifies inquirers of all kinds, whether for patent medicines, or wild-cat stocks and shares. The letters are rarely sold outright, but let out on hire with a sliding scale of charges governed by recency of date, by the subject-matter, and the number of originals among each lot. A mail-order house will pay from $5 to $10 for the loan of a hundred thousand letters; but I have known $1500 given for the names of fifty thousand possible victims in a crazy speculation.

It is curious to recall the stunts of other days, and the itch for novelty which was never still. Even civic science had its freaks and finds, and editors were glad to get them for the Sunday supplement. Take the alligators of the Jacksonville (Fla.) Zoo. These idle saurians were yanked out of the sun and set to clear the city drains by crawling through them with ropes and chains. Who could invent such things as these?

The social firmament was combed for stunts—(there is no escaping the word), and all classes responded eagerly. At the zenith was my lady of Newport, who went to the fancy ball as Aphrodite, with nothing on her but a wisp of gauze—"you could *lose* it in your purse, my dear"! And at the nadir was the felon in gaol; he was tyranny's victim, I fear, in this democratic land. His terrors and tortures in Trenton were exposed. So were drink and drugs smuggled in to him at Auburn; and—worst of all—the ghastly preparations for the death-chair in Sing-Sing, a sizzling horror which I shall not describe.

These ugly themes cast wholesome light upon abuses; for the vice and graft of American prisons, no less than their crude philanthropy, were scandals that cried aloud for reform. Of late years an official ban has been put upon penitentiary yarns. Superintendent James M. Carter, of the New York State Prison Service, warned his staff against notoriety of this unbecoming kind. Legitimate news might properly be given out, but "the practice of featuring convicts and advertising persons indiscriminately is not and cannot be helpful."

Aerial and cinema feats took a reckless toll of human life, besides debauching the people who viewed them. On the political side there was the "Manless Special," a famous train which brought Suffrage armies to besiege the White House and the Capitol, and the liquor-loathing Sheriff, who watered the streets of his home town with hundreds of gallons of "blind tiger" whisky.

America loved spectacular news of this kind, but the buzz of it ceased when ten million citizens marched to register for Humanity's War. New Headlines now appeared in the papers, and mere inanity was no more seen. "Old Glory in the Firing Line" was a front-page feature. Or "The Hoe behind the Flag"—an exhortation to the farmers: "Taking Stock of Our Resources," "The Men who Get Things Done," and "Our Bridge of Ships Across The Atlantic." "These United States," whose lack of cohesion Washington himself bewailed, were now one indeed in that "privilege of self-sacrifice" which President Wilson praised. "We may regard this as a very happy Day," the Chief Executive told the veterans of the Civil War. "A Day of Dedication, a renewal of the spirit which has made us great."

America's millions were now in Democracy's War—

"With both feet," as General Pershing vowed: "To the last dollar," as M. Viviani testified after his memorable tour with Marshal Joffre, "To the last man, and the last beat of their hearts."

CHAPTER XIII

THE "PEOPLE OF NOW"

"Les anciens, Monsieur, sont les anciens; et nous sommes les gens de maintenant."—(MOLIÈRE, *Le Malade Imaginaire*).

THE collapse in Russia and the military burden it threw upon the Allies did much to deepen America's responsibility and reveal her own *rôle* in a critical liberation of forces too evenly balanced for a speedy decision. Germany, as we know, held her lightly as a possible enemy. The early satires of journals like *Kladderadatsch* and *Simplissimus* show Uncle Sam as a clumsy titan with a wooden sword:

> "Any centenarian can see
> To ring a bull's-eye when he shoots at me!"

Another cartoon showed a Mexican peon on a bucking bronco, throwing a lasso at the impotent President, who was scolding Berlin from the far Atlantic shore. America's aim to boss the world was desolate Hamburg's theme: "Not of course by military means, for these people lack the very rudiments of martial tradition. Their mentality is essentially bourgeois, yet they assume lofty airs as keepers of the world's conscience. This pose flickers through all Herr Wilson's chameleon Notes."

Herr Wilson would do well to change his ways while yet he was safe. For, lifted again and again from the diplomatic saddle, he was now in danger of being blown out of the military path. . . .. And so things drifted to a rupture which was quite calmly viewed in Berlin. Was it of much more account after all than the break with Hayti or

228

Liberia? These opinions underwent a change. I find Professor Jannasch debating the cost of war with "the Land of Limitless Resources." He regrets the Pan-American influence which can seize millions of tons of shipping, and close markets from Vera Cruz down to Valparaiso—"the result of our colonizing genius these ninety years." But there could be no turning back. Dr. Jannasch kept the Pan-German eagle flying because: "Our people have poured out streams of blood! They have hungered and shivered, and sacrificed their savings to the one Desire, of which the halting fulfilment has proved bitter enough. Let us push on to the decisive battle in which the Americans can take no part."

Other writers, too, thought the New World too thickly overlaid with Germanism to move an armed fist against the Fatherland. And therewith they traced the sway of Deutschtum in the United States, from the rabble of Valley Forge which Von Steuben reorganized for Washington with German marksmen of deadly fame, armed with bored rifles made by German gunsmiths of Pennsylvania.

From first to last what was America without its Teuton leaven! It was Andreas Klomann, a Rhenish Prussian, who founded the steel industry of Pittsburg, which Pennsylvania Germans like Henry Frick and Charles Schwab carry on to this day. Busch, the famous brewer of St. Louis; Havemeyer, the Sugar-man, Otto Kahn and Jacob Schiff, those Wall Street princes—here was German genius flowering in a bleak and graceless land. In the Civil War 187,000 hyphenates fought for the Union; their folks at home put $600,000,000 into Lincoln's empty war-chest. But what reminding should America need of all this aid? German soldiers in bronze and marble stood in mute reproach in every well-kept park from Boston to San Francisco.

By this time America shook from sea to sea with armed

upheaval, and Berlin pedants were dwelling upon new facts. This world-war was more scientific than any which had gone before. But it was also a machine-made war, and men were drilled for it with an ease and swiftness which confounded precedent and opened up disturbing possibilities. America's Day of Registration showed an enormous muster. Secretary Baker was talking of six-figure armies raised by selective drafts which favoured no class. And Joffre's appeal was being answered. "Led by her President," said the Marshal through the State Department, "this mighty people has entered the war. And by the side of France, in defence of mankind, the place of America is marked. France, to whom American valour is known, cherishes the thrilling hope that the flag of the United States will soon be unfurled in our fighting line. This is what Germany dreads!"

That dread was spreading as the President got to work and training camps appeared, each one with a city's population, and all intent upon the business of slaughter. Soon there was an Expeditionary Force in France, an American Staff established in the Rue Constantine near the Paris Ministry of War, and whole divisions of pupils were at lethal games behind the lines under the veterans of Haig and Pétain. Fabulous loans were offered to the Allies. There were steel rails and rolling stock for Russia, fleets of ships on the stocks for Britain, that she might defeat the submarine. For home defence America had a program involving billions of dollars, and a rally of power—personal, industrial, and agricultural—which must change the continent for all time.

The navy was transformed; a loose system of coast defence was pulled to pieces and reconstructed in the light of ballistic lessons. Science and invention were enlisted on a vast scale. All things lacking—torpedoes and shells, big guns and mines and explosives—were forthcoming in truly

American profusion. So were skilled hands for the bases in France; engineers, electricians, and road men; dockmasters of Hoboken, Fifth Avenue chauffeurs and lumberjacks from the far North-West. The submarine service began a headlong race for proficiency. It had a long way to go, I am bound to say; yet the pace of it exceeded the utmost hope of men who knew America's resources. Here Henry Ford deserves a tribute. He enlisted his own industrial armies, which number scores of thousands; he offered machinery quite unique in scope and scale and ingenuity.

But it was above all in aircraft that supremacy was planned. The eyes of the German armies were to be blinded by American squadrons, so machines were talked of in ten thousands. For this purpose a first appropriation for $64,000,000 was no sooner passed than Congress tabled another for $600,000,000. The German war-aims were often expounded by the President. The Kaliphate of Berlin was dissected by him with its implied dominion of Europe and Asia from the North Sea to the Persian Gulf. "The great fact that stands out," Dr. Wilson explained, "is that this is a peoples' war for freedom, justice, and self-government among all the nations. . . . And that it rests with us to break through these hypocrisies—the patent cheats and marks of brute force—and help set the world free; or else stand aside and let it be dominated by sheer weight of arms, and the arbitrary will of self-constituted masters."

"To do this great thing worthily and successfully," the President pointed out, "we must devote ourselves to service without regard to profit or material advantage, and that with an energy and intelligence that rise to the level of the undertaking." But would this efficiency be forthcoming? The Germans doubted it, and fell back on a survey of past American wars. All was different now, however; confusion was stilled like the twitter of birds in a rising storm.

Colonel Roosevelt's offer of an independent levy was
politely declined. He was a gallant man, a fine public
servant, but . . . "the business now in hand," declared
the President plainly, "is practical and undramatic,
scientifically definite and precise." There was no scope
here for the *beau sabreur;* rough-rider methods, well
enough in Cuba, were sadly out of place in the fields of
France. "I shall act at every step," Dr. Wilson declared,
"under expert advice from both sides of the water."

Even Germany began to see that this leader was carrying
his people with him. "It is not an army we have to train
and shape for war," the President told Congress when he
moved the Conscription Act; "it is the entire American
nation." And that miracle was growing; the States
"United" in a sense that Washington never saw, nor that
Lincoln left when his task of Reconstruction was completed.
"What our country needs," said Dr. Murray Butler, President of Columbia University, "is an intellectual hero, an
outstanding poet or a seer, to move hearts and heads as
Emerson did our fathers." America was sure she had such
a man at the White House in this her Day, and German
thinkers were inclined to agree.

It is curious to follow the Berlin process of giving the
devil his due. What astonished friend and foe was the
personal ascendancy of the President, his fixity of purpose
and supple grasp to which men in Congress who opposed
him paid unstinted homage. "Wilson *may* have a one-
track mind," they conceded, "but it seems to have ample
switching facilities!"

His *rôle* was the pontiff's, his word infallible in American
faith and morals. "Why have our people changed overnight?" asked Congressman Byrnes of South Carolina.
In this case an opponent of the Conscription Bill went
home to face constituents who favoured it as by an abrupt
caprice; it was bewildering. "Simply because the papers

urge them to back up the President. Whatever he asks for he gets by an overwhelming vote." And indeed his sagacity had won. Now for the first time one heard business men agreeing with Martineau that: "Reverence for human life is carried to an immoral idolatry when it is held more sacred than justice or right, and when the spectacle of blood becomes more horrible than the sight of desolating tyrannies and triumphant hypocrisies."

The forty-eight States ranged themselves behind their chosen leader "with plain heroic magnitude of mind." In New York the German Liederkranz serenaded Mayor Mitchel with "The Star-Spangled Banner." Southern negroes marched to the booths with martial song; in Western deserts the Indian braves went on the war-path— not indeed in plumes and paint, but in the latest caper of Kirschbaum togs, with dandy hats and loud shirts of *ultra* design.

It is no skin tepee that houses the Indian chieftain of today; that saddle-coloured savage draws thousands a year from gas and oil lands leased to the big Standard or some other interest of the East. The Osage lord rolled up to the Agency in a Ford car and registered as an American soldier. Then he drove back to a fine house, with fauteuils and parquet floors, and a costly gramophone in which Gounod and Verdi were followed by ragtime airs from the Broadway musical shows.

I must say there are less "civilized" specimens than these. In Colorado the Utes were unwilling to serve, the remote Navajos of Arizona would not "fight in Germany," and were therefore tactfully excused. Otherwise all the races of the Melting-Pot rose at their President's appeal. The Hungarian of Chicago wrote patriotic letters to his native paper, the *Amerikai Figyelő*, whose leading article was a pæan to the Day. It was the same in Lowell (Mass.)—"our vest-pocket Athens"—where the

Greek *Erevna* gave stirring news to the native coffee-houses. Registration was also explained in Italian, Spanish, Yiddish, and Norse. Even hyphenate journals turned upon the Fatherland with regret, recalling its furtive strokes at Uncle Sam. These began with the Samoan affair, and passed to the Hayti intrigue of 1914, not forgetting Herr Zimmermann's bait to Mexico and Japan.

Every sort of citizen hailed the privilege of service, which the President hoped would receive the widest publicity. And the press responded with a "Wake Up!" campaign which spoiled the farmer's picnic on the Kansan plain. It was for sluggish rural centres that the Committee of Public Information prepared a national booklet, *How We Came Into The War.* Propaganda swept the continent with tireless ingenuity and zeal. It pierced the prairie apathy; it struck sparks from the dullest, and set Great Britain in a new light. An official order was now issued deleting the offensive third verse of "The Star-Spangled Banner." And a typical Western newspaper summed the situation in these words: "Mr. Balfour's reception by Congress ought to convince the English that *we* are willing to forget George III—if *they* can!" So at long last President Wilson was rewarded for that patience which Pitt defined as the first virtue of statesmanship.

I have called America a continent of contradictions. That "all men are created equal" was set down as a self-evident truth in the classic Declaration. Yet a Rockefeller may amass a thousand millions, whilst the "poor white" of Tennessee drags out a life of savage squalor on his lonely rocks. Then Jefferson, in his first Inaugural Address, laid down the principles of democracy, which as a "bright constellation has gone before us and guided our steps." A particular star of that galaxy was "Justice for all men

of whatever persuasion, religious or political." Yet the
State laws jar strangely on this Jeffersonian latitude. Last
year a citizen of Olympia, Wash., was sent to gaol for
calling George Washington a drinker. And three thousand
miles off—in prosaic Waterbury, Conn.—a Lithuanian
freethinker was tried and convicted for "blaspheming the
Bible," making light of its miracles and the divinity of
Christ. The Free Speech League of New York took up
this case, pointing out that the law went back to 1642
and was coupled with witchcraft, entailing the death penalty.

How are such vagaries possible among the People of Now
—the "common people" whom Lincoln said God loved
because "Ile made so many of them"? The sovereignty
of the people is the first principle of Americanism, and no
leader has stated it more forcibly than Woodrow Wilson.
"I take it," he says, "to be a necessity of the hour to open
up all the processes of politics and public business—open
them wide—to public view: to make them accessible to
every force that moves, every opinion that prevails in the
thought of the people: to give society command of its
own economic life again—not by revolutionary measures,
but by a steady application of the principle that the
people have a right to look into such matters and to control
them. . . . Wherever political programs are formulated
or candidates agreed, over that place a Voice must speak,
with the divine prerogative of a people's will, the words,
'Let there be light!' " Here is the antithesis of Kaiserism!
And in similar vein was the message which Mr. Gompers
sent to revolutionary Russia on behalf of the Federation
of Labour.

Meanwhile, from Madrid to Prague, from Calcutta to
Quebec, "the silent mass of mankind" for whom Dr. Wil-
son spoke, were raising voices louder than the guns. And
America showed the way with growing determination.

"At one bound," our Prime Minister told her Pressmen in Downing Street, "the United States became a world-power in a sense that she never was before." Her President was hailed by France as the eloquent interpreter of outraged right and civilization. All Europe rang with homage. The halls of the Sorbonne were full of American praise, so were illiterate barracks of the Ukraine, where the mujik blinked in the new light of freedom and extravagant hope. Marshal Joffre was a pilgrim to that sacred grove on the Potomac, where he laid a palm-spray of bronze upon Washington's tomb, with the wistful hope that America would soon sound a trumpet-call like his own classic Order of the Day: "L'offensive va se poursuivre sans trêve et sans relâche!"

Courage, self-mastery, and continuous effort—here is the formula that sustains the American soul in the great game of life. "O' course," as the darkie explained to the learned German, "ef you sho'ly *hunt* Trouble, an' stay ter shake han's an' ask how's all de lil' Troubles at home —w'y den ye can't blame Joy ef he take ter de woods wid his banjo!" To think pink and look prosperous are factors extolled and favoured as conducing to Success. On the other hand, the grouch—he who croaks and kicks—is known and damned at sight, like the movie villain who flickers to a lurid end in the last picture of a popular reel.

Therefore preparedness for the battle of life is a forceful affair. To begin with, it involves many experiments in education; the President of Columbia bluntly declares that "Our present system is worn out." For this reason the General Education Board, backed with thirty-five millions of Rockefeller money, began to remodel elementary and secondary education on lines laid down by Dr. Eliot of Harvard, and by Dr. Abraham Flexner, who would cut out all the trimmings of the Platonic ideal and get down to the brass tacks of today: *"Nous sommes les gens de Maintenant!"* The Flexner plan lays stress upon science and industry. It would abolish that formal discipline which moved the humorist to remark with reminiscent sadness, "It makes no dif'rence *phwat* ye shtudy, 's long's ye *hate* it!" Mathematics of the utilitarian type are to be taught; the training is to be largely vocational and on strict business lines with little regard for the larger humanities.

Of course the intellectuals opposed this scheme, citing the wisest sage of antiquity, who turned from the physical sciences and gave himself to the life of man. The contest between the two schools still rages sharply, as it does among ourselves. But the Greeks may have to give way, with all their allies from Ignatius Loyola to Heinrich von Treitschke, who defended the classics as a guide to intellect and taste. "Imagination will be cramped and stunted," American scholars mourned as they surveyed the Flexner scheme. "Knowledge and enlightenment will be abridged and shorn of those delights which have made them so rich a possession." The experiment is therefore assailed as a disastrous stroke—"the opening wedge of a frankly sordid, materialistic education which will make of us a race of efficient Hottentots."

On the other hand, American parents raise a counter-plea for their twenty million boys and girls. "Give our children a practical education," they urge. "We want them fitted for the fight." So the system of 1898 must go; it is already out of date, although hailed in its day as the heritage of all the ages. Secretary McAdoo of the Treasury would have the teaching of Spanish made compulsory in the common schools; two-thirds of America's youth leave these at the age of fourteen, and never return. In this day of plain speaking hard things are said of the mental and moral equipment they take with them into the busy American world. After all, the high-brow was a poor enough citizen for war-time—unless indeed he knew something of the Science of Slaughter. Even conservative England had found this out. Had she not now a Chair of Aviation at Oxford? There was at Leeds a Depart ment of Tinctorial Chemistry, at Liverpool a School of Tropic Medicine, and at Sheffield—that home of high-speed steel—a Professorship of Metallurgy, as well as a Chair of Russian, endowed by the armament firm of Vickers. Surely these were significant signs of the times?

Colonel Shirley, Director of Military Studies at Cambridge, was aghast at the ignorance of high-brow English boys. "Is it not absurd," he asked—for all the world as Dr. Flexner might!—"to make a boy do Latin verse before he can express himself clearly in his mother tongue!" So there was vigorous blowing in Britain upon the Latin cinders and Greek dust; a floundering out of blind alleys and buffalo-tracks of learning into the broad American way, and the workshop of a brighter and better world.

The college man in business is often debated in New York, where tradition and the facts go steadily against him. An industrial prince, like Charles M. Schwab, will take the high-brow for his theme in get-ahead talks with slum lads over on the East Side. Mr. Schwab—no college man himself—favours Science in a general way, because it tends to eliminate chance from the material affairs of men. The cultured youth, Mr. Schwab is afraid, has inflated notions of his own worth; he seeks to capitalize at once his costly years of study. Hard slogging on the up-grade, the steel-master believes, goes against the college grain. The high-brow gets a disagreeable jolt in his new job; his own superiority is a standing bar, with all its top-hamper and unnecessary sail. It is quite otherwise with the poor lad, hammered night and day in ambition's forge. He pores over books when others are in bed; he foregoes the usual pleasures, he does menial tasks in the summer months to pay for his technical tuition.

Mr. Schwab made out a plausible case, and American life fairly bristles with the proof of it. That brusque giant and patron of the arts, John G. Johnson, of Philadelphia, was a blacksmith's son who scampered through a suburban board school. He became the leading corporation lawyer of America, and two Presidents pressed high office upon him.

Another poor boy was James A. Farrell, President of the U. S. Steel Corporation, the master of 270,000 men and a business worth a thousand millions a year. Jim Farrell is the incarnation of American drive; no man's advice is more eagerly sought on the all-absorbing topic of Success. He has a memory of abnormal grasp, as the greatest of advocates found when heckling him in a Government suit against the Trust he controls.

The lives of these men, paragons of energy and shrewdness, have long allured the American masses and inspired the arid literature of efficiency schools. *Forging Ahead* is a typical title. *How to Figure Fast* is a ready reckoner which is described as *The Book That Counts!* Another is *Wealth in Waste;* it deals with potential gold from the factory smoke, with potash from seaweed, paper from sugar-cane stalk, silk from sawdust, and valuable nitrates from the atmosphere. Was not War Secretary Baker building a four million dollar plant for this "crazy" purpose?

These books have an immense sale. There are get-ahead periodicals, too, like *Success and System* and the *American Magazine;* this last is conducted on novel lines. Here we have inspiring yarns, with real heroes and real names. Here is Jim Hill driving his dog-sled over the Canadian rivers in mid-winter—the Cecil Rhodes of the

United States, of whom a spell-bound reader wrote, "Hill's adventures make fiction seem vapid stuff. I have never hung by the eyelids to any climax as I did to this man's battle with the Hudson Bay Company for the Red River Trade." Equally moving (to the American reader) was Hill's exploit with the St. Paul and Pacific. The American titan took that road in hand when it was but "two streaks of rust and a right of way," and with the derelict he built an empire in the North-West.

But the Great War is shaping other heroes. America's Hall of Fame has now shifted from University Heights to the battle-fields of France, with expectancy of new leading worthy of more spacious times. This feeling was voiced by President Butler in the halls of Columbia, when he conferred degrees upon Marshal Joffre and Arthur Balfour, the envoys of a new Holy Alliance for security and peace. Big gaps in the graduates and Faculty spoke of Columbia's contribution to the new Day. Five hundred students were at Plattsburg, Newport or Fort Myer, training for Army and Navy commissions.

"The American youth who pass out today," Dr. Butler said, "enter a strange world at a crucial hour of history. Time will soon tell whether man has crossed the Great Divide and begun his decline, or whether he is still ascending to universal freedom. It is more than a world at war— it is a world in social revolution. From the Russian steppes clear across Europe, and the United States round to Japan and China, men and nations are not only locked in fearsome grappling,—they are also examining, readjusting, and reorganizing their olden habits of thought and action, private as well as public."

Hence the need for new leading; for larger vision and devotion such as the people perceive in Woodrow Wilson, who "reigns" as no President ever reigned before. "It is an heroic age," says another American thinker, Dr. Eliot of Harvard—"an age that prompts the question: 'What do I love? What do I live and work for? And for what am I ready to die?' Quite naturally the answer comes: 'For justice, for freedom, for the increase of natural human joy, and the fairer distribution of the legitimate fruits of labour.'" Here is Americanism defined; the laic religion of tomorrow's reconstruction to which all the democracies subscribe.

Meanwhile, an epic stage is set in the United States with mute beckoning to unknown players. What manner of man will the stress and strain bring forth, as the Revolution brought forth George Washington as patriot, soldier, and statesman? It is strange, America muses, how war discovers genius in unlikely quarters. Andrew Jackson stepped from the Bench to the battle-field in the chaos of 1812. It was an obscure failure, Ulysses Grant, who was destined to lead the Union Army to victory at last. The splendour of Lincoln has a background of blood and flame, and imminent ruin. It was the rough-rider charge up San Juan hill that gave Roosevelt a glimpse of the White House and future renown. Therefore the flush-time idols are neglected. The standards of Success have shifted, and citizens rally for service as they did when the farmers of Concord Bridge fired "the shot heard round the world." "The whole nation," the President ordained, "must be a team in which each man shall play the part for which he is best fitted."

Achievements once thought great were forgotten now. The Panama Canal is America's greatest "short cut," yet the man who made it—General G. W. Goethals—had a prouder task in the Emergency Fleet which was to foil the German submarine. The crowning work of Edison's career is being done in war-workshops of the Westinghouse concern. Herbert Hoover forsook his mines for the rationing of nations. Julius Rosenwald, the Selfridge of Chicago

—a man rich enough to give away $687,000 on his birthday
·—left his mammoth store to join the Council of National
Defence.   And Daniel Willard turned his back on railways
to organize American industries for war.

As for the women, I could fill pages with their practical
work.   "Stop passing resolutions," a shrewd lady advised
a very exclusive Society.   "And go home and plant something!"   It was pointed out by the Department of Agriculture that housekeepers control eighty per cent. of
America's food expenditure; they could therefore do great
service by eliminating waste.   Secretary Houston was
informed by his experts that poor cooking and over-lavish
provision at table dumped in $700,000,000 a year into the
garbage-cans.   This vast sum was now to be saved, and as
much more added to it by the children, whose "door-yard
gardens" were soon a national feature, full of vegetables
and small fruits with hygienic space on the side for chickens
and rabbits, pigeons and ducks.   The U. S. Commissioner
of Education, showed that by intelligent direction a twelve-
year-old boy or girl could easily grow $50 worth of food in a
garden of five hundred square feet.   There need be no
interference with regular school work, nor too much time
taken from the hours of play.   Moreover, the new hobby
had an educational value; it added to health and strength,
and filled the child with wholesome pride as a helper of
the State.

Then a million women were asked to do men's summer
work on the farms.   To all volunteers the Department of
Agriculture sent a concise and simple primer of instruc-
tions.   For the first time economy and thrift were Government themes, urged upon homes where these virtues had
never been known.   The women were told it was possible
for them "to aid our economic preparedness when the
Great War summons an immense Army to the colours."
With a good team, and·a riding-cultivator equipped with a

sun umbrella, ploughing corn was a more pleasing job than washing clothes. The spring seat of a binder was contrasted with the useless piano-stool, and "few household chores are more fun than riding a hay-rake."

It need hardly be said that the Red Cross had feminine armies of its own, as well as funds to the extent of $100,000,000, and as much more as might be desired. Never, surely, was money so profuse in flood. Only the Quakers were exempted from combatant service, and these took up works of utility and mercy. "No Friend will fail in his duty at a time when the world is torn and bleeding. We must show by our example that we love America in very deed and truth."

It is a long way from the Quakers of New York and Vermont to the Filipinos of the Asiatic Archipelago, yet here also the same signs were seen. Fifty thousand islanders answered America's call, and marched to the Malacang residence of Governor Harris, who rules in the President's name. "We take our stand," said island chieftain Manuel Quezon, "on the democratic principle that he who will not aid his country as a soldier in the hour of need is unworthy of citizen privilege."

Such was America's will to war; it came with a bracing sense of shock and the awed perception of a sterner Day. No man voiced this more earnestly than General John J. Pershing, Commander-in-Chief of the First Expeditionary Force. "This is the beginning of a wonderful era," the veteran declared when both Houses of Congress passed the Conscription Bill with great majorities. "I would rather live now and have my share in today's events than have lived in any past period of the world or witness any development which the future may have in store."

The upheaval in America was more foreign to habit than in older nations of homogeneous race and traditions of war. It is hard to convey the sensations of a New York matron, when shopping in Sixth Avenue and suddenly faced by a big effigy of Liberty, with minatory finger and the startling legend below: "*You* Buy a Bond, or I perish!" One of these days a native humorist will write a droll book on the "Wake Up" campaign which President Wilson waged to ensure an effective war and to imbue the Central West and South with martial incentives. For it was in these sections that the farmer scratched his head, irresolute over the many scientific recipes for the "bread bullets" which he was to provide for the Allied peoples. Rube cheered with the rest, of course; yet in his heart he was afraid the Executive ran too fast and was over-autocratic in Freedom's war. Witness the new regulations for the produce markets, the bossing of railroads and factories and mines. Mr. President, the farmer feared, was filching more and more power from Congress until that body bade fair to become a war-time rubber-stamp. Nor were signs lacking that Congress itself felt that way too.

"We're shooting democracy into the Germans," said the caustic Socialist of Milwaukee. "We've a Tsar of our own over here, so let Nicholas send us his cast-off crown." In this way were the rueful and truculent, the remote herds of brotherhood and peace, as well as artful traitors and duty-dodgers worked upon with auras of conflict and confusion. It would be absurd to say that the Great War was "popular" in the jingo sense, as war was when petty victories over Spain shrieked from the *New York Journal* in monstrous type made up of Stars and Stripes. America's War called for patient education. The Council of National Defence called a conference of all the States, and Secretary Lane spoke plainly to the delegates. Germany, he declared, was not to be starved out; she would put up the greatest fight the world has seen. "But whatever the size of the job, we must be equal to it." The envoys present should therefore impress upon their home folks the need for immediate action, and lay plans for a long and obstinate struggle.

Secretary of Labour Wilson made a personal appeal to the workers. Mr. McAdoo, of the Treasury, toured the country with his wife on a "Why We Fight" mission. He dealt also with the national penalty: "If Germany wins . . . she would come here and set the conqueror's heel upon us all! We might have to pay an indemnity amounting to half our total wealth, which is $250,000,000,000. You would have taxation upon your shoulders for a hundred years to come." There were also lectures on the Chautauqua system which brought home to the masses how vital was victory in this far-off fight.

But if "Business as Usual" was an early obsession of our own, is it any wonder that the Melting Pot—a continent thousands of miles off—should be slow movers in a universal war? Americans find life hard enough in normal times. "Our toll of industrial deaths," said the Director of the Museum of Safety, "equals fifteen full Army regiments every year. Over three hundred regiments of toilers are so seriously hurt as to be laid off for four weeks." "America at peace," said another authority, "lost in two years and a half of death, mutilation, and lowered production, the $3,500,000,000 first asked of Congress on the eve of our entry into the war."

At home and abroad today there are nobler interests for America's gilded youth who at one time aspired to a De Maupassant leisure of parties and veiled ladies, practical jokes and games in the vicious ephebia of Broadway glare and tumult. A Thaw of Pittsburg became the senior American flying officer in France. Alan Seeger, the Harvard poet, gave his life for the cause like our own Rupert Brooke. Vernon Castle, the famous *salon* dancer, had America "at his feet," yet he hurried over to take part in sky quadrilles against the Boches. Young Marshall Field, a lad of enormous wealth, became a trooper in the

Illinois Cavalry; young Vanderbilt joined the ammunition train as a private soldier.

There was a time when the rich youth sought to outshine all the dandies, since Alcibiades went out to supper with golden grasshoppers in his hair. This folly can nevēr quite regain its tinsel glory. The mermaid feast, the hectic play at Palm Beach tables—all the staggers and lapse of moneyed license—these belong to America's isolated past, when young Hotspur made a torch of his purse to light his narrow round—*Las de toucher toujours mon horizon du doigt*. The American youth of 1918 has the world for a field.

CHAPTER XIV

THINKING PINK AS A NATIONAL OUTLOOK

"I call a new testimony—yea, one better than all scripture, more discussed than all doctrine, more public than all publications. . . . Stand forth, O Soul!"—(TERTULLIAN).

WHEN Henry James returned to New York after years of absence he had much to learn about his native land, its joyous growth and clamorous aims. "Perhaps you'll write us the Great American Novel," was the hope of a friend, who guided the weaver of words through the noisy maze. But the artist demurred. "I'm afraid I can't," he said, "for I don't know the American world of business."

Now my survey of a pink and practical outlook must go back to a time when the *anima mundi* of these people was not duty or sacrifice, but mainly Success, and that of rather a barren kind which left the winner unfulfilled.

To compare the present American aspect with that of pre-war days is like setting the Britain of 1918 beside the England of Ascot Week in 1913, when our "week-end habit of mind" was a German taunt. America as well as Russia has known the throes of revolution. The uprooting of tradition, the adventure overseas and its reaction upon life at home—these are already reflected in American life and letters. The Great American Novel, it is felt, may after all be written in blood, like Draco's law. And haply by some exiled Ovid, like young Norman Prince who died for France, or Alan Seeger, the poet-soldier, whose reverie called up Love and pillowed ease:

"But I've a rendezvous with Death
At midnight in some flaming town!"

It is the voice of America's new-found soul, a nobler note than that of the petty trader who "couldn't pass a bank without raising his hat and walking on his toes." This waggish worship of the money-shrine has been appreciably chilled. Dollars are become as dirt to be swept in billions into the maw of war. Therefore a sober journal like the *Sun* can now say, "We are reading seriously." The reviewer glanced at "this Season's books," and sighed as one who knew them by heart. How could the public swallow the old stuff in this new day? But it was not the old stuff; there was here less of the milk for babes and more strong meat, such as belongeth to them that are of full age. Books of broader vision lay on the critic's table. Something of Mazzini's flame in '63— "Nationality is an end, a collective mission from Above." Writers were harking back to the fervour that lifted the North in '65 when the security of the Union had been assured by the sword. And men pointed to France, quoting the Parnassians of Fort Vaux and Douaumont: "Notre race toujours a su reverdir!" Over American literature a change had come, as it had over industry itself. There were now merchant fleets to build, and U-boat destroyers; aeroplanes in thousands, sea and land harness for millions of men. The steel plants of Pittsburg were turned from the ways of peace. So were the motor-shops of Michigan, the rubber-shops of Ohio, lumber-camps of the North-West; the farms and ranches, the stock-yards, oil-fields and mines.

The wholesale jeweller was busy with periscopes, the sash-chain man making cartridge-clips; and from underwear factories came bandages in ribbons that would reach to the moon. Machine-gun aid was expected of the corset people. Cash-register plants and makers of infants' food were also in the killing or curing line. Thirty thousand firms had asked for a share in the Big Job, and Uncle

Sam was doling out "practice orders" of an educational kind. Thus a threshing-machine man got a contract for a hundred six-inch shells, and with it Government guidance in the necessary jigs and tools and gauges. There was room for every citizen in Democracy's war—for the Wyoming cowboy as well as for commercial lords who were on the Washington pay-roll at one dollar a year.

It was this upheaval which accounted for the new books on our reviewer's table. Of course there were pamphlets on physical condition. "In this world-crisis," said the dope-and-diet ad. of a health-culture course, "you must be a national asset, and *not* a liability." Even the fiction promised, by title or puff, to illumine matters—that swayed the new American thought. There was still pink reading, of course, but its pride of place was gone. The novels were less exuberant; minor poets had more flints than flowers in their little triolet offerings.

Strangest of all, here was naval and military science—a work on *Trench Warfare*, for instance, by Major James A. Moss, U. S. A. This author was concerned with obstacles and ditches, mining and countermining; bayonet-fighting, the use of grenades, and bombs and liquid fire.

At the same time there were a few works that reflected peace-time interests wholly given to war. The cottage spinster still gabbled from her cabbage-patch with a background of hollyhocks and hens. The small-town parson told of business methods in the local church. He took space in the paper to advertise his spiritual wares. There were bulletin boards at the cross-roads, and Barnum parades to boost the Sunday School—that problem of a stormy day when Christ ethics were decried with Nietzschean ferocity.

There are Western yarns in the Season's list—"fine, big novels of simple sweetness and virile strength," with corresponding heroes on the coloured wrappers, and private guidance from the publisher to the reviewer. Here is "a ten-strike in fiction, a miracle of mental cleanness, and that rarest of all achievements—a really pure love-story, mined from the grand old moral bed-rock." Of one novel we are told that "not a man in it wears a collar." It is a tale of gold-seeking, with the Arizona desert for a scene. Life on the ranch and range has always been a big seller; simplicity makes a strong appeal to the sophisticated of this land. Fanatics of the speed-up are allured by languor under the giant tree-ferns of Hawaii, where the heart's thirst is satisfied by the hand's thrift, and unwedded lovers eat frugally of taro and dried fish. It is a standing marvel to the New Yorker what a dollar can do in these cradled nests. *He* pays a dime for each egg in the restaurant caviare; three children at private schools run him into nine thousand dollars a year.

But the best seller of all is the *Wholesome* in fiction. I know a man who sold seven million copies by virtue of a God-given secret which was defined by his Chicago publisher in a special brochure of boosting. In this pamphlet, ministers of religion pay generous homage to this maze of letters. Had they not preached from the Big Seller's text? So great a man was in more than one sense a handful for his publisher. That lucky tradesman jour-neyed 2500 miles into the waste with his contract. For genius held that the heart of the great reading public could only be touched from a hermit hut in the sage and sand far away from all distraction. The source and fount of big sales was duly pictured in the booklet; it was a dinky abode, eighteen by thirty-five, thatched with arrow-weed and furnished with Socratic severity. Here prose epics for the million were turned out. Here the Big Seller played upon America's soul—"soft and low," as Chicago tells us, "like a magnificent organ is played."

Pre-war America had no great love for heavy reading;

it held with Byron that the end of all scribblement is to amuse, or at any rate to point a rosy moral. "I haven't read a serious book for fourteen years," President Wilson owned in one of his rare moods of intimacy. "I read detective stories for fun, but very little modern fiction. It concerns itself with problems, and I have enough of these." So the war-time President falls back upon his old favourites. "There are things of Tennyson which have comforted me," he owns. "Where will you find the theory of popular government so finely expounded as in *The Princess?*"

> "A nation yet, the rulers and the ruled—
> Some sense of duty, something of a faith,
> Some reverence for the laws ourselves have made,
> Some patient force to change them when we will,
> Some civic manhood firm against the crowd."

There is much Americanism here, with aspiration towards the ideal State; a benign democracy in which sorrow and evil are but calls to valour and dignity, that these things may cease. "I intimate in a hundred ways," is a Walt Whitman impulse, "that man or woman is as good as God!" Yet Secretary Harlan could oust that whimsical poet from a humble clerkship as "the author of an indecent book!" It is a fact that realists have never been popular over there. "The stream of events which we call actual" was to Thoreau an abominable mess—"a sort of vomit in which the unclean love to wallow." There was another and sweeter stream which hurried the spirit into the flowery way. Edgar Allan Poe was long classed as a wallower; it was not until 1910 that he was admitted to America's Hall of Fame. Poe was among the disreputables—an outcast from clean-living America when he returned from Philadelphia with a sick wife and four dollars fifty in his wastrel pocket. Yet respectable authors were doing well at this time—witness Hawthorne and his

Puritan themes of sin and the soul. He had a fine home in
the Emerson parsonage at Concord, where *Mosses from
an Old Manse* breathed the New England note that "God's
in His heaven; all's right with the world."

Or there was Lowell, Professor of Belles-Lettres at
Harvard; abolitionist, diplomat, poet of *The Cathedral,*
surveyor of a well-made world from "My Study Windows."
Lowell could haggle over terms with that magazine harpy,
Sarah Josepha Hale, who was paying the unfortunate Poe
fifty cents a page, and receiving grateful letters from
him. "The price you mention will be amply sufficient,"
the pariah wrote to her. Would Mrs. Hale keep five
dollars' worth of space for a special feature, "which I will
endeavour to adapt to the character of *The Opal"?* So
the way of the transgressor was hard, the way of a Longfel-
low serene and smooth, with fear of God and the love of
man to commend "A Psalm of Life" such as that which
America loved.

It is curious to consider Columbia as the Britomart of
purity, hailed as such by all her poets from Bryant to Bliss
Carman. The moral tap must be kept running, the arts
can only defy its cleansing at their peril. In some of the
States Shakespeare has been banished from the schools: a
production of *Antony and Cleopatra* was raided in Chicago, where culture and civic pride are peculiar obses-
sions. The Heine fountain in New York was fiercely
assailed; paintings in Denver and Kansas City have been
slashed with the axe of an outraged proletariat. *Tess* and
Jude were withdrawn as improper books.

The successful American writer will resent comparison
with European realists, however great their fame. Thus
the late O. Henry was aggrieved when an admirer called
him "the De Maupassant of the United States." "I never
wrote a filthy line in my life," this author protested to
Professor Alphonso Smith. "And I won't be classed with

bawdy writers." America's foremost periodical is proud to claim that its stories "strike twelve, but not sex o'clock!" The welter of State laws have at least this in common—that they reveal authority "smelling for smut" with the professional zest of a wheat-inspector in Minneapolis. There are as many censors of the movies as there are religious sects. The lavish *Birth of a Nation* was banned in Ohio on the ground that it stirred up hatred and racial strife. Nor will Ohio allow snakes to be shown on the screen; the bandit may flourish through a five-reel crime only on condition that he comes to a bad end.

In Iowa the clubwomen censored a story that showed a bride at breakfast in a sumptuous home. Her husband, it was pointed out, was "only on a salary." Therefore modish gowns, fine silver, and parquet floors set a dangerous example to the young women of the community. Down in Missouri the State is severe upon the amorous motorist. His car, it seems, is all too apt to pull up at night with all lights out, to the peril of joy-riders behind him, who come hurtling through the dark to certain wreckage. The man at the wheel, Missouri maintains, may forget himself, but he should at least remember the lives and limbs of others. Why should the love-god fare forth in a high-powered car, and use it as a man-trap in the gloaming? So Sheriff Bode and Attorney Ralph declared war upon the "one-armed" driver—that public terror whose soul was centred on the girl beside him, and not on the road or the joyous traffic of it.

Now and then a literary rebel will scathe all this Puritan peering. Thus Theodore Dreiser breaks a lance with the vice crusaders; it is only fair to say that he speaks as one of the vetoed and forbidden, involved in public odium and pecuniary loss. "The average American," this novelist complains, "is intellectually bounded by the canons of church and Sunday School, as well as by the conventions of his native town. The darkest side of democracy is that it permits the magnetic, the cunning, and unscrupulous to sway our masses—not so much to their own undoing as to the curtailment of natural privilege, and the ideas which they should be allowed to entertain if they could think at all." Mr. Dreiser is very severe on the intellectual poverty of "a land so devoted to the material, though dedicated by its Constitution to the Ideal."

Another realist whose name carries weight is Abraham Cahan; and he also spoke his mind about "our divorced life and literature." It was only in the newspaper, Mr. Cahan said, that the cultured reader could get a faithful reflex of the American scene. Life was faced squarely enough in business, in politics, and in the home; yet the ablest writers continue to produce little but fluff and prettification for that terrible tyrant, the average reader. In this discussion professors and critics took a hand; so did publishers, novelists, and moralists of the Comstock Society—these last concerned to protect "female readers of immature mind."

Mr. R. W. Chambers drenched the debate with common sense, scathing American literature as he passed. "What is read and criticized as such reflects nothing but the self-consciousness, ignorance, and impotency of those who diligently produce it." Another forceful critic answers the self-set question: "What are the judicious to do?" "They will do what they have always done—read the literature of less pious countries. Why should I bawl and beat my breast because Dr. Howells has written nothing comparable to *The Revolt of the Angels*, or *The Nigger of the Narcissus?* It is much more polite and comfortable to heave Howells at the cat—and read Anatole France and Joseph Conrad"!

However, Americans are not easily shaken from their

sense of well being.   They do love the literature of rosy
thought; they savour goodness—

> "As one who stays the sweet wine in his mouth,
> Murmuring with eased lips, and is most loath
> To have done wholly with the sweet of it."

There is wide agreement to ignore ugliness and evil, and
let laughter drown the surge of cosmic mystery and the
cruelty of things.   The "ostrich-literature" is more than
a tradition: it is the national symbol of huge endeavour,
and the brave Bossuet-faith which sees our tangles as so
many golden chains that meet beyond mortal sight at the
conventional Throne.   There are too many people, as O.
Henry reminds us, who wear life as "a reversible coat,
seamy on both sides."   America has no use for these doleful fellows.   They are nearly always high-brows, like John
Caspar Branner, Professor of Geology at Leland Stanford
University in California.   Let this scientist tell us of the
ostrich pose, in so far as it relates to earthquakes on the
Pacific Coast.

Here was a group of problems which nature had left at
the door of a lovely and favoured land.   Surely the railroads would encourage research, and the collection of data
that might help?   Or what of the telegraph and telephone
concerns—the electric power and water companies whose
dams and mains were in constant danger?   Insurance
offices, too, were puzzled over rates and risks.   Yet the
policy of hush "put it over" on them all.   Only two concerns in a land three times the size of England showed any
interest in Professor Branner's quest, which was the
rational study of earthquakes.

"It seems incredible," this bold man avers, "that the
business interests of our State should willingly and weakly,
year after year, allow a permanent threat to hang over their

industries, their transportation-lines and public utilities, without making an intelligent effort to investigate the subject, or to help those who are willing and anxious to do it. Yet such are the sad facts. The result was that the great 'quake of 1906 caught us unprepared. Water-mains were broken when the city of San Francisco became a raging furnace; we were fairly trapped in snares of our own weaving.''

In a word, California prefers to take her chances and go on thinking pink. This was America's chosen outlook till the world flamed with war. For two years and more she surveyed the wide anguish with expectancy worthy of a bench of bishops. The battle-field of France loomed as a new Sinai, to be watched afar as from a sanctified camp. On that Mount of thunder new laws were being graved for the wiser ruling of the race in years to come. America lent a sympathetic ear to the Primate of All England, preaching in Westminster Abbey on a task of reconstruction that glowed through the smoke of ordeal like a pillar of fire. . . . ''Fear not, little flock; it is your Father's good pleasure''! So the blood of sprinkling spake better things than that of Abel. A portent of this time was the insistence upon universal slaughter as a panacea for spiritual and social ills and the ultimate betterment of humanity. Rainbows of Christ were seen gleaming from green clouds of the poison-gas. Nests of new-born sweets were found in the shell craters; the perfect man would yet be gathered from horrid fragments that swung from the barbed wire.

Certainly America, in her neutral day, was kindled with shining prophecy of quenched tears. To her the dreadful blast was

> "A trumpet in the distance, pealing news
>   Of better; and Hope, a poising eagle, burns
>   Above the unrisen morrow."

I know nothing stranger than the buoyant alchemy which turned our shame and torment to new grace in this rosy way. It was not confined to Americans—though I know no people more nimble in transmuting woe into joy, or sublimating boons from the ashes of dread.

That spirit smiles at us in the work of Mr. W. D. Howells, the dean of American letters, whom the whole nation honoured on the celebration of his eightieth birthday at the National Arts Club in New York. All his life Howells shrank from moral disease with the pudor of Jane Austen. He disliked violence, and rarely dwelt upon unpleasant themes. In his early days he renounced a tidy job as a reporter, though he knew the value of this "school of reality," and "the many lessons in human nature it could have taught me." "My longing," this typical American tells us, "was for the cleanly respectabilities." After all, the goodly outside of life was best. Why stray into gloomy recesses where silly gnomes hammer out of their own hearts the seeds and sparkles of new misery? This was America's view. *Je me presse de rire de tout,* she confesses, with Beaumarchais' hero . . . *de peur. d'être obliger d'en pleurer!*

Nowadays the old pink thinking is less ebullient. America is a conscript nation; her cities are armed camps, with slackers in gaol or fled over the Border into Mexico. The continent of peace is converted to force of arms and war's philosophy—surely a German triumph of peculiar poignance?

"We must begin with a fresh sheet of paper," President Wilson said, as he removed General Goethals from the Shipping Board. "And we must do the things that are most serviceable." Here we have the bustling motive which America imports into all activities, from the church to the slaughterhouse. Even her religion is business-like, and one must examine it if her spirit and literature are to be understood. There is no mutiny against a heedless God, no tears in eyes that fail with looking upward; no murmur of baffled breath, but only the practical prayer of Heine—"Give me health, O Lord, and a sufficiency of money—'tis all I ask!"

America has no quarrel with any cult, from the Quietism of Laotze to the devil-dance of Billy Sunday and his pulpit slang. An industrious reporter counted a hundred and fifty faiths between Mormonism and Christian Science. Some of them were winners in a worldly sense. Look at John Dowie, who made millions of money in Zion City, and came to grief wrestling with sin in New York where no sin is (they say), but only will and gratification. Or consider Elijah Sandford, the penniless madman who began to build a temple on the sandhills of Maine with no other possessions than a wheelbarrow and a spade. Soon men were selling their farms to support a rascal of whom his dupes at last declared that he "hadn't enough religion to grease a gimlet." Sandford claimed to raise the dead; he talked with the Deity in aisles and minarets where at length the rats swarmed in eerie desolation. In his decline this man and his Holy Ghosters set seaward in a crazy fleet bound for Beirut and the Way of the Cross in Palestine.

The Holy Rollers were ruled by hell-fire and fear; their antics surpassed the contortions of an Indian village *mela*. The Brotherhood of Light left the grosser communities, and took to the desert four hundred miles south-west of Denver, where they lived on apple sauce, dates and water. There is no end to these eccentrics.

"Religion," said Oliver Wendell Holmes, "is the flag under which the world sails, but not the rudder that steers its course." And America has very many rudders. Here religion adapts itself with all the elasticity of Hinduism and the rugged wisdom of Islam.

Hence all the drastic editing of the Bible; the restating, rearranging, and transvaluing of outworn theologies. The Protestant Episcopal Church, in General Convention at St. Louis, laid easy hands upon the Ten Commandments. Clauses that were meaningless or turgid were cut out, since the spirit of the age called for brevity and sense. Both the marriage and burial services were altered. The word "obey" was undesirable, the commendation of St. Paul redundant as the wedded loyalty of Isaac and Rebecca.

And at funerals, why should not more cheerful Psalms be chosen? The Twenty-Seventh, say—the Forty-Sixth, and Hundred and Twenty-First? That gruesome thought, "Though after my skin, worms destroy this body," must come out altogether. Why depress dutiful citizens at the graveside? So the elements of fear and fuss are eliminated; they are out of place in the New World Prayer Book, as they would be in a balance-sheet or a prospectus. In short, the American is a radical in religion. Like Holmes, he aspires to a wider, more humane and modern interpretation of Christianity.

American intellectuals do not mince their words in this matter; let me cite Professor G. Stanley Hall, President of Clark University. "Two millennia under the Prince of Peace," says this psychologist, "have not prevented this colossal and atrocious war. And the Church of Christ cannot fail to incur reproach and neglect unless it be relaid from the foundations. It stands by; it looks on—aimless, helpless, paralysed; convicted of failure to a degree that all the heresies in its history could not have caused. True, it mitigates suffering by beneficent ministration; but it did nothing to prevent the nations from flying at one another's throats, and has been impotent in all its efforts to restore peace. Time was when the Church made and unmade wars. Today it is a proven bankrupt, an all but negligible factor. And we have in Christianity, as at present understood, very little guarantee that the world may not at any time lapse into the barbarism and paganism of a war of extermination.''

It is common knowledge that this "failure" has been canvassed throughout Europe, from Lambeth Palace to the Holy Synod of Moscow. The American Churches have felt it keenly, and are striving for unity with a view to the brotherhood of nations and the prevention of future strife. Thirty communions, with eighteen million adherents, now form a Federal Council, with committees of wide range from the liquor-laws to relations with Japan. The immigrant is taken in hand; so are divorce and labour conditions, farm life, home and foreign missions, corrupt politics, the Lord's day, slum tenements, and the physical and moral well-being of America at large. Yet somehow these efforts lack "punch"—to use an expressive Americanism. Or if they have it, the country is too huge, too busy with doing, to straighten up and reflect upon ghostly things. After all, to get ahead is the principal goal; and the greatest of sins is the Greek one of missing the mark.

No complex philosophy sways this people; no hierarchal dogma of life and death, destiny and evolution. American clerics are in no way dismayed by the spectacle that met Newman as he considered the world, its various history and the races of men. "Their mutual alienation, their conflicts . . . the disappointments of life, the defeat of Good, the success of Evil; physical pain, mental anguish, the prevailing intensity of Sin—all this is a vision to dizzy and appal, and inflicts upon the mind a sense of profound mystery which is absolutely without solution.''

The American saint has no such worry, for his primary concern is with social salvation here and now. Quite likely, his church has a library and a gymnasium; a swimming-pool too, with billiard and card saloons—even a "spooning parlour" where a lad may woo his sweetheart under the smiling eyes of the parson's lady. There is music and laughter over all; the oxygen of good fellowship is here infused, and the church community rejoices in it. The perfect pastor of such a flock is Dr. Henry M. Edmonds of Birmingham, Ala.—a fearless hustler with a world of sympathy in his glance. Differing with the Presbyterian Board on Old Testament tales, on Sunday games, and the question of drink, Dr. Edmonds founded a church of his own, which even the negroes may attend. Here local ministry reaches out to the mines and gaols, as well as to the roaring industrial plants of this great steel city of the South.

A trained nurse instructs poor mothers in infant care, and milk is supplied by the church funds. The men of the congregation have in their minister a business friend and adviser. On certain days Dr. Edmonds sits in a downtown office as the father confessor of traders in trouble. And the city pays tribute to his skill in freeing people from financial toils. It will therefore be seen that American religion has little interest in wingy mysteries or omens of terror come down to us from far-off times. Superstition is largely confined to the alien and coloured races; it is also a pastime in the more lavish "native" circles. For the Newport cottagers have "recourse to them that have familiar spirits, and unto wizards that peep and mutter." No modish gathering is quite complete without its Eastern mage installed in a tent on the lawn.

The masses display a mild interest in theoretical science. Sunday supplements of the newspaper will have an astronomical feature in which this earth of ours is belittled as a speck of cosmic dust, with joys and woes too insignificant for words when considered *sub specie æternitatis*. How the sun is a million times bigger than our globe. How Arcturus is fifty thousand times greater again, and so remote that light takes two hundred years to reach us, though travelling at a speed equal to the New York-London journey and back in the twentieth part of a second. This is excellent high-brow stuff, and fetches an appropriate price from the Sunday editor.

In one corner of the page are vague creepy-crawlies; in the other a portrait of the cheerless Haeckel, or even Sir Oliver Lodge, whose views upon Death and Survival provide the American ghost story of today. The higher physiology sets out soundy theses on "Vitalism," "Materialism," and the like. It accounts for everything; presenting a surgical case in the Crucifixion of Christ, Who is said to have died "from pericarditis with effusion, accelerated by the javelin-wound." Or again, here are ingenious bridges built by science between the microscopic amœba and the higher man, represented by Dr. Wilson and Mr. Edison. The gap is abysmal, of course, but the Sunday caterer is equal to it. From the ape to Plato is conceded to be a long, long way; but is it any longer than that from Clausewitz to William Jennings Bryan?

A palæolithic fashion-page will show the flounced robes, the jackets and jewels and sashes, of faded ladies painted æons ago in the Cretan caves. There is also a column of sanitary science, with diagrams from the palaces of Minoan priest-kings. All this makes first-rate reading in the Sunday *American*, whose editor draws the salary of a Cabinet Minister. The secular religion of these people reacts upon their literature, and the two must be considered together. It is the religion of that scientific inquirer who recently stated his aim as follows:—"To make discoveries which shall, bit by bit, add to the interpretable, subtract from the incomprehensible, enlarge the practicable, and thus improve our estate upon earth—that is, if we have the good sense not to employ our invention to worsen it."

The scientist may tell quaint tales of men's arboreal

ancestry. It is quite possible, he will declare in the Sunday paper, that the primate stock came of Therapsid reptilians which had become bipedal, and perhaps arboreal. Now here is a dandy opening for the write-up man of Mr. Hearst's papers. That artist makes ready an impressive page which appears in a whole chain of journals from Boston to Chicago and thence to Los Angeles on the Pacific.

"Arboreal uprightness came first,"—the ingenious writer makes this his foundation. And he builds as he goes, boosting the half-human monster who is already three parts Man in column four of the yarn and is still growing —like the giant at the fair.

The arboreal climber is hunted through æons of time, and the reader's imagination aided in the process by photos of baboons from the Bronx Zoo. The creature's fore-limb is soon a mobile arm, his hand a plastic instrument for grasping, hanging on, reaching ahead and catching hold. Thus early in human history does acquisitiveness appear; and from this stage to the portraits of Carnegie and Rockefeller is only a matter of a column and a half. There is a big public for pseudo-scientific stuff of this kind. But the moral is America's unfaltering faith in man. It inspires all the pink thought and the philosophy of smiles; it is the secret of impatience with nescience and pessimism of every shade. No doubt the world-war has jarred this fond belief. America herself is plunged into the orgy with armed establishments on the grand scale such as will not pass when Peace reigns again in a sore and smoking world.

For all that, the United States is slow to put off her rosy glasses. She finds comfort in the optimism of Speucer that, in some way or other, a future race of men will become automatically moral. Among the foremost thinkers one finds a soul-state of agnostic stoicism. They pick to pieces the older Christianity; they examine dogma by the glare of guns, and recite in No Man's Land the sublime paradoxes of Christ. Their demand is for a lowlier cultus, one more in accord with human suffering and sin; a religion of mutual aid and earthly understanding, to be clasped and woven into the day's work, and not writ in the starry unattainable. "I have the sense of these things," the American says with Saint-Beuve, "but not the things themselves."

They are not other-worldly, these high-brows of the United States; they hold, with the late William James of Harvard, that "true ideas are those we can assimilate, validate, corroborate, and verify." There is the same pragmatist appeal to experience and the individual, the same self-abandonment to life and the experiment it entails in contact with reality. Not long ago Professor J. H. Leuba, of Bryn Mawr College, sent out test questions upon religion to a thousand men, all more or less distinguished in physical science as well as in sociology, history, and psychology. The results were published in Dr. Leuba's work: *The Belief in God and Immortality;* and the effect on the reader's mind is to persuade him that American leaders are in the main freethinkers, or at all events unorthodox and various to a degree.

The sombre Haeckel of Jena preaches the beauty of resignation to the hap of chance—a brave acceptance of the unavoidable in a scheme of things where heedless Nature for ever makes and breaks with a futility which eludes our scrutiny. To the American mind this is monstrous. The scientist that counts over there is the "sensible" man. Why should the electrician waste his time chasing the positive ions when he could send high voltage to the Californian vine and kill the costly blight of phylloxera?

It is now asked of Science that she leave ineffable problems, and fall in for service at home or abroad. Let the chemist drop his molecules and try to abolish famine by laboratory research. Let the inventor abandon liquid air and solar heat, to get busy with farm tractors, and a mechanical cotton-picker which shall catch the lint and leave unripe bolls on the uninjured plant. Such gear as this might be the making of the South, and free her from economic slavery to the negro whom she abhors.

I may say that bodily soundness has a literature of its own; the present year will see six hundred books on medicine and hygiene published in the United States. How is a sick man to go on thinking pink in the traditional American way? Systems and theories are set out for him by experts like Professor Irving Fisher of Yale, Chairman of the Hygiene Board; Dr. Eugene Fisk, of the Life Extension Institute; Dr. G. W. Crile, of the Cushman Laboratory; and Dr. Robert Morris, whose *Microbes and Men* tells how bilious folks are despondent because the "sad" germs—the colon bacilli—are too well fed and swarming in the intestine. "I never think of Nietzsche or Schopenhauer as philosophers," Dr. Morris says, "but only as afflicted men expressing the toxins of anaerobic bacteria."

There are books and pamphlets against dope and drugs; stoke-up counsel for the high-speed job, with a few words from Edison at the start, and much about Mithridates—a hero who, it seems, had Jim Farrell's memory, the stamina of a Texan jack, and the devil's own flair for dodging poisons in his food. The foreigner wilts at last under this literature of health, with its fusillade of Do's and Dont's from every department of life; baby's bottle and the garbage-can, the papering of rooms, the licking of postage stamps, the swatting of flies, and the cuspidor or spittoon, which is by no means banished from America in 1918.

There are national laws about food; State laws, the laws of towns and cities and private concerns. The New York Department of Health scatters far and wide free booklets in English and Yiddish; there are lectures and movie-shows on eugenics, genetics, and dietetics. Sickness, one gathers, will soon be a crime; a clear century of active life is claimed as the birthright of every citizen.

With all this incitement it is no wonder that quackery flourishes, from the Park Avenue palace to a shack in the Kentucky hills; from the New York surgeon of costly stunts down to "ole Aunt Lize," the herbal witch, with her dog-fennel and weird roots, her toads and snake-skins, cobweb-pills, and charms beyond the Chirurgia Magna of Paracelsus. No civilized nation that I know is so intent upon mending and moulding, training, dosing, and fortifying the horse-power of man. Here in America the drug-store is become a saloon in disguise—one already known as an agency of mischief. It is to the chemist's shop that the citizen turns for free treatment when grit blows into his eye on the gusty street. Here also he can buy stamps, or use the telephone while his wife and the girls sip iced drinks at the soda-fountain. But Congress has no illusions about the drug-store, its tonics and bitters, its remedies, cordials, elixirs and compounds. Many of these contain a high percentage of alcohol, and sell the more freely as prohibition laws are pushed to fanatical extremes.

Representative Meeker of Missouri shocked the Lower House with a list of 746 patent medicines that warmed the cockles of the heart, if they did nothing else. More than half of them were twenty per cent. alcohol; a few were as high as ninety per cent. It is not to the ailing, but to tipplers that these nostrums appeal, and the rogues who sell them manœuvre skilfully between the vast complex of State laws. Then the question of drug addiction grows more and more serious, apart from the bracer and pick-me-up of the business man. I refer particularly to the craving for morphine, heroin, and cocaine which is found among all classes, from the rich *flâneuse* of Newport and New

York to the "bad nigger" of New Orleans: his whisky trade vanished when a raid on the fruit-storer disclosed quart bottles of rye inside noble pumpkins priced at $1.60 each.

I began to fear, after residence and research in the United States, that pink thinking is not so much a native trait as a defensive armour for life's battle—that it was, in fact, no spontaneous aura, but a rather hard exaction; an implicit law punished in the breach and favoured in the observance.

It is true, as Bacon noted, that "the pencil of the Holy Ghost hath laboured more in describing the afflictions of Job than the felicities of Solomon." But such pencils are gaily edited in this New World. Even its early Puritanism, as Professor Channing reminds us, was not so much a system of theology as an attitude of mind. It was "idealism applied to the solution of contemporary problems." No doubt the war, with all its attendant change, will modify this passion, though to what extent it is yet too early to determine. Up to now, religion, philosophy, and literature have all been tinged with betterment and the uplift of man; the elimination of pain, of unnecessary labour and those tiresome chores which swallow up the good time and cloud our little span of life. In America the greatest doctors, psychologists, and men of science seek the limelight as popular writers, and contribute their quota to the Greek "full" of joy which is the national goal.

Here a familiar theme is the triumph of great men over physical infirmities. These range from the stomach troubles of John Rockefeller to the fatness of Roscoe Arbuckle, that merry monster of 320 pounds, who makes $100,000 a year as a movie-star. Fatty Arbuckle's grin lights up the billboards for three thousand miles; and the secrets of success were wrung from him for the benefit of lesser men. "If work and worry could have made me

thin," he told the sympathetic reporters, "I guess you'd be
hunting for Fatty this minute with a microscope!"

Or here again is *An Autobiography* by Edward L.
Trudeau, M.D. Certainly the American spirit shines
throughout. At two and twenty this man broke down
with tuberculosis. He fought hard for every day he lived,
"contemplating the ceiling" from his bed for twenty years.
At sixty-three Dr. Trudeau died, after saving thousands
of lives and building the greatest open-air sanatorium in
the West. His *Autobiography* is pink unto shrillness, with
insistence upon every page that your true conqueror is he
who fights with a broken sword. "The fellow who's fully
equipped," the author maintains, "has no battle on his
hands, but only a walk-over."

Here is the *religio poetæ* of the United States. This is
the laughing mask with which America covers the sinister
face of things. Every singer warbles the "Excelsior" note.
No vicious panders of the Martial type are these poets; no
bitter Juvenals, no doleful bards in the sombre black of
Tasso, but blithe zealots like Willard Wattles of Kansas,
who hails a new constructive Christ amid the rippling
leagues of wheat and green-bannered corn of the Sunflower
State:

> "Who art thou, Carpenter,
> Of the bowed head?—
> And what buildest thou?
> 'Heaven,' He said."

One must know these regional poets if the real America
is to be gauged. I consider Vachell Lindsay of Illinois
a more "American" voice than any Anacreon of New York
who only sings of love. Lindsay is a truer index to the
seething of the giant Pot than all the mannered *vers
libristes* of the East. Sectional poets now confine their
fancy to homely themes, as Edgar Lee Masters did in his
Spoon River lyrics. The prairie town now glows with

unwonted splendour. In his "Springfield Magical," Mr. Lindsay finds mystery and glamour in prosaic streets; the American city is to the poet what Florence was to Dante, or Shiraz to the rosy hedonism of Hafiz:—

> "In this, the City of my Discontent,
>   Sometimes there comes a whisper from the grass,
>   'Romance—Romance is *here!*' No Hindu town,
>   Is quite so strange. No citadel of Brass
>   By Sindbad found held half such love and hate,
>   No picture-palace in a picture-book ⁻
>   Such webs of Friendship, Beauty, Greed, and Hate."

Turn where you may in the United States, the desire for sweetness and light is seen.

The uplift is very loud on the Chautauqua platform—that orgy of instruction which may begin with Iroquois tales for the children at ten in the morning, and go on till eight at night, when a lecture on the torpedo's gyroscope winds up an overflowing day. A mushroom city of three hundred souls will have its culture-club. In due time the Browning cult appears, to flower at last into a Shakespeare celebration under the Drama League of Chicago. This is a nation-wide concern, affiliated with hundreds of libraries, universities, and civic societies for both sexes and all America's races.

Today the levelling-up of taste extends from the child's book to the crusade against ugly hoardings which threaten to spoil the new national roads which are being laid from sea to sea. There is the Lincoln Highway, in which twelve States are interested; it will be 3284 miles long, linking New York and San Francisco for the motorist in a direct line. The South plans a Dixie Highway, which will be longer still; the West has more than one such road, notably the scenic stretch known as the Columbia, which runs for two hundred miles through the Cascade Mountains of Oregon.

It was here that the billboard man was warned off. A
new race of æsthetes will have no giant cows shrieking
somebody's milk on the sky-line. No Heinz cans should
disfigure the glorious landscape, no monstrous babe calling
for a favourite food, or forty-foot Fatimas lolling on the
bluffs to boom a famous cigarette. To their credit be it
said that most of the advertisers agreed. A few rebelled,
of course, and set up claimant horror by lake ánd hill and
torrent. But the Oregonians were not to be trifled with.
They turned out in force with flame and violence; moreover, there was to be a boycott of these offending wares.
Tar and feathers haunted the billboard man till he agreed
that Beauty was best—at any rate in the Grape and Apple
State.

I cannot deal at any length with the American stage,
which was so well guarded for forty years by the late
William Winter, the famous critic of the *New York Tribune.*
When this man frowned a play was damned; his favour
had the "Broadway appeal" in it, and fat bank rolls alike
for author and producer. Mr. Winter could be very prudish; he was nearly always pugnacious, loathing "immoral"
themes and scathing them in terms that shocked his milder
brethren. This despot had a horror of Ibsen; he set his
face against most of the translations—French, German,
and Russian. Not even the acting of W. H. Crane could
save a comedy of Octave Mirbeau, though it bore the
promising title *Business Is Business.* Here the play itself
passed the Puritan muster, but it was a sombre theme
of bitter unjoyous aspect, therefore success was impossible.

Everybody knows that men of genius are appreciated in
the United States. The famous painter is made much of
there; so is the tenor of lyric passion, the pianist of rhapsodic fireworks, the Wunderkind who takes the town by
storm with a Guarnerius violin and a Tourte bow that
would tame the devil himself.

It is curious how these high priests of art take to the dollars, however dreamy and unworldly they may be at home: America has no illusions upon this score. A picturesque alien of renown was offered $40,000 for eight concerts at which none but the So and So piano was to be used. Did the musician accept it? He did, although none too gladly. The great man's face, we learn from the cynics, fell "like a cook-book cake," for he thought the fee was to have been bigger. "He'd play on a tin kettle if you made it worth his while," the agent confessed with shocking frankness. No wonder the American humorist considers music "the most expensive of noises." But even he agrees that America will hire the world's foremost artists at any price—the sculptor, the designer of dress; the Slav boy-fiddler with a left hand of flawless magic, such as draws tears down the iron cheek of Success and raises to life the spiritual death which is Vulgarity.

A generation ago Matthew Arnold gave high-brow counsel to the United States where he perceived an inveterate drift towards commonness. "What the Americans most urgently require," their superior visitor said, "is a steady exhibition of cool and sane criticism." In this matter Arnold himself led the way, quoting Goethe's warning against mob-movement and excessive homage to King Demos and his noisy train: the Americans, our apostle of culture found, had too much esteem for the average man and deferred unduly to his wishes. Their Press was "an awful symptom," their education of the "brisk and flourishing" variety, which the critic feared was "more than doubtful" in results.

Matthew Arnold praised Emerson for his roseate views, but he was afraid they went too far. Nor did the English visitor agree with the Ohio lady who found Syrian roses on each common bush, and excellence in lavish riot. On the contrary, Arnold held that "excellence dwells among rocks hardly accessible, and a man must always wear out his heart before he can reach her." That is the lesson which is being driven home today. And as the old illusions wither, a new hope grows that the reconstructed world will find in American ideals that "moral equivalent for war" which William James desired.

"Each one of us literally chooses," the American philosopher said, "by his ways of attending on things, what sort of a universe he shall appear to himself to inhabit." From the first America's choice was a goodly Eden which no serpentry could wholly spoil. It is unlikely that pink thinking will easily pass or that this people will be quickly convicted of error in its radiant creed. You may demonstrate the futility of it; you may point to ravening war as a proof of incurable evil. But America will always cut you short with her eager Browning outburst: "Ah, but a man's reach should exceed his grasp—or what's heaven for?"

CHAPTER XV

THE WORLD MUST BE SAFE FOR DEMOCRACY

"By the rubbish in our wake, and the noble noise we make,
Be sure, be sure we're going to do some splendid things!"

IT is in no flippant vein that I set down these lines of Kipling. Every American knows how well they express the hub-bub and friction of official Washington in the time of Preparation for war. The fervid clamour for Congress and its advisers, the prodding and protest of newspapers, the shrilling of cranks and patriots in conflict with wiser counsels; the efforts of willing or wilful men, no doubt in earnest, but still a real hindrance, no less harmful than the plot and rumour of German agents and tools. There was uproar everywhere; a cheery tumult in which everybody fed the flames with such fuel as he had, until responsible men called a halt in the anxious riot. "Less shindies and more ships," was the shrewd appeal in this distracting season.

America groped and staggered after splendid things without regret for the unfamiliar mists enfolding them. An unmartial people was now rough-hewing Armies and equipping Navies of the sea and air for service abroad against the most warlike people of all. These things democracy must do in its own way, imbibing discipline in doubtful gulps as it floundered into battle. This is naturally the way of blunders; our own Prime Minister hinted as much when he drew America's attention to Britain's unready record and the lessons it afforded the latest champion of our cause.

In all ages leaders have complained about Liberty's

273

legions; they are hard to handle, and apt to become tyrannous in a crisis. History teems with instances of this, from the city-State of ancient Greece to the Ireland of Sinn Fein and the tragi-comic violence of revolutionary Russia. The trials of Cromwell and Washington come back to us now with new force. Danton's struggle with the Girondins and Lincoln's with his ''Copperheads'' have a parallel in Kerensky's stand against the Bolsheviki that overthrew him.

As for America, it is plain that the early Fathers put no great faith in the common people. Richard Henry Lee was all for a ''regulated liberty, so that the ends and principles of society may not be disturbed by the fury of the mob.'' Jefferson was anxious to curb the supremacy of the new Legislature. ''One hundred and seventy-three despots,'' the famous democrat was afraid, ''would surely be as oppressive as One.'' It was to guard against these perils that the State Constitutions were provided with elaborate checks based upon the division of power favoured by Montesquieu. Hence a curious distinction between Constitutional and Statute law, such as is unknown in our own polity; it has given peculiar authority to the Judges, who replaced the Legislatures as the ultimate guardians of popular liberty.

In 1911 President Wilson, then Governor of New Jersey, spoke very plainly on this subject. ''If we felt,'' he said, ''that we had genuine representation in our State Legislatures, no one would propose the 'Initiative' and 'Refercudum' in America. They are now being proposed as a means of bringing our representatives back to the consciousness that what they are bound in duty and policy to do is to represent the sovereign people whom they profess to serve, and not the private interests which creep into their councils by way of machine orders and committee conferences.''

The past few years have seen astonishing reforms. Thus the Non-Partisan League swept North Dakota with a Socialist demand for public utilities under State control— grain-elevators and milk supplies; markets and slaughter-houses, with hail-insurance for the farmer and rural credits on a new ingenious basis. So drastic a program called for alteration in the State Constitution, but this has already become a mania with the Commonwealths.

This appetite for change, together with the lingering sectionalism of the continent, accounts in part for the war-time confusion that raged in Washington. Certainly the men in authority were aware of the peril of this tumult; witness the humorous inversion of President Wilson's dictum by Governor McCall of Massachusetts— ''Democracy must be made safe for the world!'' Individualism was well enough in the abstract; it was mere suicide when face to face with the German *Wille zu Macht,* intent upon conquest and exploration. Here the collapse of Russia was cited, and America's millions rallied to militancy for Freedom's sake. At one time the Eastern States rebuked the West for an alleged war apathy—which was said to put the Mississippi Valley ''behind the field-kitchens'' of the battle-line. They were a flabby folk, out there, provincial and pacifist, sodden with selfishness and materialism; pro-Germans, flush-timers, and the like. I quote the ironic comments of the West when the recruiting records had turned the tables upon those censors of the Atlantic coast.

It was Alfred Zimmermann, the German Foreign Minister, who stirred the trans-Alleghany farmers to vivid wrath with the egregious letter he wrote to Von Eckhardt, his envoy in Mexico City. In this' it was suggested that President Carranza should seek the aid of Japan, and then with German backing make an onslaught upon the United States with a view to the reconquest of ''lost territory in New Mexico, Arizona, and Texas." America was staggered at this. Her irrepressible humorists fell mute in the face of a perfidy that jarred the nation into vengeful unity overnight.

That letter was in President Wilson's hands when Bethmann Hollweg was cooing about those "friendly relations with the United States which have come down as a heritage from Frederick the Great." Zimmermann dates his letter January 19, 1917. And twelve days later Johann von Bernstorff handed Mr. Lansing a Note in which the following appears: "The German people repudiate all alliances which serve to force the nations into a competition for power, or to involve them in a net of selfish intrigue."

The Zimmermann letter was the most dramatic discovery of the war, so far as America was concerned.

It was a God-send to President Wilson, for it grappled the West to him as nothing else could have done. For the first time "America's war" lowered up on ranch and prairie with searching blast. It was Prussian intrigue that stiffened Wilson's Reply to the Pope's Note. "We cannot take the word of the present rulers of Germany as a guarantee of anything that is to endure. . . . Treaties of settlement, agreements for disarmament, covenants to set up arbitration in the place of force; territorial adjustments, reconstitutions of small nations, if made with the German Government, no man, no nation, could now depend on." When was a great Empire so branded and shamed? And how startling was the confirmation found in those "Willy-Nicky" telegrams of 1904, published by the *New York Herald*. In them was a plot aimed by the Kaiser at "the Anglo-Saxon group."

Next came the frigid orders for wholesale murder sent by Count Luxburg from Buenos Aires with secret Swedish aid. There was also Baron von Rautenfels. This man arrived at Christiania with two hundred bombs in his baggage, and Foreign Office seals to ensure their use in sinking ships and drowning non-combatants at sea. America was bewildered. So the German Emperor, his envoys abroad, his officers on land and afloat—what were they all but a gang of callous Thugs for whom the rope and shot-gun of the lynching party were altogether too mild a fate? The Republic was awake at last; aware of her own danger too, and very angry indeed.

Her first Army in France represented every element in the United States, from the alien volunteer to the millionaire conscript. The students of Yale were there with The Bowery toughs, Virginian planters, Rocky Mountain miners, and lumber-men of the North-West. There were stock-riders, and stockbrokers; there were Red Indians—like F. W. Riches, a full-blood Cherokee of Oklahoma, who was already a *decorée* of France and a noted flier since 1914. Lieut. O. Loft, in charge of the redskin Forest Service in France, was himself a chief of the Mohawk tribe; the Sixth Wisconsin Regiment had whole platoons of Chippewas from the Lac Courte Oreilles Reservation.

So the revolution was complete, confounding the prophets and politicians. There was no frothy rage or red fire. "We go into it gravely," said the *New York Times*. "Our mood of 1917 is not that of 1898 (the Spanish-American War). Yet America's mood in 1917 is that of France in 1914: our enemy can take no comfort from the fact." There is no desire to impress unwilling soldiers, the ideal of a consecrated army was emblazoned on the first recruiting banners—"Be a Went, Not a Sent!" In his hints to the Exemption Boards President Wilson defined the delicate duties entrusted to them, between "the most sacred rights of the individual and the untarnished honour of the nation." "Our armies at the front," he felt, "will be strengthened and sustained if they be composed of men free from any sense of injustice in their mode of selection." And to this end the draft system was altered again and again.

The margin of man-power was immense. There are in the United States 22,000,000 males of militia age—that is, between eighteen and forty-five. No more than five per cent. of these were to be called until the establishments were ready for more. Objectors who quoted the "involuntary servitude" clause of the Thirteenth Amendment to the Constitution were reminded that this did not apply to soldiering in time of national stress. There were Exemption Boards for every 30,000 of the population, with the right of appeal to a Board of Review in each Federal District. Civil servants and divinity students were excused. So was the conscientious objector; the sailor, the artificer, and all industrial and agricultural hands. No man with a wife and child, or other dependents, was enlisted; neither was the resident alien who had not yet taken out his first papers of citizenship.

Of these drifters the last Census showed two and a quarter millions, many of them subjects of Germany, Austria, Turkey, and Bulgaria. A special Act of Congress raked in the Allied nationals for service under their own flags; but on the whole America was disgusted with her *sans-patries*, and pressed for drastic measures against them. "This is a poor time," the shirkers were reminded, "for a man without a country." Freedom was tossing and straining upon stormy seas, so the alien was asked to "bail, row, or go ashore."

I must also mention political influence in the working of the Exemption Boards. Congress was stirred with rancour over the assignment of local quotas according to population. The most startling allegation came from the Northern States. Their spokesmen declared that the Draft Census had been so juggled as to throw a disproportionate burden of service upon them, with a corresponding immunity south of the Mason and Dixon line. So hotly was this grievance pressed that Mr. Samuel Rogers, Director of the Census Bureau, was summoned to the Senate to explain how he arrived at his estimates for 1917, basing them on the returns of 1900 and 1910.

But all this sectional stress—this "oppression" of the North by a Democratic administration—melted away when the President appealed for unity with incomparable dignity and tact. Human freedom was at stake "to be wholly won or meanly lost," as Lincoln said when he stood alone among betrayers, resisting them all. This was no season for fruitless talk. "We have a chance to show," Dr. Wilson urged, "that the principles we profess are living principles; we are glad to pour out our blood and treasure to vindicate these things."

No one in this country, and not many in the United States, have a clear idea of the forces arrayed against the Federal Government in its task of waking the nation's war-will and developing and maintaining its power. For a hundred years America has been a land of refuge, an asylum where Liberty was given extravagant interpretation. And this was treated with lenience till the Day of trial came.

The anti-American forces may be divided into pacifism, Socialism, Irishry, Germanism, indifference, and downright anarchy. All of these—apathy alone excepted—were very noisy; each had its own press and hordes of adherents intent upon clogging the war machine by every known means, from sabotage to wholesale matrimony. The cause of Peace so multiplied its labours as to become unwieldy. Therefore a Clearing-House was formed to co-ordinate the activities of the Emergency Peace Federation, the Church Peace Union, the American Union against Militarism, the Neutral Conference Committee, and the Woman's Peace Party. To the last named that veteran social worker, Jane Addams of Chicago, lent her strenuous aid.

Peace at any price had a backing in the Senate among that "little group of wilful men representing no opinion but their own," whom the President declared had left America "helpless and contemptible in the midst of a crisis of extraordinary peril." I recall this episode as one of the many milestones on the *via dolorosa* of Preparedness. For at last that stormy way grew thick with unlooked-for converts and devotees. There came a time when the mildest of pilgrims preached a Pacifist War against Prussianism. Had not Hoover and Gerard trailed the vileness of it from the slave-pens of Wavre in Brabant to the drear typhus-hell of Wittenberg, where British prisoners died obscenely, crawling with lice and torn by savage dogs? It was a holy and wholesome thing to war with an organized terror which seventy million people backed so long as it promised them power.

Gerard's account of the lawless Kaiser eclipsed that of Ambassador Dana in 1781, when Frederick the Great was flaunting his brazen guns as the last reasoning of force and fraud. Dana considered Frederick "as complete a despot as hath ever been sent into this world for a curse to mankind." It was Frederick's successor who told Gerard that no laws of war existed between the nations—"and to this statement the Chancellor agreed."

To America, therefore, it grew clear that Kaiserism must be stamped out if Freedom was to survive the calculated pounce of 1914. It was a reluctant lesson; but Woodrow Wilson—the "Princeton Professor" of the Berlin satirists—had ten million men in his class when the application of it became an imperious need.

Then was the new America born. Then it was that Bryan himself preached war from the Chautauqua platform —that peculiar vehicle of bourgeois culture in the United States. "The more any one favours peace," the Nebraskan orator said, "the more loyally should he support the Gov-

ernment.'' In Chicago—that stronghold of hyphenism—
Mr. Bryan went much further. ''I've been a pacifist all
my life,'' the ex-Foreign Minister owned in a famous apologia; ''but the sort of peace I'm after is one that lasts.
There's only one way to attain it now, so we should all get
together and fight the devil!'' Here also was Henry Ford,
of peace-ark fame, ''prepared to go to the limit in this
struggle.''

But the unlikeliest of all belligerents was surely the Peace
Society, which rallied to ''the cause of humanity at large'';
its placid organ, *The Advocate,* was now hailed as a good
loser by the laic press. ''If our members,'' *The Advocate*
said, ''can conscientiously engage in active service they will
do so; if not, they will lend their efforts behind the firing
line. . . . We must all help in the bayoneting of a normally
decent German in order to free him from the tyranny which
he at present accepts as his chosen form of government.''

This change of heart was mainly a domestic process. It
owed little or nothing to Allied suasion, and a great deal to
American pacifists employed on relief work in all the zones
of havoc from the Danube to the Meuse. This is not the
place to speak of benevolence which covered Europe and
crossed over into Asia at Beirut to keep the Syrians from
starving. American Jews heard the Kadish or prayer of
mourning from the Polish provinces. They replied with
millions of dollars, as well as with foodstuffs and warm
clothing, doctors, nurses, and business administrators.
The same work went on in stricken Serbia, in Albania and
Montenegro, in Flanders and Northern France, where ''the
kiddies'' were crying; their cries reached the Iowa prairie,
where the Farmer's Acre was soon sacred to their wants.

Americans engaged in relief work took dreadful testimony home with them, when they went to report or appeal
for funds on the lecture platform. Take Vernon Kellogg,
Director of the Belgian Commission in the two neutral

years of war. He is Professor of Biology at Leland Stanford University, and as fervid a peace-man as his colleague, Dr. David Starr Jordan. No man living has seen Prussianism in the raw as Victor Kellogg has, from Warsaw in the East to Great Headquarters at Charleville, where he was the guest of German officers of all grades—the veteran general and the subaltern of eighteen straight from Heidelberg with sabre-slashed face. Here, then, was unique opportunity to seize the German point of view, the perverted *Weltanschauung* which had strewn the earth with corpses and now skimmed the baby's milk for explosive glycerine.

"The discussions," Dr. Kellogg says, "would begin at dinner and last far into the night. As we talked we tried to understand each other." But Deutschheit, the American concludes, "will never allow any land controlled by it to exist peacefully beside a people governed according to our ideals." The guest perceived in his hard-drinking hosts "a whole-hearted acceptance of the worst of neo-Darwinism—the *Allmacht* of natural selection rigorously applied to all human life, society and Kultur.". . . "I was convinced that this war must be fought to a finish which will determine whether or not the German system is to rule the world." It was for this reason that the Director of Belgian Relief went home a converted man—"an ardent supporter," he was careful to say, "not of war, but of *this* War." It was a distinction that spread like a flame. Not without protest, however, from "those dangerous elements," as President Wilson called them, "who hide their disloyalty behind a screen of specious and evasive words."

So numerous were these, so reckless and determined in anarchy, that I can only outline their malignity. The draft-resisters of Central Oklahoma called themselves the Working Class Union. They were a serious trial to Governor R. L. Williams of the Wonder-State, for they enlisted " bad niggers," Indians, and alien tenant farmers, in a league of terror that flashed through three of the wilder counties. It may be well to remind the reader that in the United States a regular police force is unknown outside the larger cities; so that sparsely-settled regions have to rely upon the Sheriff and his civilian posse, who are too often a law unto themselves. This is one of the root causes of lynching.

Cranks of a tamer breed invaded Minnesota under Louis Lochner, of Peace-Ark notoriety; this man claimed to speak for two million workers. Lochner's convention was vetoed by Governor Burnquist, who declared "it would have no other effect than to aid and abet our enemies." So all facilities were denied. Herr Lochner's train—the "White Rabbit Special"—rolled back and forth in vain quest of asylum for the so-called People's Council. The hotelkeepers of Milwaukee and St. Paul closed their doors against the party. At last Lochner's followers were asked to bring their own tents, as well as pots and pans, for a desert meeting far from the tyrannous crowd.

The Socialists were truculent and shrill till the Federal Government handled them roughly. Their bosses were Morris Hillquit (born in Russia), Victor Berger (born in Austria), Julius Gerber, and Boris Reinstein—the delegate to Stockholm whose passport was at last rescinded. The passing of Conscription caused disruption in the Socialist ranks. Real Americans like Upton Sinclair, Allan Benson, and J. S. Phelps Stokes broke away from the party. A very able member, Charles E. Russell, was expelled for going to Russia with Elihu Root's Mission. Therefore little was left but a cultus of pro-Germanism upon which the Department of Justice descended with a heavy hand, because of its treasonous propaganda. Irish-American editors were now ordered to refrain from attacks upon England, whom the United States had joined in Democracy's war. The Irish also were divided. Patrick Egan, a former Minister to Chile, charged John Devoy, the editor of the *Gaelic-American*, with plotting the Dublin Rebellion with the aid of German money, as well as exporting arms and ammunition in defiance of American neutrality.

It is certain that Anglophobia of this kind passed decent bounds. The "flag of the Irish Republic" was presented to Lieut. Wacker, of the U-53, who sank ships in American waters. "We shall hoist this flag in honour of Ireland," the assassin said as his boat left, "when we sink the next English ship." Folly of this kind added to President Wilson's burden. The Clan-na-Gael orators cried "Death to England!" from a soap-box at the street corner. The Irish-American press preached open sedition; at a hyphenate meeting in New York, an officer of the Irish Volunteers struck a reporter with his sword because the man refused to rise when "Die Wacht am Rhein" was played by the orchestra.

All this faction was unanimously condemned; American common sense would have none of it. "It is incomprehensible to me," the President said, "how any frank or honest person can doubt or question my position with regard to this war and its objects. . . . I can conceive no purpose in seeking to becloud the matter, except the purpose of weakening our hands and making the part we are to play in this great struggle for human liberty an inefficient and hesitating part."

Mayor Mitchel of New York, himself the grandson of an outlawed Irish patriot—forbade anti-Ally speeches, and refused police protection to Jeremiah O'Leary and other firebrands of the Clan-na-Gael. Of course, mob fights ensued. An Irish captain of police gave an order to his Irish squad—and the New York streets beheld civil war of a new kind, with citizen "Vigilantes" aiding the forces of order against the Clan-na-Gael mob. Mr. T. P. O'Connor poured oil upon these troubled waters. Ex-Ambassador

Gerard (whose life was threatened in Chicago) told the Irish that their pro-German leaning would change to fury if they could but see the camp at Limburg where "Irish prisoners are dying of starvation and tuberculosis." . . . He got secret news that the Prussian Guards were shooting and killing their Irish captives. One prisoner was killed whilst Mr. Gerard was inquiring into the murder of another. "There is no telling how many were shot down by their custodians." This was after the fiasco of Roger Casement's recruiting visit.

Meanwhile "America first" was a national watchword of rising sternness. Again and again the President insisted upon unity of aim; the gigantic conflict he was directing would (he declared) not only remove the last vestige of difference between North and South, but also "any lines, of race or association, cutting athwart the great body of the nation." He met hindrance still, however, from the Senate Chamber to far Viatka in Russia, where returned emigrants were abusing America and a democratic régime which, these renegades vowed, was more cruel and tyrannical than any Tsardom. These Russo-Americans did much to nullify Mr. Root's Mission; the Bolsheviki were told it was nothing but "a Wall Street venture conducted by the Chief Tory of the country."

Impatient people in Paris and London knew little of the dark forces with which President Wilson was battling. He had the Press on his side, however. The intellectuals hailed him as America's Man of Destiny; the ideal Executive whom Lowell pictured years ago—"so gently guiding public sentiment that he seems to follow it; so instinctively grasping the temper and prejudices of the people as to make them gradually conscious of his own superior wisdom." Wilson's opportunity was now declared greater than that of Washington or Lincoln. The saviour of the Union, it was pointed out, was at first thought a White

House misfit by reason of his rough exterior and backwoods breeding. On the other hand, it was as a high-brow that Wilson was mistrusted. How should a book-worm steer forty-eight rugged and striving Commonwealths through the storms ahead? What sort of President should an historian make when the world was aflame?—a man of letters, a fine gentleman, and no mob-orator at all? Yet hearken to his voice in the thunder's mouth: ''Woe be to the man or group of men that seeks to stand in our way in this Day of high resolution, when every principle we hold dearest is to be vindicated and made secure for the salvation of all!''

The foes at home were more difficult to deal with than any foreign enemy. Their tactics changed from day to day. Their tools and catspaws were Protean shadows sheltered by State laws; it was impossible to disentangle motives in treason's twilight zone. The German Embassy, we know, was the headquarters of a dynamite diplomacy. It was efficient in its way and spent tens of millions in wicked work ranging from alarmist rumours to infernal machines. Three thousand miles off, in San Francisco, Consul-General Bopp and the Saxon Attaché, Von Brincken, were hiring bombers at $300 a month and a bonus on each successful job—say a ship bound for Vladivostok or a train-load of horses for the Allies, bridges and tunnels on the railways; munition works, warehouses, and docks. The forces of Deutschtum were at one time blatant, at any rate in the German-American journals, of which there were not less than four hundred and fifty in the United States. I fancy these misread the average hyphenate; he was wary and prudent throughout, and sat on the fence, mindful of his stake in the richest of countries. Ninety per cent. of him came down on the American side, leaving a band of plotters, incendiaries, and strike-fomenters upon whom Chief

Justice Covington moved with all the might of the Federal Government.

The fact should not be forgotten that America is partly German, and that, however loud hyphenate loyalty may be, there remains an alien menace of great boldness and sway, shifting with the fortune of war and current feeling in the Fatherland. There were spies in the White House itself, as the leakage of the Wilson Peace Note showed. The Naval Affairs Committee of the Senate were told by Secretary Daniels that important letters had been stolen from confidential files of the Ordnance Bureau. Senators Tillman and Chamberlain, men high in the War Council, admitted the daring and success of traitors; no military or industrial secret could be hidden from them. The German hope—as Secretary Lane expressed it—"of mastering the world by high explosive and low intrigue," was luridly pursued in America, which offered unique scope and immunity.

The hyphenate danger was complicated by the dual allegiance sanctioned by Paragraph 25 of the German Citizen Law, passed by the Bundesrath and Reichstag and made effective on January 1, 1914. This measure—*semel Germanus semper Germanus*—superseded the old law of 1870, whereby nationality was lost after ten years' residence abroad, or by declaring fealty to a foreign State. The new Bill was framed by Baron von Richthofen, who explained that "it permitted Germans who, for motives of an economic kind are compelled to acquire a foreign nationality, to retain at the same time their *Reichsangehoerigkeit*." Of course this duality nullifies the Bancroft Treaty, and establishes a conflict which, as Senator Lodge pointed out to State Secretary Lansing, "is contrary to American law and incompatible with our oath of allegiance."

The President was also troubled by labour violence of an anarchic type, and by the high-handed methods of State

Governors in suppressing it. I refer especially to that outlawed body, the Industrial Workers of the World, whose
organ declares that: "Property, whether material or in
the form of specialized labour, has ceased to exist for the
proletariat."

The I. W. W., as this singular body is called, works with
bomb and torch and terrorism. "They can't stop us," was
the boast of Boss Heywood. "We—the rough-necks of the
world—will go on till we take control of all production,
working how and when we please. The man who makes
the wagon shall ride in it himself." Another leader hoped
the I. W. W. "would keep the soldiers so busy in the industrial centres of the West, that they'll have no time to fight
the Germans." There was warfare in the Desert States,
and it is worth while to consider it if one is to grasp the
bewildering complexity of American conditions. Twelve
strikes were engineered in the anthracite coal regions.
Anti-conscription literature was freely circulated, together
with pamphlets urging riot and gaol delivery for the men
who had refused to register for military service. In South
Dakota vast grain-fields were mapped out with a view to
burning the crops; and Food Controller Hoover had the
grain-elevators of the State protected with barbed wire
and armed guards.

"There's the devil to pay out here," came across the
Rockies to New York. "Strikes reasonable and unreason-
able occur, and they spread and multiply. Fires have been
started, and wells poisoned. Helpless workers are stoned
and beaten. Treason is openly preached. Our Army is
reviled; and soap-box orators, foaming with anarchy, are
bedevilling the cow-town communities." Federal officers
conferred with Samuel Gompers, of the Labour Federation,
and it was proved that German money backed the wickedest
designs. At seditious meetings a portrait of Karl Marx
would be displayed, with his favourite motto in many lan-

guages: "Workers, unite! You have only your chains to lose and a world to win."

There was never at any time a genuine Labour movement against the President's plans. On the contrary, Labour stood behind the Government "like a stone wall," as James Duncan said, "in its fight against autocracy."

Meanwhile the President, radiant in summer garb, and carrying a big flag, led his early conscripts from the Peace Monument to the White House. Here he addressed them from the reviewing-stand with his usual sense of fitness and felicity. "The eyes of all the world," Dr. Wilson said, "will be upon you, because you are in a special sense the soldiers of freedom." The first half million were soon housed in sixteen model townships, each with 40,000 recruits in training. These and other specialized camps rose as it were miraculously in their chosen sites. At Quantico the Potomac flats and Virginia hills had a new Aldershot set in their midst. Dense woods disappeared, roaring war opened in the tranquil spaces with French and British experts directing it.

At Dayton, O., great farms were obliterated by thousands of teams, and by workmen both black and white. Six weeks saw an aviation camp laid out here, with miles of hangars, acres of machine-shops, barracks, lecture-halls and offices. For the aerial arm alone Congress appropriated $640,000,000. It was in tens of thousands that machines were ordered so as to ensure that "crushing superiority" which the French High Commissioner declared would break the trench deadlock and end the war. Under General G. O. Squier (a formed Attaché in London) aerodromes were built at Mineola, L. I., at Newport News, Pensacola, Detroit, Champaign, and San Diego. Admiral Peary took charge of the Aerial Coast patrol, with its sentinel cordons and squadron stations. The Mexican Border was soon to be made safe in this way. Had not Pershing praised the wings of war that carried his mails over the Sierra Madre from Sonora, and awed the bandit troops of Pancho Villa with a sight of ''yellow hawks that dropped flame from the skies!'' One machine, the General testified, ''was worth more to me than a whole division of infantry.'' There were Allied advisers at Headquarters in Washington—Colonel Rees, R. F. C., a noted English pilot; Lieut. de la Grange, an aerial champion of France, and other aces of renown. The docility of America in all her efforts was a sign to be remarked; her willingness to learn war methods impressed all her foreign teachers, as well as her aptitude in grasping the novel conditions of war.

As for the Navy, President Wilson pointed to vast defensive areas in both oceans, and urged a suitable program with all speed in contracts and construction. A single Bill, passed unanimously by the Lower House, voted $1,500,000,-000 for this purpose alone. It called for capital ships of over 40,000 tons; these include new types like the electric *California,* and giant cruisers of 35 knots mounting 16-in. guns. There are also scout cruisers and coast patrols, submarines of 1000 tons, swift U-boat chasers, as well as seaplanes and dirigibles. New dockyards and naval stations are designed; powder, shells and armour plants, as well as underground oil-tanks at Guantanamo, Pearl Harbour, Puget Sound, San Diego, Mare Island, and Narragansett Bay. An energetic drive is being made to bring the naval *personnel*—ever a weak point—up to 150,000 men. One may soberly say that money is being poured out like water; the first year of war cost America over twenty billion dollars. Merely for destroyers Secretary Daniels has asked Congress for $1,000,000,000.

But money alone will not produce modern warships and trained crews at short notice. Naval construction has up to now been slow and costly in the United States—at all events when compared with British, or even German sources.

From the time Congress authorized the Dreadnought
Oklahoma until she joined the Atlantic Fleet, nearly five
years and a half elapsed. Four years were allowed for the
battle-cruisers, and $16,000,000 for the hull and engines
alone. In many cases private bids from concerns like the
Fore River, the Newport News of Quincy, and Cramps' of
Philadelphia fell through altogether, and Secretary Daniels
had to lay down the ships in the national yards. Then
Hadfield's of Sheffield secured a $3,000,000 order for 14-in.
and 16-in. armour-piercing shells. Their bid was no less
than $200 each below that of the Bethlehem Steel Company
of Pennsylvania. And these Sheffield shells passed the
severest test of the Ordnance Bureau, when fired at plates
turned at an angle of ten degrees, so as to deflect the
striking force.

Of course in these matters it is war-experience that wins.
But America is fast learning on the naval as well as the
military side, adapting and developing her industries and
resources in a style that amazed the foreign missions. The
Japanese Plenipotentiary was greatly impressed by the
titan efforts which America was making ''against the insane
despoiler of our civilization.'' . . . America's will would no
longer be expressed in words alone. To frustrate the submarines, emergency fleets of merchant vessels were put in
hand by the Federal Shipping Board. For this purpose
Congress voted $750,000,000, but the purchase of new
vessels and the commandeering of others took the total
estimates to $1,134,500,000. All the great steel plants—
all the lumber of the South and the North-West, as well as
new armies of skilled labour, were pressed into service under
Admiral W. L. Capps and Mr. E. N. Hurley of Chicago, new
nominees of the President, after inevitable disputes and
delay.

This colossal program was to do more than defeat the
trump card of the Von Tirpitz policy. It would also

revive America's merchant marine, which may be said to have passed with the Civil War. The Confederate raiders wrought havoc among the clipper-ships of that time, and left the nation with no zest for changed conditions of the sea, brought about by the introduction of steam and iron, for which America's "wooden" yards were not adapted. Therefore capital was withdrawn from maritime investment and turned to the exploitation of natural resources, as well as the building of railroads and the development of industries which promised a rich and speedy return.

In this way America fell off as a seafaring nation. Sailors and their sons now took to the land out in the Middle West. They went into the factories, they engaged in coastwise or fishing trades. In world-commerce the United States became more and more dependent upon the bounty-fed and cheap-wage vessels of other nations. She was at last paying $300,000,000 a year to alien owners for the transport of her own products.

After the Civil War a few subsidies were granted to shipowners, but these new lines failed, partly through unskilful management, and partly owing to economic conditions beyond any owner's control. The Pacific Mail was rescued by strong financial interests, but this concern also went out of business owing to the Seamen's Act which the President signed in 1914. Primarily a labour law, forced through Congress by an autocratic Union, this measure added seriously to shipping costs, which were already the bane of American owners. The trans-Pacific lines could only live by employing Chinese, Japanese, and Lascars, at $10 or $15 a month. "Safety at sea" was the watchword of a new Bill which radically altered the sailor's status. The foreign provisos were so complex that American Consuls required the modification of thirty-seven Treaties and Conventions in order to carry them into effect.

Thus it was that the Pacific became "a Japanese lake";

and in two years 405 American vessels, totalling 351,000 tons, were transferred to foreign flags. A steamer manned by Asiatics would cost only $777 a month to operate; the same ship with an American *personnel* cost $3270; the officers' pay alone was more than double. The new Act had orders about the seaman's food and quarters, his freedom at home and abroad, and his ability to understand orders in English—a rule which applied to seventy-five per cent. of the crew. Therefore the outbreak of war in 1914 saw maritime enterprise at its lowest ebb; the last grudging aid. to builders and owners quenched in apathy or downright opposition. No wonder the American flag had become a rare sight in foreign waters, and the native sailor a still rarer sight. A recent Government estimate showed but five men seeking sea employment from every hundred square miles of continental America, as against forty-three in Germany and two hundred and forty in England.

This dwindling was especially regretted in regard to the South American trade, and statesmen quoted remarkable figures to drive the lesson home. Elihu Root instanced the port of Rio de Janeiro. Thither in a recent year came 120 steamers and sailing-ships under the Austro-Hungarian flag. Norway sent 142, Italy 165, Argentina 264, and France 349. Germany was represented by 657 vessels, and Great Britain topped the list with 1785. But not a single steamer had flown the Stars and Stripes! Seven sailing-ships was America's contribution to Rio's teeming trade, and of these, as Mr. Root remarked, two were in distress.

Four years ago there was little enterprise in the American yards. In August, 1914, ship-plates were selling at Pittsburgh at $26.66 a ton, and in Middlesbrough at $34. Yet a 5000-ton steamer, costing $40 a ton in the English yard, cost at least $60 in the American—a difference of $100,000 on this small vessel alone. The price of labour too was far higher; there was also the comparative inexperience of American builders, due to the long decay and national discouragement.

Shipping was a neglected, even a discredited industry, beset with disability and penalty. Yet such are the resources of America that all obstacles went down before the wand of war and the beckoning freights, which were a thousand per cent. higher. The present year will see America with a merchant fleet of over 1600 ships, trebling the tonnage of 1917, and including enemy vessels in operation by the U. S. Government; these aggregate 700,000 tons. A grand total of 10,000,000 tons is said to be in sight.

America felt the full force of the war-time shipping boom. There were stories of steamers paid for by a prosperous maiden voyage. An old tub that went begging a decade ago at $72,000 now fetched half a million. The German tramp, *Walküre*, sunk by Con Spee in the shallow harbour of Papete (Tahiti), was fished up and patched. Soon the rusty wreck rolled into San Francisco under her own steam, and there, after further repairs, she was sold for $700,000. Anything that floated was the surest gold mine, for the shadow of scarcity lay upon the world through the Prussian policy and the economic pinch it brought. Here, then, was America's chance to foil the German aims. She could strike a blow for Freedom with the shipwright's tool, at the same time setting up a new marine of her own with Government aid—belated indeed, but now with no stint of capital or national energy. Six million tons is America's promise for the current year.

Hence the clattering orgies of construction. Hence the steel ships of 8000 tons launched in a little over two months, and freighters of 3000 tons built on the Great Lakes, and brought down through the locks of the Welland Canal to the St. Lawrence and the Atlantic. The whole continent soon crashed with this work from the old-world

yards of Maine, westward to the inland seas, and down to
the Delaware flats and new Florida slipways at Jacksonville
and Pensacola.

Shipyards sprang up overnight round the white rim of
the Mexican Gulf.   Likewise in Louisiana bayous, in remote Texan ports, and up and down the Pacific Coast
from San Diego to Portland, Seattle, and Tacoma; here
virgin forests are at hand and the steam saw is never silent.
America's crop of ships is an astonishing portent, the
most timely of the many harvests intended for a world
besieged and menaced with hunger.   New legions of labour
were called for and drilled, standard parts assembled
and uniform types designed, as in the motor-shops of
Detroit, where motor-cars are turned out by progressive
magic.   In this way it was possible to produce ocean-going
vessels in a few weeks—ships with a fair turn of speed and
a variety of uses; cargo-boats and tankers, transports,
wooden auxiliaries, coastwise tugs, lighters and harbour
craft.   The one aim was to create the carrying fleets with
ever-increasing speed, to confuse and whelm the German
submarines with the sheer number of possible victims until
naval invention and counter-measures should check the
underwater weapon, and once more adjust the balance between attack and defence.

The automobile torpedo is a delicate weapon, and each
target missed increases the cost and risks of a destructive
cruise.   It was America's aim still further to reduce the
U-boat's chances.   Better five little vessels of 3000 tons,
it was argued, than one big ship of 15,000, which a single
shot might sink.   Such was the motive of the Shipping
Board's energy.   On seven hundred launching-ways, it
roused workers of all degrees, from the Pennsylvania steel-
king to the riveters of a lonely sand-pit on Puget Sound,
where ships were launched for the new Vladivostok service
which served Russia in her hopeful days.

But what of navigating officers and men, say for a thousand ships? New schools appeared, afloat and ashore, under public and private auspices. Henry Howard of Boston started classes at Harvard; these spread through New England and thence down to Baltimore, Norfolk, Charleston, and New Orleans. Recruiting stations were opened on the Great Lakes, as soon as the ice formed and the big freighters tied up for the winter. Chicago, Cleveland, Detroit, and Buffalo soon had their academies. Commodore Frank Hastings, the New York banker, began tuition at Greenwich (Conn.), and gave likely men a fair knowledge of theory in six or eight weeks. There were also calls for marine engineers, and many a chauffeur responded, leaving luxurious service for the fearsome lure of a war-time sea.

Let me say in passing that the chief engineer of a Standard Oil tanker was paid up to $5000 a year, with a bonus of fifty per cent. The Navy Department gave the cruiser *Newport* to the State of New York as a school for officers of the merchant marine. Massachusetts equipped the *Ranger* under Captain Emery Rice, who in the *Mongolia* fired the first shot of America's war at a German submarine. The coastwise States—Pennsylvania on the East, Oregon and California in the West—passed laws establishing sea-schools with the support of the Federal Board. As for deck hands, cooks, stewards, and firemen—"We shall provide them," was the pledge of Andrew Furuseth, the ruling spirit of the Seamen's Union; he fell into line at the President's appeal for unity and aid, and he sent through the Central West the stirring slogan—"From farm to fo'c'sle!" which brought thousands of recruits for the new ships.

The war-spirit of the United States drew remarkable tribute from British statesmen of ripe experience and measured speech. "It is a theme which absorbs my thoughts day and night," Mr. Balfour told a crowded House of Commons with unwonted force and fervour. "It is a theme which moves me more, I think, than anything connected with public affairs in all my long experience."

CHAPTER XVI

THE WATCHMAN AND THE SWORD

". . . O son of man, I have set thee a watchman unto the House of Israel; therefore thou shalt hear the word at My mouth, and warn them from Me."—EZEK. xxxiii. 7.

FOR two memorable years Woodrow Wilson was torn between the bandits of Mexico and Teutonic Thugs in Washington and Berlin. These last had unlimited funds and Imperial license. No law restrained them, no scruples of decency or humanity. They found willing tools among the German-American millions whose attitude in the mass no man could predicate, since they were confronted with a dilemma as novel as it was unexpected. The President, in his Declaration of War, thought it well to draw distinction between the German people and their autocratic Government, whose warfare was against mankind. Towards the German race America had "no feeling but one of sympathy and friendship." In the face of all the facts, and fierce avowal of the contrary by the Berlin press, President Wilson was sure the German masses had not backed the militarists in this calamitous war. "It was not with their previous knowledge or approval," the President declared.

Of course high reasons of State prompted this distinction; it was more than once set out with ostent and evident anxiety. For if Germans do not form the backbone of America—as hyphenate leaders claimed in their truculent time—they do play a leading part in the economic and industrial life of the United States.

Now the hyphenate position was obscure and delicate

to a degree. Moreover, the forty-eight States were far from being "United" in a foreign policy. The East was chafing under humiliation at sea and at home; the West sang pæans to the President who "kept us out of war." State Secretary Bryan handed minatory Notes to Bernstorff and Dumba, at the same time assuring them that America's eagle screech was not to be taken seriously, since its purport was mainly to impress sentiment at home. It is quite clear that as Foreign Minister at such a crisis the Nebraskan orator was a misfit, if not a national misfortune. His nods and becks and smiles, his incurable pink thinking and Jeffersonian views, did America the gravest disservice. The State Secretary was played with as a child might be in a brigand's den; his geniality encouraged the Central Powers to a course of outrage which could only have one result.

On his way home in 1915, Constantin Dumba reviewed America's attitude with a sort of naïve wonder. Was it really possible, the ex-Ambassador asked one of "these idiotic Yankees" who was a fellow-passenger, that the President and his State Secretary thought the Central Empires bound by any international law in a fight for their very existence? If so, it was too grotesque. As for American mediation, it had a fair chance at first, Dr. Dumba thought—"if Wilson had been big enough for the job."

Mediation was certainly in President Wilson's mind at first, and—the disgraced Ambassador notwithstanding—he was as "big" a man in 1915 as he afterwards proved. But he had first of all to educate and rouse his people.

Wilson's heart was set upon peace, despite his own growing fears and doubts; this is evident from his public utterances. His intimate friend, Secretary Lane of the Interior, says with perfect truth that "the President sees the world, not as so much money, land, and machines, but as so many men, women, and children." However, apart from Wilson's inclination, we must also consider America's military weakness, and the tradition of moral suasion which State Secretary Bryan urged, even when the *Lusitania* crime thrilled America with wrath and horror.

Officially, at any rate, Dr. Wilson set his face against war, and began the long watch and wait which the angry East styled "Government by periscope." Three months after his "Strict accountability" Note, and three days after the hugest atrocity in the sea's annals, the President made his unfortunate "Too-proud-to-fight" speech at Philadelphia. At that moment the bodies of American women and children were being washed ashore on the Irish coast. The whole continent was stirred, and "big" leadership at home lost a rare chance. But the President was confused with the surge of threats and motives; he was for a time distracted and overwrought—"rattled" is the American word. Indeed, his long ordeal, had we but known the facts, would have earned our loyal support instead of the note of satire which our editors took from colleagues in New York who ought to have known better. For if France and Britain were unprepared for the German onslaught and the web of craft that went with it—what of America, to whom war of any kind was a shameful nightmare which the oceans and her own ideals had alike combined to render impossible?

In February, 1915, the Berlin Reichs-Marine-Amt ordained the "Sink-at-sight," and all neutral vessels were warned from a certain zone around the British Islands. This drew a Note from the State Department, claiming for citizens and ships "the full enjoyment of their acknowledged rights on the high seas." Any violence "would be very hard to reconcile with friendly relations," and the Imperial German Government was thereby held to "strict accountability" for any lawless acts of its naval officers.

On 29th March the *Falaba* was destroyed, and on May 1 the *Gulflight*. Six days later came the immense tragedy of the *Lusitania*. This was followed by the *Nebraskan* on May 24, the *Arabic* on August 19, the *Hesperian* on September 4, the *Persia* on December 30, and so on to the *Silius* and *Sussex* in March of 1916. In all these cases American citizens were drowned or injured. The list is not complete, but it shows the German disregard for successive protests from Washington. "What can America do?" asked the Berlin press, as the President's Notes grew stiffer. To the German mind it was a purely academic discussion, tinged with mild amazement. For here was a nation of a hundred millions whose Chief Executive confessed he could not even police the Mexican Border, so small and ill-equipped was the Federal Army!

Theodore Roosevelt inveighed against "the Pontius Pilate neutrality" of Washington, and the milk and water of America's reply to the blood and iron of the German *Wille zu Macht*. Elihu Root shot many a rankling shaft which inspired the most caustic cartoons. "A Government," the ex-Senator said (he has a large and influential following), "that shakes first its fist—and then its finger—is bound to fall into contempt." Indictments of the Wilson policy were published by diplomats like David Jayne Hill, and by historians like Franklin H. Giddings, Professor of Sociology and Civilization at Columbia. The White House was a target for angry theorists, yet all of them ignored two cardinal facts: (1) That the continent was not unanimous, and (2) That if it were, the military means to enforce its will were wholly lacking.

Moreover, the flush time and the Golden Year had done much to blunt the nation's sensibility. The fall of 1916 saw money raining in billions and New York herself embarrassed by the deluge. At this period President Wilson gave a cryptic hint of his own position in a letter to the late Seth Low, a civic magnate and philanthropist of note. Mr. Low was referred to the first few verses of Ezekiel xxxiii., wherein is laid down the duty of a Watchman to a rather heedless flock: "But he that taketh warning shall deliver his soul." Of course, so long as unity was lacking, and adequate force remained a pious wish, the President could only ensue peace, whatever his private judgment might have been. He professed to ignore the root causes which had set the world ablaze; he was still concerned with moral issues only, at the same time giving a subtle lead to Western apathy, which continued to block the way. "You are looking for some cause," he told the Nebraskans at Omaha, "that will make you raise your spirit and not depress it; a cause in which it seems a glory to shed human blood if need be, so that all the common compacts of Liberty can be sealed with the blood of free men."

The Speech with which the President opened his Second Term prepared his people for the upheaval that was at hand. They now stood firm in armed neutrality, but might be drawn still further into uncontrollable currents which shook the earth with passion and apprehension of organized wrong. It was a wistful, reluctant address. There was much to do at home, Dr. Wilson reminded his hearers, but these things were shelved; there were still mightier ends to achieve "with the whole world for a stage." The Chief Executive was above all things anxious to be America's authentic·Voice, the instrument of her considered will.

This is the *rôle* he praised in Grover Cleveland in 1897, and again in 1913, when writing to Mitchell Palmer about "the most delicate dealings of the Government with foreign nations." There should be no knight-errantry on a President's part, no ebullition of feeling, but swift and loyal interpretation of the country's desire. "America first," was Wilson's concept, as it was Lincoln's in 1862.

It was Wilson's hope to settle the Mexican welter and

keep out of the European war. This was the period of his abstract posing which puzzled the Allies and confirmed the Germans in their estimate of America's impotence in war.

The President's views sprang from the complex of a statesman and a man of letters engaged in political tasks at once delicate and huge. He was profoundly influenced by the teaching of Immanuel Kant, for, as lecturer on international law, Wilson often expounded the well-known Kantian theories of Permanent Peace. The German philosopher considered war a degrading barbarity. "Seek above all," he urges, "the domain of pure practical reason." Kant agrees that a violation of Right may be felt throughout the world, but he does not argue from this that recourse to war is necessary. He appears to go further indeed, and to deny that international wrong has any objective character. States are entirely independent of one another. They have no superior, therefore who shall decide between the just and the unjust?

Still less can States judge of their own cause. The two concepts of Justice and War do not touch at any point. That does not mean that the rights of one State cannot be violated by another. But when war breaks out, who shall say which of the parties has Justice on its side? Two moral forces are in conflict. Each may subjectively believe in the virtue of his cause. There is no judge, therefore no law.

Yet even in Wilson's academic day, belaboured by all belligerents and by many of his own as well, it is plain that he had America's war in mind and was shaping the people's will to it. "God forbid that we should be drawn in," he told a training-camp of nurses. "But if we are, we shall shake off our dreams and stand up for humanity." His domestic schemes were now fading in the battle-smoke, military weakness dogged his larger aims with shadowy indecision. This was glaringly seen in the Mexican chaos, to which I must here allude. It is none too clearly realized that Mexico marches with the U. S. border for two thousand miles, much as Scotland marches with England. In the towns of Nogales and Naco the main street is the international boundary. Now border conditions have for many years disgraced America's name, and roused a real hatred for the "Gringos" in the Republic of the south.

It is also well to point out that States' Rights have time and again hampered the Federal Government in this Border affair; much of the blame must lie with Texas, Arizona, and New Mexico. Here the Sheriff and his posse; the raid, the feud, the "bad man" and his pocket artillery are still familiar features. And the *lex talionis* still has a wide sway.

I may not linger over this Border life. At its worst it surpassed the wildest flights of a Western movie-play, with cattle-thieving and wholesale homicide; the smuggling of arms, the train-wreckers and masked bravos, the plots and frauds, all the terror and reprisals which strew the chaparral with dead peons and desperadoes, as well as with innocent victims of American greed. How Mexican ranchers and farmers have been squeezed out of land and stock by the white men of the Border is a squalid tale. From 1910 onwards refugees fled from the fire and sword of the *pelados* in the Mexican States of Sonora, Chihuahua, and Tamaulipas. Many of these settled in the strange No-man's Land of the Rio Grande, between Laredo and the Gulf, where the river plays erratic pranks and offers shifty problems to the Boundary Commission in Washington.

Now in neither Republic had the hapless peon any political existence. His treatment on the Border stung him to revenge, and kept alive the hatred, contempt, and mistrust of both races. The bandit Villa spoke for the Border serfs when he swore he would raise a wall of terror which the Americanos would never cross.

Wilson's attack upon Vera Cruz, Pershing's punitive mission and the persistent talk of intervention, all served to fan the flame and unite rival factions against America's wavering dictation. *Abajo los Gringos!* became the watchword of all. "Mexico for the Mexicans!" was another patriotic cry, potent as the iron sway of old Diaz in healing feuds and closing the ragged ranks of outlaws, from Manuel Pelaez in the oil-belt to Lower California, where Cantu reigned as king with a comic opera army in full song.

As Venustiano Carranza gained in power, defying Wilson and forcing recognition on the United States, a new Mexican Constitution was coming into force, with anti-foreign clauses so sweeping as to exclude missionary work, as well as ownership in lands and mines. There is, of course, historic warrant for Mexico's mistrust. This goes back to the Texan War of Independence and the confusion it entailed. In 1847 the frontier troubles caused armed conflict with the United States. The troops of General Winfield Scott reached the Mexican capital; they scaled the heights of Chapultepec, imposing America's terms in the Treaty of Guadaloupe-Hidalgo, as a tablet on the Castle wall reminds the citizens of today.

The long Border remains a problem, especially with a weak, unstable Mexico ruined by bandit chiefs and played upon by Germany—as the Zimmermann letter showed, and the record of Franz von Rintelen, who was paymaster-in-chief of the plotters south of the Rio Grande. So much for the Border, which President Wilson tried to police with the State Militia in 1916.

To the south of it lies a State which Humboldt called the treasure-house of the earth. Mexico is larger than the German and Austro-Hungarian Empires, with France added to them. Nearly one-third of the world's silver comes out of this land. Her mineral riches are incalculable; her petroleum a precious asset of the Grand Alliance in a universal war to which oil is a vital need for new engines of ever-increasing power and number. American oil supplies are running short, owing to the increased demand of a pleasure-loving generation which has millions of cars. California's output rose from four million barrels in 1900 to a hundred millions in 1916. Oklahoma's increased from six thousand barrels to sixty-five millions, yet the shortage grows more and more acute.

Therefore it was more than ever necessary that disorder should cease in Mexico, where the Tampico belt alone bids fair to equal or surpass the oil production of the world. These great fields follow the Gulf for three hundred miles, and extend sixty miles inland. Experts say there are signs of oil all down the coast as far as the Guatemalan border, and that borings on a wider scale will have astonishing results. The whole yield of the United States for last year was 307,000,000 barrels. Fifteen Tampico wells had a capacity of 250,000,000 barrels. A single gusher at Poturo del Llano gave a hundred thousand barrels a day, another could fill an ocean tanker overnight.

It was thought well to maintain armed guards against the ever-present German incendiary; for her ten million barrels may go up in smoke, as happened at the Dos Bocas gusher in the Tampico region. I need hardly say that Mexican brigands levied tribute on this wealth. The armed gang of Candido Aguilar demanded $10,000 from each producing concern. Only Lord Cowdray's syndicate refused; the result was that pumps were stopped, and great leaks caused. Then surface fires broke out and lasted four months, involving a far greater loss than Aguilar's proposed blackmail.

Before the Terror—which dates from the decline of the Diaz régime in 1910—there were 40,000 Americans in Mexico, handling property worth over a thousand million dollars. Of Mexico's imports fifty-five per cent. came from the United States; of all that Mexico had to sell, her big sister took seventy-seven per cent.

In Victoriano Huerta's day, President Wilson was anxious over American prestige, which was then at a low ebb. It is clear that the Washington Bureaux had a fair inkling of German designs in the fall of 1915. German reservists were crossing into Mexico and directing petty "wars" too bewildering to follow. German ships were stealing into lonely ports with lethal cargoes hidden in cases of hardware, typewriters, pianos, and ice-cream freezers.

Mexico under Huerta offered a German vantage-ground of unique scope. For this reason the Mailed Fist was soon stirring the hell-broth, and Von Rintelen poured millions into it through the Deutsche Bank. Meanwhile Huerta's manœuvres—the Vera Cruz affair and the abortive pursuit of Villa—gave the ignorant peon a low opinion of American might. Thus the too-tame bull that refused to fight in the crowded ring—the tawny Longhorn or red Hereford of massive and kindly mien—was now hustled out by angry *chulos* to the contemptuous shrieks of the mob: *Toro Americano!*—Why, it was a Yankee beast that turned to nibble straw when the picadors spurred on top of him, dropping their lances and stooping to slap his stupid snout!

It cannot be denied that the Mexican mess was badly handled by the U. S. Government. In 1914 Huerta, a Mixtec Indian of pure blood, was ruling well enough when President Wilson resolved to break him. Huerta's sway was, of course, despotic—like that of his master, Porforio Diaz. The American Fleet, under Admiral Mayo, was sent down to Vera Cruz to compel this tyrant to salute the flag. Huerta haggled for a return salute; the result was that none was given on either side. Mayo's squadron sailed away after a pitched battle ashore, in which there were many casualties.

Meanwhile Wilson was pointing out to Congress that "if we are to accept the tests of its own Constitution, Mexico has no Government." It was argued that Huerta was a usurper who had overthrown with treachery and crime the previous régime; but then, that has been Mexico's way since the Constitution of 1857 went into force.

Carranza was favoured by the Washington Cabinet—though it also leaned to Pancho Villa, a free-lance who had hopes of the precarious "throne" in the National Palace. But Villa's aims were blighted by Wilson's final choice after Huerta's resignation. Thereupon the bandit chief took a bloody revenge by invading American territory and "shooting" up the border town of Columbus, N. M. This was the outrage which called for the Pershing expedition, and an outlay of $200,000,000, which was worse than fruitless. "Get Villa, dead or alive," was the order given to the American General. But he came back empty-handed, his retreat hastened by the minatory tone of First Chief Carranza, who now threatened a national war. Such was the problem confronting Wilson in his neutral time; and Prussian devilry in both Republics heaped fuel on the flames.

Mexico was now exhausted; one of her railways with a gross revenue of $34,000,000 earned but $22,441 in paper money of more than doubtful value. Claims on Carranza's Government soon climbed to a billion dollars. At long last President Wilson drew out of this political morass. He reinstated Ambassador Fletcher in Mexico City; he received Carranza's envoy, Señor Ignacio Bonillas, who had been a member of the Joint Commission that settled terms between the two Republics. Mexico now settled down to business as the Border itself does when the tide of woe has turned and the good time smiles again. Railroads and mines were dug out and repaired. There was reconstruction everywhere on the old familiar lines. The native press began to change its tune, and was quite polite to America. Anti-Gringoism was bad form in this brighter day. The State mints were working overtime; so were the theatres and cafés of the capital, where Americans left the club and strolled up to Sanborn's drug-store for ice-cream, and pastries and tea. *Où sont les neiges d'antan?* Where were the bandits and butchers of yesteryear?

President Wilson was well aware of the geographical and political importance of Mexico, but he mistook the mass of peons for a people, which they certainly are not. No accurate census of the country has been taken, nor should we accept the official estimates and classification of 1900. There are, perhaps, 15,000,000 souls in the Republic, and of these fewer than 2,000,000 are of Caucasian race. The number of half-breeds is rather larger; the rest are Indians, belonging to fifty tribes speaking as many dialects. Mentally, morally, and physically the peon of today is what he was centuries ago. "There can be little doubt," says Senator Beveridge, "that, speaking by and large, he is far below the culture of the ancient Aztecs." An American protectorate appears to be the sanest solution of the Mexican question upon all counts. And the next upheaval will find the United States equipped to make an end of endemic anarchy at her door—the desolation of a State which is unique among the prizes of Latin America, and therefore a standing lure to arrogant Powers trained in war and forced to territorial expansion.

Mexico commands the Gulf, which is at once the outlet

and approach to the southern harbours of the United States. It has been the dream of American statesmen that this sea should one day be wholly American—the more so in that it now controls the Panama Canal. Moreover, as Mexico dominates the near Pacific, this turbulent State has a bearing upon America's Western Coast. A modern army landed there could invade the Border at many points where fortification is impossible or prohibitive in cost. Therefore its integrity, stability, and internal order are prime factors in the policy of the greater Republic.

Wilson's dilemma when the Great War came, was a repetition of history—that of April, 1793, when the First President declared America's neutrality in the French wars and sought "to gain time to our country" which was quite unfitted to play its part. The "suitable establishments" which Washington urged upon the infant Republic were still ignored; even the "respectable defensive posture" which was his minimum was not yet in sight. For this reason he steered clear of entanglements and pursued the "different course" which "our detached and distant situation" appeared to render possible.

Washington had not been dead twenty years before America was faced with entirely new conditions which entailed a radical change. Monroe, Madison, and Jefferson were already counting upon British sea-power as a barrier against European intrigue. Aloofness was even then known for a myth, and the Two Americas closed their ranks, resolved to exclude any and every Old-World domination. So the problems of the Fathers were in part repeated by the issues which Wilson faced in his neutral day. The Farewell Address of Washington is not more unruffled than Wilson's Message to Congress a few weeks after the German onset broke. ''We are at peace with all the world. . . . We mean to live our own lives as we will.'' So said the Pilgrim Fathers when they set sail from Plymouth in 1620, weary of the homeland and its religious persecution.

America has always been a place of dreams, and no dollar-hunt has ever quite dispelled them. No less a witness than Henri Bergson has lately testified to this. ''He who has lived in America,'' the philosopher told the intellectual peers of Paris, ''comes to realize that in no nation does money mean less; it is only a certificate of efficiency. The American soul is saturated with idealism—even with mysticism. Their history shows that abstract thoughts of morality and justice have always held first place.'' This is the plain truth. Pacifism split the House of Deputies of the Protestant Episcopal Church when new prayers for the National Army were to the fore. Thus the God of Hosts was asked ''to strengthen and protect the soldiers of our country; to support them in the day of battle, and in time of peace to keep them from all harm.'' ''If we adopt this prayer,'' said Dr. J. H. Melish of Brooklyn, ''we shall be doing irreparable injury to the youth of our land. It is impossible for soldiers—as the Prayer asks—to 'serve without reproach.' Moreover, it is not a Christian prayer, but one addressed to the iron Deity whom Joshua invoked when he set forth to invade.''

Pacifism was carried to queer extremes; its apostles in all ages were cited, from Buddha to Mr. Bryan. Non-resistance was expedient, the fanatics said; it was also economically wiser than war. It was quite workable too, according with the Christ ethics, teaching humanity and justice as well as conserving men's energy for sane constructive labours. America should, therefore, adopt the peace-ideal and act upon it until the older nations, led by this example, should pass into Emerson's ''region of holiness," where no ignoble passion marred the social serenity. This was the counsel which Theodore Roosevelt decried for three years or more as "the diluted mush of a make-believe morality."

This Utopian land has had many wars, and muddled through them all with no great zest for the business. The Revolutionary War lasted seven years, the War of 1812 three years, the Florida War seven years, the Mexican War two years, and the Rebellion four years—to say nothing of frontier affrays with the Indians during the whole of this period. In 1898 came the clash with Spain, thirty-three years after the surrender of Lee to General Grant at Appomattox. America was wholly unprepared for the war with Spain, but it would be a graceless task to recall the scandal and confusion which marked it at home and abroad—the sea affair as well as the land campaign. The navy was in a bad way; its gunnery record at Santiago was exposed by the late Professor Alger, a leading American authority. "At 2800 yards," this scientist states, "nearly half the shots fired went wide of the mark." Service powders, the discipline of crews, battle-practice, co-ordination, and construction all were unsound at that time. Yet Congress was unmoved at each revelation.

Nevertheless reforms were stirring. Young Sowden Sims was bombarding the Bureaux and the Senate Naval Committee, thereby imperilling his own career. "When we launched the *Kentucky*," Sims declared, "we ought to have shed tears over her instead of breaking a bottle of champagne." This was the battleship of open turrets and unprotected guns, a design that was soon officially condemned. But if Sims spoke plainly in those days (he became an admiral, and worked with our own fleet in European waters), what shall be said of candid friends who are today rewriting America's school books till the military record glares with crudity?

It is a wholesome sign, this banishing of mythical exploit; the spread-eagling of minute-men and rustic heroes who could "lick creation" with a pike and gun snatched from the farm-house wall when the drums began to beat. *The Unpopular History of the United States* is a piquant novelty of our time, and a token that the great democracy is building from the depths in order to cure the Prussian madness.

"Why," asks the new historian, "has the sovereign voter of America remained so heedless? I was a grown man of thirty, hoeing my beard with a safety razor, ere it dawned upon me that the fighting record of our country had not been one long, unbroken record of star-spangled victories. Like other boys, I'd been fed upon Fourth of July orations. . . . I believed that one lone, grey-haired farmer with a drum, a bloody rag round his head, and a son and a grandson behind him, had chased the British Army from our sacred continent. I believed that—did you? I thought that a single American patriot, with a muzzle-loader and both hands tied behind him, could beat any horde of foreign hirelings that ever marched down the pike. I had no doubt of it—had you? I was sure the Redcoats outnumbered the Colonials. Yet in that glorious year of '76 we mustered 89,600 men against the British 20,121! I didn't know that—did you?" Much of this "Unpopular History" has lain *perdu* in General Emory Upton's *Military Policy of the United States*. The late Homer Lea's *Valour of Ignorance* carried the truth a step further, and General Leonard Wood, a former Chief of Staff, rounded off the peril of reliance upon moral force in a sullen world of torn-up treaties and rattling swords.

But a prosperous and easy-going America had long forgotten the famous Draft by which the Colonies filled their fighting quotas in Revolutionary days. In the 'Sixties both the Union and the Confederacy used the Draft, and the courts of North and South upheld its validity. Conscription does indeed raise the sharpest issues in a modern democracy: we saw this in Australia, where Mr. Hughes put a Referendum to his people. Yet he lost by a narrow margin because Labour and the women electors were against him.

In Canada the cleavage was more serious, led by the Catholic hierarchy under Cardinal Bégin of Quebec and Mgr. Bruchesi, Archbishop of Montreal.

In the United States conscription came as a real shock. The example of Quebec was quoted by one set of partisans; another pointed to "a military Canada, with veteran legions trained in the sternest school and contemptuous of their unmartial neighbours." When President Wilson delivered his War Message every point was cheered till he came to the first levy of half a million men—"who should, in my opinion, be chosen upon the principle of universal liability to service." Congress was taken aback. Staunch supporters of Wilson demurred, and there was resolute opposition for a time.

Southern Congressmen were against the arming and training of negroes, who were all too prone to run amuck, as they did at Houston, Tex. Here coloured troopers shot up the town, killing seventeen and wounding twenty more before they could be disarmed. Senator Vardaman of Mississippi was quite justified in his earnest warning of this danger. Then American Labour looked askance at conscription; influential newspapers attacked it as "unnecessary, undemocratic, conducive to militarism, and a violation of that 'involuntary servitude' which the Constitution forbids."

President Wilson stood firm throughout this agitation;

he was supported by the Federal Army Staff, by most of the Eastern Press, and all the intellectuals. "No one can hate militarism more than I do," said Dr. Nicholas Murray Butler of Columbia in his Allocution to the University. "None would resist more actively and emphatically any movement to change the peace-loving industrial temper and spirit of our people for any of the older forms, which are now slowly going to their death—let us hope never to be resurrected—on the battlefields of Europe. But there is a call to national service and a preparation for it which, so far from sharing the Prussian motive, is only the voice of Democracy conscious of obligation and duty, as well as of rights and opportunities." This is the voice that prevailed.

German folly and frightfulness helped it in surprising ways, till at length America was roused, from the schoolgirl to the negro surgeon; from the Polish mechanic to the Wall Street millionaire. James Wood the Quaker was now on constructive work. Thomas Edison was at sea, studying anti-submarine devices; Frank Vanderlip, America's foremost financier left the greatest of banks to enlist in War Loan service. Conscription was an accepted fact; it brought in State quotas of men that filled the camps to overflowing. And with it came the *bushido* code of loyalty which Americans have so long admired in the Japanese. The sons of Cabinet Ministers—Daniels, McAdoo, Houston, Lane—were now serving with the humblest lads. "Conscription," as young Rockefeller said, "is the one thing needed to abolish class distinctions among us." Judge Gary of the Steel Trust, welcoming the Japanese Mission, put America's military resources at fifteen million men and a hundred billion dollars, without seriously crippling the country.

These are stupendous figures, but the record of the Sixty-Fifth Congress confirms them. In six months' session an

Army of a million and a half was mustered, besides overseas forces which were transported with little loss. Fifteen million hands were mobilized for industry. The Navy was trebled, the Regular Army modernized, vast aerial forces planned, together with mercantile shipping on a great scale.

Admiral W. L. Capps, of the Emergency Fleet Corporation, promised 2100 ships by the end of 1919, or 14,500,000 tons in all. This includes enemy and commandeered vessels, as well as new construction and ships from the Great Lakes, which are cut in two and brought down through the Welland Canal. Twenty thousand million dollars were voted by Congress in direct appropriations, including seven thousand millions in loans to the Grand Alliance. In the same half-yearly session the President acquired unique prestige. Men marvelled at his "despotic" powers, asserted in such measures as the Selective Draft, the Espionage and Embargo Bills; Priority, Transport, War Revenue, the Food Control, and Soldiers' and Sailors' Insurance.

"Give us victory," wrote Lincoln in a famous letter to General Hooker, "and I will risk the Dictatorship!" Dr. Wilson made up his mind that if war came he would avoid Lincoln's anguish and insist upon conscription at the outset.

The long-drawn chaos of the Civil War should have settled this matter, but democracy has a short memory for things that ruffle its ease.

"The real difficulty," says Sherman in his *Memoirs,* "was to get an adequate number of good soldiers. We tried every system known to modern nations—voluntary enlistment, the draft, and bought substitutes." Very reluctantly did President Lincoln sign the Draft Act on July 11, 1863; it pressed unfairly upon poor men, and gave exemption to any recruit who could produce $300. Two days later fierce riots broke out in New York, and the casualties exceeded those of many an American battle. So abhorrent was military service that out of 77,862 names drawn from the wheel in the metropolis, only 2557 joined the Northern Army.

We may be sure that Lincoln's ordeal was in Wilson's mind as early as the panic winter of 1914–15. It was of course the submarine campaign which hurried him into war—the reckless German gamble which was to humble Britain, and give naked *Macht* a vindication that would silence every protest and establish the Prussian code. Now this U-boat bid was simple enough, and by far the bravest menace ever aimed at civilization. The last shred of law was to be dropped, every ship afloat destroyed, whether belonging to neutral or belligerent. Red Cross vessels too, argosies of food for the starving Belgians, steamers full of refugees, the Dutch fishing-boat, Spanish liners and coasting vessels—all the tonnage that sailed the seas—was to be sunk for a complex of reasons, military, political, and economic. The invisible craft could not conduct a cruiser warfare according to established rules. Of its very nature it could only strike and disappear. It used torpedoes as the mad Malay uses a *kriss* in the crowded bazaar, with no regard for victims or his own fate.

Such was the German plan for breaking British might and planting the Trident in the Mailed Fist with appropriate flourish. U-boat "warfare" was to give the Fatherland a flying start when a German peace was signed and other nations, crippled for ships, faced a shortage of food and raw materials. This was the plot which unfolded before America. She was slow to grasp it, even with U-53 doing fell work in her own waters. It was an over-prosperous America of many views and voices. Moreover, the German element had great sway; German efficiency

(*Tüchtigkeit*) was the pattern of all, as the President himself reminded a Labour audience. "As a university man, I have been surrounded by men trained in Germany, because nowhere else could they get such thorough and searching training, especially in the principles of science, and those which underlie modern material achievements." The German farmer was known for a wizard who produced ten pounds of pig-meat from a bushel of corn. Where the American got thirty bushels of oats from an acre, the German got fifty-eight; the potato-yields were respectively ninety-five bushels against two hundred and five.

However, this business friendship was cooling fast as the two ideals of government fell asunder with glaring cleavage. Germany watched the process with unconcern, confident of her own "strong position" (*Machstellung*) and America's sprawling hugeness which no war-danger could ever arouse in time. Germany was sure of this—Hindenburg himself explained it; parrots of the press played scornful variants on this theme for a season. The Americans were "a naïve colonial-like people," led by a dreamer who talked daggers with a bodkin in his hand.

So matters drifted until January 31, 1917. On that day Alfred Zimmermann handed Mr. Gerard the "ruthless" Note which caused President Wilson to sever relations. He could do no less in view of his own threat after the sinking of the *Sussex*, and the pledge which his warning extorted from Berlin. That pledge was now voided for the sake of "tortured mankind." The troubled conscience of the German Government could leave no means untried "to hasten the end of the war." . . . "It must therefore abandon the limitations which it has hitherto imposed upon itself in the employment of its fighting weapons at sea."

I have said that America was slow to realize a purpose so monstrous. Even in his address to Congress, announcing the rupture, President Wilson renews his "inveterate confidence" in "the sobriety and prudent foresight" of Kaiserdom. . . . "I refuse to believe that it is the intention of the German authorities to do, in fact, what they have warned us they will feel at liberty to do. . . . Only actual overt acts on their part can make me believe this even now."

The night crime of the *Laconia* was such an act, and thenceforth the United States was committed to war, though little or no preparation had been made for it. That the Watchman in Washington was perplexed is evident from the Notes he sent between the *Lusitania* and the *Sussex*. He took each German quibble seriously: the liability (with blood-money offered) in the *Lusitania* case; the "regrettable mistake" of the *Arabic,* the proposed "inquiry" into the *Persia,* and the conditional "concessions" which followed the *Sussex* affair in the Channel.

Merchant vessels (the German promise ran) were not thenceforward to be destroyed without warning, and the saving of human lives—provided that America insisted upon the freedom of the seas as laid down by her in Notes sent to Great Britain on December 28, 1914, and upon the freedom of the seas as laid down by her on November 5, 1915. Should American pressure fail in this respect (as German catspaw for sea "freedom"); should Great Britain continue to violate "the rules of International Law universally recognized before the war," then "the German Government would be facing a new situation in which it must reserve for itself complete liberty of decision."

More than once the Imperial Chancellor asked Mr. Gerard how America could protest against the submarine without equally resisting Britain's tyranny at sea? The diplomat was not posed at all, but ready with a shrewd reply. "If two men entered my grounds," said he, "and one stepped on my flower-beds, whilst the other killed my sister, I should first pursue the murderer.''

In his Message to Congress declaring war (April 2, 1917), Dr. Wilson defined the cause for which he led this ''great and peaceful people into the most terrible and disastrous of all wars.''

''We shall fight,'' he said, ''for the things we have always carried nearest our hearts. For democracy, for the right of those who submit to authority to have a voice in their own government; for the rights and liberties of small nations, for the universal dominion of Right by such a concert of free peoples as will bring peace and safety to all nations, and make the world itself at last free.''

Years ago, as Governor of New Jersey, Woodrow Wilson laid down his creed, declaring himself ''enlisted for life'' against all reactionary systems thrown athwart ''the triumphant hosts of the great Democracy. . . . We must move forward,'' the Governor told an audience at Hoboken, after a three-thousand-mile tour of the West as Presidential candidate for the first time, ''and any man who blocks this concerted movement of humanity will be swept aside.'' America, he said, was no longer choosing leaders because they were fine fellows, but because they understood the best interests of the nation at a critical juncture in her history.

It is absurd to suppose that this born leader was at any time an advocate of peace-at-any-price, or that he carried the doctrine of non-resistance to visionary extremes. But he knew, as none other did, the full complexity of the many problems before him. As historian of George Washington's epoch, Dr. Wilson pictures the anguish of the First President, with an unruly rabble as the only available force and a victorious enemy in the land. ''He found neither the preparations nor the spirit of the army to his liking. His soldierly sense of order was shocked by the loose discipline, and his instinct of command by the free-and-easy insolence of that irregular levy. And his authority grew stern as he laboured to bring the motley host to order and effective organization.'' Wilson little dreamed, when he wrote this Life of his fellow-Virginian, that he was himself destined to create a colossal militarism among the masses he loves so well. ''Let the result be so impressive and emphatic,'' he urged upon them on Liberty Day, '':that it will echo through the Empire of our enemy as indeed what America intends to do—to bring this war to a victorious conclusion.''

That enemy styled Wilson the greatest ''despot'' of all, and truly history repeats itself in the strangest way. Less than ten years ago Woodrow Wilson was immersed in books; his greatest battle was fought in University affairs in the Gothic halls and tree-shaded campus of Princeton. Today he sways, with unprecedented power, an armed democracy which may well prove the decisive factor in the most stupendous of wars. In his college days Wilson wrote *A History of the American People,* and in the chapter dealing with Lincoln's second term he gives a picture of dictatorship which is closely applicable to his own.

''The war had not run its extraordinary course without touching the Government itself with revolution. The Constitution had been framed with no thought to provide for such days as these, when States were breaking away from the Union, and the Government was struggling for life itself. And with unlooked-for exigency had come unlooked-for and arbitrary acts of power. The whole authority of the nation seemed to be concentrated in the Executive without restraint of law. . . . Many an undoubted principle of the Constitution seemed as if for the time suspended in order that the executive and military powers might move supreme to meet a supreme necessity.

Individual rights seemed for a time in abeyance. Even
politicians of his own party thought the President unsafe.
. . . Fortunately the rank and file had caught the spirit
of the war. . . . They looked confidently to see all things
restored, as of course, to their old poise and balance when
the storm of war had passed.''

But the turmoil of the 'Sixties was a small affair compared with the present effort; its conscript service and
control of the railroads, its authority over food production,
distribution, and prices; its embargoes and taxes and
censorships. There was at first much carping at these
''surrenders to Kaisertum and Tsarism.'' All this interference, the dubious were afraid, would set America on
the road to Marxian Socialism—or even, to the Fourier
ideal of communal happiness, with ''home'' in a vast bar-
rack under the watchful eye of impersonal sovereignty.

The power of the President has grown enormously since
the time of Washington and the elder Adams. Chief
Executives of the early school concerned themselves with
laws, the appointment of officials, and the direction of
foreign affairs which were mainly formal. Formal also
were the White House relations with Congress; and the
Constitution was rigidly observed. It is Jackson, Lincoln,
and Cleveland who are chiefly associated with the broaden-
ing of Presidential sway. Officials were now abruptly removed, the veto power was used, the national policy
moulded, and legislation led along bolder lines.

It was felt that Congress needed skilful handling if it
were not to split into regional elements and cross-purposes
fatal to any real national progress. Roosevelt took a vigorous hand in this control; Taft was of the *laissez-faire*
school, and consequently left the White House with his
political fortunes ruined. In 1913 Wilson inaugurated
a ''reign'' so sagacious and strong that the whole continent rallied to him. Even the Eastern press, in its most

impatient moments, could review the Prussian affronts with unshaken faith in the Chief Executive. "We're behind you, Mr. President," was a timid assurance of this time. *"Only, for God's sake, don't step on us!"*

The high Wilson note was sounded on Inauguration Day. "This is not a day of triumph," he told America, "but a Day of Dedication. Here muster, not the forces of Party, but of Humanity. Men's hearts wait upon us; men's lives hang in the balance; men's hopes call upon us to say what we will do." Yet it is as a militarist that this Apostle of Peace will live, and not as the social and political reformer.

The President has power to lead the country into war, though the formal declaration is left to Congress. A case in point was President Polk's despatch of General Taylor's force to the Mexican Border in 1846; it was a step which made straight for war. Another instance is Cleveland's bellicose message to Great Britain in 1895 over the Venezuela-Guiana boundary. And three years later, when McKinley sent the *Maine* to Havana, he knew it meant a war with Spain. Wilson's Note to Germany after the sinking of the *Sussex* committed America in the same irrevocable way.

When war breaks out the President becomes Commander-in-Chief of Army, Navy, and State Militias. Men, money, and ships are voted by Congress, but thereafter the Chief Executive is an autocrat. He can make or break commanders; he can move troops and plan and direct campaigns, as well as dictating matters of life and death to the civilians at home. I relate these things because opinion in Europe is unaware of any precedent for the stern paternalism of the Wilson régime. Even the America of today knows little of the "Tsarism" which Lincoln, the country attorney of Illinois, assumed in three tragic months of the Civil War. And in the words of the historian Rhodes: "Never has the power of Dictator fallen into safer and nobler hands."

It was loudly asserted in Central Europe that Americans were incapable of that selfless discipline without which all their strength would be frustrated.

Yet under Wilson the miracle was achieved. It culminated in "Garfield's Day"—an order from the Fuel Administrator which shut down all industries (save those of war) east of the Mississippi River. Millions of workers stood at ease. The theatres were closed, there were candles in skyscraper offices; and in the Stock Exchange the brokers shivered in a freezing atmosphere wearing greatcoats, sweaters, and ear-muffs. The object of this order was to relieve congestion on the railroads, and get waiting ships away to France. At one stroke the distilling of whisky was stopped, and 40,000,000 bushels of grain added to the available food.

The sovereignty of the State was steadily encroaching, and loyal acceptance of its rule was mainly due to the personality of the President. Business men submitted with grace to unexampled dictation. They agreed to the Government price for copper and steel and ships. The coal retailer was obliged to sell at the 1915 margin plus an increase of thirty per cent. Priority in railway transport was insisted on; men saw their own goods lying derelict in warehouse or siding, whilst material of war went swiftly forward. Huge taxes were paid, costly plants turned over to the Government, unnecessary products cut down arbitrarily.

Boards and Committees innumerable now bossed the man of affairs. They criticized his cost-accounting; he was told he must standardize his output on a model which his rival had evolved. Or he handed over his factory entire; he built or manufactured according to Board ideas of price and labour conditions. The head of a Produce

Exchange had to warn his members against speculation in futures, lest that hydra-headed Board shut down upon trading in that particular commodity.

The new paternalism was helped by propaganda such as impressed the lessons of America's War upon many races dwelling in a continent of three million square miles. In these appeals every language was used, from Czech to Chinese. The issues were set out in the Greek *Atlantis* of New York, and all the polyglot journals of that city: the *Russkoye Slovo*, the Italian *Progresso*, the Yiddish *Forward*, the Magyar *Figyelő*, the Polish *Dziennik Zwiazkowy*. For America is a very Babel of newspapers. This work was decentralized, with State Governors and civic leaders on their mettle to devise ways and means of reaching every home—even in the desert.sage-brush, the mining camps of Colorado, and forest clearings of the lone North-West. "Save a shovelful of coal every day," Mr. Garfield told the housewife, "and we shall have fifteen million tons to show for it at the year's end."

Mr. Herbert Hoover wrote novel theses about food economy for the schools. "We have in our abundance and in our waste an ample supply to carry them and ourselves to Victory. There is no royal road to food conservation. It can be accomplished only through whole-hearted co-operation in the 20,000,000 kitchens and at the 20,000,000 tables of the United States."

Foreign Minister Lansing drew upon his unique knowledge of Prussian evil, and addressed millions of citizens through the daily and weekly press. It was a tale to move the most lethargic: "Yet—God help us! these things have come to pass, and Iron Crosses have rewarded the perpetrators of these crimes." . . . Pulpits and "the pictures," aerial bombs full of leaflets, methods spectacular and sedate—all were enlisted with unresting *brio* and purpose. Veteran soldiers had a hand in the educative game. "We must finish it on the other side,'' General Leonard Wood warned America. ''Otherwise they will finish it over here.''

This propaganda succeeded. Apathy was slowly fired with love of country; the hostile elements were stilled, the hyphenate millions forced into lip-service at least to the great American mission. Even the Irish began to warn their brethren overseas not to expect sympathy for anti-British ebullitions.

All this suasion can be traced to President Wilson. He sat alone in his study on the second floor of the White House, tapping an old typewriter whose peculiar script is a token of confidential communication. In this sanctum was the slogan born: ''Food will win the war!'' Here, in Lincoln's Cabinet Chamber, Wilson wrote his famous Notes; his historic Messages to Congress, too, and less formal exhortation to the care-free people whose guardian he was. ''We are upon a war footing,'' he urged, when supporting his Fuel Controller. ''And I am confident that the people of the United States are willing to observe the same sort of discipline which might be involved in actual conflict itself.'' Sitting here alone (always alone), the Chief Executive expounded the Prussian drift with perfect grasp of its pervasive devilry.

This moral preparation took a long time, and little was done on the material side until the President could say, ''The eyes of the people are opened, and they see.'' Faction and conflict faced him everywhere. He had ''big'' men to choose—and to dismiss, as he did Chairman Denman and General Goethals when they fell out over the details of emergency ships. Most difficult of all, there was the froth of sedition and pacifism of every hue to whip from the Melting Pot of races.

This Dr. Wilson did with due severity. ''I hear the voices of dissent,'' he owned—''Who does not? I hear the criticism and clamour of the noisily thoughtless and troublesome. . . . I hear men debate peace who know nothing of its nature, nor the way in which we may attain it with uplifted eyes and unbroken spirit. But I know that none of these speak for America, nor do they touch its heart. They may safely be left to strut their uneasy hour and be forgotten." He spoke more plainly to the Federation of Labour at the annual Convention in Buffalo. "Any man in America, or anywhere else, who supposes that free industry and enterprise can continue if the Pan-German plan is achieved and German power fastened upon the world, is as fatuous as the dreamers of Russia." So did the self-styled Watchman of the White House "blow the trumpet and warn the people" of the coming Sword.

Perhaps one day, in his lettered leisure, this scholar-statesman will tell us how he kindled a mixed continent to the Pacifist War of the world, so that in his Thanksgiving Proclamation he could say at last—"In this Day of revelation of our duty" . . . "there has been vouchsafed to us, in full and inspiring measure, the resolution and spirit of united action. We have been brought to one mind and purpose. A new vigour of common counsel and common deed has been revealed to us all."

The President had tussles with Congress after he came before the Joint Session to asks for credits and extraordinary powers. More American ships had been sunk; the position was very critical. A request had been made for the co-operation of neutral Governments—"But I fear none of them has thought it wise to join in any common course of action."

The War Revenue Act passed the House after the cotton-tax of $2.50 a bale had been violently rejected by the solid South. The Food Bill was tangled up with prohibitiou; for in this measure extremists saw a heaven-sent opportunity to make the continent "bone dry," and abolish strong drink for ever. Here again the President took a hand, urging a speedy decision in view of food speculation and rising prices, due to over-eager bidding from Allied agents to the detriment of the American people.

The Senate resented this constant forcing of its pāce; behind closed doors there was hot retaliation upon the Cabinet, who were said to thrust important measures upon Congress without due form or consideration.

The fact is, the U. S. Constitution is out of date; the Great War will overhaul it drastically. Every intelligent American is aware of this; therefore Lord Northcliffe was on safe ground when he said that in many ways the Republic was today much as she was in 1776.

For many years the executive branch of the Government has been gaining upon the legislative in actual power, and it is the separation of these two which is now revealed as a serious disability. Close association with France in Revolutionary days brought the Montesquieu theory to America, and it was written with fervour into the State and Federal Constitutions.

A generation ago Woodrow Wilson himself described the baleful effects of this system upon the Government. It was also decried at the Constitutional Convention of 1915 by men like Elihu Root and Henry L. Stimson. "I believe," said the last-named statesman, "that by far the greatest part of the inefficiency and corruption from which we suffer in our Federal and State Governments can be directly traced to that venerable heresy which keeps the influence of our Executive out of our halls of Congress and assemblies. That this is a political heresy has been long and abundantly proven. . . . It lingers on in the United States, however, as the fount of most of our troubles, although cherished like a veritable Ark of the Covenant."

But rude hands are being laid upon that ark in an era of militarism and anti-cultural expenditure. Already Secretary McAdoo has warned the nation that "the future holds a less roseate prospect for Government finance." Senator Martin, Chairman of the Appropriations Committee, urged a closer scrutiny of the prodigious sums which Congress was voting with such enthusiasm. Five months of war showed appropriations totalling $20,000,-000,000. "We are compelled to shut our eyes," Senator Martin feared, "rather than hamper our men on the battlefield; but our duty to trim these estimates grows more imperative every day. Impoverish the country if you will, so that victory be ours; but, for God's sake, let us not lavish money blindly, or we shall drift at last into peril and panic."

In the Lower House yet another committee was proposed to check the vast appropriations and—as the veteran Senator Aldrich hinted—to save thirty cents on the dollar, whilst getting the same results.

Here the two "divided" branches of Government clashed. The President protested, as he had done before over the Amendment to his Food Control Bill, and later over Senator Chamberlain's suggested War Cabinet and Ministry of Munitions. Dr. Wilson has no illusions about the Congressional Committee. "There is a very ominous precedent in our history," he pointed out to Chairman Lever of the Lower House, "which shows how such a supervision would operate. I refer to the Committee on the Conduct of the War, formed by Congress during the administration of Mr. Lincoln. It was the cause of constant and distressing harassment, and rendered the President's task all but impossible." That Inquisition became the censor of both Army and Ministers for four years following its first inquiry into the disaster of Ball's Bluff. It summoned statesmen and soldiers before it, questioning them "like refractory schoolboys," and overruling the military judgment of Generals Grant and Meade.

It will therefore be seen that, as historian of the United States, Woodrow Wilson had significant lessons before him. And from the first he joined issue with fussy amateurs and well-meaning meddlers who had no grasp of America's war or the efforts it would entail.

In three months sixteen cantonments were built, each one of them housing an Army Corps. On the mechanical side were devices like the Liberty motor for high-powered planes; a standard lorry, trench-diggers, motor batteries, and new appliances for poison-gas, liquid flame, and lachrymatory fumes. Congressional appropriations leaped to ten or twenty times the sums normally voted, and contained items never seen before, such as $277,000,000 for aero-bombs. For the fiscal year ending June, 1918, the huge sum of $8,911,000,000 is required for the Army alone.

It was the same with the Navy, which was to have a *personnel* of a quarter of a million men. Yards are enlarged, or new ones built, with shipways for vessels of all grades. There are new naval foundries and machine-shops, new piers and warehouses; seaplane shops, operating bases, and training camps for a further 85,000 seamen. The new armour-plate and projectile factory at Charleston, W. Va., is the first to be erected west of the Alleghany Mountains. An inland site was chosen for this naval forge in view of attack from the air, with hostile warships as a possible base.

These are official facts from the Bureaux of Secretaries Baker and Daniels; but it would be misleading to suppose that America geared herself for so vast a conflict without serious lapse and error. "Democracy," says Secretary Lane of the Interior, "is not so efficient as Autocracy." The fact was shown before the Senate Committee on Military Affairs when unpleasant stories came from the National Army. "In no camp," declared Senator Wadsworth, "are there small-arms for half the men, so they are drilling with broomsticks! At Camps Meade, Fulton, and Spartanburg, I talked with machine-gunners who had never laid eyes upon a machine-gun. Many of our boys have no overcoats; thousands wore light summer underwear in the bitterest of weather." The Governor of Oregon complained that his guardsmen were housed in floorless tents, and there was an alarming shortage of blankets. Three years ago General Leonard Wood attacked the War Department for its inertia in such matters, and became a target of persecution for his pains.

The Committee of Inquiry called before them General Crozier, the Chief of Ordnance, and Quartermaster-General Sharpe, whose evidence showed the American war-machine overtaxed and borne down. General Crozier confessed that no American artillery could appear in the European field before the summer of 1918, and even then only 6-inch guns, "middle-heavies" and lesser pieces. There was vacillation and delay over rifle manufacture; details of rechambering and interchangeability of parts were badly confused.

But when all is said, these are familiar stories in the militarization of democracy. In America, as with us, there was drastic house-cleaning in bureaucratic circles. President Wilson is perhaps over-loyal to his Cabinet staff; he selected them in 1912–1913, when America never dreamed of the cataclysm at hand, with all it involved of politico-social revolution. His War Minister was once the Pacifist Mayor of Cleveland, O.—a civic reformer concerned with three-cent tram-fares, and to "safe" the dance-halls for exuberant youth. The First Lord of Wilson's Admiralty was the editor of a country paper; and Mr. Daniels' ideals of discipline in a democratic Navy were too genial to last. The Presidential Council of Ten was chosen on strict party lines. All regions were represented with due bias towards the South, to which Dr. Wilson owed his victory. So far as Congress is concerned, Cabinet appointments are purely personal to the President, and therefore apart from the Legislature, in which the Ministers have no seats.

This curious aloofness has been debated for fifty years, and is now known for a flaw in the Constitution. Jefferson never spoke face to face with Congress as Wilson does today; written Messages were sent by a White House clerk to give the lawmakers "information of the state of the Union." The Ten Executive Departments, though within a stone's-throw of the Capitol dome, might as well be in Paris or London so far as Congress is concerned. The result is a diffusion of energy which makes for delay and muddle to a lamentable degree. Of course it cannot last. President Wilson himself is in favour of seating Cabinet officers in Congress for the better expedition of affairs, particularly at a time like this.

It is at least possible that the present Watchman of the White House will see the passing of the Prussian Sword, and some attempt to establish that League of Nations which is the prior and fundamental feature of his enduring peace, and not—as the German Chancellor would have it—a matter to be considered "after all the other questions in suspense have been settled." Wilson's second term expires in 1920. Already America is scanning the political horizon with no great hope of finding a successor to the ablest Executive who ever led her to the vindication of her ideals. At this writing the United States is still in "her honeymoon of the war," but her Allies need have no fear of her fortitude in the hap ahead, with its seesaw of calamity and triumph, its test and trial of endurance on the part of civilians as well as soldiers. "We are out to win," is the Wilson note. And if I know anything of

America, each set-back will only burn her purpose deeper to make an end of that German curse which the President has branded as "the enemy of mankind."

CHAPTER XVII

"So soon as we communicate and are upon a familiar footing of intercourse, we shall understand one another. And the bonds between the Two Americas will be such that no influence the world may produce in future will ever break them." (President Wilson to Delegates of the Pan-American Financial Conference at Washington.)

The United States has three foreign problems which are peculiarly her own:—(1) The integrity and stability of Mexico, (2) the inviolability of the Latin Republics in Central and South America, and (3) the policy of the "Open Door" in China, which involves the question of relations with Japan. The matter of Mexico is of the first importance. So far back as 1826 Daniel Webster laid stress upon this fact in the Lower House of Congress, pointing out that whilst a foreign landing, say in the River Plate, might be only a matter for diplomatic protest, a similar attempt in the Mexican Gulf would call for drastic action on the part of the United States.

But the factor of distance has shrunk since those days; the hidden hand of Germany has raised afresh the spectre of foreign aggression which alarmed Jefferson, Monroe, and Calhoun. Germany's expansive policy, coupled with pacific penetration in Central and South America (especially Brazil), has of late years roused the Washington Government to a decisive course. The German aims were plainly stated to the Imperial Reichstag by Bethmann-

Hollweg on March 30, 1911—the .year of the Agadir *coup* and imminent world-war.

"The condition of peaceableness is strength," the Chancellor laid down. "And the old saying still holds good that the weak shall be the prey of the strong. . . . We Germans, in our exposed position, are above all bound to look this rough reality in the face. . . . Therefore the world, and especially the weaker countries, should take this warning to heart. For it implies more than passive recognition of a fact; it is the declaration of a policy— the policy of expansion which we consider indispensable to the cause of world-peace and the existence of the German Empire."

Here was the brigand code set forth in the twentieth century. "Gentlemen," said the same high spokesman to the same assembly three and a half years later, "we are now in a state of necessity (*Notwehr*). And necessity knows no law." Such was the Chancellor's apologia for the martyrdom of Belgium which Germany was sworn to protect. What wonder, then, that the Monroe doctrine of "Hands off the New World" became an urgent concern of President Wilson in his second term? America had had her own Agadir alarms due to the *dira necessitas* of expansive Deutschtum. There was the Samoan dispute in 1889; the menace of Von Diederich to Admiral Dewey at Manila in 1898; Roosevelt's ultimatum to Von Holleben in the Venezuelan affair of 1902. And there were German efforts to get a foothold in Haiti, and to acquire the Danish islands in the Caribbean with a view to establishing a naval base on St. Thomas or St. John, and with it a great entrepôt for Central and South American trade which should command the eastern entrance of the Panama Canal.

Already the harbour of Charlotte Amalie was an appanage of the Hamburg-Amerika Line. In 1902 Roose-

velt and John Hay could have bought the Danish group
for $5,000,000, but the German "hand" nipped all nego-
tiation, and the treaty was defeated in the Copenhagen
Landsting by only one vote. By 1917 the price had risen
to $25,000,000; and on April 1 Mr. Lansing handed a
cheque for that amount to the Danish Minister in Washington, thus closing a deal which had been vaguely debated
for fifty years.

That Germany has long looked upon Latin America as
her Promised Land admits of no doubt; the evidence is
overwhelming, apart from the intrigues published by the
Foreign Relations Committee of the Senate. The design
is naïvely stated by all the Pan-German apostles. Wilhelm
Sievers points out that the "Empty Continent" is the only
white man's territory left—"therefore we must hasten to
take possession of it." Ludwig Riemer proposed an expeditionary force of "technicians and engineers, scholars,
business men, and managers," who might effect the bloodless conquest of this prize by the push-and-go of Prussianism. Von Liebert was for concentrating Deutschtum in
the Argentine, Uruguay, and Brazil, so that "a powerful
body, united to the Fatherland by every tie, might organize that Greater Germany of which the Emperor spoke to
us in 1895."

The Pan-German Atlas of Paul Langhans, published at
Gotha in 1900, shows three-quarters of a million Germans
in the Latin Republics. And of all "our Antarctic Colonies," the most flourishing and cohesive were those of
Rio Grande do Sul, Santa Catharina, and Paraná in Southern Brazil.

These settlements owe their origin to an invitation from
the Brazilian Government in the first half of the nineteenth
century, with a view to developing vacant provinces of
vast extent and potential riches. In 1849 the Hamburger
Kolonisationverein was formed, and the following year a

barber named Blumenau founded the Brazilian colony which bears his name today. It contains 40,000 Germans, isolated like the rest from "inferior" Latin elements around them. German schools and traditions foster the ideals of Deutschheit in this land. Visiting merchants who use the ports of Pelotas and São Pedro scout and scorn all things Brazilian. Lutheran pastors come and stay for years as politico-social missionaries; they are maintained from the homeland, and preach the divine right of Kaiserdom and the doctrine of *Allmacht* on the usual biological lines.

There are associations in Germany which support the teaching of German in these colonies; substantial grants, up to half a million marks, figure in the Imperial Budget for the same purpose. On their part the colonists have their Vereine and patriotic clubs, as well as the ritual of the Bierkomment to foster the sentiments of the Fatherland in remote highland pastures, in the ranches and coffee-fazendas. The Federal Government in Rio is prevented by the Constitution of 1891 from interfering with public instruction in the States; here is another parallel with the hyphenate problem in North America. The Brazilian authorities have, however, closed the German shooting clubs and confiscated over 100,000 rifles belonging to exuberant colonists who talked of armed insurrection and complete independence (*Unhabhaengigkeit*).

Long before she severed relations with Berlin, Brazil was aware of her hyphenate embarrassment. Herr von Pauli, the German Minister in Rio, played the part of plotter which Count Bernstorff played so long in Washington. Strikes and riots were fomented so as to hinder and discourage the Government. Arms were smuggled down the coast, wireless stations were discovered, with crafty ramifications north and south. The State Government of Rio Grande moved Loyalist troops to Porto

Allegre in view of a German rising. Uruguay took similar steps on the frontier; she had news of a projected raid, and took official counsel with Argentina with this event in view.

Meanwhile the destruction of Brazilian ships (the *Macao* was the fourth) with every circumstance of horror—especially in the case of the *Paraná*—roused native feeling to a dangerous pitch. Deutschheit was declared a national danger to Brazil. The Germans were assailed by mobs in Curitába. Three hundred German buildings were burned in Porto Allegre alone; and Colonel Schmidt, the Governor of Santa Catharina, was denounced as a traitor and a spy. The Brazilian press was very bitter indeed; it assailed its own Foreign Minister, Dr. Lauro Müller, because of "the terrible doubt of Brazilians as to the predominance of Germanism over his nationality." Dr. Müller resigned, and was succeeded by Senhor Nilo Peçanha, a former President of the Republic.

There was in this huge land the same awakening that America felt; the same alarm over unpreparedness, for there were barely 25,000 soldiers to defend a country as large as Europe. But there was also a patriotic surge, led by poets like Olavo Bilac, and statesmen like Senator Ruy Barbosa, the author of the Brazilian Constitution, and a leading figure at the Second Hague Conference in 1907.

"The juridical questions of the present war," declared Barbosa in the Municipal Theatre of Rio, "and the burning problems of neutrality, afford common ground for all America, and especially for South America, where is found upon Teutonic maps a Southern Germany. . . . If the Central Empires are victorious in this war, the German nation, intoxicated with pride and with Europe prostrate at her feet, will not hesitate to settle accounts with the United States; and then, violating the doctrine of Monroe, which our great neighbour is not yet strong enough to uphold, she will proceed to seize in South America those regions which the cartography of Pan-Germanism has so often claimed as the natural seat of its sovereignty. Such is my mature and profound conviction."

It is common knowledge in Latin America that Teuton settlers despise their hosts and seek to dispossess them. The notorious Karl von Luxburg warned the Berlin Foreign Office, from his Legation in Buenos Aires, that "our easy-going good nature" was a poor policy in South America—"where the people are only Indians under a thin veneer." So the advocate of "Sink without a trace" favoured an occasional flourish of the Mailed Fist if "our political aims in South America" were to be successfully achieved. As these included "the reorganization of Southern Brazil," it is clear that the excitement in the big Republic was amply justified.

It is this shadow of Prussianism which accounts for the ".continental solidarity," which Señor Francisco Tudela, Foreign Minister of Peru, announced in a Note to Secretary Lansing in Washington. Grave duties confronted Peru, and the "necessity of defending her rights against the new form of maritime warfare set up by Germany." So Dr. von Perl was handed his passports, and he made tracks for Ecuador, to which Republic he was also aceredited. The Foreign Minister in Quito promptly telegraphed to his Legation in Lima, saying that the German Minister would *not* be received in Ecuador. Cuba and Panama declared war; Costa Rica, Haiti, Honduras, Nicaragua, Bolivia, and Uruguay broke off relations. Chile and Argentina swayed back and forth, a prey to German influence and intrigue—though in the last-named State poets, people, and the press were all but unanimous for war. The vote in the Senate at Buenos Aires was twenty-three to one in favour of a rupture; Dr. Romulo Naon, Argentine

Minister in Washington, resigned his post in protest against the neutral policy of President Irigoyen.

The Anti-German demonstrations following the Luxburg *exposé* were very violent, but the President continued to block the people's will, as the Constitution permits him to do. German interests in this Republic are exceptionally strong; the Hamburg-Amerika Line has a steamer on the stocks (the *Cap Polonio*) of 40,000 tons, intended for the Argentine trade alone. In German hands are the most thriving electrical concerns, banks, breweries, and meat-packing plants, as well as a large share of the sugar, wine, and quebracho industries. Many prominent Germans, among them the present Under-Secretary for Foreign Affairs, Baron von dem Busche-Haddenhausen, have married into wealthy Argentine families. German nobles and industrial magnates own immense lands, one of the largest holders being the Kaiser's brother-in-law, Prince Adolf of Schaumburg-Lippe. Other great estates belong to commercial concerns in Berlin, Düsseldorf, and Hamburg.

German designs upon Latin America took a new turn after the Spanish-American War, when all other Powers had acquiesced in the Monroe Doctrine. In October, 1900, we find the Emperor laying the foundation-stone of the Roman Museum at Saalburg and outlining his grandiose scheme: "May our German nation in future, aided by princes and people, their armies and citizens, become as powerful, as strongly united and unique in sway, as Rome's universal empire!" In this year also the new Navy Bill was introduced to the Reichstag, and the Preamble plainly stated that "Germany must have a fleet of such strength that a war, even against the mightiest naval Power, would involve risks threatening the supremacy of that Power." The indiscreet Höhenlohe put this into plain English when he said in his *Memoirs* that the new Navy was meant for purely offensive purposes.

The position was simple enough in Teuton eyes. Britain, the Saxon historian declared, was "a decrepit Power living in lucky aloofness on a wealthy island." And Germany was the bold inheritrix (*Rechtsnachfolger*) of her world-dominions. No wonder, then, that the "Monroeismo" took a new turn in this baleful light. Secretary Lansing told the Latin delegates in Washington that it was now the national policy of the United States, and Pan-Americanism the prior principle of her international policy.

But until the Great War revealed Prussian methods, it cannot be said that the Latin Republics hailed their northern protector with any great enthusiasm. Brazil alluded to this fact in a Note to her envoys abroad on the revocation of her neutrality and her new alignment with the United States. "If there has hitherto been a lack of reciprocity among the South American Republics, it is because the Monroe Doctrine permitted a doubtful interpretation of their sovereignty." Current events now ranged the greatest of all the Latin States beside her powerful sister, since the foreign policy of all had a practical orientation towards the common end of liberty and development. The minor Republics followed the lead of Brazil. President Tinoco of Costa Rica discovered German intrigues to overthrow his Government. Guatemala unearthed similar plots "aimed at the safety and independence of the whole of Central America." Even erratic Haiti had her citizens slain by German torpedoes; and as her demands "in the name of humanity" were ignored, the negro State severed relations—to the great amusement of Berlin.

The predominance of the United States in the Western Hemisphere may be said to date from the close of the South American War of Independence, which lasted nearly fifteen years and closed in 1824.

At that time Spain still had powerful armies in South America; and the reconquest of her colonies was the avowed purpose of the crowned conspirators of the Holy Alliance who, at Verona in 1822, secretly vowed to destroy representative institutions and uphold the preposterous principle of the Divine Right of Kings. At any rate this is the version taught in the United States.

British aid, military as well as financial, was felt in the Empty Continent from the earliest days of its independence. And compared with Britain's commercial and industrial development, that of other nations is relatively small. In listed securities today British investments total at least £700,000,000, and to this must be added immense sums in trade credits and private enterprise. From Mexico to Chile British capital financed the Governments, built railways, ports and harbours, opened up new lands, tilled the soil, established plantations, worked the mines, raised flocks and herds, and furnished banking facilities for domestic and foreign use. European rivals came on the scene only when the pioneer work was done. So that our prestige has always been great; the "palabra de Inglés"— the Englishman's word—is still a respected bond from Vera Cruz to Valparaiso.

On the other hand Monroeism, with the implied trusteeship of the United States, has never been welcomed in Latin America, which is extremely sensitive where sovereignty is concerned. This was very noticeable after the Mexican trouble, when President Wilson claimed to act as *censor morum* and to lead the lesser Republics, by force if need be, along the path of constitutional reform. It is pointed out that America herself has long outgrown the Monroeism and become an Imperial Power, by virtue of the Washington Treaty of Dec. 2, 1899. This gave her certain islands of the Samoan Group; there was also the annexation of Hawaii and the Philippine Islands after the war with Spain. So far back as 1826, when Bolivar wished to liberate Cuba and Puerto Rico, America vetoed the project and it collapsed. In 1848 the United States expanded at Mexico's expense, and at Colombia's in 1903.

So the Big Sister, it was said, was by no means free from those designs of conquest which were thought peculiar to the Old World. An alliance of the so-called A. B. C. States (Argentina, Brazil, and Chile) was at one time widely mooted for preserving the balance of power; and Roosevelt's tour in 1913 was mainly intended to allay these alarms and preach a new and modified version of Monroeism. But the U. S. policy in Cuba, Nicaragua, and Mexico left the Latin nations more suspicious than ever. President Wilson's statement that America would not tolerate any financial or industrial control of these States was openly denounced in the Brazilian Chamber. It was taken to mean "that under pretence of emancipating our Republics from the highly fanciful peril of European Imperialism, the United States would simply submit them to its own control."

Awkward evidence on this score was Secretary Olney's assertion in the Venezuela-Guiana boundary dispute with Great Britain. "Today," Cleveland's Foreign Minister declared, "the United States is practically sovereign upon this continent; and its fiat is law upon the subjects to which it confines its interposition." All authorities agree that this claim is void unless America can back it with armed forces commensurate with her imperial duties. To an historian like Hiram Bingham the Monroe doctrine is "an exploded shibboleth." To Roland Usher even the Pan-American movement is a sentimental dream by reason of racial barriers, language, religion, civilization, and infrequent intercourse. It is not Europe that Latin America fears, Professor Usher tells us, but the United States with its new schemes of political and commercial aggrandizement.

The emergent fact is America's continuous growth since

the precarious day of James Monroe; hers is no exception
to the rule of nations, and she must needs adapt herself to
her changing destiny. So early as 1821 she showed a desire to expand; the following year Florida was ceded by
Spain and organized as an American Territory. In 1825
and 1829 attempts were made to acquire Texas by purchase; Louisiana had been bought in 1803 for $15,000,000.
And so the process went, with Indian, Mexican, and Civil
wars, and steady expansion westward till Alaska was acquired from Russia in 1867. As a profession of chivalry
and defence of the weak, Monroeism was left behind; it
was never an international treaty, and became at last a
purely American policy, based on the welfare and con-
venience of the United States.

The Inter-oceanic Canal marked a new era of Imperialism. In 1902 Congress empowered President Roosevelt to
acquire the derelict French ditch for $40,000,000. The
Spooner Act called into being the six-mile strip known as
the Isthmian Zone; and next emerged the new Republic
of Panama, shorn from Colombia by native rebels, backed
by the armed forces of the United States. The lesser Republic was bitterly aggrieved; and though the Colombian
Pact, drawn by Mr. Bryan in 1914, bound America to pay
$25,000,000 as a *douceur,* mutterings of German intrigue
continued to reach the U. S. Senate, and delayed the ratifi-
cation. "We are told," declared Senator Lodge, "that
Colombia will furnish submarine bases in order that Germany may assail our shipping and the Panama Canal.
Therefore we must buy off this Latin State and make
apology!" . . .

I may not stay to consider so gigantic an undertaking as
the Canal; it was the grave of many American reputations,
and has disappointed the American people. Admittedly it
was a mistake to build a lock canal in a precarious region
of earthquake and tropic floods. The choice is all the

stranger, seeing that the engineers of five nations (including our own) were called into consultation, and favoured the sea-level system.

M. Philippe Bunau-Varilla, a man of unique authority—he was chief engineer of the Second Panama Company—points out how this essential artery of military navigation is now at the mercy of aerial bombs. And the wrecking of gates and walls might separate for months the fleets of the Atlantic and Pacific Oceans. Moreover the Canal, as at present constructed, could not give passage to those capital ships of 110 ft. beam and 200,000 horse-power which America has in view. It is therefore suggested that the famous ditch be further excavated for 100 ft. and turned into "the Strait of Panama." This would, of course, be a sea-level affair, and its completion need not seriously interfere with the working of the existing Canal—into which, by the way, our Minister beheld two ranges of hills sliding with uncanny persistence. Howbeit, America has a second string to her bow in the Nicaragua route, which unofficial estimates showed would be cheaper than the constant removal of land-slides from the Culebra Cut of the Panama Canal. The Nicaragua venture was suggested years ago by Senator Morgan and Admiral J. G. Walker. Work was begun, but the project failed through lack of funds in 1893.

"We need all the friends we can attach to us in Central America," President Wilson wrote to Senator Stone, Chairman of the Foreign Relations Committee. Yet the touchy Latin States continued to find affronts. Costa Rica complained that her territorial claims in the Nicaragua Canal option had been ignored. Salvador, Honduras, and Guatemala lodged protests over the new American naval base in Fonseca Bay, on the ground that their approval had not been sought. Then Colombia put in a shadowy claim to the two islands in question, asserting that the King of Spain had awarded them to her 113 years ago. But enough has been said to show the mistrust with which the *Yanqui* was viewed in Latin America before the Great War broke out. His moves were disconcertingly abrupt. A lack of punctilio marked them all, a certain want of *simpatía* which the Germans were not slow to emphasize.

For years before the war, official America was puzzled at the mysterious antagonism of many of the Latin Republics. This is now known to have been due to German-owned newspapers printed in Spanish and edited on anti-American lines. The new *Militarismus* of America—an Imperial America with the habit of war and great offensive establishments—was artfully presented to the Latin States as that of a new Colossus from whom everything was to be feared. Sinister motives were ascribed to each visit of the U. S. fleet: "To put the fear of big guns into little countries," was how the Latin-American patriot, Chavero, described it. Peru took offence when the cruiser *Tennessee* called at Callao, and Secretary McAdoo refused to land: there was rumour of bubonic plague in the port. This touchiness was kept alive by a host of German leagues and clubs from Mexico City, where the Society of the Iron Cross was busy, down to Valparaiso; here the central Deutsch-Chilenischer Bund is affiliated with forty-four branches in as many towns. The aim of all intrigue was to inflame public opinion in the Latin nations and present German influence as a counterbalance to the new "Monroeismo" and the growing aggression of the United States. Hence the trouble in Cuba—in Honduras, Salvador, and Nicaragua, too, with Lehmann, the German Minister to Guatemala, as chief plotter and master mind.

These plans were periodically published by the State Department in Washington, and also by the Foreign Relations Committee of the Senate. The process of "tunnelling the Monroe Doctrine" was plainly shown all the way from Paraguay to Haiti, where Germany had her eye on a naval base·at Mole St. Nicolas. Hidden schemes were now brought to light—the cancelling of Allied contracts in South America, the stirring of sedition and resentment, as well as the chain of wireless stations which played so fatal a part in the destruction of Admiral Cradock's squadron. In Nicaragua, German agents were outbidding the American Treaty offer for a new Canal route, offering two million dollars more.

All these moves were supported by a native press, by local German Chambers of Commerce, too, and by energetic bodies in Germany, such as the South American League, of which Herr Dernburg is President, and Gustav Schmoller, of Berlin University, the most eloquent advocate. "South America is the land of the future," this economist declared. "There is more for us in the Empty Continent than in any part of Africa." Schmoller pictures a new German Empire in the Western Hemisphere when the Great War is over, and the formidable forces of Deutschtum are once more loosed in industry and trade.

Hamburg has its Iberian-American Union, with a review of its own published in Spanish—the *Cultura Latino-Americana*. There are also pamphlets and guide-books for commercial houses interested in the ambitious program "when we build up afresh in South America on the lines of Hanseatic tradition and experience." The vast web of German propaganda, closely linked with Weltpolitik and the military machine, called for counter-efforts on the part of the United States. Long ago Director-General John Barrett, of the Pan-American Union in Washington, warned his Government that such measures were urgently needed in view of swarming German agents, whose efforts might "completely nullify all the apparent advantages of Pan-American co-operation and support in the war."

As the war progressed and Wilson's leadership was weighed, a notable change came over South American opinion. It is a fact that German methods of war shocked all these nations, however lurid their own histories might have been. No denunciation of the Kaiser equals in fury the "Apóstrofe" ("To a Crowned Assassin") which the Argentine poet, Almafuerte, published in *La Plata*. Novelists, essayists, classical scholars, and men of science were soon pleading the Allied cause with less invective and much more cogent reason: Dr. Luis Drago, who brought a South American doctrine of his own to The Hague; Paul Groussac, Director of the Biblioteca Nacional in Buenos Aires, José Enrique Rodo, the Uruguayan writer, and Professor de Medeiros e Albuquerque, who spoke for Brazil.

These intellectuals laid stress upon the impassable gulf between Deutschheit and their own material interests, their racial affinities and cultural traditions. "The psychology of the Brazilian people," Professor de Medeiros pointed out, "is radically and fundamentally opposed to that of the German people. Their mutual antipathy is not a sentiment such as newspapers may inflame one day and quench the next. It is a profound and essential antagonism, more deeply seated than that of any European people, not excepting even the French." This writer reviewed the repeated German efforts in Brazil, beginning with the military mission which the Kaiser proposed, and Marshal Hermes de Fonseca was cajoled into backing, as a means of reorganizing the Brazilian Army. The next offensive was against the native press. Newspaper debts were bought up, and skilful moves set afoot to compel embarrassed journals to espouse the German cause. After that, pro-Germanism raised its head in the Rio Congress; but national feeling ran too high, for Brazil was too well aware of the Prussian danger in her midst.

Gradually the influence of President Wilson began to reassure these Latin nations. Pan-American Congresses were called to Washington, one of them with the specific object of improving financial relationships. And in outlining his policy, Dr. Wilson implied that domestic peace between the Latin States was a condition precedent to the new era of Pan-American co-operation and prosperity. First of all, the political independence and territorial integrity of every Republic should be guaranteed. All outstanding boundary and other disputes were to be handled by patient investigation, and settled by friendly means. No State should abet or permit the equipping of revolutionary expeditions against the Government of any other State, nor allow munitions of war to be exported for that purpose.

America now had millions to lend for the development of her sister nations. Her merchant marine was being restored; and as an earnest of it a new freight and passenger service was started from New York to Valparaiso by way of the Panama Canal, which saves four thousand miles over the old Magellan route.

But when all is said, it is impossible to forecast the drift of this Pan-American movement. The lesser Republics are quick to resent any interference. Canada is not interested at all. There are, moreover, foreign colonies and islands— British, French, and Dutch—which Pan-American zealots would purchase or "restore," as the Falklands to the Argentine Republic. This is the view of Mr. Charles H. Sherrill, Chairman of the Foreign Relations Committee of the U. S. Chamber of Commerce in Washington. Another ambitious scheme is the Pan-American Railroad from New York to Buenos Aires, a distance of 10,471 miles. Many links are already in existence, but 3309 miles remain to be built, and it is doubtful whether the project will ever be completed.

Other thinkers believe that time and fate will bring an American Protectorate over all the territory between the Rio Grande and the Isthmian Zone. The late Admiral

Mahan was for limiting the Monroe doctrine to the defence of the Canal itself. No foreign Power should be allowed a foothold within striking distance of that strategic waterway. Mahan thought that Monroeism, applied to the whole South American Continent, would impose a weightier burden than the Great Republic could bear. In any case it is clear that President Wilson's first concern is to ensure peace among the Latin States and to sublimate good from the Great War by drawing the two continents together as "an example to the world in freedom of institutions, freedom of trade, and intelligence of mutual service."

It is more than doubtful, however, whether peace can be indefinitely kept among the Latin Republics. Chile is especially feared, as an oligarchy with a truculent record. In the war of 1879–83 she attacked and defeated both Bolivia and Peru, taking from the latter the nitrate fields of Tarapacà and the provinces of Tacna and Arica. The Chilean Army is German-trained, the country poor, but undeniably ambitious. In 1898, over disputed goldfields, she mobilized for war against Argentina; but British arbitration went against her, awarding her rival valuable lands in Southern Patagonia. High up in the Andes the two nations erected a dramatic statue of Christ, the Peacemaker, and a bronze tablet below records the vow: "These mountains shall crumble to dust ere Chile and Argentina break the solemn pact which they registered at the Saviour's feet."

Bolivia desires an outlet on the sea, and would no doubt take over Tacna and Arica in case of further trouble between Chile and Peru. Colombia has a grievance of her own against the last-named State; Venezuela could be relied upon to invade Colombia and seize lands which are likewise in dispute. Lastly, Paraguay has territory to redeem from the Argentine, and believes that she might count upon Brazilian aid in the attempt in view of yet

another long standing feud. He is indeed a pink thinker
who imagines perpetual peace among these proud and
primitive Republics. Their finances are still chaotic, and
caste is glaringly marked. Beside a small and lavish aristocracy is a politico-military party, variable as the moon
and freaked with lawless "dictatorships," like those of
Cipriano Castro in Venezuela and José Santos Zelaya in
Nicaragua. Below this ranks are the masses, commonly
sunk in ignorance and squalor, and all too easily led by the
loudest pretender. Illiteracy in Guatemala reaches 92 per
cent. Therefore the new armed might of the United States,
well and wisely used as it will be in defence of Democracy
and Right, cannot fail to be a blessing to the South American peoples, whose delegates President Wilson greeted in
Washington with no formal welcome, but one "from the
heart as well as from the head."

The Empty Continent, as it is called, contains one-eighth
of the land-surface of the earth, and has barely the population of the British Islands. Argentina alone is almost as
large as our Indian Empire. Roughly speaking, Brazil has
the same area as the European continent; a single province
of Peru (Loreto) is larger than Austria-Hungary by 40,000
square miles. It is a mistake to suppose that Spanish and
Portuguese are the only languages spoken. In Tierra del
Fuego, a country no bigger than Scotland, three distinct
dialects are used, and five or six in the Paraguayan Chaco.
It is no wonder that Germany mapped out an Empire in
these parts, for there is no limit to the riches of this un-
developed world.

Since food has proved a vital factor in the Great War, it
is worth while to consider South American supplies—always bearing in mind that not one-tenth of the area suitable for the raising of such products is at present under
cultivation. Countries bordering on the Caribbean and
the Mexican Gulf alone stand ready to supply 300,000 head

of cattle every year. Three-fourths of the Latin States have in recent years become exporters of food-animals or meat; and foremost among these are Argentina, Uruguay, Paraguay, and Venezuela. Mexico sends the United States 4,000,000 lbs. of meat each year. Of beef, Latin America exported last year 340,000 metric tons, valued at $104,000,-000. This came largely from Argentina and the south; but the immense plateaus and uplands of Central America and northern South America are perfectly adapted for the raising of flocks and herds on a huge scale.

Of wheat, maize, and other grains the export was 6,000,-000 metric tons, worth $160,000,000; of sugar, 3,236,000 tons, worth $271,000,000; of coffee, 18,000,000 bags, worth $191,000,000; of cacao, 126,000 tons, worth $35,000,000. Coco-nuts and pines represented $3,500,000; every week saw 116,000,000 bananas delivered to the United States alone. These products are capable of indefinite expansion, and in this work America is now taking an energetic hand.

Apart from meat, Latin-American exports for last year totalled $774,000,000. Special efforts are now being made to grow sugar. Suitable areas in Brazil are thirty times greater than those of Cuba, which last year produced three million metric tons. Peru and San Domingo could increase ten-fold their present cane cultivation, and great tracts of Mexico, Central America, Colombia, Venezuela, and Ecuador are likewise suitable for this valuable crop.

Three-fourths of Latin America can easily furnish substitutes for the staple grains. Yams, for instance; manioc and banana-flour, rice, beans, figs and coco-nuts. On both sides of the Equator are lands with extraordinary climatic advantages. Even in waste places valuable products are found, like the stunted tagua-palm, whose big seeds yield a vegetable ivory for which Hamburg devised special machinery of manufacture. Three corn crops a year are often possible in Latin America; and Washington is now sending agricultural chemists and experts into the sister States to demonstrate new ways of farming and marketing. Mr. C. H. Townsend, of the Bureau of Entomology, points to the State of Amazonas, in Brazil, as by far the richest on earth in regard to possible human subsistence. Every conceivable food-stuff could here be grown. Yet the capital city of Manáos, and other important centres, are actually compelled to import supplies, such is the lack of development in a peerless State more than three times the size of the German Empire, though with a smaller population than the city of Bradford.

Pan-American advocates point out that up till 1914 almost all the Government and private loans of the Latin States were raised in Europe. This supply has been cut off, and is unlikely to be renewed for many years after the war. Therefore the financing of Latin America is become a matter for the United States, and must in every way be beneficial on the prudent lines laid down by President Wilson. It is thought that if $500,000,000 were invested in the twenty Republics during the next five years, it would result in an increase of Pan-American trade to a like amount.

But first of all, the banking interests of the United States and their bond-buying constituencies must be educated in Pan-American possibilities. Nor should this be difficult, thanks to the impetus given to bond-buying by the famous Liberty Loans. One of these was taken up by four million investors, whereas less than 300,000 Americans had previously owned Government bonds; they preferred municipal issues at home, and mining, railroad, and industrial stocks, which were subject to erratic fluctuation and market manipulation. Unfortunately the Latin States are associated in the American mind with periodic revolutions and political instability. Cartoonists have long pictured the bravo who seizes the reins of government with no larger following than a few ragged peons and a mule. Pan-American apostles now point out that this comic-opera régime is over, and the United States intent upon the economic soundness of the whole hemisphere.

In round figures, American trade with the Latin States for 1917 showed an increase of three hundred per cent. over the figures for 1914. Nine months' imports (especially copper) from Chile were greater by $53,000,000 than they were two years previously. Those from Peru were $17,-000,000 up, and so in proportion with Uruguay, Colombia, and Ecuador. The increase in exports from the United States was equally large. Peru is extending her cotton production, Brazil is exporting five times more beef cattle than she did in 1916; Argentina is striving to make up for Australia's restricted export of wool.

It is the belief of Director Barrett of the Pan-American Union that five years after peace is declared, Latin America's commerce will reach five billion dollars, evenly divided between Europe and the United States. The National City Bank of New York, America's most powerful financial concern, has inaugurated the new era by opening branches in Rio and Buenos Aires, in Santos, São Paulo, Bahia, Montevideo and Santiago. This is but a beginning. The same bank publishes a magazine called *The Americas,* and this contains valuable information for traders who wish to enlist in the new "economic offensive" which the United States is planning after the war on both Government and private lines.

Meanwhile the Pan-American Union in Washington has taken a fresh lease of life for the coming Day. This is an International Bureau of Information, maintained by the twenty Latin Republics and the United States. It is housed in a very handsome building, which Mr. Carnegie gave at a cost of a million dollars. American diplomats like Mr. C. H. Sherrill, a former Minister in Buenos Aires,

and consular agents like Mr. E. B. Filsinger write books
and pamphlets to promote the growth of Pan-Americanism. The last-named was president and commissioner of
the Latin-American Trade Association. These prudent
guides explain the tariffs and customs laws, the perils of
unstable exchange and the peculiar tastes and prejudices
of South American importers, with whom Yankee hustle
may be grievously out of place. Therefore stress is laid
upon the social side of business deals; the value of cour-
tesy and tact, which "cut so little ice" north of the Mexican Line, where goods and price are the most appealing
factors.

The whole of this trade offensive—it is by no means
confined to Latin America—has shrewd backing from the
American Government and its bureaucracies. Gone for
ever is the shirt-sleeves diplomacy and "political" Consular Service of the United States; both were overhauled
during the four terms of Roosevelt and Wilson. The Reorganization Act of April 5, 1906, graded all the American
consuls. It provided for inspection and supervision, it
required all official fees to be accounted for and turned
into the Treasury, at the same time providing adequate
salaries, and thoroughly Americanizing the service by in-
sisting that all officers of over $1000 a year should be citi-
zens of the Republic.

As usual, unlimited power in this matter was vested
in the President. With these reforms went a new merit
system devised by Secretary of State Root. This consisted
in an efficiency-record of each consul: his ability, prompt-
ness, and diligence; his personal conduct whilst in office,
and the character of his trade reports to the Department.
These records are consulted by the Secretary of State,
and brought to the President's notice with a view to promotion, transfer, or retention in office. In this way a
good man was assured that his work would not be for-

gotten by a new Administration; and his service to the nation's commerce was made independent of the ebb and flow of party politics. The Department of Commerce and Labour publishes a daily brochure of Consular Reports and Foreign Trade Opportunities. Here is a college in Buenos Aires asking for school and laboratory supplies. A Dutch house inquires about maple rollers for making wall-paper; the Chilean Government is about to invite tenders for seventy-nine miles of railway (with important bridges) from Asorno to Puerto Montt.

Shoes for the Balkan States, horses for British artillery, motor-cars for India, a meat-packing plant for Serbia; trams for Salonica, water-pipes for Tsing-tau, candles for Uruguay, cheap jewels for Korea, with hints on packing and pilfering *en route,* together with sad reflections on the Turk and the guileful Chinee. These reports, acute and terse, are extraordinarily interesting. They tell of markets for all goods, from a gramophone to a case of chewing-gum; orange-wrapping machinery, street sprinklers, and portable houses for Central and South America. Moreover, the consuls take note of every foreign institution likely to be of service; and from the frequency, variety, and intelligence of these remarks, a man is judged and weighed. Of course the great staples sell themselves—cotton, petroleum, grains, and ores. It is in finding markets for manufactured goods that the American consuls are so clever; and due meed is properly given them in State Papers when the Government deals with the huge increase of trade which recent years have seen.

In the Latin States the rivalry between American and German consuls became intense before the Great Republic declared war and gave a lead to her sister nations, grappling them to her with new ties—"now that all trust in treaties and international loyalty is gone." I quote from Brazil's regretful Note to the Holy See.

It was America's task to attack the net of commerce and finance with which Germany had covered the Empty Continent. A start was made with a "black-list" of nearly two thousand enemy firms—banks, business houses, merchants, public utility concerns, and the like. America never thought she would have a black-list; her President and State Secretary had said as much. Had she not already protested over similar measures taken against her own firms by the British and French Governments? But war is a great teacher. In July, 1917, Washington began to black-list the largest and most dangerous combinations of German capital in Latin America; billions of dollars were here represented. Exports to these concerns were forbidden by law or made subject to license. Imports from them were only permitted in liquidation of American debts.

In this work the War Trade Board was assisted by commercial attachés and consuls, who, in order to minimize inconvenience, furnished the names of non-enemy firms as substitutes for the proscribed concerns. The latter had been politically active, aiding German raids and plots, fomenting strikes in the familiar style; furthering German aims and paying for propaganda which had reached amazing proportions. The new theory forced upon England and the United States by the German *patriotismus* was that an enemy was an enemy—not only in his own country, but wheresoever he was found. To what extent German interests in South America will recover after the war, it is not yet possible to say. Certain it is that the United States will use her opportunity to the utmost—not in mere trade alone, let me hasten to say, but also in firm and tactful leading of these nations towards political stability and reconstruction.

As a belligerent Power on a great scale, America's mission has often been stated by President Wilson. "It is for us a war of high principle,'' he claims, ''debased by no selfish ambition of conquest or spoliation. Our object is to vindicate Peace and Justice in the life of the world . . . and to set up among the really free and self-governed peoples such a concert of purpose and action as will henceforth ensure those principles.''

CHAPTER XVIII

("THERE had undoubtedly arisen between the peoples of Japan and the United States an unfortunate misconception of each other's motives in regard to China. . . . The tendency to mistrust spread to such an extent as to assume alarming proportions.

"We know now that it was fostered by a campaign of falsehood, secretly carried on by agents of the German Government, which, as part of its foreign policy, thought it well to alienate America and Japan, hoping, in the event of trouble with either Power, to have in the other at least a friend, and possibly an ally. . . ."—Secretary of State Robert Lansing.)

Looking into the future, America is a little anxious over her military transformation. Is it likely to be permanent? Will the times return to their primitive gold when this era of blood and iron has passed; or is the divine precept, "Bear ye one another's burdens," to be carried out indefinitely with bayonet and bomb? The veteran, Dr. Eliot of Harvard, is afraid the great Lesson will leave untouched the unholy feud which Lucretius saw in the fiercely battling forces of the world. Already Bills have been brought into Congress to fasten military service upon the United States. War Secretary Baker, in his annual report, soothes a pacific people by deferring policy in this regard until peace comes again, and perhaps with it a rational measure of disarmament and guarantees.

This is also the President's view, and that of the masses in the main who are content to wait and see, bearing in mind the old racecourse maxim, "When it's wet, do not bet."

There still lingers in the United States a body of opinion which dreads preparation for war, and would somehow compromise with the monster of militarism, lest Force come to be regarded as the sole hope of liberty in the twentieth century as it was in the seventeenth. It is worth while to notice this wistful sentiment as I pass, for although quiescent now it is likely to reassert itself at the first opportunity. The military machine, these pacifists contend (they are found in Congress as well as out of it), is a dangerous possession—explosive, impersonal; responding to the lightest touch, as the avalanche moves to the perching bird or the slam of a cottage door in the Alpine valley. It is a feeling of this kind which Congress has always opposed to the arming of the United States, quoting the desideratum of William James with inveterate hope. "One hears," the philosopher said, "of the mechanical equivalent of heat. What we now need to discover in the social realm is the moral equivalent of war—something heroic that will spread to men as universally as war does, and yet will be as compatible with their spiritual selves as war has proved to be incompatible."

Of this wordy stuff and the hindrance it entailed, General Crozier, of the Bureau of Ordnance, spoke quite frankly in his evidence before the Military Committee of the Senate. For years, the witness pointed out, Congress had cut down the appropriations for artillery until they were "absolutely inadequate." The result was that the work of years had to be crowded into a few hurried months, with the inevitable "difficulties and present partial delays," to which the President alluded in his reply to Count Hertling and Count Czernin. The American Press passed all the errors and muddles in angry review—the personal friction and resignations; the absurd red tape, the disappointments and failure to accomplish enormous programs in hand. Blame for these things, as the *Washington Star* pointed out, should not be laid upon present-day officials, but upon "past Congresses, acting under the influence of ranting spell-binders and dreaming millennialists."

It must be said that these are today a shrinking band—especially since Viscount Ishii sprang his Japanese "Monroe Doctrine for Asia" on the United States in 1917. This supplements the Root-Takahira Agreement of 1908, which in turn reaffirmed Secretary Hay's policy of the Open Door in China to which the Powers agreed in 1900. The text of the Ishii-Lansing Memorandum is in part as follows: "In order to silence mischievous reports which have from time to time been circulated, it is believed by us that a public announcement once more of the desires and intentions shared by our two Governments is advisable.

"The Governments of the United States and Japan recognize that territorial propinquity creates special relations between countries, and consequently the United States recognize that Japan has special interests in China—particularly in the parts to which her possessions are contiguous.

"The territorial sovereignty of China, nevertheless, remains unimpaired, and the Government of the United States has every confidence in the repeated assurances of the Imperial Japanese Government that, while geographical position gives Japan such special interests, there is no desire to discriminate against the trade of other nations, or to disregard the commercial rights heretofore granted by China in treaties with other Powers.

"The Governments of the United States and Japan deny that they have any purpose to infringe in any way the independence or territorial integrity of China; and they declare, furthermore, that they always adhere to the principle of the so-called 'Open Door,' or equal opportunity for commerce and industry in China.''

Now the good faith of America in this matter is beyond dispute, whereas the record of Japan is one of aggression. Her Twenty-One Demands, put forward by the Okuma-Kato Ministry in 1915, were calculated to destroy the sovereignty of China altogether. The notorious ''Group V'' of these demands aimed at complete control by Japan of the public life of China, together with its army and munitions of war. So that American opinion, especially on the Pacific Slope, was far from pleased with the new Eastern Monroe Doctrine, which the ''yellow Prussian'' put forward at a time when the white Powers were locked in deadly conflict.

Let me say at once that I deal first of all with America's version, passing later to that of Japan, and explaining friction and mistrust of long standing over the great world-markets of awakening Asia. For China is a land of incalculable riches; it comprises one-twelfth of the earth's surface, and has a population of 400,000,000 souls. With Japan in possession, the pessimists say, she would in time become a menace to the world. She would realize her Pan-Asiatic dream, with industrial wealth beyond compute; an immense navy, and an army of possibly twenty million men recruited chiefly from her Chinese vassals, whose fighting quality, given modern weapons and scientific leading, have been proved in many fields. Unhappily this martial spirit has been mainly shown in civil wars.

The break-up of China, so long expected, may well be at hand by some *coup de main,* such as these lawless days have made familiar to us all. For China is a loose chaos of many tongues, with no national spirit informing it. A single province—silken Sze-chuan—is larger than France, and in its red basin lie the largest coal-fields in the world. Food crops grow twice, and even thrice in a year. Here, then, is an unexploited world—a derelict which expansive Japan, through all her statesmen from Hayashi in 1895 to Terauchi in 1918, has marked as the proper sphere of an economically poor and cramped, though proud and ambitious people.

The late Sir Robert Hart, who gave his life to China's service, was for ever haunted by the fate of his adopted land. "The ship may go down in the night," he would say, as he paced the floor in the small hours. Assuredly the night of world-war has not bettered China's chances of weathering the storm. Nor has America any illusions, as she reviews the history of the past twenty years, culminating in Viscount Ishii's mission, which was a portent of momentous change. Precisely what pressure and promise were brought to bear upon the United States in this matter is a diplomatic secret, and must remain so for a time. "None of us doubt," writes the typical American humorist, "that Japan has Pacific intentions!"

Californian papers were more downright, reminding their readers of Korean "scraps of paper," now added to the historic heap. Three of these guaranteed the "integrity and independence" of that debased and wretched State. The last of them was made only two years before the total absorption of the Hermit Kingdom by Japan. The very name of Korea was then blotted from the map; it was rechristened Chosen, and became a province of the expansive Empire by reason of that same propinquity which America now concedes as a ground of special interests. And so with Manchuria, wrested from Russia a few years later under public promise of its restoration to China. It is now a Japanese sphere. So also is Eastern Inner Mongolia, together with Fukien and the Shantung promontory —this last taken over with the conquered German zone, including perpetual rights, and the railway from Tsing-tao to Tsinanfu, the provincial capital.

America complains that propinquity and special interests appear to be links in an endless chain which, with avowed purpose, Japan is pursuing into the very heart of helpless China. Before the war, the Yang-tse Valley was regarded as a British sphere, even as Fukien was Japanese. But the Twenty-One Demands included joint ownership of the Han-yeh-ping holdings near Hankow.

After forty centuries China remains a nebulous welter with no Government as we understand it; the main street of her heedless capital is today policed by foreign soldiers. It is impossible to convey the lack of nationhood which this Asiatic prize presents—"the only country on earth," as one of her intellectuals said, "which finds it necessary to give compensation for the withdrawal of wholly untenable demands."

Has China any disinterested friend? Undoubtedly she has in the United States, which, on John Hay's recommendation, remitted half the yearly indemnity payable on account of the Boxer havoc of 1900. This money—nearly $12,000,000—was devoted to the education of Chinese boys in academics and technical schools of the first rank in the United States. It would take too long to instance all the goodwill manifestations of America for the Chinese people. In June, 1900, when the Allied ships opened fire on the Taku Forts, it was the U. S. commander, Admiral Kempff, who alone refused to take part in the bombardment, warning his colleagues that it would unite and inflame all factions against the foreigners.

That China was mindful of this friendship is seen by the vote in the Pekin Parliament to erect a monument to John Hay, who, in 1899, gave a practical turn to America's concern over the impending break-up of the Empire. The war with Japan, five years before, had demonstrated China's military impotence in the face of a foreign foe. And now the Powers of Europe were plainly bent on spoliation. Japan had seized Formosa and imposed a fine of $185,000,000 on her late enemy; the original demand was much larger. Russia had taken Port Arthur, and was extending her influence in Manchuria. Germany had occupied Kiao-chau, Britain had appropriated Wei-hai-wei, France added to her Asiatic domains certain Chinese territory in the south. Concessions for railways, mines, and special privileges were being extorted month by month; and the nineteenth century closed with the dissolution of the Chinese Empire predicted on all sides.

It was on September 19, 1899, that John Hay, then Secretary of State, addressed his Open-Door Note to the predatory Powers. It was an adroit move, and, for a time at least, stayed further encroachment as well as enhancing American prestige. Hay was trying to develop an alternative to those "spheres of influence" which bade fair to devour the Asiatic domain. Replying to him in an exchange of Notes, the Powers agreed to base future policy, not upon individual spheres, but upon the common interests of all. Nevertheless the military might of Japan —already proved against a great European Power—her pressing needs, and trade energy were soon assailing the "Open Door."

So far back as 1895, when peace with China was concluded, Count Tadasu Hayashi stated the conqueror's plan in these words: "What Japan must now do is, remain quiet for a while in order to lull the suspicion of her which exists. Let her meanwhile strengthen the bases of her national power; let her watch and wait for the opportunity which will one day surely come to her in the Orient." It is plaintive America's case that the Great War has furnished this opportunity; and the Manufacturers' Export Association said as much to Secretary of State Lansing in a notable letter, written in 1916. All indications, the members declared, "pointed to the fact that Japan, taking advantage of the occupation of other world-Powers with their own affairs, was about to take strong measures in carrying out her designs in China, and that in a manner which may seriously affect the interests of American trade, and promises to nullify the 'Open Door' policy to which Japan, in common with other Powers, is committed."

The Association did not confine itself to vague fears, but reminded the Foreign Minister that "the history of Japanese activity in Manchuria is the history of an all but complete extinction of American commerce." The weapons used were preferential rates and vexatious hold-ups of foreign goods. Here was a sphere in which a trade of $24,000,000 speedily dropped to below $3,000,000, and is still on the downward grade. So far as America was concerned, Manchuria was another Korea. In 1907 the trade in grey cotton shirting and sheetings for that State was evenly divided between Great Britain and Japan. Six years later our share was eight per cent., and that of Japan ninety per cent. In the same interval American trade with Korea fell off seventy-five per cent. Here again were special freight rebates for the Japanese, special customs dues to their own people at Au-tung, and loans from the Yokohama Specie Bank at four and a half per cent., which was much below the prevailing rate.

Another element which disturbed America was the secret Treaty between Russia and Japan, signed on July 3, 1916. This appears to have had a definite military aim in keeping China free from the influence of a third Power. Manchurian railroads and munitions of war were also included in a deal which may well have conflicted with Article III of Great Britain's own alliance with Japan, renewed five years previously. Here the high contracting parties declare that neither shall enter into another agreement without consulting her partner.

It is well known that secret diplomacy of this kind is very repugnant to the United States, whose love for above-board methods and popular assent have been so often set forth in President Wilson's speeches. It will be remembered that the Bolsheviki of Petrograd published all the secret treaties they could lay hands upon in the Russian archives. These embarrassing papers dealt with the fate of the Dardanelles and Persia, the future of Asiatic Turkey and the left bank of the Rhine, as well as inducements to Greece, Rumania, and Italy. In the latter case the whole Dalmatian coast was added to the Trentino, South Tyrol, Trieste, and Istria. Thus the Adriatic was to become an Italian lake, with Austria-Hungary cut off from her seven strategic gulfs and naval bases. President Wilson referred to these furtive bargains, warning statesmen not to ignore the wide-awake opinion of democracy, nor to attempt "any such covenants of selfishness and compromise as were entered into at the Congress of Vienna. The thought of the plain people, here and everywhere throughout the world—the people who enjoy no privilege, and have very simple and unsophisticated standards of right and wrong, is the air all Governments must henceforth breathe if they would live." Only upon that basis was there a promise of stability beyond that of the bad old order—"the arbitrary decisions of a few negotiators striving to secure, by chicanery or persuasion, the interests of this or that dynasty or nation."

It was this passion for the square deal which led to publication of the Ishii-Lansing Agreement last year. Its reception, I must say, was rather mixed, and many American thinkers sided with Chinese publicists at home and abroad who posed an awkward parallel. "We feel you have departed from your traditional friendship," these last complained, "in conceding the Japanese demand. China is an independent nation and ought not to be made the subject of negotiation between foreign countries. Now suppose Japan and the United States signed another agreement—with 'Mexico' substituted for 'China.' Do you think that would improve Mexican-American relations?"

German comment on the Ishii Agreement was that it deferred indefinitely "that war between Japan and the United States which has become a fixed idea with the average German, and a definite element in our Government's political calculations." Another expert thought that Germany would have Japan to deal with at the peace-table as regards Tsing-tau, and that place in the Orient sun which divine right had decreed to the *Herrenvolk,* as the Kaiser so often declared in his character of seer and prophet. "Who can foresee," Wilhelm put to his people, "what events may take place in the Pacific in days to come—days not so far distant as some believe, and for which we must steadily prepare?"

The *Frankfurter Zeitung* had an able article from its former correspondent in the Far East, and this may be taken as typical of German trade aims. "China is the land of the future for the industry and enterprise of the world; we must allow no blocking of our road in that spacious quarter. After the war we shall see fierce vying in the Asiatic field, and we Germans will face not only individual competition, but also State-aided concerns, like the American International Corporation." The *Cologne Gazette* went over the same ground, and then turned to a grander theme—a German-Russian-Japanese coalition which was "a syndicate for the division of the world," with promising partners for the German job, which was of course to secure the lion's share.

It may be recalled that Mr. Gerard, as U. S. Ambassador in Berlin, heard a good deal about this Tento-Russo-Japanese offensive. Financiers and members of the

Reichstag assured him that Germany "would be forced" into such a pact if America threw her weight into the Allied cause, and thus brought about what Von Tirpitz called "the Anglo-Saxon tyranny." It was Germany's wish that the United States should "stay at home," as Bismarck thought Russia ought to do. All the world knows how German intrigue worked to keep America "at home." She was constantly reminded that she now had Imperial problems of her own, including an Eastern Question in which her Teuton "friend" took an extraordinary interest. Mr. Gerard himself tells of a strange talk with the Kaiser at the New Year's reception of Ambassadors in 1914, six months before the outbreak of war. The Diplomatic Corps were lined up like dragoons, six feet apart, in one of the palace halls when the Emperor entered with his staff. "He stayed longest with the Turk and myself, thereby arousing the curiosity of the others, who suspected that the Kaiser did more than merely exchange the compliments of the season. And he did. What the Emperor said to me is of interest to every American, for it shows his subtlety of purpose. The Kaiser talked at length about what he called Japan's designs upon the United States. He warned me that Mexico was full of Japanese spies and an army of Japanese colonels." America must be kept at home, and at all costs prevented from joining hands with Great Britain in an "Anglo-Saxon domination." Later on the German press took up the theme, and dealt simultaneously with this new menace to the Fatherland. For it might well offset the European system where docile States were to be ranged like satellites around the central German sun. In this connection a certain telegram of the Kaiser to Tsar Nicholas should be recalled. It was dispatched after the Dogger Bank affair, and made use of the term "Anglo-Saxon," as if to show that even then

Wilhelm pictured Britain and America united against him on his trampling march from Antwerp to the marts and strongholds of Eastern Asia.

Evidence was also published in revolutionary Russia— that *enfant terrible* of the chancelleries—showing that the German Emperor made overtures to Japan. The latest of these was on the eve of the fall of Tsing-tau, when a separate peace was mooted on the Mikado's own terms; the only stipulation being that Japan should attack Russia as a preliminary to the Pan-Asiatic scheme which Okuma's Government was supposed to cherish. This proposal was scornfully rejected, and the Kaiser's message turned over to the British Ambassador in Tokio. For German intrigue in the Far East, especially with a view to commercial rivalry after the war, had been throughout inimical to Japan. Propaganda was carried on in the right Chinese quarters, which is to say among Pekin officials; merchants of the Treaty Ports who handle foreign trade, and Young China representatives in Parliament and the Provincial Assemblies, where Western thought is developing.

It is not to be denied that German prestige stood high with the Chinese military caste. Great play was made with the war-map; subsidies were granted to native journals which were supplied with German news by the Ost-Asiatische Service. Nor was there any lack of agents drilled in what America calls "the gimlet ways of a spy-and-bully system." Witness the two years' tour of Otto von Hentig from far Yarkand back to the security of the German Consulate in Hankow, leaving a trail of slaughter and confusion behind him. Something like $15,000,000 a year was paid by the Chinese Government to the Deutsch-Asiatische Bank: this included Germany's share of the Boxer Indemnity, and also interest on the two Anglo-German loans. So there was plenty of money available for evil work against the Allies; for support of the Manchu movement (there were German gunners in that *coup d'état*) and above all for the fertilization of future commercial fields. "Germany looks ahead," as the Emperor remarked in his "far-stretching horizon" speech. It is therefore clear that the elimination of such a rival was a necessity for Japan, and she set about the task with rare vigour.

When Marshal Terauchi's Government saw America committed to war, it was decided to send a Plenipotentiary who should state in clear terms the new Asiatic policy of Japan, and at the same time dispel the mistrust and irritation of years between the two nations. For this mission the ablest of envoys was chosen—Viscount Kikujiro Ishii, a man of extraordinary fluency and grace, trained under Komura, who was the father of Japanese diplomacy. Ishii was Ambassador to France in 1912, and three years later he became Foreign Minister under Okuma. "Our message this day," he declared on landing in San Francisco, "is that, through shadow or shine, America and Japan are bound together for the same goal. Your sons and ours must have good neighbourhood assured. We must live so that the word or deed of neither may be viewed aslant; that venomous tongues, hired slander, and sinister intrigue such as has victimized us both, can only in future serve to draw us closer together for mutual protection and the common welfare of all."

At the same time there was throughout this envoy's speeches a quiet insistence upon prior rights. "Circumstances for which we are in no sense responsible give us special interests in China. . . . Our Chinese friends," Ishii explained at a banquet on his return to Tokio, "tell us that China and Japan are like the two wings of a bird, the one indispensable to the other." I saw cartoons in California showing that bird in mocking flight, leaving Uncle Sam completely in the lurch! Meanwhile Viscount

Ishii, by reason of his success, was appointed Ambassador in Washington, replacing Aimaro Sato, who was barely established in his post—the graduate of an Indiana University and but recently hailed as the ideal Japanese envoy.

Sixty-five years have passed since the Roosevelt of his day, President Fillmore, sent Commodore Perry to open relations with the shy Twilight Children whom Francis Xavier had long before found "very desirous of being instructed." But Japan of the Shogunate days had no zest for foreign ways or creeds; nor can it be said that her visitors, whether traders, missionaries, or naval officers, made a pretty showing in that mysterious land. They were all cleared out in 1637, and Christianity was put under a ban. Then followed two centuries of seclusion, when Japan was fenced in a feudal world untroubled by sophists, economists, or calculators. Of course it could not last. Rumour of Russian encroachment began to reach those lovely islands. England's Opium War in China caused a faint stir; the French and Dutch gave warning that the Christian nations were looking eastward for new marts of trade. But it was America who led the way, after abortive attempts on the part of whalers and castaways to obtain concessions.

As early as 1846 official Washington took a hand—always be it noted with an "armed prayer" to the mediaeval Shogunate. Yet Commodore Biddle could get no more than an anchorage in Yedo Bay for his ninety-gun ship; the intruder was plainly told there was "nothing doing." By 1850 American interests were more clamorous. There were sailors marooned in Japan at this time, and California's gold had turned men's eyes to the Pacific and alluring isles beyond. Two years later President Fillmore's Cabinet arranged the Perry Expedition with elaborate care. Books were bought, scientists and interpreters selected; charts to the value of $30,000 were procured from Holland, and American wares got ready on a tempting scale. It is curious that the United States should have taken such a step at this time, for there was trouble in Cuba, and feeling was very bitter between North and South over the slavery question.

Perry's mission wore a minatory look. He sailed from Norfolk with a squadron of four warships, nor did he "speak softly," as Roosevelt advised America should do when she carries the "Big Stick." On the contrary, the message sent to the Mikado spoke of a still greater armada which was "hourly expected." The Commodore explained that, "should it become necessary," he would return the following spring "with a much larger force. But it is hoped that the Government of Your Imperial Majesty will render such return unnecessary by acceding at once to the very reasonable and pacific overtures contained in the President's letter." This last ran as follows: "These are the only objects for which I have sent Commodore Perry, with a powerful squadron, to pay a visit to Your Imperial Majesty's renowned city of Yedo—Friendship, commerce, a supply of coal and provisions, and protection for our shipwrecked people.

MILLARD FILLMORE."

Having thoroughly shaken up the Shogun, together with the Emperor and his people, Perry sailed away and went back again in February, 1854, with an imposing fleet of ten warships. The result was the first Treaty with Japan —America's earliest "Open Door" in the Far East. England, Holland, Russia, and France were soon elbowing each other in that door.

But Japan herself was by no means unanimous over the

passing of her ancient order. Friction arose between the
Shogun in Yedo and the Mikado in Kyoto—a shadowy
figure who dwelt apart, leaving mundane rule to his
hereditary lieutenant. The feudal lords and warriors were
in favour of continued isolation: the Liberals urged intercourse and compromise with pushful nations overseas.
Ten years of rancour and civil strife drove the division
deeper; and in 1863 the Shogun issued an order expelling
all foreigners. The arrogance and greed of these intruders
recall the righteous blaze of St. Francis Xavier, the apostle
of India and also of these "Islands in the Hope of God."
"Every one here," said the sixteenth-century Jesuit, "takes
the same road—*rapio, rapis.* And I am terrified to see
how many moods and tenses of the wretched verb those
who come this way can invent."

New envoys and Treaty Rights called upon the Mikado,
under threat of war, to rescind his deputy's decree. Then,
at the suggestion of Sir Harry Parkes, the Powers took
steps to eliminate the Shogun altogether; in 1868 the
Emperor Mutsuhito abolished his *alter ego,* and became
the actual as well as the formal head of the Government.
The capital was now moved to Yedo, which was renamed
Tokio or "the Metropolis of the East." Four years later
the feudal lords, together with their Samurai retainers,
gave up their rights in order that Japan might be brought
into line with modern progress. How effectually this has
been done may be seen in any picture-book of today.
For the pretty people are no longer concerned with ex-
quisite trifles and cherry-blossom festivals, but with factory and forge; with skyscrapers and docks, department
stores, and mushroom fortunes, like that of Shinya Uchida
of Kobe, who made five million yen in a single year of
war, chiefly out of shipping, which returned him a dividend of six hundred and fifty per cent. The *narikin,* or

"man turned into gold," is an envied figure in the industrial Empire of today.

Japan's assimilation of Western ways, her rise to power, with armed assertion and suave diplomacy—here is a portent without parallel in the drama of history. No sooner was the so-called Restoration complete than the Mikado took a public oath "to seek for wisdom in every quarter of the earth." Gradually a Parliament came into being; a new bureaucracy, a system of education, and military service on the French and German lines.

Meanwhile the lesson of force—first taught by American ships and guns—was quietly developing. The quarrel with China over Korea revealed a new Power schooled in modernity to the alarm of her teachers and those who had broken into her feudal life. Eight months of war saw China overwhelmed and suing for a peace of territorial cession and indemnity. Korea was cleared by the "toy people," who now loomed as alarming warriors. Manchuria was invaded, the Liao-tung peninsula ocenpied, together with its stronghold, Port Arthur. The Japanese were preparing to advance upon Pekin when China gave way and signed the Treaty of Shimonoseki on April 14, 1895.

Here the Powers of Europe stepped in—especially Russia, whose concern for Far Eastern peace pressed upon the upstart conqueror the return of Liao-tung to humiliated China. There was no course open but submission to this demand; it rankled keenly, however, and sowed the seeds of a new war, for which Japan prepared by sea and land, as well as by industrial activity. The five years that followed showed the European Powers scrambling for rights, leases, and naval bases in China. Port Arthur itself was now acquired by Russia, who had forced Japan to restore that fortress to its rightful owner. Then came the Boxer Rebellion with its national motto: "Uphold the dynasty and drive out the foreigners."

It was at this time that America moved in the matter of China's "Open Door." Japan was watching Russian moves in Manchuria, where railways were being laid, troops poured in, and defences strengthened. The little men, nursing resentment and conscious of growing strength, began to fear for their mainland markets, so the hour of challenge was very near.

In 1902 Japan received a momentous lift through her alliance with Great Britain; for the first time an Asiatic nation was received in the European comity on equal terms. Thus fortified, Japan fixed a period for the Russian evacuation of Manchuria. But Russia quibbled, and put forward demands of her own. For two years diplomacy did its best, and then the sword was drawn—with disastrous results for the Tsar's forces by sea and land. When all was over, President Roosevelt was appointed mediator between the belligerents. They met on American soil, at Portsmouth, N. H., where Count Witte and Baron Rosen faced Komura and Takahira in a "reasonable" bargain. From that day Japan advanced by leaps and bounds. Her imperial progress made little noise in the Western world: it had for its goal the hegemony of the Far East, and recognition of the "little people" as a very great people indeed, with a future of splendid sway.

Before the war with Russia, Count Okuma laid down the new law as a hint to the United Sates: "A Japanese must be respected wherever he goes, for we yield to none in our citizen pride." Now the Sage of Washeda is the Bismarck of Japan—the idol of the nation and supposedly of anti-American bias: this was seen when the sale of the Philippine Islands was mooted in the Washington Congress by Senators with little grasp of foreign affairs.

Okuma remains a Samurai of the Ages, revering the

Emperor and upholding the sword. He can recall a Japan that was impotent as Siam; he has watched her exports grow from next to nothing to $800,000,000 a year. The aged statesman has seen the native junk replaced by home-built Dreadnoughts, like the mighty *Fuso* from the Kure Yard, and her sisters the *Yamashiro, Ise,* and *Hiuga* respectively from Yokosuka, Kobe, and Nagasaki. Each of these great ships carries twelve 14-inch and sixteen 6-inch guns. In Vice-Admiral Kondo the Empire has a naval architect whose pioneer designs are watched with professional interest by foreign experts. It is Japan's desire that all structural work and equipment of her navy shall come from domestic sources. Therefore the Government foundry at Wakamatsu supplies the steel. From the Kure arsenal come armour plates, with forgings and castings, which are also made by private concerns, of which the largest is in Kobe. Guns are made at Mormoran, in the Hokkaido.

Okuma's life-span has also witnessed a railroad miracle, of which the Korea-Manchuria Express is perhaps the most impressive symbol. There is no more luxurious train in the Old or New Worlds. At Fusan pier it connects with the channel steamer service of the Imperial Government Railways. The train runs to and from Chang-chun by way of Mukden and the South Manchuria system, crossing a stately swing bridge over the historic Yalu River, and thus offering the safest and quickest route between Japan and Chosen (Korea), Manchuria, China, and Europe over the Trans-Siberian Railway. No wonder America views with concern this "social climber among the nations," who moves without haste or rest to her appointed goal. For in her own sphere Japan can now defy the world, hedged about as she is by the stormiest seas, and armed with natural features which lend themselves to impregnable defence.

Yet observe this infant Power in 1870, when, as it were, hat in hand, she tried to borrow a paltry million in the money market of London. It was grudgingly given her— at twelve per cent. interest. As security the Customs revenue was pledged, and the loan rigidly earmarked for specific purposes. Even so, our leading financial paper poured derision upon credulous capitalists who could lend money to a people whose national bankruptcy and industrial incapacity were notorious. We are today over £30,000,000 in Japan's debt; and the little people now have an export trade of 1,600,000,000 yen, or £160,000,000 a year. The war has indeed brought Japan unprecedented prosperity. Her "flush-time" dates from the spring of 1915, when Allied orders were first placed and the Island Empire began to profit by the universal dislocation of trade, and the absence of German and Austrian competition. Electric wire and appliances, antimony and sheet glass, paper and toys, celluloid, matches, and raw silk— these are but a few of the commodities for which the nations turned to Japan.

The Government's policy of State initiative and dircetion is being anxiously watched in the United States. Japanese commissioners have been sent abroad to study local trade conditions, and inform the authorities at home on scientific lines. Root-and-branch elimination of German and Austrian trade is aimed at in the Far East; but it is absurd to suppose that this campaign will make no effort to supplant British and American interests of long standing.

The transformation of Japan is complete, her genius for colonization demonstrated during Marshal Terauchi's seven-year clean-up in decayed Korea. Nothing that America ever did in Cuba, Panama, or the Philippines can eclipse that orgy of social, administrative, and agricultural reform, which the Mikado himself inaugurated with a gift of seventeen million yen from his privy purse. Meanwhile Japan's Army was growing fast; it is today at double divisional strength, armed and staffed with Prussian foresight and skill. Her military strength is but dimly apprehended by outsiders, even those who have seen this marvellous race pass from the Stone Age to the Flying Age in their own time.

Whether this material progress is a good thing is open to doubt in our present mood of disillusion. "Hitherto," says Mill, "it is questionable if all the mechanical inventions yet made have lightened the day's toil of any human being. They have enabled a greater population to live the same life of drudgery and imprisonment, and an increased number to make fortunes." The war-millionaire of Tokio; stock speculators of the Kabuto-cho, the narikins of shipping and dye-stuffs, iron and steel—these have lavish mansions on the Ginza, with gorgeous cars and works of art: they will pay five thousand dollars for a single Nabeshima plate. But the working girl remains a slave; the Japanese printer, if paid at the American rate for a forty-eight hour week, would draw no more than a dollar for his labour. A cotton-mill doctor of the Nagano prefecture found forty per cent. of the young girls affected with consumption. They worked fifteen hours a day; they were poorly fed, with only five minutes for a meal. "These hands dwell promiscuously in tiny rooms which scarcely know the sunlight. And at night they sleep face to face, two girls on each six-foot mat. . . . Employers are too engrossed in their own profits to pay heed to these terrible conditions of labour."

The Japanese wage-scale bears no comparison with that of Europe or the United States. A female silk-spinner gets 15 cents a day, a male weaver 21 cents, a dyer 25 cents, tailors 27 cents, shoemakers 30 cents, carpenters 36 cents, stone-cutters 50 cents. Here I approach the eco-

nomic and social problem of the yellow man, which has
for many years made bad blood between Japan and the
United States.

The position is stated by Viscount Kentaro Haneko, a
Privy Councillor and former Minister of Justice; he is
also an LL.D. of Harvard University. "Had we remained
a China or Korea," this statesman says, "the clamour of
this race question would never have reached so acute a
pitch. As it is, Japan emerged from her foreign wars
with a splendid organization, and as civilized as the foremost nations of Europe and America, imposing respectful
consideration upon them all, and breaking—to the resentment of some—the tradition that the white peoples are
essentially superior to Asiatics."

It is well to remember that we are here dealing with a
proud and energetic people, acutely sensitive to foreign
criticism and desirous of admiration and praise. During
the Russo-Japanese War, American feeling favoured the
"little men," but the signing of the Portsmouth Treaty
brought about a change. Japan, it seemed, was no longer
docile or submissive. She declined the proposal of Secretary of State Knox that she should hand over the South
Manchurian railways (which had cost a hundred thousand
lives), and accept instead a settlement in money. The
implied threat of insistence was this time ignored; for
Japan was no longer to be browbeaten by the older Powers, one of whom she had just humbled by force of arms.

Once again, then, America saw the "Open Door" in
China closing, and markets of vast potential value in the
shadow of a new Oriental sword. Japan protested there
was room for all—with herself as the dominant partner.
"It is a great mistake," said Kikisahuro Fukui, one of the
Empire's foremost merchants, "for any nation to do business in the Far East without considering Japan's commercial and geographical advantages. She should be regarded

as a colleague rather than a competitor. The Germans are already aware of this; and the General Electrical Company of Berlin entered into successful co-operation with the Shibaura Engineering Works of Tokio. For we have need, and long shall need, the technical skill and genius of the Western world."

As for America, she wanted the yellow man's trade, but not the yellow man himself. Hence many years of friction, with newspaper "wars" and jingo flourishes in Tokio, as well as in New York and San Francisco. For Japanese settlers were all too successfully competing with the white man in the three Pacific States of Washington, Oregon, and California. Still farther north is British Columbia, which also has its yellow problem. Here the Chinese Exclusion Act shut out the earlier intruder unless he possessed £100; but the question of Japanese immigrants is much more delicate because of the power behind them, the racial pride, and growing vehemence of Government claims. Australia, too, has a jealous eye upon her Asiatic neighbours. "It is well known," says the *Frankfurter Zeitung*, "that Japanese longings are directed to the Northern Territories which a dog-in-the-manger attitude cannot indefinitely withhold from colonization." A "White Australia" is undoubtedly the Commonwealth's ideal!

Here the Immigration Act of 1901 blocked all Hindus, Chinese, and Japanese, for it ordained a literacy test of fifty words' dictation "in a European language." Which one was not specified, so the failure of the most cultured Asiatic is a foregone conclusion. Early in the war, German New Guinea and Samoa fell to expeditions from Australia and New Zealand respectively. Japan disposed of Tsing-tau and the Marshall Group, so that "Das Deutsche Südsee Schutzgebiete" was soon a thing of the past, buried with due honours by the Berlin press. Japanese warships were policing the Pacific lanes, and escorting the transports and food-ships of Australasia. Great Britain was much beholden to the little people—but Australia was still entirely White, and quite unmoved by hints of expediency and concessions.

For example there was German New Guinea, a rich land which the Japanese could develop amazingly. But nothing could induce Australia "to bring the Asiatic menace to our back door." The other alternative—colonization of the Northern Territories by the Japanese—was still more dreaded, and the mere idea rejected with scorn.

I allude to Australia and the opposition of her Labour Unions, because the analogy with Western America is complete in this regard. Both democracies accept the black man because he is there and does not count; it is grotesque to suppose that the negro has equal rights with the white man in the United States whatever be the Constitutional theory. But at all costs the "yellow streak" must be kept from spreading. Labour has always been a precarious commodity on the Pacific Coast of America. An unlimited source of supply was closed in 1882, when Congress passed an Act prohibiting Chinese immigration. This was in response to a demand from the three States affected. Asiatic labour, it was pointed out, lowered the standard of living. What decent American could hope to compete with the ten-cent standard of the "Chink"?

After the Exclusion Act the price of labour rose, and fruit farmers were at their wits' end for season pickers and packers of enormous crops which called for rapid handling. In 1887 four Japanese appeared in the Vaca Valley region of California: These were the pioneers. Between 1890 and 1900 twenty-five thousand came—nimble, intelligent fellows, who moved in gangs under clever bosses, and solved, as it seemed, the labour problem of a rich land. Death and departures were soon reducing the proscribed Chinese.

There was no law against the new yellow men, who were not long in finding their American legs. They began to buy up land, to form unions and demand larger wages. And they had a passion for tenantry, these quiet invaders of the Coast.

If the owner of a farm or citrus orchard would not sell, he was faced with a labour boycott, and gave way at last perforce. That was the beginning of Japanese colonies. White neighbours moved away; new homeseekers would not settle in a yellow region. Orchard displacement in the Vacaville and Newcastle sections was soon on a sweeping scale, and in time most of California's strawberry crop was in Japanese hands. They also controlled the celery output of the south, and the great market gardens which supplied the cities of Los Angeles and Sacramento. And the Japs were uncannily efficient with prehistoric tools which, applied to unlikely swamps bought for a song, presently yielded a huge harvest. Meanwhile in the towns the Japanese invasion was causing alarm, not only in common white and semi-skilled labour circles, but also among the small traders—barbers, cook-shop men and storekeepers.

The white laundry folk formed Anti-Japanese Leagues; the yellow men met these with protective unions, and won the day with their steadfast resolve to "do it for less." Economic defeat deepened racial prejudice into downright hate, and the Japanese was ostracized with penal restrictions which he was quick to resent. Thus the little men were excluded from the public bathing places of San Francisco. Their children were segregated in Asiatic schools; and at last the Pacific States, led by California, proposed a Federal Law shutting out these Asiatics altogether. This was very embarrassing to the Washington Government, because there was a definite treaty permitting the Japanese to come and settle in the United States like any other race of the Melting Pot.

However, there was no arguing with California, where
riot and disorder, arson and murderous outrage were directed against the yellow men, despite grave warning from
Tokio, and protests from the Ambassador in Washington.
California pleaded her State Rights as a sovereign commonwealth of the Union. This was exclusively her affair.
She must settle it in her own way, and threatened President Roosevelt with secession if he insisted on coercing the
Coast people in a matter which concerned them alone.
After all, was not the naturalization law limited "to aliens
being free white persons, and to aliens of African nativity
and persons of African descent"?   Here was the last straw
in heaped-up injury. Japan was debarred from a citizen
privilege which the lowest negro could claim in a huge democracy where equal opportunity for all was the first
commandment of the national creed! After many alarums
and excursions, including the dispatch of sixteen warships
round the Horn into the Pacific, Roosevelt and Root made
a bargain with Japan that no more passports should be
issued to labourers.

In 1913 the Californian Parliament passed the Anti-
Alien Land Bill, a vague measure which limited Japanese
tenure to a three years' lease. Four other States passed
similar laws, to the growing anger of the Tokio Foreign
Office and a clamorous native press. "We must have room
to grow," these papers pointed out. "More than seventy
per cent. of our people get a living on the land—poor
enough land at that. We have a population of 357 to the
square mile, as against America's 31 and California's 17.
Our excess of births over deaths is 600,000 a year. Then
where shall we turn?" Ernst Haeckel, the German, was
right when he predicted wars of dispossession, with crowded
nations struggling for existence in a pegged-out world,
"where the strongest and most resourceful will alone survive."

It is well to state both sides of the case. That of Japan is a claim to peaceful expansion in quest of the raw material so vital to her manufactures. "What wrong has she done America?" she asks. Six thousand miles of sea separate a poor group of islands, containing over fifty million souls—only sixteen per cent. of whose lands are arable—from a fabulously rich people of over a hundred millions, owning a fertile continent as large as Europe. And America's national wealth, when compared with Japan's, is like John Rockefeller's billion beside the coppers of a gutter newsboy. Japan insists that the maintenance of peace is a cardinal principle in her development of new Asiatic spheres, now opening to her beneficent sway. She rests upon her proven quality in war, and points to the patience with which she has endured years of insult from the United States, who in turn regards a solemn treaty as a scrap of paper, and shuts out the Japanese as though they were felons of the Black Hand or the Camorra.

"When we strike," the little man informs America, "we do it without counting the cost, in the true *bushido* spirit. And when our heroes fall in battle, their families do not droop in mourning, but put on gala dress to receive the visit of friends who congratulate them on the high honour which their sacrifice has brought. A formidable outlook, it may be, judged by Western standards; it is one to be reckoned with in the continual baiting and thwarting of Japan. It is only economic pressure that drives us from home. We produce the finest rice, but we can't afford to eat it. We ship it abroad, and import inferior stuff for our own people. China was our last chance—'the opportunity of ten thousand years,' as Okuma called it. We shall do there on a vast scale what Terauchi did in Korea, what Lord Cromer did in Egypt, what Governor Taft did in the savage Philippines. Supremacy in China is naturally ours, because of racial affinity with the people and geographical contiguity. We shall not close your Open Door, but only set our watchmen in it—the sturdy little fellows you despise and reject because they are better farmers than your own. Consider Kinya Shima, of Stockton, Cal., who cornered the potato market with a million dollar deal, out-manœuvring his American rivals. Another of our people hired some land near Los Angeles, at a cash rental of twelve dollars an acre. The owner had offered it rent free to the poor of the town, yet there were no takers. Soon the yellow man's trucks were creaking cityward with produce, and your people stood sourly by. 'Look at that damned Japanese,' they muttered, 'taking the bread from our children's mouths!'

"San Francisco started the Japanese Exclusion Leagues. Reckless mobs, inflamed by the Labour Unions, ran amuck in the yellow quarters. Now mark the difference between the Asiatic peoples in your midst. The Hindus wept helplessly when assailed. The Chinese ran away and hid, but the Japanese stood their ground and fought, leaving their mark upon the ruffian horde, which outnumbered them a hundred to one. It is well to remember that we are of the warrior caste; you can ignore this only at your peril. 'Scratch a Japanese,' as Inazo Nitobe reminds us, 'and you will find a Samurai.'"

For years the Japanese peril figured in American newspapers and magazines. "In May, 1913," Captain Hobson told the House Committee on Naval Affairs, "and for weeks afterwards, our gunners on Corregidor Island were busy day and night. The harbours were mined, Federal troops were dispatched. Our warships were got ready for the Pacific Coast. Secretary Daniels is present. Does he deny the imminence of war with Japan at that time?" There were also rumours of preparation in Manila, where a Japanese descent was feared, with transports convoyed by a great fleet for the seizure of the Philippines group, which Dewey called "the key of the Pacific."

When Rear-Admiral Yashiro was at Pasadena, and a ball was arranged at the leading hotel, the Californian belles were heard to say "They would just as soon dance with niggers." That festivity was cancelled; so was the visit of school children to the Japanese fleet, all dressed in their best and carrying the flags of both nations. A curt telegram from the "nigger" Admiral, and his sudden departure, added another unpleasant episode to the long list. At this time the press of Japan was rehearsing them all, and calling upon its rulers in a fashion which could not be ignored. Apology and redress—or war with America was the popular Japanese demand. It was not alone voiced by "yellow" journals like the *Yorozu Choho*, but by sober organs like the *Asahi* of Osaka, and the *Hochi* of Tokio, which reflects the views of the Doshikai party, of which the Marquis Okuma is the leader. The Newspaper Law of the Restoration was invoked to restrain this newspaper fury. It subsided somewhat, in view of the Gentlemen's Agreement which shelved the immigration question, without deciding it at all. "If as a result of this visit," Viscount Ishii said at the Japan Society's dinner in New York, "the two peoples will but believe that their mutual distrust, suspicion, and doubt are the result of careful German Kultur during the past ten years, then we shall have done much for ourselves and for you."

But America fancies that the Prussian name has seen too much service in this connection. She found nothing German in the repugnance which her Pacific States displayed towards the yellow man. And she got a great shock in 1915, when the Twenty-One Demands were sprung upon China, and at the same time concealed in part from England, France, Russia, and the United States. China herself hastened to supply the omissions, and the discrepancy in the two versions created a very bad impression which no subsequent "conversations" quite removed.

America draws a parallel between German designs upon derelict Russia and Japanese encroachment upon China's weakness. Both victims are dangerous, the Americans think. Both have enormous reserves of strength, despite their seeming looseness; each of these patient races may gird themselves afresh in the vast interior of their country, so as ultimately to smother the invader. The Chinese are a long-suffering folk, with no love for foreign wars. They are well aware of their own lack of nationhood; they are ready and willing to co-operate with others in the work of their own guidance and regeneration. But if Japan denies China a controlling voice in her own destiny, then indeed there is danger ahead. "Better be dashed to fragments as a jewel of jade than held together as a lump of brick," so said Liang Chi-chao, the reformer of Canton, when Japan declared war in 1894.

Since the war began, the diplomacy of Japan has been carefully watched in Pekin and Washington, where Tokio's act and deed are taken as sounder guides than the mellifluence of political missionaries. Japan's "extra-textual" readings have long worried China, who believes with Kung Fu-tze that "sincerity is the beginning and end of all things." Japan has throughout protested the peacefulness of her aims—provided her expansion is not blocked. For this reason America carries the parallel with Prussia a step further. Undoubtedly Japan is now a military power of the first rank—formidable, scientific, and precise. Here, as in Germany, loyalty to the State and the sacred person of the Emperor is erected into a religion. That able writer, Iichiro Tokutomi, editor of the Tokio *Kokumin,* defines the cultus as a "centripetal Mikadoism." "The Mikado is the centre of our nation," this author says in his work, *Japan to America.* "Considered as a body politic it has him as its sovereign. Considered as a race, it has him as leader; and as a social community it has the Emperor for its nucleus."

It cannot be supposed that ecstasy of this kind wakes any sympathy in Republican China or the United States. Neither does the Prussian worship of force which is enshrined in the imperial psyche of Japan. *"Bushido,"* says Professor Inazo, the foremost authority on the subject, "made the sword its emblem of prowess and power. When Mohammed declared the sword to be the key of heaven and hell, he was but echoing a Japanese sentiment." America remembers that the German sword has a monstrous statue of its own—surely the only one extant—a broad blade reared skyward in a mailed fist on the lake at Friedrichshafen, where Zeppelin built his gas-bags for civilian murder in the night. It may be well that President Wilson's war-aim—to "make the world safe for democracy"—applied equally in the East as it does in the West.

The intellectuals of Japan admit that Germany is admired in their country, as it is among the military cliques in China, who block and blight every prospect of unity and reform. According to Professor Anesaki, who was exchange lecturer at Harvard in 1913-15, many leaders of Japanese politics and industry sympathize with Germany's aim to win a place for herself in the sun. "The only remedy for Pro-Germanism among us," the Professor thinks, "is to convince our people of the futility of Teutonic methods. To do this the Allies must be successful—not only in the naval and military way, but also in social, moral, and educational reconstruction after the war." In other words, the Allies must produce a superior Kultur of their own.

Another witness is Motosada Zumoto, proprietor of the *Japan Times,* of Tokio. "It is natural," says this alert and able man, "that the scientific mind and thoroughness of the Teuton should appeal to us Japanese. Moreover, Germany's martial efforts move Japan through the *bushido* ideal of blooming and falling quickly; of heroic effort at any cost—the *Weltmacht oder Niedergang!*—even though it be foredoomed to defeat." It was this affinity of the two Powers, coupled with the mention of Japan in the Zimmermann-Eckhardt plot, which suggested to the United States the peril of a possible German-Japanese Alliance, in which disintegrated Russia might figure as a passive tool. On their part the Germans respect Japan, and warn her that her chance is passing "to conquer the great unmilitary America in a short surprise war."

"One must admit," we read in the semi-official press of Berlin, "that Wilson is wise in harnessing his man-power and industry at this time. It is an extraordinary opportunity, and, of course, only half aimed at Germany. Moreover, once accomplished, Japan's advantage will be over. Therefore America's moment is skilfully chosen. She puts off her weakness without the reproach of militarism at home and abroad. Nor can Japan protest, but only clasp the new friend to her heart. Hence all the palavers and understandings. Hence the sending home of Ambassador Guthrie's body on a warship and the mission of thanks on the part of America's Asiatic squadron, with the Mikado lunching with Admiral Knight, and making the usual pretty speeches."

The Germans maintain that it was Guthrie's successor in Tokio, Dr. Paul Reinsch, who persuaded the Chinese Government to declare war. The President, Li Yuan-hung, was convinced that Germany would be victorious. Vice-President Feng was of like mind for a time; Premier Tuan and the conservative generals were undecided. But Young China followed America's lead—first in protest, then in severance of relations, at last in open hostility, with all it entailed of repudiation and confiscation; of dismissal of German officials and general elimination of Teutonic influence. In this way was Japan outwitted, for she had announced her intention of speaking for China at the Peace Conference of the Powers.

It must be owned that since 1914 the affairs of China present a tangle which defies unravelling. There were coups and counter-coups, mandarin plots, and continuous strife between the radical South and a reactionary North. And always in the background were the ant-like millions leading the same old life in Asiatic spaces, knowing little of the political game, or the very meaning of a Republic. "We are like cabbages with our roots in the air," explained the illiterate despot, Chang Hsun, the "Butcher of Nanking" and feudal lord of Hsu-chow-fu; once a *mafu*, or groom, he became a king-maker in this topsy-turvy land, with a following of forty thousand men.

Through all the turmoil America's voice was raised in earnest exhortation; her efforts were unceasing to restore order in the chaotic "cabbage-field" of Asia. It was the "sincere hope" of the State Department, officially expressed to the Chinese, "that factional disputes may be set aside, and that all parties will work to re-establish and co-ordinate the Government and secure China's position among the nations." I need only refer in passing to the attempt to restore the Manchu dynasty in the person of the eleven-year-old boy, Hsuan Tung, who was hauled from his bed in the small hours to mount the most precarious of thrones. His sponsor, the bandit chieftain Chang Hsun, was soon denounced as a traitor, and fled for shelter to the Dutch Legation with a price upon his head.

But Chinese politics are too bewildering to follow. That strong man, President Yuan, himself plotted for the throne for twenty years, and at last passed a hundred days as uncrowned Emperor—losing his nerve in the interval, and

at last dying miserably of Bright's disease. That was
the end of the Hung Hsien, or Era of Brilliant Prosperity,
in which Yuan's American adviser, Dr. Frank J. Good-
now of Baltimore, had a professional—or rather a profes-
sorial—hand.

America is a long way off: Japan is at China's door,
and now committed to exploitation—if possible with American money, as Baron Shibusawa's mission showed in the
autumn of 1915. Japanese expansiveness is by no means
a new policy; it goes back to the dream of conquest cherished by the great dictator, Hideyoshi, at the close of the
sixteenth century. It was urged in 1859 by Yoshida
Shoin, the Choshiu Samurai, who may be called the
Treitschke of awakening Japan. It was from this philosopher that Kido, Ito, Inouye, and the rest of the "Meiji
Heroes" learned their earliest lessons in statecraft and
national destiny. "The foreign policy of Japan does not
change with the Cabinet," Marshal Terauchi said, when
he succeeded Okuma as Prime Minister. The soldier-
statesman spoke very curtly about the charges of "militarism and territorial aggrandizement" which had been
bandied about in Europe and the United States. "It is
unnecessary for me to assure any one of Japan's good
faith, or to waste words in contradicting and denying the
mischievous rumours and unwarranted presumptions of
those who misinterpret my motives, or forecast my future
actions."

Will Japan realize her project of a protectorate over
China, with all that it entails of power-politics and change?
Who can say with any certainty? The boldest prophets
have been confounded in the course of this war. Even
the cock-sure German is often subdued, and talks of the
Incalculable in human affairs—the folly of forecasting the
fate of nations, or measuring their drift by nicely reckoned
laws of more or less. "It is part of probability," says

Aristotle in the *Ethics,* "that many improbabilities will happen." Who could have predicted the heroic stand of little Belgium or the collapse of mighty Russia in the face of the same foe—with millions of men, in the latter case, flatly refusing to fight, and lynching their own admirals and generals? As for China, no two opinions, native or foreign, coincide about its future; though many observers who have spent their lives in the land detect a new sense of unity—a definite transition from the "family" to the national stage, such as may portend the fusion of four hundred million people into a polity which no alien race could ever hope to control.

Meanwhile China's millions live in a state which American travellers describe as "only half a hop ahead of hunger." The currency is a maddening thing; in Pekin alone nine imaginary taels are in circulation, yet accounts are actually settled in dollars. The measure of silk varies with the city in which you bought it. Language, politics, and problems, all are provincial rather than national. And China remains a roadless land, with each journey an adventure, and many perils in the way.

It is true that change is astir; but can these hordes be roused before the domination of Japan is complete? Here is America's fear; this is her own Eastern Question. It should be remembered that the Panama Canal, by developing the Western Seaboard of the United States, has opened immense prospects of Asiatic trade. America is a Pacific as well as an Atlantic Power, with strategic bases of imperial reach in both oceans.

She has hitherto been weak in a military way, unable to help the helpless nations save by moral means which are now seen to be worse than ineffectual. America's treaty with Korea, signed at Seoul on May 18, 1893, could only offer "good offices to bring about an amicable arrangement . . . if other Powers deal unjustly or oppres-

sively with Korea.'' Yet America was the very first nation to express approval of Japan's decree of suzerainty
over that crumbling kingdom. Again, the United States
was committed to protest on China's behalf when Tsarist
Russia began to absorb Manchuria. No such protest was
made, for it could have nothing behind it but a pious
wish: the champion of Liberty was always without helm
or sword. ''If you can't protect your own citizens in
Mexico,'' said a typical Chinese intellectual in Washington,
''how can we expect you to stretch across the Pacific to
protect us?''

So it came back at last to brute force and the Big Stick,
which no nation may neglect save at the risk of ruin, as the
Russian visionaries found when it was too late. Senator
Chamberlain of Oregon brought out this fact in a three-
hour speech which moved the Upper House profoundly,
and reverberated from sea to sea among a resolute people
arming for Democracy's War. ''From Washington's Letters,'' Mr. Chamberlain said, ''from Bunker Hill to the
Mexican Border affrays of 1916—throughout our whole history—we have never had a military organization or a military policy. Nothing but luck and aloofness have saved
us, and now we must save ourselves.''

War Secretary Baker put up a brave defence of his
Department; but it is clear the machinery broke down in
all directions under unexampled strain. ''It was like trying to run a British tank,'' one heard in the Senate lobbies,
''with the engine of a Ford runabout!'' Sober historians
like Albert Bushnell Hart of Harvard rehearsed again the
unreadiness of 1775, 1861, and 1898. In all cases ''material had to be made ready after the war began.'' . . . ''In
April, 1917, we went to war with the most powerful
oligarchy the world has ever seen, on the basis of a fairish
Navy and a Regular Army of a hundred thousand men.

But there was not a single aeroplane. Not one battery of big guns, not enough rifles for the first Army, no regiment of them trained to the trench, wire, and bomb methods of the new warfare. That is why we now pour out men, money, and munitions to erect the proper engine of war and catch up with our own enthusiasm."

Japan also is a student of war by sea and land and air. As early as September, 1914, her cruisers and destroyers left Yokosuka to search the Marianne, Caroline, and Marshall Groups for our common enemy. When Tsing-tau fell, after a ten weeks' siege, Japanese naval activity widened. It patrolled the Pacific; it co-operated with us in the Indian Ocean and the Bay of Bengal. Important missions were undertaken at the Straits; over transport routes of the South Seas, in the South Atlantic too, and lastly in the Mediterranean under Admiral Tetsutar Sato, whose destroyers rescued British troops and nurses from the torpedoed *Transylvania*.

The Mediterranean squadron brought with them seaplanes, which were soon scouting for submarines with all the scientific *élan* which we take for granted in this race, to whom no Western miracle comes amiss. Japan had her own aviators aloft over the German fortress of Tsing-tau in China. Riddled with bullets, the machines continued to observe, and sailed away when their work was done. I need hardly emphasize the professional zeal with which Japanese attachés follow the colossal struggle on land, and communicate its lessons to the Supreme War Council in Tokio. Meanwhile the Japanese Army was re-armed with a new rifle, the invention of Colonel Kijiro Nambu, a professor of ballistics of international repute. This weapon is a notable improvement upon the Murata rifle, which it has now superseded. In all directions the machinery of war was improved. "The world will be astonished," said

Baron Hayashi, now Japanese Ambassador in Rome, "when it learns all that we have done, and shall do in the future." This significant hint no doubt referred to the projected operations in Eastern Siberia, with Vladivostok as a base.

Both Japan and the United States will therefore emerge from the war as great military Powers. Their future relations depend upon the fate of China and Pacific problems bound up with it, political, economic, and strategic. Earnest efforts, following the Ishii Mission, are being made to improve these relations. Thus Japan has her "East and West News Bureau," an association for promoting cordiality between the two nations. Its director is Dr. Iyenaga, who is also linked with the University of Chicago as a lecturer. Mr. Samuel Gompers of the American Federation of Labour now cables fraternal greetings to President Suzuki, of the Workers' Friendly Society of Japan: "The most important duty of our movements is to maintain frank and friendly terms between our respective countries, and endeavour amicably to solve vexatious problems."

Asked whether America would fight for the Open Door in China, President Roosevelt declared that she would. His successor, Mr. W. H. Taft, held the contrary opinion, doubting whether Americans were sufficiently interested in Far Eastern affairs to make any substantial sacrifice for them. The present Administration sent Notes of great vigour to Tokio and Pekin over the Twenty-One Demands. President Wilson's Government confessed itself "greatly disturbed" over the further Japanese aggression which followed the squabble in Chen-chia-tun. But those were the days of America's "wooden sword," when protests from her were filed or ignored as a matter of course. With the habit and harness of war she will receive a very different hearing. America will in future have something stronger than "good offices" to offer her Allies and protégés, whether

Britain or Belgium; France, China, Mexico, or the Latin-Republics,—to whom by the way the Monroe Doctrine was become a somewhat threadbare mantle of protection from foreign foes.

CHAPTER XIX

THE NEW ANGLO-AMERICAN UNDERSTANDING

"WILL you not convey to His Majesty my appreciation of his sentiments, my confident expectation that the great principles of truth, liberty, and honour, which the people of this country hold so dear, will increasingly serve as a broad, solid foundation upon which the friendship and cordial relations of the two Governments may rest and develop?

"I believe that the righteous cause we are now prosecuting will bind more closely the people of the United States to the people of Great Britain."—(President Wilson to Earl Reading, British High Commissioner in Washington.)

.   .   .   .

The above speech is a momentous break with tradition. Before the Great War there was no European nation which America esteemed so highly as Germany; there was but one nation in all the world for which America had an hereditary dislike, and that was England. The Scotsman escaped this feeling. As for the Irish, whether as citizens or as an "oppressed" people overseas, they were, of course, viewed with peculiar sympathy. Were they not living symbols of that "absolute Tyranny" which is impressed upon every American child in the Declaration of Independence, with its scathing indictment of King George the Third as a prince who "is unfit to be the ruler of a free people"?

The fallacy of "cousinship" with the United States was persistently held in this country in the face of all the facts, and the irritation it roused, by reason of the implied

398

condescension of which Lowell complained. War with America was stoutly declared to be unthinkable by British writers—as though it had not loomed again and again since 1814, when John Quincy Adams met Lord Gambier in the old Carthusian Convent at Ghent, both sides smarting under humiliation, and signed at long last a treaty which left open more questions than it settled, especially the right of search at sea.

Our ruling classes of that time despised the young Republic. They believed it would soon break up, just as Gladstone, Russell, and Derby did at a later day, when Lincoln was at his wits' end to save the Union from disruption. The Treaty of Ghent left bad blood between the two nations, and it was a sullen affair in the making. After four months of obstinate haggling, it was only popular pressure on both sides which forced the Commissioners to. sign a covenant of peace. On our part we declined to grant the United States the privilege of trade with the British-American colonies. Canada's haunting fear was not yet laid with regard to her neighbour's territorial designs.

On her side America resented British "arrogance" with Jeffersonian warmth, and rejoiced that she had for the second time humbled the haughty mistress of the seas. Then in the "roaring forties"—a period of expansion and pioneering to the South and West—there were boundary disputes and border incidents in Oregon and Maine which once more threatened Anglo-American relations. There were quarrels over Mexico and the Isthmus, and over the steps which our officers took to repress the slave trade. The Civil War saw latent antagonism flame up afresh. Rupture was very near when the Confederate envoys, Slidell and Mason, were seized at sea on an English ship and carried off as prisoners to Fort Warren by Captain Wilkes. Palmerston demanded an "instant apology for a violation

of international law." Troops were despatched, war was
declared inevitable, and prayers were offered in the Washington Senate. It was one of those occasions when America mourned her impotence at sea, and wished she had a
navy capable of curbing "the sway of an arbitrary trident."

From the very first a peculiar touchiness is discernible
in the State Department's dealings with Great Britain: a
liability to sudden anger with little provocation, as Cleveland's Message showed in 1895 over the Orinoco swamps
of Venezuela, to which British Guiana laid claim. This
alleged infringement of the Monroe Doctrine was declared
in the Message to be "a wilful aggression upon the rights
and interests of the United States." American protests
to Great Britain, by the way, are seldom couched in the
suavest terms—even those received after 1914, over the
hold-up of American mails, our "hovering" cruisers, the
Black List of traders, the status of "merchant" submarines like the *Deutschland*, and lastly our "so-called" Blockade, which was dealt with in a Note of quite forcible language.

Yet for a hundred years Anglo-American peace has remained unbroken, thanks to the sound sense of both democracies, who insisted upon finding a way out before
extremes were reached.

During the American Civil War our neutrality was of a
kind that vexed both belligerents and left us with few
friends at the close, either in the North or the South.
This irritation grew more intense when the struggle was
over, thanks to unscrupulous angling for the Irish vote,
and partly through the growth of American imperialism.
The Irish question, I may say at once, has always lamed
our relations with the Republic. Since 1914 German
propaganda has made damaging use of it, pointing to the
gulf between Britain's precept and practice in her treat-

ment of the weaker nations. Ireland, Egypt, and India
are specifically named in pamphlets and speeches addressed
to people who have little or no knowledge of the facts.
In America the Irish have a political power out of all
proportion to their numbers. And having joined forces
with disloyal German elements in the early days, they
were able to hinder America's war-will, adding to the confusion of her neutral time.

At home and abroad Irish hostility has been unwaver-
ing, and it cropped up in each Anglo-American dispute.
As leader of the Nationalist Party, Mr. John Redmond
sent the following message to New York at the time of
Grover Cleveland's threat over the Venezuelan affair: "If
war results from the reassertion of the Monroe Doctrine,
Irish national sentiment will be solid on the side of America. For with Home Rule rejected, Ireland can have no
feeling of friendliness for Great Britain."

It were absurd to deny that such seeds as these fell
upon stony ground in the United States, whose very
founder threw off the "despotism" of a British king who,
with his hireling soldiers, was accused of "cruelty and
perfidy scarcely paralleled in the most barbarous ages,
and totally unworthy the head of a civilized nation."
Nor did George Washington acquit the British people of
a share in "these usurpations" when he wrote his wrath-
ful Declaration. "We have appealed to their native justice and magnanimity," he said, "and we have conjured
them by the ties of our common kindred. . . . They, too,
have been deaf to the voice of justice and consanguinity."

Here we see the root of an Anglophobia which lasted a
hundred and forty-one years. It coloured all intercourse,
social, economic, and political; and as America grew, it
was kept alive by the most assertive aliens in her midst.
Dislike of England hampered the ablest and sanest of
State Secretaries—men who had vision enough to put prej-

udiec away, as Jefferson did, and were willing to "marry ourselves to the British fleet and nation" whose championship America had already known in serious crises.

John Hay's Anglo-Saxon policy received no support; the cry of "Subservience to England" spoiled his sagacious drift, especially during the Boer War. Hay gives us many hints of the strong currents against him at this time. "That we should be compelled," he mourns, "to refuse the assistance of the greatest Power in the world in carrying out our own policy, because all Irishmen are Democrats and some Germans are fools, is enough to drive a man mad!" Already the hyphenate problem was acute, clogging American statecraft, and renewing the ancient bitterness every Fourth of July with hymns of hate which did more harm than the fireworks: and *they* were very deadly indeed, as every American knows. Writers in our newspapers who took the "cousinship" line appeared to ignore the fact that America's greatest holiday was an orgy of Anglophobia. The sight of a British flag on "The Fourth" could and did provoke a serious riot. Anglo-American history in the schools recalled heroic deeds of the minutemen and farmers against the red-coats, whom England's German King sent "to complete the works of death, desolation, and tyranny" in his own long-suffering Colonies.

Speaking at Plymouth ("where the *Mayflower* last left land"), Ambassador Page alluded to this fallacious teaching and the mischief it wrought. "On the American side," Dr. Page was glad to say, "the disproportion and wrong temper of these books is fast disappearing. Newer texts are correcting this old fault." The Ambassador also proposed for British schools a modern book about the United States; its foremost men, its social structure, and ideal aims for the betterment of humanity. In short, a work which should be to children what Lord Bryce's *American Commonwealth* is to students of a more mature age.

There is no gainsaying the need for this restatement on both sides, and particularly the part which Great Britain played as America's friend during the German intrigues of 1898. Cleveland's ringing renewal of the Monroe Doctrine was resented by the Central Powers; and when the quarrel with Spain developed, Von Holleben and Hengelmüller—the Bernstorff and Dumba of their day—were soon urging intervention upon the whole Diplomatic Corps in Washington. America knew that Germany had designs of her own in the Caribbean; she was nevertheless determined to liberate Cuba and vindicate her own claim to the hegemony of the New World. In the critical weeks that followed the sinking of the *Maine,* German overtures were made to France and England with a view to thwarting American aims. John Hay was then Ambassador at our Court; he was presently able to inform his Government that Britain, far from being a party to the plot, took a sturdy stand by the side of the United States.

Of course if Germany had had her way nothing could have saved America from humiliation. For with three of the greatest fleets barring the Cuban coast, she could never have approached the island, much less landed an army there. The war with Spain must have ended ignominiously, for resistance could only have brought about disaster. The Atlantic seaboard would have been at the mercy of a new Triple Alliance; all the cities from Eastport down to Charleston lay open to attack and occupation, with possible indemnities and national abasement.

John Hay persevered with his Anglo-Saxon scheme, and found a staunch friend in Joseph Chamberlain, whose speech at Birmingham on May 11, 1898, is now widely quoted in the United States. "What is our next duty?" Mr. Chamberlain asked. "It is to establish and maintain bonds of permanent amity with our kinsmen across the Atlantic. For there is a powerful and a generous nation.

They speak our language, they are bred of our race. . . .
I don't know what the future has in store for us; I don't
know what arrangements may be possible. But this I do
know and feel—that the closer, the more cordial and fuller
and definite these arrangements are, with the consent of
both peoples, the better it will be for us both and for the
world. I will even go so far as to say that, terrible as
war may be, war itself would be cheaply purchased if, in
a great and noble cause, the Stars and Stripes and the
Union Jack should wave together over an Anglo-Saxon
alliance.''

Writing to Senator Lodge from London, Ambassador
Hay referred to ''Chamberlain's startling speech'': ''It
was partly due to a conversation I had with him, in which
I hoped he would not let the Opposition have a monopoly
of goodwill expressions for America.'' This goodwill took
a dramatic turn in Manila Bay. Here the truculent German commander, Von Diederichs, assumed a threatening
attitude towards Admiral Dewey, who was greatly perplexed thereat. That veteran sailor told the story to the
late Earl Grey at a Senatorial banquet in Washington
in 1905, and Lord Grey repeated it in the House of Lords:

''Admiral Dewey told me that the presence of German
cruisers of heavier displacement than his own caused him
to realize the danger menacing his country in the event
of those ships taking hostile action; and of this he had
reason to be apprehensive. He described how the American Fleet watched in silent anxiety the visit of the German Admiral to Captain Chichester's ship, and the intense
relief with which they saw, shortly after Von Diederichs'
return, the two British cruisers, *Immortalité* and *Iphigenia,*
hoist their anchors and move to a position which placed
them in the direct line of fire between the German and
American vessels. No action has ever done more to promote the friendly feelings of one nation for another than

this of Captain Chichester, which is well known to every officer in the United States Navy.''

Yet outside that Service the old dislike of England persisted, greatly to the disappointment of John Hay. He was now America's Foreign Minister. ''All I've ever done with Britain,'' he wrote in plaintive key to his predecessor in that high office, ''is to wring concessions from her with no compensation. And yet these idiots say I'm no American, because I don't cry 'To hell with the Queen,' at every breath!''

Hay was abused as an Anglomaniac, as Lowell had been, and by the same Irish irreconcilables. Even close friends of his, like Lodge, were afraid there was something in the air of St. James's which turned the sturdiest Yankee into a bit of a courtier, with undue leanings to the English side.

I have said that Germany was esteemed by the American people, and that dislike of England was a persistent tradition. The reversal of these sentiments is a curious study in national psychology, and the cause can be traced to reasons of American safety. Quite apart from the fact that Germany was a very good customer, taking $235,000,-000 worth of cotton and copper alone each year, she had come to be regarded as the post-graduate schoolhouse of the United States. Every ambitious youth who could afford it took a course at a German university, because this gave him a better send-off in a career than any diploma from an American technical school. And hyphenate professors, like the late Hugo Münsterburg of Harvard, worked hard to heighten the prestige of the only Kultur which was one day destined to improve with guns God's moulding of the world.

Münsterburg's *Psychology and Industrial Efficiency* is something of an American classic. It was William James who invited this scholar from Freiburg, and at the same time Von Holst, on the strength of his American history, was called to the newly-founded University of Chicago. These imported high-brows soon saw "the failures and deficiencies of American civilization," and set about mending them with characteristic zeal. According to Münsterburg, they were due to "a lack of that social idealism which gives meaning to our German life"; and in the summer of 1898 he confided to Ambassador von Holleben his plan of foisting the true Fichtean brand of Kultur on the United States.

Germany's "official contact" was promptly secured for this missionary work, first for Harvard and then for Chicago. At length Münsterburg was able to chant his triumph, for on March 6, 1902, the Kaiser's brother, under that hyphenate roof in Ware Street, Cambridge, handed over the documents and gifts of the Germanic Museum at Harvard. "The official Americans," the Professor tells us, "were led by David Jayne Hill, who was later on Ambassador in Berlin. Towering over the German group stood one of the mildest-looking of men, Alfred von Tirpitz, and next to him, Admiral Robley D. Evans. Many other Americans and Germans of renown listened to the speeches, which culminated in Prince Henry's spontaneous plea that the friendship between America and our Fatherland might never be broken."

Débris de toiles d'arraignée que le vent emporte!

There was no talk in those days of Prussian militarism. The thing was known, of course, but Americans laughed at it as a peculiar hobby—a national aberration, marked with schlager-slashes on the faces of students from Alte Heidelberg.

But the German was thorough: he was a fellow of ineradicable purpose: a first-class stayer and timber-topper in the long and tricky Grand National race, of which the prize was supremacy in the world of commerce. Compared with this apostle of *Die Thätigkeit*—the restless activity which Goethe said proved the Man—his English rival cut a poor figure, resting as he did upon his father's oars and "glorying in the name of Briton"—like George the Third of obstinate and execrable memory.

The English (America thought) were the most insular of peoples, and that in the narrowest, most irritating sense of the word. "They don't say much," as the French statesman remarked when dealing with the notorious *morgue Britannique*. "And you can't *tell* them anything at all!"

Such, then, were the estimates which America held of the two foreign nations in which she was most interested. This estimate held good in 1914; it was not greatly disturbed during the "flush time," nor did the fulminations of the Eastern press bring about any noticeable change. Indeed, to speak frankly, there seemed to be one law for Germany and another for Great Britain where dealings with the State Department were concerned. The mere presence of our cruisers was a vexatious fact; yet a German submarine (the U-53) could enter an American port, collect information, and then sally forth to sink merchant vessels, leaving the work of rescue to destroyers of the Narragansett Bay station under Admiral Knight: this was in October, 1916. Protest from four of the Allies, including Japan, drew a sharp reply from Washington, which expressed its "surprise" at the implied dictation, and "reserved its liberty of action in all respects." Mr. Lansing's naval advisers told our Ambassador "there was no reason for treating the submarine otherwise than is customary in the case of an ordinary warship visiting a foreign port."

It may seem ungracious to recall the American Notes dealing with that thorny question, the "freedom of the seas," which President Wilson put in the forefront of his fourteen proposals for an enduring peace after "this, the culminating and final war for human liberty." But those Notes inflamed feeling against us, especially in the Southern States, where our declaration of cotton as contraband of war came as a great blow. In both Houses of Congress retaliatory embargoes were proposed upon commodities useful to the Allies—first munitions of war, and then foodstuffs. In the latter case rising prices made the masses welcome that move as one likely to reduce the cost of living, so it had a fleeting measure of popular support.

Then the Battle of Jutland was hailed in New York as a German victory; the "re-write man" of the Hearst journals used the word "overwhelming," and was thereafter denied the use of mails and cables by our Government for systematic distortion of official news. No doubt our Admiralty was in part to blame by reason of its maladroit reports. For even the New York *World,* which never had pro-German leanings, came out with a big cartoon showing the British Lion emerging from the waves with a black eye and a tin can tied to his tail. "In spite of conflicting reports from Berlin and London," the *World* leader said, "and a common suppression of details, it is plain that the British Fleet was outmanœuvred, outshot, and outfought by its adversary."

In those early days Germanism swept the United States with gusty ecstasies of all-pervasive tinge. Deutschheit was backed by a propaganda which covered the continent from sea to sea, and was aided by the Irish—by Sinn Feiners and Clan-na-Gaelers, Ancient Hibernians, Irish Leaguers, Friends of Freedom, and an Irish press so vindictive that it was at last forbidden the mails by Post-Master Burleson. Senators Martine and Phelan brought forward extravagant motions, like the one requesting President Wilson to intercede for Roger Casement and the "Irish Martyrs." Indiscretion of this kind did not prevent

America's leading men from sympathizing strongly with the Irish cause. President Wilson himself accepted a statue of Robert Emmett, and he received Mrs. Sheehy Skeffington at the White House with unusual warmth.

So that, swayed with emotion from millions of her citizens, it is not surprising that at one period America was inclined to believe that the German would win the war and vindicate his clamorous claim to super-manhood among the races. Even the native humorist, friendly to our cause, was afraid of the Kaiser's sledge-hammer strokes in East and West. He described them in prize-ring jargon, such as everybody understands. "The Divine Right is working like a piston," this wag was grieved to say. "And unless the Allies can put over a rib-roasting left, it's the sleep-act for theirs, and a sad count over the champion that was!" This detachment, with all its levity and unconcern, woke angry remonstrance in England and France—especially when it was known that Captain (now Admiral) Sowden Sims had been asked to revise his professional report of the Battle of Jutland, lest its eulogy of British tactics should offend the German elements in the United States.

That those elements were able to influence policy is beyond a doubt. German-American shippers and traders were loudest of all in the outcry against our right of search at sea; our seizure of neutral mails and contraband of war, and lastly over the Black List—"an arbitrary and sweeping practice," which the American Note was afraid would have "harsh, even disastrous effects upon the commerce of the United States." We had a hostile press over there at this time.

The severity of the saner papers became rabid abuse in those of the Hearst chain, and the German language journals, from Sacramento to St. Louis, became extraordinarily scurrilous. It was purely time to remind present-day America of the historic part which the British Fleet has played; so Mr. Balfour began with a dissertation on the Freedom of the Seas. "England and Holland fought for it in times gone by," Mr. Balfour told our ruffled friends, "and to their success the United States may be said to owe its very existence. For if, three hundred years ago, the maritime claims of Spain and Portugal had been admitted, whatever else North America might have been, it would not have been English-speaking. It would neither have employed the language nor obeyed the laws, nor enjoyed the institutions which, in the last analysis, are of British origin."

America's stand over the right of search at sea is an historic tradition; it goes back to Benjamin Franklin, who negotiated a Treaty of Amity and Commerce with Prussia, in which it was agreed that private property should not be seized. Of course in those days the sea affair was mere lunar politics to Prussia, seeing that she had no fleet worthy of the name, nor any call for it until 1848, when Prince Adalbert wrote his "Memorandum Concerning the Establishment of a German Navy." It was mainly our right of search at sea which caused the Anglo-American War of 1812. In 1856 the United States disagreed with the Declaration of Paris, because the contracting Powers would not admit her maritime view of "free ships and free goods."

John Hay impressed this upon his delegates to The Hague in 1899. "You are authorized to propose the principle of extending to strictly private property at sea the immunity from destruction or capture by belligerents which such property already enjoys on land." This the State Secretary thought "worthy of being incorporated in the permanent law of civilized nations." Both McKinley (in 1898) and Roosevelt (in 1903) sent Messages to Congress reaffirming this claim. It received national sanction by a joint resolution of both Houses, passed on April 28, 1904.

And three years later Secretary Root armed America's envoys again with the old sea-heresy, which they took with them for the second time to The Hague.

In 1812, as in 1915–16, the British (and French) restraint of neutral trade had exasperated American opinion. Yet in their own Civil War President Lincoln brought sea-power to bear upon the Confederacy with crushing effect. His Proclamation, dated April 19, 1861, deems it "advisable to set on foot a blockade of the ports within the States aforesaid, in pursuance of the laws of the United States, and of the law of nations in such case provided."

We were grievous sufferers by this drastic step, which, although it saved the Union, dislocated our trade and inflicted the direst misery upon our people. Lancashire drew her cotton from the blockaded States, and when supplies were cut off, thousands of mill-hands were thrown out of work. Later on they were brought to the verge of starvation, and their employers faced with downright ruin. Yet from those famishing homes the Slave Emancipator got a message of sturdy support for his cause. Lincoln replied to this in a very moving letter to our Manchester hands. "I cannot but regard your utterance," he wrote, "as an instance of sublime Christian heroism which has not been surpassed in any age or any country. . . . I do not doubt that the sentiments you have expressed will be sustained by your great nation; and on the other hand, I have no hesitation in assuring you that they will excite admiration, esteem, and the most reciprocal feelings of friendship among the American people."

It is no wonder, therefore, that America's agitation for the freedom of the seas died down before the parallel cases we put to her, with modifications made necessary by the great size of ships and the impossibility of adequate search on the high seas. A Naval Board advised the American Government that: "No difference . . . can be seen be-

tween the search of a ship of 1000 tons and one of 20,000
tons, except possibly a difference in time for the purpose
of establishing fully the character of her cargo and the
nature of her service and destination.'' The absurdity
of this contention was soon realized, and American jurists
of high repute upheld the British view. Thus Professor
S. E. Edmunds of St. Louis University, comparing our
blockade of Germany with that of the Confederate ports
during the Civil War, declared our action amply justified.
''A sense of consistency should make us mute,'' concludes
this American authority on international law.

It is a mistake to suppose, however, that the matter
is definitely settled; on the contrary, it has figured frequently in Presidential utterance as the considered policy
of the United States. As Article II in Dr. Wilson's program of the world's peace, it follows the abolition of secret
diplomacy, and is thus phrased: ''Absolute freedom of
navigation upon the seas outside territorial waters, alike
in peace and in war, except as the seas may be closed, in
whole or in part, by international action for the enforce-
ment of international covenants.''

Thus it is evident that in any future conflict America
looks for co-operation, which has been denied her during
the most merciless of all wars. President Wilson did appeal for neutral support, and appealed in vain, as he told
his people with regret. The non-belligerent nations were
all Sinn Feiners, all concerned with ''Ourselves Alone,''
and no doubt intimidated by ''frightful'' German methods as carried out in Belgium—*Jam proximus ardet Uca-
legon.* Even German thinkers have commented upon this
Levite shrinking attitude. ''The nations,'' says Rudolf
Eucken of Jena, ''are no longer ruled by ideals, but by
interests; they preach open egoism, and apply it with new
zeal to the practical philosophy of life.'' The Pope made
a moving appeal for peace—''Must the civilized world

become nothing but a field of death?" And, like President Wilson, His Holiness urged that "the moral force of Right should take the place of the material force of arms." But here, surely, is the crux of the tragedy. For in such a war as this, all the belligerents believe they have Right on their side.

Germany sees herself as *der Hort des Friedens*—the Rock of Peace, assailed by floods of jealousy and fear. Von Kirchhoff, the Bavarian General facing the French near Peronne, during the battles of the Somme, broke down and cried before the American pressmen when he recalled the Allied taunt of "Huns and barbarians," applied to the legions under him who were dying daily for the Fatherland. "Justice, loyalty, and truth are fighting on our side," the Emperor told his Brandenburg Grenadiers on the Tagliamento plain. And in an Order to both services, he declared that "the gallant exploits of our submarines have secured to my Navy glory and admiration for ever." What argument is possible with sentiments like these? The fatal fact is that they are sincerely held, and that the clash of Right against Might must make war a condition of eternal recurrence.

America herself—the most peaceful of all democracies—felt this in her Civil War, when North and South fought with a furious conviction which became a religion. "The men were in dead earnest," we learn from that scholarly pacifist, David Starr Jordan of Leland Stanford University. "Each believed that his view of State Rights and national authority was founded on the solid rock of Righteousness and fair play." So it must be to the end, when feeling runs high and there is hopeless divergence of causes.

In peace proposals addressed to the Powers, Pope Benedict would assure "the supremacy of Right" by simultaneous and reciprocal disarmament, and a system of arbitration backed by a League of Nations. This follows the American plan. But the Pope as well as President Wilson contends for "the true liberty and community of the seas, which on the one hand would remove many causes of conflict, and on the other would open to all new sources of prosperity and progress." Now this aim strikes at the very root of the British Empire and bids fair to be the gravest of all the problems before the plenipotentiaries of Peace. The German Government referred to it when replying to the Pope's Note; it was among the "definite rules and safeguards" which were to ensure "the fortifying moral strength of Right." Germany was ready to support "every proposal which is compatible with our vital interests." The Imperial Chancellor was in ostentatious agreement with President Wilson over the freedom of the seas in war and peace. Was it not "also demanded by Germany as one of the first and most important requirements of the future?" "There is, therefore," Count Hertling continued, "no difference of opinion here."

But there is ambiguity everywhere in scope and definition of this aim. Few of its advocates are so frank as Herr Dernburg who, as propagandist in New York, explained why sea-power should be hobbled and land-power left free: why war should be banished from the element in which Germany was weak, and left to ramp in the region of her proven strength. When the *Lusitania* was destroyed, Von Jagow, who was then Foreign Minister in Berlin, described that fearful crime as a blow for the freedom of the seas, and consequently a service to the whole world. But as these "services" multiplied, with American victims drowned again and again, the logic of the argument grew more than doubtful, even in the American West, whose moral indolence a German industrial magnate like Walter Rathenau surveyed with grave amazement.

"The most important element in the freedom of the seas," declared Mr. Roosevelt bluntly, "is freedom from murder. And until our Government takes an effective stand, its talk of freedom can only expose it to ridicule." This view gained ground with each succeeding outrage, and at the same time the ancient estimate of Britain underwent a profound change. Count Bernstorff's prompting about British "navalism" was now coldly received—as Mendoza's was long ago when he complained to Elizabeth about the intrusion of her ships into the waters of the Indies. American experts like Admiral Mahan were read again, and sea-power began to loom in quite a new light.

It was now recalled that without a blockade, ruthlessly enforced, the rebel States of the 'Sixties would never have been subdued. The sale of their cotton would have bought munitions of war, and America as we know it would surely have broken up. Then there was Mahan's testimony to Britain's benign use of her sovereignty at sea. He admits that from the Arctic Circle to the Gulf, and from the Atlantic to the Pacific, freedom has been maintained by captains of English breed, such as have for centuries impeached the would-be conqueror afloat.

"If it were not for this British mastery," mused the Wall Street journal at last, "where would our export trade be today?" In other quarters the Monroe Doctrine was historically reviewed, together with the opinions of it held by reactionary statesmen of the Central Powers. Thus it was to Metternich a calamitous consequence of free-footed democracy. Bismarck called that doctrine "an international impertinence." But Great Britain was behind it throughout, and for this reason history itself took on new meanings; Americans marvelled how that legacy of dislike could ever have come down to them.

Why, it was German despotism which America fought in her Revolutionary War! Two of the Georges were Germans who hated England and barely spoke her tongue. The Third of that line was brought up by a narrow-minded German mother to be "King," as she impressed upon him. And he it was who steered the State into what Goldwin Smith called "the most tragical disaster in English history." It was therefore a civil war, that of 1776, with the liberties of all at stake, whether at home in England, or in the American Colonies. Had not Chatham withdrawn his son from the Army "so that he might not fight in the unhappy war with our fellow-subjects"? The Earl of Effingham resigned his commission, and received the civic thanks of London and Dublin for his action. General Amherst also declined to serve; Sir William Howe was reluctant, but King George insisted, and the soldier obeyed under the duress of his military oath. This is the new English history, as taught today in the United States.

The late John Redmond took it down to 1910. Mr. T. P. O'Connor brought the story to this present year; and the result is a change of heart which may fairly be called epoch-making. There were no signs of it in the Catholic press of America which now scathed the "All-for-Ireland" sabotage and plots which the Department of Justice had discovered. The Chicago *Citizen* mourned the fact that "Irish names, some of them prominent, have been tainted with disloyalty and tarnished with German gold."

The Catholic *Transcript* of Hartford recalled the Pastoral Letter of Cardinal Logue dealing with Young Ireland's "pursuit of a dream which no man in his sober senses can hope to see realized—the establishment of an Irish Republic . . . by hurling an unarmed people against an Empire which has five millions of men under arms, furnished with the most terrible engines of destruction which human ingenuity could devise."

However, Irish-American citizens were less concerned with folly in the Motherland than with treasonous action against the Stars and Stripes—"the flag which has given asylum and liberty to so many millions of our race." These loyalists formed a new party, and sent out an earnest appeal to compatriots at home and abroad not to embarrass the cause of the Allies by vindictive action against England.

The German intrigue was far more formidable, and for many reasons it kept the State Department in a state of indecision. Large American supplies were reaching our enemy through neutral ports. Thus in the early days, when we held up cotton cargoes on their way to Sweden, the quays and warehouses of Gothenburg were heaped high with the staple, yet Swedish spinners were complaining they had none for their own use. One significant contract with a German firm came into our hands; it was for 50,000 bales at double the price which cotton was fetching in any other country. All of it was consigned to neutral ports, and when we seized a shipment there was no trace in the papers of enemy destination. Every device that guile could suggest was employed in this nefarious traffic from the United States. Thousands of tons of meat, documented for a neutral port, were sent to non-existent firms. Other consignments were addressed to lightermen or dock labourers. Others again to a baker, an hotelkeeper, and a maker of musical instruments.

In the three years prior to the war Sweden's average import of lard from America was but 638 tons. In 1915 the figure leapt to 9029 tons. Norway's imports of pork and bacon showed a similar bound; in 1916 she supplied Germany with 868,500 tons of food. The Allies protested, of course, but their demands were in various ways evaded, as by the erection of canning factories at Hamburg for Norwegian sardines and oil. As for Denmark, so late as June, 1917, she was sending across the frontier seven thousand head of cattle every week; and her American imports of indispensable fats presented a glaring case. Thus the intake of cottonseed oilcake was thirty times greater in 1915 than in the preceding year. Sweden's traffic was mainly in munitions of war. It was Holland's popular boast that she was "Germany's bread-basket"; and when the Allies tried to stop the supplies of pork, Richard von Kühlmann, who was then German Minister at The Hague, said he had no objection to offer, since "a Dutch pig was only American maize on four legs."

These facts were brought to the notice of the Washington Cabinet, for the United States was regarded by these neutrals as an inexhaustible source upon which they might draw after having sold to the Central Powers at enormous profit. After declaring war President Wilson shut down upon this traffic. He declared an embargo upon American products in order that these might not be made "the occasion of benefit to the enemy, either directly or indirectly." Washington was soon filled with plaintive missions from "the necessitous little nations." The envoys presented specious documents, but America's Export Council was inexorable. Fifteen Dutch ships were held up at Baltimore, and fifty more at New York laden with millions of bushels of wheat and maize, as well as oilcake, bacon and lard.

Mynheer van den Wielen had a piteous tale of misery in Holland; but the intelligence Bureau of the State Department proved to him that Dutch food imports had shown an excess over home consumption which was enough to provision 1,200,000 soldiers for a year! The Norwegian Mission, under Fritjof Nansen, was severely heckled by caustic Americans. "You have it in your power to starve us," the famous explorer said, "but we hope and believe you will help us instead. A million tons of our merchant fleet have been sunk, and six hundred of our seamen drowned." America asked why Norway had fed her murderons assailant, and even provided the nickel for the German torpedoes which did the work? Here is one of the darkest problems of the war, and a fruitful theme for misanthropy.

It will be seen that step by step the United States swung into line with the British view of sea-power. We plied her with precedents in her irritable time, quoting facts from her own Civil War and the war with Spain. "If the ship's papers," American cruisers were instructed in 1898, "indicate the presence of contraband, the ship should be seized." In Lincoln's day Secretary of State Seward said he was very sorry for the distress in England occasioned by the blockade; but who could expect him to sacrifice the American Union for cotton? And therewith he baffled the blockade-runners of neutral ports. Moreover, the Supreme Court extended the doctrine of continuous voyage, so as to cover all cases of trickery intended to break the blockade. This became more and more effective; until Seward could say that, "Cotton commands four times the price in Manchester and Rouen that it does in New Orleans."

These cogent arguments were working in the American mind, and they served to offset the mischief-making efforts of Germany, both directly from Berlin and also through the Embassy in Washington, whose influence was at last on the wane. In one of the Notes which Von Jagow handed to Mr. Gerard—it was a reply to further protest against the submarine—America was reminded that she had it in her power to confine the war to belligerent forces, had she been "determined to insist against Great Britain, on incontestable rights to the freedom of the seas." As matters stood, the German people saw only protests against the "illegal methods" of their enemies, and an American demand that Germany "who is struggling for existence, shall restrain the use of her effective weapon."

On our side surprise was expressed that Secretary of State Lansing did not see eye to eye with us about the new status of the submarine, especially after the havoc wrought by U-53 off Nantucket. But impulsive action is wholly foreign to the tradition ·of the State Department. It is a slow-moving Bureau, entirely undemocratic, and charged with domestic as well as foreign duties—including the over-sight of a Presidential election every four years. American vacillation in regard to armed merchant vessels and submarines was due to representations from naval advisers who were watching the development of the under-water craft with a single eye to national needs of the future. A Memorandum was handed to Mr. Lansing pointing out the enormous coast line of the United States, and the peculiarities of many of its harbours, which might well make the submarine a suitable weapon, alike for attack and defence.

The auxiliary cruiser, the strategists said, could work havoc in war-time with American commerce, so it might be well to avoid any policy which could be cited here-after to hamper the free use of the invisible boat. So defective were the coast defences, that it would be im-possible to resist the landing of an army backed by pow-erful warships unless the underwater weapon were given the fullest play.

Moreover, to insist that a submarine should visit and search a liner before attacking her might one day place America at the mercy of an enemy with a large merchant marine, and therefore able to equip raiders incomparably more destructive than even the notorious *Alabama*. Alto-gether the sea affair was fraught with perplexing possi-bilities to a great democracy beset on every side and con-sidering the future in the light of a lurid war-time day. In the meantime America was suffering from a German blockade. Her ships were held up in port; tankers of the Standard Oil had been recalled and added to the dock congestion, which was already serious. At length there was nothing for it but to put guns on board and to assume that armed neutrality which is the half-way house to war. For this purpose a hundred million dollars was voted by Congress, and the liner *St. Louis* set forth as a pioneer equipped for any encounter.

So at long last the warnings against British *Seeherrschaft* and maritime tyranny recoiled upon Germany: she was soon to figure as the "furious and brutal Power" in a Presidential Note, "whose word we cannot take as a guarantee of anything that is to endure." American travellers began to ask what complaint had Germany to make about the freedom of the seas before she made her pounce in 1914? "I sat on the club verandah at Singapore," Mr. Poultney Bigelow testified, "and counted twenty-seven funnels of a single German line. Then I crossed to North Borneo, also on a German line which carried the British mails. Later on I went to Siam— likewise on a German line. After that to Australia, to Java and the Eastern Archipelago. And always in ships of that same concern."

New York newspapers published the large-scale maps which the Hamburg-Amerika and Norddeutscher Lloyd Steamship Lines used to display so proudly in their London windows, showing every known sea-lane traversed by them, from China to Peru. "Absolute freedom," as defined by Germany, means the abolition of blockade (*Absperrung*) except within the limits of territorial waters; and this modern weapons have made impracticable. It forbids the right of search for enemy goods or munitions of war. Contraband is not to be seized. German maritime trade should therefore swarm unchecked, leaving the naval preponderance of the Allies a helpless nullity in the greatest of all wars. These contentions looked absurd to America—though she was hurried into war without having decided the question to her entire satisfaction. For this reason she regards the freedom of the seas as only in abeyance; we shall no doubt see her envoys, for the third and last time, take a decisive stand upon the subject at the Conference of Peace.

It is well to remember that America wishes to keep a free hand in her war against the German autocracy. President Wilson's deputy, Colonel E. M. House, made this quite clear at Downing Street and the Quai d'Orsay. For the old mistrust of entangling alliances is still strong, and the devious statecraft of Europe can never be agreeable to the United States, whose distaste for expedients is almost prudish when these conflict with her standards and ideals. This was seen in her reluctance to give formal assent to Japan's move in Eastern Siberia, with Vladivostok as a base and the railway junction of Harbin as an objective of high importance in the preservation of Far Eastern peace. In American eyes such an invasion was morally indefensible without a direct mandate from the Russian people: and no foreign guarantees could take the place of this national sanction.

It is America's pride that she went to war for no material gain, but through love of liberty and sympathy with the struggles of all the peoples, both great and small. For this reason a typical English statesman like Arthur Balfour called the Day of her entry "one of the most important in the annals of mankind." Mr. Asquith, in the historic debate of felicitation in our Parliament, ventured to doubt "whether even now the World realizes the full significance of the step which America has taken." France weighed the wealth of her sister Republic; the man-power and material resources, allotting her at last the supreme *rôle* of a decisive factor in the war.

But no sign was so significant as the drawing together of Great Britain and the United States, of which the symbol was the Stars and Stripes floating from the Victoria Tower of Westminster—the first foreign flag ever displayed by the Mother of Parliaments. The periodical literature of America soon teemed with tribute to the effort and purpose of Great Britain. Our new armies were praised; our Navy's shield over all the seas, our genius for colonizing, and a commercial policy throughout the Empire which was a standing marvel to our German rivals in the old days. University Presidents dwelt on the ethical side of English rule in India, Egypt, and the Africas. The Britain of today was presented in glowing propaganda, and the pæans of Emerson recalled—he was afraid that if he lingered too long among us his patriotism would suffer!

"Mother of nations," wrote the pink-thinking Sage of Concord, in his apostrophe to England, "Mother of heroes, with strength still equal to the time; still wise to entertain, and swift to execute the policy which the mind and heart of mankind require at the present hour!" These transports passed, of course, and left the idealist with a considered verdict upon the Englishman, whose "stuff or substance seems to be the best in the world. I forgive him all his pride. My respect is the more generous in that I have no sympathy with him, only an admiration."

But the martial spirit of our race in the gravest trial, and its achievement in the three elements of war since 1914 have aroused more than admiration in the United States. Her ablest writers, together with historians, labour leaders, and members of Congress, were sent over to report this unsuspected psyche, and with it the industrial surge which has turned our country into an arsenal, and so quickened its productive power as to make the Britain of tomorrow the keenest of all commercial rivals in the fields of peace.

How mistaken was even so able an observer as John Hay, when he lamented the "degeneracy" of England in

1900. This was the burden of many messages which America received, with a wealth of detail that woke the reader's wonder and warmed him to enthusiasm at last. After all, he mused, there must be something in Hegel's claim that "wars invigorate humanity, just as storm preserves the sea from putrescence." America had but to look at home to see the shock of war working out her people's destiny. For the first time duty and sacrifice were put above the dollar, alike by the rich and the obscure, in matters of great moment and in trifles too. Here was the boy soldier in Lorraine advising his mother to "quit sending candy." "It tastes fine," he agreed in a wistful letter home. "But it seems we're short of ships, and we want all the space we can get for cartridges."

And, stripping to the fight, America shed her old illusions and traditions. Her prescient statesmen and thinkers now openly urged her to join hands with Great Britain as "the conscious and leagued custodians of the world's peace"; I quote from the Plymouth speech of Ambassador Page. "To undertake this," he pursued, "our comradeship must be perpetual, and our task is to see that it be not broken, nor even strained . . . for we are laying new foundations of human freedom." With profound feeling the senior American diplomat vowed himself to this work: "Whatever years remain of my working life I propose to devote to this and nothing else—to the bringing about of a closer fundamental and lasting acquaintance between the people of this Empire and those of the United States. . . . We understand each other better than any two great nations, so let both turn to the task. For upon our united shoulders henceforth and for ever, so far as we can see, the peace of the world must rest."

Surely these earnest words, and the dangers that loom ahead, foreshadow an Anglo-American Alliance? For this was the "marriage" which that famous democrat, Thomas

Jefferson, found the most natural of all when he looked across the seas for a partner to share America's peril. Nearly fifty years before that crisis came, Jefferson had drafted the historic Declaration of Independence.   He was later on President Washington's Secretary of State; and in his long career he had moulded the young Republic, and held every office in its gift, retiring at last laden with honour and prestige, to direct and advise his successor at the White House.   Naturally, then, it was to Jefferson that President Monroe turned for counsel when Richard Rush, U. S. Minister in London, sent over the two letters of Canning which offered the support of England against the New-World designs of Metternich and the Holy Alliance. "With Great Britain on our side," Jefferson told Monroe, "we need not fear the whole world!"

THE END

Lightning Source UK Ltd.
Milton Keynes UK
UKHW020824031218
333381UK00012B/1533/P